CONTINENTAL EUROPE

Country Inns
and Back Roads

CONTINENTAL EUROPE

Country Inns
and Back Roads

Including some castles, pensions,
country houses, chateaux, farmhouses, palaces,
traditional inns, chalets, villas,
and small hotels

Norman T. Simpson
The Berkshire Traveller

Harper & Row, Publishers, New York
Grand Rapids, Philadelphia, St. Louis, San Francisco
London, Singapore, Sydney, Tokyo

TRAVEL BOOKS BY NORMAN T. SIMPSON

Country Inns and Back Roads, North America
Country Inns and Back Roads, Britain and Ireland
Country Inns and Back Roads, Continental Europe
Bed and Breakfast, American Style

COVER PAINTING: Chateau de la Chevre d'Or, Eze Village, France, by Janice
Lindstrom
DRAWINGS: Janice Lindstrom

ISSN 0893-1291
ISBN 0-06-096341-7

89 90 91 92 93 RRD 10 9 8 7 6 5 4 3 2 1

Contents

A special note of thanks to Virginia Rowe for her invaluable contribution in the editing and writing of the books of the Berkshire Traveller Series

Introduction

Welcome to Europe!

I'll never forget my first visit, and neither will you. Go now, so you can go back several times. I did.

This book is not intended as a one-volume, overall guide to the countries of Europe. Rather, it is my adventures on a series of itineraries. My main purpose is to encourage travel in any form, although for the most part it is ideally suited for use by two or four people using an automobile. Travelers can follow my suggested itineraries or branch out for themselves, particularly at times other than the high season. I encourage my readers to feel free to move about with maps, guides, and a light heart, expecting the best because they will find it. Basically, the good people of the countries included herein are courteous and helpful, and the accounts of my experiences are liberally sprinkled with how I was aided by many individuals.

I do not speak any foreign languages well, although I rapidly learned to communicate wherever I went.

Renting a Car for Europe

For many years I have made all of my automobile renting arrangements through AutoEurope. Through them I found I could pick up a car in one country and leave it in another, and there are AutoEurope agencies available in every one of the countries covered in this volume. The toll-free AutoEurope number in the U.S.A. is 800-223-5555 (from Maine, call 800-342-5202). I have always found their service very satisfactory.

Traveling to Europe

I heartily recommend a visit to your travel agent for unraveling the tremendously intricate special fares that seem to be undergoing constant changes these days. A travel agent can be very useful in simplifying the myriad details by making advance reservations for most of the inns in this book. The travel agent receives a commission from many of the accommodations, but where this is not true, you should expect to pay a reasonable reservation fee for the handling of such details.

Incidentally, a Eurailpass can be purchased only in the United States.

Rates

The rates vary, with an emphasis on the upper middle range. All the rates are in the Index, and these are changed, as necessary, in subsequent reprintings so that they should be fairly current.

The rates quoted in this book are meant as guidelines only. Basically, they are the cost of one night's lodging for two people, and many times include a continental breakfast. They are quoted in the money of the country involved unless otherwise indicated. Please bear in mind that the rates listed are designed only to give the reader a general idea.

A Few Final Words

If you have been waiting to visit Europe until after the kids are out of college or a new roof has been put on the house, don't wait—go now. It is an absolutely fantastic experience. But for goodness' sake, don't try to do too much in one trip.

I carry tape recorders, not only to record all of my impressions (you should do the same because they match up extremely well with photographs), but also to play cassette tapes of the music of the various countries. Imagine listening to Grieg's *Norwegian Dances* while traveling the fjords of Norway; the *Suite Espanola* of Albéniz while high in the mountains of Spain; Ravel in Paris and Mozart in Vienna!

Pack under the assumption that you are going to have to carry all the bags yourself. Personally, I take only carry-on luggage and do a small laundry every night.

Don't bother to learn twelve new languages, but at least be able to say "Please" and "Thank you," wherever you may go.

I found I could use my Visa credit card almost everywhere. American Express is also widely used.

For many years I've had an extensive correspondence with the places mentioned in this book. These European innkeepers love it when you show them a copy of *CIBR, Continental Europe,* and it is a good opportunity for you to give them my personal best wishes.

Spain

ITINERARY 1 (PAGE 22)

INNS AND LOCATIONS
ALMAGRO, Parador Almagro, 36
ARCOS DE LA FRONTERA, Parador Casa del Corregidor, 47
AYAMONTE, Parador Costa de la Luz, 43
CARMONA, Parador del Alcazar del Rey Don Pedro, 45
CAZORLA, Parador del Adelantado, 35
CORDOBA, Parador La Arruzafa, 38
GRANADA, Parador San Francisco, 29
JAÉN, Parador Castillo de Santa Catalina, 32
MADRID, Hotel Ritz, 19
MADRID, Hotel Tryp Palacio, 19
MADRID, Hotel Victoria, 20
MÁLAGA, Parador Gibralfaro, 22
MAZAGON, Parador Cristobal Colon, 44
MERIDA, Parador Via de la Plata, 41
MONACHIL (Granada), Parador Sierra Nevada, 31
NERJA, Parador Nerja, 26
SEVILLE, Hotel Doña Maria, 44
TARIFA, Hotel Dos Mares, 48
TORREMOLINOS, Parador del Golf, 50
UBEDA, Parador Condestable Davalos, 33
ZAFRA, Parador Hernan Cortes, 40

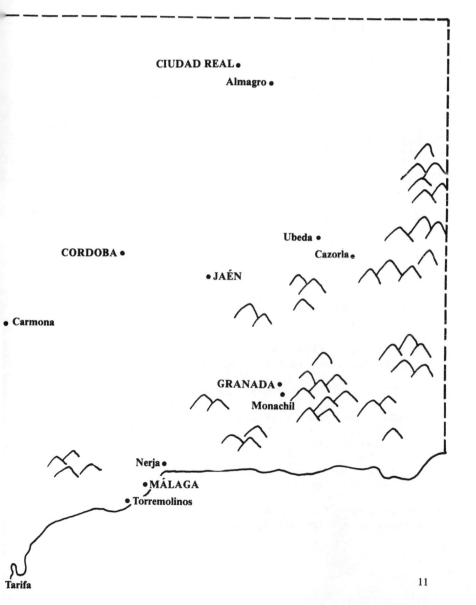

MADRID

CIUDAD REAL

Almagro

Ubeda

Cordoba

Cazorla

JAÉN

Carmona

GRANADA

Monachil

Nerja

MÁLAGA

Torremolinos

Tarifa

11

Spain

ITINERARY 2 (PAGE 51)

INNS AND LOCATIONS

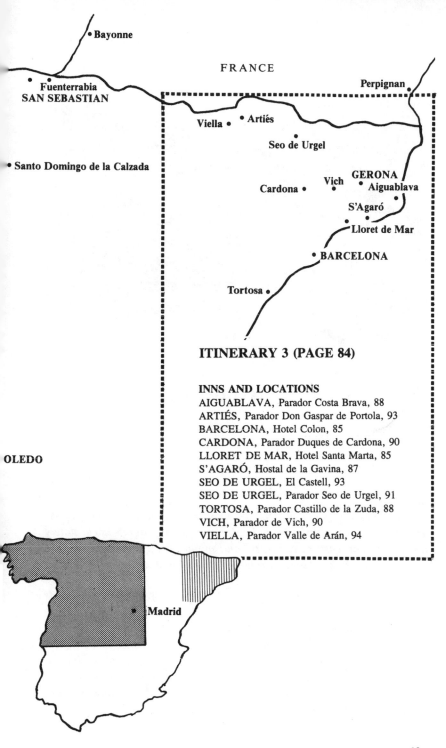

Bayonne

FRANCE

Fuenterrabia
SAN SEBASTIAN

Perpignan

Viella • **Artiés**

Seo de Urgel

• **Santo Domingo de la Calzada**

GERONA
Cardona • **Vich** • **Aiguablava**

S'Agaró

Lloret de Mar

BARCELONA

Tortosa •

ITINERARY 3 (PAGE 84)

INNS AND LOCATIONS
AIGUABLAVA, Parador Costa Brava, 88
ARTIÉS, Parador Don Gaspar de Portola, 93
BARCELONA, Hotel Colon, 85
CARDONA, Parador Duques de Cardona, 90
LLORET DE MAR, Hotel Santa Marta, 85
S'AGARÓ, Hostal de la Gavina, 87
SEO DE URGEL, El Castell, 93
SEO DE URGEL, Parador Seo de Urgel, 91
TORTOSA, Parador Castillo de la Zuda, 88
VICH, Parador de Vich, 90
VIELLA, Parador Valle de Arán, 94

OLEDO

Madrid

TRAVEL SUGGESTIONS FOR SPAIN

Country Inns in Spain

Most of the accommodations in this section are inns owned and operated by the Spanish Ministry of Information and Tourism. These are known as paradores, where it is possible to stay for an unlimited time.

These are not youth hostels or humble wayside accommodations. They have been established in old palaces of historic significance, stately homes, ancient castles, convents, and monasteries. Some are modern in design. These have been carefully restored with a maximum respect for their heritage, and fortunately for all travelers in Spain, they have been fitted with modern conveniences. Each bedroom has twin beds and a sumptuously furnished private bathroom.

There are almost a hundred of these truly remarkable accommodations scattered throughout Spain, and they present the best face of Spain today. To stay in them is to return to the glories of a Spain of the past, while at the same time enjoying the conveniences of the present.

Each parador offers breakfast with the cost of the accommodation. Lunch and dinner are also available.

Relais et Chateaux: Iberia

The Relais et Chateaux group of first-rate independently owned inns mentioned in the section on France extends throughout Europe. In Spain and Portugal they are called "Relais & Chateaux: Iberia," and all are handsome, well-located properties with especially fine dining rooms. Reservations may be made directly through your travel agent or David Mitchell, 200 Madison Avenue, New York, NY 10016; 800-696-1323.

Reservations at Paradores

I strongly advise that reservations be made in advance during all seasons for the Spanish paradores. This can done through Marketing Ahead, 433 Fifth Avenue, New York, NY 10016; 212-686-9213. They can also arrange for your reservations at Portuguese pousadas, which are the equivalent of the Spanish paradores.

Car Rentals

Don't hesitate to travel anywhere in Spain by automobile. The main roads are excellent and even the secondary and tertiary routes are well maintained. Advance reservations may be made before leaving North America for an AutoEurope car to be picked up, not only in Madrid and Lisbon, but in many other cities on the Iberian peninsula. For full information about AutoEurope, see the introduction of this book.

Spanish Menus

Each of the paradores offers regional dishes featuring local specialties, and their menus consist almost entirely of Spanish food. For example, paradores on the Costa del Sol offer a great variety of delectable fish dishes, including pickled tuna and bonito, shellfish cocktails, and sardines, which are cooked both on a spit and in a frying pan. Frying fish is an art in Andalusia. This region is also well known for gazpacho in many varieties. Other possibilities on the menu could be octopus served in many forms, ham and beans, or the famous Sacromonte omelets from Granada. There are cookies from Antequera and egg-yolk candies from Ronda.

Each parador has two menus, a table d'hote and an à la carte. On the table d'hote, for one piece there are several choices within each of the four courses. The first course usually has a choice of hors d'oeuvres or soup; the second course might include poached eggs, noodles, or other light dishes; the third is the main course and offers dishes such as hake (a Spanish fish), tuna, roast chicken, stewed oxtails, or York ham and salad. The last course is dessert.

The à la carte menu allows the guest to choose at random, when all four courses seem too heavy.

Except under unusual circumstances I did not take many lunches in the Spanish paradores. I found it very satisfactory to stop at the small grocery stores that can be found in every Spanish town. They provide fruit, bread, cheese, and mineral water for a roadside picnic. I also took a few light lunches at snack bars and smaller restaurants.

Everyone should have at least one meal of the famous paella de mariscos o pollo. This is rice cooked with garlic and spices, combined with countless tasty ingredients from the sea or farmlands, and infused with the spirit of something Spanish that goes beyond my comprehension. For centuries, paella has been served in Spain for family and visitors. It is sometimes the result of individual experimentation and each version can be a whole new experience for both the one who prepares it and the one who partakes. Its spiciness and flavor can vary from region to region.

Itineraries in Spain

This section contains three itineraries in Spain. The first is a circle tour of Andalusia (southwestern Spain) that begins and ends in Málaga.

It includes the famed Costa del Sol, Granada, the nearby Sierra Nevada mountains, the rolling plains and olive groves, Cordoba, and the fortified towns of western Spain, as well as Seville and Cadiz.

The second itinerary begins in Madrid and proceeds south a short distance beyond Toledo and then veers into the mountains northward to Avila, Zamora, Verín, and on to Galicia, including Santiago de Compostela. The route continues across Asturias, the northern coast to Santander, the caves of Altamira, and San Sebastian at the French border. It turns south through the Peaks of Europe to Burgos and Segovia, and returns to Madrid.

The third itinerary begins and ends at Barcelona International Airport, making a loop through Catalonia, the ancient kingdom, now an autonomous province within the Spanish democracy. After several days in Barcelona, I went north along the Costa Brava, then crossed along the foothills of the Pyrenees to the northwest corner of Catalonia. I then cut southeast again to the toe at Tortosa and back along the Costa Daurada to the airport.

Madrid

There are several references in this book to the emergence of Spain, and to the "old" Spain and the "new" Spain. Perhaps nowhere in Spain were the changes more obvious to me than in the Madrid airport. When I first came here in 1975, the airport was in tremendous confusion and there were even several leaks in the roof. It was necessary to take buses between airports, and in general I was bewildered. Today, the Madrid airport is a model of efficiency and everything is under control.

Buses leave from the airport, although it is possible to rent an AutoEurope or other car to be picked up there if it is more convenient. I don't advise anybody to drive in Madrid, or for that matter, Lisbon, London, Paris, Rome, or any other major European city if it can possibly be avoided.

The airport bus arrives at the Plaza de Colon, marked by very impressive fountains, which commemorates the feats of Christopher Columbus. This is one of the great intersections of Madrid, where at least six major roads all come together. The traffic is capably handled by rather attractive señoritas wearing blue coats, blue hats, and blowing vigorous whistles.

One of the broad streets that lead to the bus terminal is the absolutely magnificent Paseo Castellana, the "Champs Elysées" of Madrid. I enjoyed several invigorating walks along this avenue, as it was within walking distance of the hotel where I was staying. It was early May and the trees were beginning to come into leaf and the sun provided a

foretaste of warmer things to come. This is a perfect time for tourists because it's not too warm, or too cold, or too anything. The men of Madrid wear suits and jackets and the women wear dresses and light coats. In a few weeks hence the streets would be even more beautiful, enhanced by the blossoming trees.

There are occasional small cafes along this route and in one of them, instead of sitting around tables, the patrons enjoyed their refreshments on porch swings, rocking gently back and forth. The cafes sell a complete comida *(lunch). I ordered a drink whose name is totally international: Coca-Cola. These little restaurants are called* kiosco.

Of course, there are literally hundreds, even thousands, of things of interest to the tourist in Madrid, and I submit to one and all that the Michelin Green Guide *is a good place to start.*

Before I share some of my observations about a few hotels in Madrid, I might point out that if you look at Madrid on a map of Spain, you realize that it really is the hub of the country, and the main roads feeding into it are packed with traffic every morning and night. In my case, it was necessary for me to come off of one main road, go into the middle of the town, and go back out another main road in order to leave my car at the airport upon my departure from Spain. Instead of trying to cope with the complexities of traffic and routes, I repeated the solution I had used in Rome; I hired a taxicab to lead me across the town's shortcuts. This will work almost anywhere.

HOTEL TRYP PALACIO
Madrid

This is a very nice hotel on a lovely street and is central to most of the things that would interest a tourist in Madrid. It's a sort of half-business and half-tourist hotel, and the prices are average for a four-and five-star establishment. As is the case in other hotels in Europe, the incoming guest checks in at the desk at the reception area and from then on does his business with the *conserjeria,* who arranges for transportation, tours, keeps the keys, collects the mail, and does a hundred-and-one other things that add up to service.

The hotel menu has a fixed-price dinner with eight or nine international items but, as in the case of other Spanish hotels, there's also an à la carte menu. In order to accommodate the many tourists who come to this hotel, the lunch or dinner hours have been moved back, because ordinarily the Spanish eat lunch at 2:30 and dinner at 9:30, and director Señor Alvarez explained that his visitors from North America simply couldn't wait that long for those two meals.

I enjoyed the Hotel Tryp Palacio. I'm glad that I stayed there.

HOTEL TRYP PALACIO, Paseo de la Castellana 57, Madrid. Tel.: 442-51-00; Telex: 27 207 Luze. A 182-room luxury hotel on one of Madrid's most pleasant avenues. In a city that has scores of such hotels, I found the Tryp Palacio to be very pleasant and accommodating. Rates: See Index.

HOTEL RITZ
Madrid

Almost every major city in the world has a hotel called "The Ritz." As a matter of fact, the term has been used since the 1920s to indicate a sort of high style of living as popularized in a song of that time titled "Puttin' on the Ritz." During the 1930s, when the small city hotel was much more common than today, almost every town in the United States had a Ritz Hotel.

Well, the Ritz in Madrid is very ritzy—it has five stars for everything. The *Michelin Red Guide* gives it top billing. It's across the street from the Prado.

On the day of my unexpected visit, I was able to browse about in the reception area and an adjacent room, but when I tried to go through the glass doors into the rooms where afternoon tea, drinks, and meals are served, I was restrained by a junior-high-school-aged staff member who explained I would need a jacket and tie to continue my tour. Such formal apparel is not required in the terrace dining area, which opens to the street and operates during the summer, serving lunch only.

Just a few steps from the front door of the Ritz was a small kiosk selling ice cream. Both the strawberry and the mocha were excellent and made a good short lunch. It was amusing to see some of the children coming out of the Ritz Hotel and dragging their parents over to get the ice cream before stepping into their Mercedes-Benzes.

HOTEL RITZ, Plaza de la Lealtad 5, Madrid. Tel.: 221-28-57. U.S. reservations: 212-686-9213. The Michelin Red Guide lists two hotels with five stars in Madrid. The other is the Villa Magna. I would suggest checking with your travel agent or Marketing Ahead, a reservation service in Manhattan, for full details. Rates: See Index.

EL PRADO

I'll have to admit that art treasures of the world remained fairly obscure for me until I took the freshman course in art appreciation given by Blanchard Gummo at Bucknell University in Lewisburg, Pennsylvania.

As they did for many other people, the slides in the darkened lecture hall of my first college course opened my imagination and widened my horizons. I only wish I had paid better attention.

I certainly paid rapt attention during my afternoon at the Prado, one of the supreme art museums of Europe. I have no intention of doing a review of the masterpieces by Goya, El Greco, Velásquez, Titian, Van Dyck, Rubens, and a host of others. To see the originals in the context of other inspired paintings lifts the spirit and makes the travel experience far more meaningful.

HOTEL VICTORIA
Madrid

No one seems to know why this pleasant, very well-located hotel began to attract bullfighters and aficionados, but during the season it has become an accepted residence. Most of the guests, however, are just experienced travelers who know a good value.

The Victoria is a five-minute walk from either the Puerto del Sol or the Plaza Mayor and is just across the Plaza Santa Ana from the Teatro Español, where you can see classics of Spanish drama. It is also very near the restored house of Lope de Vega, the poet and playwright (1562–1635). It is a ten-minute walk to the Prado.

The Plaza Santa Ana is a pretty square with park benches and flowers, surrounded by shops and, on one side, an old German beer hall popular with tourists. Reading, visiting, and people-watching seem to be the prime concerns of its regulars, and on a sunny day it is a wonderful spot to spend an hour or so just watching the citizens of Madrid go by.

Incidentally, if you want to see a genuine bullfighter in ordinary street clothes, ask a waiter in the hotel cafe to point one out.

HOTEL VICTORIA, Plaza del Angel 7, 28012 Madrid. Tel.: 231-4500. U.S. reservations: 212-686-9213. A 110-guestroom pleasant 3-star hotel rated "very comfortable" by Michelin and well located for the sights of central Madrid. Entrance is on Plaza del Angel, but the hotel stretches along one side of Plaza de Santa Ana. Restaurant. Barajas Airport is 20 min. by taxi. Rates: See Index.

ITINERARY 1

I made a circle tour of southwestern Spain in a counterclockwise direction, starting from Málaga and visiting Granada, Jaén, Cordoba, Seville, Cadiz, and Algeciras. There were also side trips to Ciudad Real, Zafra, Merida, and Huelva.

PARADOR GIBRALFARO
Málaga

In retrospect I realize that Parador Gibralfaro was a most fortunate choice as my first country inn in Spain. It is located a few steps below the Moorish fortress through which I had been wandering during the late afternoon.

Originally, the building was a most impressive home that now has been carefully restored and enlarged to accommodate travelers. The most memorable thing about it, of course, is the view of the harbor and the city below. However, even in another less spectacular location it would still be an outstanding experience.

The setting, so high above the tumult of the city, creates a total atmosphere of peace and tranquility. In redesigning the building to meet the needs of travelers, the architects made every possible use of the magnificent view; hence, most of the lodging rooms share the spectacle along with the second-floor outdoor terrace. I found that many Mála-guenans are fond of having their midday meal or dinner at this parador.

As in all paradores there was a very comfortably furnished parlor with a fireplace, where guests frequently gathered at the end of the day. Lots of books and magazines made the place more homelike.

At most paradores the bedrooms and sitting rooms follow a carefully

chosen individual decorating theme. At Gibralfaro the colors and textures were in harmony with the closeness of sea, sky, and sun, with many beige tones as well as brown and accenting touches of green. My bedroom was basically designed around the large double doors leading to the balcony.

That evening, after dinner, I walked out on the veranda to look at the lights of Málaga below. The balcony apartments of the city were small pools of yellow light in an otherwise velvety blackness. The moon over the Mediterranean created silvery paths along the crescent shores. The boulevard circling the waterfront had quite a few automobiles. The lights of the cruise ships anchored for the night continued to intrigue me. My eyes kept going back to them and wondering what activity was taking place within these floating palaces that reminded me of the cruise ships in the harbor in Saint Thomas, Virgin Islands.

PARADOR GIBRALFARO, Málaga (Málaga). Tel.: Málaga 22-19-02. A most comfortable former home on the heights overlooking Málaga, 556 km. from Madrid. RR., airport. Rates: See Index.

THE ALCAZABA IN MÁLAGA

Here I was at last. My first castle in Spain. I had climbed to the very top of the highest tower in the Moorish fortifications known as the Alcazaba above the city of Málaga.

Beneath me lay the city stretched out in a gorgeous crescent beside the Mediterranean. The sandy beaches extended up and down the coast as far as I could see. I leaned out over the parapet and looked down into the town. I felt like the captain general of all I surveyed—the commander, nay the sultan or king! My domain was the Costa del Sol—the coast of the sun. How the lush hills, valleys, and warm beaches must have beckoned those Moorish invaders in the 8th century who eventually overcame all of Spain. They held it in their grip for 700 years until Ferdinand and Isabella climaxed many years of war with a final victory at Granada in 1492 and began a new period in Spain's history.

Looking down from the tower into the ruins of this castle, preserved and reconstructed in many places, I could see the evidences of the

Moorish influence, an influence I was to see throughout Spain. The walls and crenelated towers were of Moorish design. The Moorish arch, now an integral part of Spanish architecture, was restated in the galleries, balconies, and staircases, and the courtyards were paved with small black and white stones, repeating an intriguing, symbolic Moorish design.

MÁLAGA

The Parador Gibralfaro was at the top of the heights overlooking Málaga, so after following the circuitous road down the mountain, my driver and good friend, Miguel, and I arrived at the bottom of the hill and found ourselves immediately involved in the activities of a Monday morning in a Spanish city. There were just a few tourists, but the number would increase considerably during the following Holy Week.

It was about ten o'clock and a number of people were having a second cup of coffee in some of the sidewalk cafes overlooking the plaza. The one-way traffic around the plaza was about seven cars wide, but most of the cars were small. The pace was rapid but not harrowing. There were quite a few motorbikes, and here and there a horse-drawn cart for tourists. Buses came by frequently and more and more shoppers poured into the center of one of Spain's major cities.

Málaga is blessed, as is most of the Costa del Sol, with a very even climate. In the summertime the breezes from the Mediterranean make the entire coast most desirable, and this section of the coast from Algeciras to Almeria is one of the most popular summer resorts in Europe.

THE ROAD TO NERJA

This section of the Costa del Sol is very popular during the summer season. It occurred to me that April and May would be an excellent time to visit southern Spain because the traffic is much lighter and the weather is mild. There is more room on the beaches and it is much easier to shop than during the summer months of June, July, and August.

We traveled from the suburbs out to the countryside, and it was on this road that I first saw a Moorish tower. Some of these were built by the Arabs over 1,000 years ago as lookout points and communication centers. Miguel explained that since the coast was subject to raids from North Africa, throughout southern Spain there was a network of these towers, which were used to summon aid quickly by heliograph when the coast was threatened with invasion. It was fascinating to realize that some of these towers, which are in surprisingly good repair, were built before the year A.D. 1000. I found that almost every sizable village in Andalusia has some type of Moorish fortification or castle left over

from the centuries of occupation. The Phoenicians, Romans, and Greeks also occupied this section of Spain, and on the road to Nerja, Miguel pointed out the remains of the Roman viaduct.

As we approached Nerja the terrain became more mountainous as it skirted the sea, and in many respects it reminded me of the coast of northern California. There were many marvelous overlooks, some of them 150 feet above the ocean. Then the road would drop down almost beside the sea for a few kilometers and suddenly twist its way back up to the cliffs. On this beautiful day the sun bathed the landscape, bringing vigor to the olive and almond trees, warmth to the sea, and life and beauty to everything that it touched.

PARADOR NERJA
Nerja (Málaga)

"In the popular summer months it is necessary to have reservations here for at least a year in advance." I was sitting on the terrace of this beautiful seaside parador in Nerja, talking with the parador director. We could see the beach stretching out in both directions, and I could well understand why guests from so many countries find this inn an attractive place for a vacation.

The village of Nerja is one of the jewels of the Costa del Sol. It is a picturesque town on a cliff in the foothills of southern Spain's mountains and is famous for sea and mountain views. Besides being a resort community, it is also a fishing district and sometimes bathers share the beach with fishermen and their nets. There is sailing, motor boating, and sport fishing here as well.

The director had already given me an excellent tour of this inn, which is contemporary in architecture. It is built around a hollow square with a modest swimming pool and a beautiful reflecting pool. The gardens, already beginning to bloom, were exquisite.

The inn, situated on a cliff, seventy-five feet above the seashore, provides an elevator to transport inn guests to and from the beach. "Of course, the beach is one of our great features," he said. "Many of our guests have been returning year after year to get a beautiful Costa del Sol tan."

Miguel told me, as we began our journey to Granada, that because of its nearness to the sea and the great beauty of the flowers, the Parador Nerja is one of the most popular inns in all of Spain.

PARADOR NERJA, Nerja (Málaga). Tel.: Nerja 52-00-50. A contemporary seaside parador, 51 km. from Málaga, 559 from Madrid. Aquatic sports, beach, swimming pool. Rates: See Index.

FROM NERJA TO GRANADA

"Now," said Miguel, "we are on the road to Granada." We had departed from Nerja approximately an hour and a half earlier and were now on a road that passed through a group of small fishing villages. The panorama reminded me of traveling south from Carmel, California, on the Pacific Coast Highway. We passed through the village of Almunécar and were now in the province of Granada. Along the coast the Moorish towers continued, each in sight of the other, most of them still in excellent repair. There was one small village after another clinging precariously to the sides of these hills by the sea.

At Motril, we turned north toward Granada. Twilight was beginning to set in and I kept looking out the rear window of the car for my last look at the blue Mediterranean for almost two weeks. There were groves of almond trees on each side. In most of the communities the people had gathered at the town square for an hour or so. It is a time for socializing and talking about the day's activities. This is a custom of the country and one that I found quite appealing. Children were playing and young people were strolling about in pairs. Dinner is not served in the average Spanish household until after eight or eight-thirty, so there is plenty of time in the early evening for the lighter things of life. I saw this scene repeated on many evenings in Spain.

We sped toward the mountains of Granada. The valleys became more steep and the road narrowed considerably at some places. I caught my first glimpse of snowcapped mountains, which were still dramatically lighted by the setting sun.

Now, the oranges, greens, purples, and reds of twilight were almost entirely replaced by the blue-black of night. My watch said 9:15, but Miguel assured me that we would be in Granada well in time for a late Spanish dinner.

THE SOUNDS OF GRANADA

Granada.

Say the word one hundred times and it has a hundred different shadings and meanings. Visit Granada one hundred times and each visit will be a new experience. Granada . . . Granada. It can be dreamy and reflective, or it can be demanding and provocative. Trill the ''r'' and you'll feel like a real Spaniard.

Granada is the home of the Alhambra, the palatial city of the Moors spread grandly across the hill bearing its name and protected by a network of walls and towers. Volumes have been written about it. Washington Irving immortalized it in his Tales of the Alhambra, *and Columbus must have spent quite a few days there waiting anxiously for an audience with Queen Isabella. It's been photographed from every angle, and the gardens and palaces are one of the most exquisite experiences in the world. Incidentally, I found that the best time to visit it is after three in the afternoon, when most of the tours have been*

completed, and the Alhambra can be enjoyed for all of its beauty and tranquility.

Granada is a city of monuments—the guidebooks list fifty-three. It has museums, galleries, churches, palatial homes, and sections of simple Moorish houses that date back to A.D. 1000. I have heard it said that Granada, rather than being a product of the culture of the Moorish civilization of Spain, was the shaper and builder of that culture. When the Moors came to Spain, they had spent centuries on the desert and were essentially a warlike, nomadic people. Seven hundred years later, when Ferdinand and Isabella reconquered the city, they found a sensual, refined, dreaming race whose chief delights were in art and nature.

PARADOR SAN FRANCISCO
Granada

"Sometimes when people ask whether it's noisy in the morning I tell them that when they wake up they will hear the beautiful singing of birds." I was seeing this beautiful parador, on the grounds of the Alhambra, through the eyes of the assistant director.

This parador is one of the most famous in all of Spain. Originally an Arabian palace, it was used as a Franciscan monastery under Ferdinand and Isabella, and has been a parador since 1945. The original buildings have been preserved and new additions have been made to provide twenty-six lodging rooms all in the style of the original architecture. Great care has been taken to be sure that the texture and the color of the brick used is as close to the original as possible.

"Queen Isabella was entombed in this monastery from the time of her death in Granada in 1504 until 1521," he explained. We were in a secluded courtyard, looking at a marker indicating her burial place, and I, too, felt a sense of quiet respect for this woman who played such an important role in the history of the world.

Parador San Francisco is enhanced with many fountains. I learned from the assistant director that each of the fountains in the Alhambra has a different musical tone. "The Moors," he said, "developed a feeling for peace and tranquility and believed that fountains were one way to achieve it. We have many fountains in the parador." At this particular moment we were standing in a courtyard that had four fountains, each with a different musical pitch. There were tall cypress trees swaying in the wind and birds flitting from tree to tree.

We concluded our tour at the terrace, where we walked to a point overlooking the Alhambra, just a few steps away. We could see the old quarter of the city and the Generalife Gardens, across the river.

The roses, which would be in such profusion in a few weeks, were just beginning to bud, and in the distance I could see the always snowcapped Sierra Nevada Mountains.

PARADOR SAN FRANCISCO, Granada (Granada). Tel.: 22-14-93. Originally an Arabian palace on the grounds of the Alhambra, 429 km. from Madrid. RR., airport. Rates: See Index.

THE ROAD TO PARADOR SIERRA NEVADA

After a most enjoyable lunch at the Parador San Francisco, Miguel and I were leaving Granada on our way to Sierra Nevada. There were two reasons to visit this spectacular mountain area—to see a parador located above the snow line, and to visit this particular section of Spain, a popular winter resort area, with skiing that attracts people from all over the world. It is possible to ski at 8,000 feet from November to May, and even year around at higher altitudes. The road that we were on, the Granada-Veleta highway, is the highest in Europe.

PARADOR SIERRA NEVADA
Monachil (Granada)

Spain is a land of contrasts. Just twenty-four hours ago I had been in a parador on the seacoast at Nerja where it was necessary to reserve a year in advance during the months of July and August. Here, perhaps no more than ninety kilometers distant, I was in a parador above the snow line where reservations for December through March have to be made three or four months in advance. I could, if I wanted to, ski here in the morning and drive to Motril for a swim in the Mediterranean in the afternoon.

The design of this parador has been created to conform with the contour of the mountains. The dining rooms and parlors have white plaster walls and natural wood ceilings with a high glossy finish. Lodging rooms, many in duplex style, overlook the snow-filled valley in front and the mountains in back.

I walked through the impressive dining room up to a balcony where there was a small fire laid in an open fireplace. As I settled back in one of the comfortable chairs and put my feet up on the hearth, a group of school children in ski outfits trooped in with a look of hunger on their well-tanned faces.

I asked them how the weather had been and they told me it had been sunny all week and that the conditions for spring skiing were perfect.

"Oh, it's excellent. We think it is the best skiing in Europe," said one. "We're on a holiday and our parents bring us here every year. One year we couldn't get reservations here at the parador, so we stayed at the ski village just below."

"It's pretty fast in the morning but along about noon, when the sun warms up the snow, it slows down and that's when we generally stop and come back here for lunch."

I decided to ask all of them where they lived and where they went to school and I had a chorus of answers in many languages and locations. They said they were going to ski the next day and asked me if I could join them. Regretfully, I said no. Tomorrow I would be in Jaén and Ubeda. They asked me why I was in Spain and I explained that I was writing a book about the country inns in Europe and they all thought that was "real cool."

I do myself.

PARADOR SIERRA NEVADA, Monachil (Granada). Tel.: 958/42-02-00. A contemporary mountain parador, 35 km. from Granada, 464 from Madrid. Rates: See Index.

THE HIGH ROAD TO JAÉN

"There is the parador we're going to visit," Miguel said, with a twinkle in his eye. *He pointed to the towers and walls of an ancient castle in the distance at the top of a steep, rugged mountain dominating the town below. "You mean that's it, on top of that mountain?" I asked. "Yes, that's it," he replied. "If you remember, I promised you something different from anything we have seen so far."*

We had driven up the high road from Granada to Jaén, passing first through the orchard country with small farms and beautiful homes, then through the low hills, and, finally, up into the mountain country. It was here that I entered the land of the Spanish olive tree. The olive tree is green and shapely, a tree of beauty and grace that is also of tremendous importance to the economy of Spain. On this road the olive groves alternated with cork oak trees.

The road threaded its way between high mountains and precipitous canyons. Occasionally, I saw shepherds with their sheep or goats. We passed through tunnels and zoomed alongside tumbling mountain brooks. In many respects the terrain resembled northern New England, except that the highlands here are not used as pasture, but cultivated for groves of olive trees extending almost to the mountain tops.

The city of Jaén proved to be a surprise because I didn't expect to see such a large, sophisticated town in this mountainous area. The road directing us to the parador passed immediately in front of one of the most beautiful cathedrals in Spain, a masterpiece of Gothic, Renaissance, and baroque architecture that took over 300 years to complete. We stopped long enough for a quick look.

Following the parador signs we found our way through the city and up the side of the mountain, the road twisting and turning as we approached the summit. Always in view, first on the right and then on the left, were the massive stone walls and tower. We passed through an old archway. We had arrived at the Parador Castillo de Santa Catalina.

PARADOR CASTILLO DE SANTA CATALINA
Jaén

My first feeling upon seeing this parador was complete awe of the building, with its massive Spanish Renaissance interior and tremendous, inspiring, mind-boggling view.

It was built by an Arab king who must have keenly appreciated its strategic military situation in the mountains. Ferdinand III laid siege and captured it from the Moors in 1266 on Saint Catalina's Day, af-

terwards reconstructing it. About twenty years ago it was converted into a parador and during recent years has undergone extensive restoration.

The first thing I saw when I walked through the massive doors of the main entrance was a three-story-high hallway. To my left was a great hall with two handsome Spanish fireplaces and cathedral windows providing a panoramic view of the mountains and the valley. Each of the bedrooms has its own balcony, which creates the sensation of being in an eagle's aerie. I had the most curious feeling that I could actually fly out over the rows of olive trees and the houses of Jaén at the base of the mountains. The cathedral that I had just visited a few moments earlier looked like a miniature from this great height. Overhead the blue skies of morning were being replaced by cloud banks and the wind was beginning to rise, causing thousands of olive trees to sway in the breeze.

In a country where castles have been converted into marvelous hotels, Parador Castillo de Santa Catalina is exceptional.

PARADOR CASTILLO DE SANTA CATALINA, Jaén. Tel.: Jaén 26-44-11. A most impressive castle parador with a swimming pool at 97 km. from Granada, 335 from Madrid. Rates: See Index.

PARADOR CONDESTABLE DAVALOS
Ubeda (Jaén)

I was singing in the shower at a Renaissance palace. The bathroom was princely, to say the least. In remodeling this stately mansion, which

would be very much in place in Florence, the architect provided the most comfortable of accommodations for two people. There were even twin washbowls.

I stepped out of the shower and wrapped myself in one of those incredible towels that go twice around. Even the most noble families who had previously lived in this palace were not nearly as well accommodated as the parador guest of today.

The bedroom/sitting room had a two-story ceiling and windows and shutters. The customary twin beds were supplemented with some interesting Spanish antiques, including a handsome carved wardrobe. At the moment the most useful piece of furniture was an unobtrusive small refrigerator, from which I obtained a welcome bottle of lime soda.

The parador is built around a glass-roofed courtyard with guest rooms on the second and third floors. There are a great many antiques, including suits of armor worn by ancient Spanish knights. The director proudly showed me the library of the parador, which is not only beautifully furnished and decorated, but has some very good books and magazines for the guests of the house. Like most of the paradors I visited, this one also has a television room.

At dinner that evening I met two retired American ladies, Mrs. Harriet Smith and Mrs. Ann Ulrich, both from the state of Washington, who were driving through Spain, and having a wonderful time. When I learned that they did not speak Spanish, I asked them how they were managing. Mrs. Smith said, "Oh, we are doing wonderfully. With a combination of sign language, maps, and lots of laughs, we have been kept on the right track by these wonderful people. I just can't say enough about the generosity and manners of everyone we have met in Spain.''

PARADOR CONDESTABLE DAVALOS, Ubeda (Jaén). Tel.: Ubeda 75-03-45. An extremely comfortable mansion at 55 km. from Jaén, 338 from Madrid. Rates: See Index.

PARADOR DEL ADELANTADO
Cazorla (Jaén)

I was having breakfast high in the Sierra de Cazorla with the Davenports—Jenifer and Clark, and their four children, Sara, Jad, Lisa, and Sam. They were Americans who were living in Spain for three years.

"We've been at this parador for three days," said Jenifer, passing a plate of rolls to Sam, "and we've had an absolutely marvelous time."

"And we've seen lots of wild animals, including an ibex. Have you ever seen an ibex?" This came from Lisa, who has very blond hair and blue eyes. I had to confess that I had never seen an ibex, which by definition is a wild goat with large, backward-curving horns.

"Well, we saw one," she said proudly, "and we also saw some mountain goats and deer."

This parador is a very cozy hunting lodge. The furnishings and decor reflect the wildlife of the region. There are mounted heads of wild boar, deer, bear, and mountain sheep. There are also some excellent black and white and full-color photographs of the region showing some of the huge rocky mountains and crags and steep dells.

After breakfast we all walked into the living room, where a welcome fire was blazing away in a huge fireplace. We made ourselves comfortable in the deep leather chairs, and I asked them if they were enjoying their holiday.

"Oh, yes, this is really our kind of place," said Clark Davenport. "And I must say that we never expected to find an intimate little inn like this so high in the mountains."

"Yes, and you should see our rooms," said Sara. "They have a wonderful view of the valley. When I wake up in the morning I can see the sun coming through the trees."

"I hope the rain stops today," said Jad, "because we have one more walking trip we want to make. Dad says that if it doesn't stop raining we'll take the road that leads back up into the mountains and is the source of the river that passes through Cordoba and Seville." Clark later confirmed that that was the Guadalquivir, which rises in the Sierra Cazorla.

Incidentally, I have one memento of the trip to Cazorla that I treasure very much. As I was leaving, Lisa Davenport presented me with a crayon drawing of an ibex.

PARADOR DEL ADELANTADO, Cazorla (Jaén). Tel.: 72-10-75. A cozy hunting lodge at 27 km. from Cazorla, 137 from Jaén, 417 from Madrid. Mountain scenery, hunting, and fishing. Rates: See Index.

DON QUIXOTE'S LA MANCHA

When I ventured north from the province of Jaén into the province of Ciudad Real, I came into the land of Don Quixote and his creator, Miguel Cervantes. I was on the edge of the countryside that is known traditionally as La Mancha. Don Quixote, Cervantes' great book, and the musical version of it, The Man of La Mancha, have brought this moving story into homes all over the world.

While I was waiting to enjoy a midday meal in the albergue at Manzanares, I made the acquaintance of an Englishman who told me some very interesting things about this area.

"It is possible," he said, "to trace the course of Don Quixote's journeys throughout La Mancha. There are towns and villages in the region to which Cervantes made several references."

PARADOR ALMAGRO
Almagro (Ciudad Real)

While visiting the parador in Cazorla I heard about one in Almagro, reputed to be one of the most outstanding paradores in all of Spain.

There was nothing to do but to head north to have a look at it. The road leading to Almagro was unusual, because instead of being blacktop it was constructed of brick and looked as though it had been there for many, many years. The countryside was flat with many fields of early-ripening grain. The houses and the villages were quite different from what I had become accustomed to in southern Spain—these had sort of a squarish look. The second-floor balconies had intricate iron grilles and many had red, green, and blue flower-filled pots hanging from them.

Almagro is a middle-sized village and a short visit to the tourist office proved to be most helpful with some literature on the area, some of it in English. Among other things, I learned that there is a 13th-century theater here, the Corral de Comedias, the only one of its kind left in Spain.

The parador was once a 16th-century convent, and it has all of the graceful architectural features that have been incorporated into the newly constructed paradores throughout Spain—graceful Moorish arches, tiled courtyards, and many musical fountains. As I found throughout Spain, a great deal of care has been taken to blend the old and the new.

PARADOR ALMAGRO, Almagro (Ciudad Real). Tel.: 86-01-00. A 65-guestroom inn in a former 16th-century convent. Swimming pool, air-conditioning (very important). It is 189 km. from Madrid, 23 km. from Ciudad Real, 230 km. from Cordoba. Rates: See Index.

Directions: Almagro is south of Madrid on C-415 between Ciudad Real and Valdepenas.

CORDOBA—CITY OF FLOWERS

Cordoba is a city of flowers. There are flowers everywhere—on the plazas, the bridges, the squares, and on almost every corner. There are some streets with flowers in all of the windows and potted flowers hanging from balconies.

One of the most engaging plazas in this city is called La Plaza del Potro (Plaza of the Young Horse). At one end there is a 16th-century fountain dominated by a colt with its front hoofs raised, holding the shield of the city. Also in this plaza stands an inn that existed before the 14th century. Miguel Cervantes lived for some time in a neighboring street with an uncle who was a saddlemaker. He mentions the inn several times in his writings.

Cordoba has many other engaging features. It is not as large a city as Granada or Seville and is somewhat more modest in its demeanor. It has an impressive mosque, excellent museums, and ancient ruins from a romantic past.

I was also fascinated by the Roman bridge that crosses the Quadalquivir River. Cordoba has a very lengthy history and this bridge was probably built during the time of Julius Caesar. Over the years it has undergone numerous alterations and has been the victim of wars and revolutions. It is somewhat ironic that of the sixteen arches now supporting the bridge, not one is Roman—most of them date from the Moorish period.

I paid a short visit to the mosque on a sunny morning and the inside was a bit spooky by contrast. There was a series of repeated arches that seemed to stretch out of sight. In the middle of the mosque is a Christian church, illustrating the merging of Christian and Moorish cultures in Spain.

In the area immediately adjacent to the mosque there were several small shops with curios and gifts of good quality. Once again, it was quite common to see mothers and daughters walking along the street with their arms intertwined. The horse-drawn, open tourist carriages were driven by men wearing the traditional flat-topped hats.

PARADOR LA ARRUZAFA
Cordoba

I will always remember the Parador La Arruzafa as the place where I had my first experience with Spanish hors d'oeuvres. It was at the midday meal (*comida*). We had arrived late the previous evening, and I had slept beyond my usual hour in the morning. Miguel had dropped me off at the mosque and I also took the opportunity to walk through the Old Quarter and up into the main square and shopping district.

I returned to the parador and was taken on a complete tour by the courteous parador director. We visited rooms on every floor and toured the kitchen, the gardens, and the recreation area with a swimming pool.

We stopped to enjoy some refreshments and the sunshine on the terrace. It had been a very busy morning and I felt unusually hungry, so I ordered the hors d'oeuvres for my first course.

Well, the dishes began to arrive. There were at least fifteen and they included delicious small clams and many varieties of small fish, very salty and extremely tasty. There were small dishes containing varieties of vegetables, small chunks of liver, and quite a few other items from the truck farm that I was unable to identify. This was only the first course.

After I finished sampling everything, I felt that I had had sufficient luncheon! But I did try the spinach omelet, one of the favorite dishes in Spain, and a light caramel custard for dessert.

The Parador La Arruzafa has all the conveniences of a four-star hotel in Spain, but the general atmosphere is far more relaxed. It is six or seven stories high, and all of the rooms have balconies facing the broad plain on which Cordoba is located. The gardens, hedges, flowers, and lemon and orange trees add to the atmosphere. There is even a play area for children. Quite a few suites are available and some of them have parlors and dressing rooms.

PARADOR LA ARRUZAFA, Cordoba. Tel.: 27-59-00. This is a somewhat larger than average parador (83 guestrooms) in the northwest suburbs of the city. There are beautiful gardens, tennis courts, and a swimming pool. Cordoba is 400 km. from Madrid, 172 from Granada, 182 from Málaga, and 138 from Seville. Rates: See Index.

LAND OF THE SKYLINE

Someday, I am going to return to the village of Fuenteovejuna. If I have to wait until I can pronounce it properly, I may never go back! However, I found that by taking it syllable by syllable and changing the pronunciation to read Fuento-be-huna *I could get it approximately right.*

It's not the name alone that has such memorable qualities. Fuenteovejuna is halfway between Cordoba and Zafra in some of the most beautiful farming country (campo) *that I saw during my trip. I call it "the land of the skyline" because at almost every point there was something to be seen on the horizon. In fact, I found that in Spain the skyline almost always seems to offer an exciting new vista. It might be the silhouettes of hilltop trees lined up like an army marching single file. It might be a ring of saw-toothed mountains, or a castle towering over the crest of a hill. On this particular route there always seemed* to be two or three Spanish villages in the distance, nestled against the hillside, each with its own church, surrounding fields, and frequently with its own guardian Moorish tower.

About an hour and a half after we left Cordoba, a village appeared in the distance. Like so many others, it was situated on a hill, with a church steeple reigning over all below. It intrigued me that there was a wall around the entire village, and the main road did not go through the village but circled it. We decided to take a look inside the walls, so we turned and drove between the sycamore trees and passed through the gate.

I was immediately reminded of Alice stepping through the Looking Glass. It was very quiet and I attributed part of this to the fact that trucks and automobiles do not ordinarily go through this village. The main streets were just wide enough for two automobiles abreast and most of the side streets could accommodate only one car at a time. I stopped to take photographs of people sitting on chairs in front of their houses, asking their permission in my stumbling Spanish. They always granted it with a smile. I was using a Polaroid camera and gave one old gentleman a picture I took of him.

The doors of the church were open and I could see the statues inside placed on the platform in readiness for the Holy Week procession through the steep streets of the village a little later. We were lucky enough to find one store open and bought some delicious Spanish almonds to ward off hunger until we reached Zafra for dinner about ten o'clock that night. Because there were practically no autos on the narrow streets, and very few reminders of today's electronic and mechanized world, it was like walking through a village of about seventy-five years ago.

Oh, Fuenteovejuna, I may never be able to pronounce you, but I will certainly never forget you.

PARADOR HERNAN CORTES
Zafra (Badajoz)

In Spain even the expected can be unexpected. Miguel told me that the parador in Zafra was located in a castle, but even with this knowledge I was positively bowled over by the Parador Hernan Cortes.

Unlike most fortresses in Spain, this was not built by the Moors, but by the Christian rulers of the region. It has been named for the Spanish explorer of the New World, Hernan Cortes, who was a protegé of the original owners of the castle.

The adaptation of this old-world castle to meet the needs of today's travelers has been most subtle. Additions have been constructed in the

same architectural style to increase the number of accommodations. Many of the rooms look out over courtyards or gardens and, of course, they are equipped with the modern conveniences, including heating and air conditioning. The parador even has its own restored chapel.

Furniture for the public rooms and guest rooms was chosen to harmonize with the dignified formality of the castle. There are quite a few large carved tables and chairs and numerous tapestries and oil paintings. Guests enjoy walking up to the tower above the third floor to enjoy the view.

This is a very popular parador and, as in all cases, reservations should be made well in advance. On the night we arrived, there was a line of people at 9 p.m., hoping that some guests would not be there in time to claim their reservation.

Hernan Cortes was famous for his conquest of Mexico, but to a growing number of aficionados his name is now synonymous with a most beautiful parador in Spain.

PARADOR HERNAN CORTES, Zafra (Badajoz). Tel.: Zafra 55-02-00. This is also a very popular stopping-off place, not only for going to the south coast, but also for the road to Portugal, 403 km. from Madrid, 85 from Badajoz, 147 from Seville. Swimming pool. Rates: See Index.

PARADOR VIA DE LA PLATA
Merida (Badajoz)

When we drove into the little square at Merida, among the first things I noticed were the storks nesting in the chimneys of the inn. (There is something very comforting about birds nesting in or near a home.) The entrance to the inn was through a gardenlike plaza filled with countless blooming flowers, whose colors were dramatically heightened by the austere white walls of the parador. Although the building had been put to a variety of uses through the years (at one time it was a prison), the most recent and longest use was as a convent. It was modified and enlarged about fifteen years ago and I was told that the furniture and decor in the lounges, parlors, and guest rooms were typical of this region of Spain.

In spite of the many centuries of Moorish occupation and subsequent reconquest by the Christians, the city has retained strong Roman influences. It was established during the height of the Roman Empire. The name of the parador, Via de la Plata, is a combination of Latin and Spanish—it was the name of an old Roman road in Merida.

Reflecting the various cultural and architectural influences, the interior of the parador has quiet corners with single Roman columns and a profusion of intricate Moorish iron work and decoration. The chairs, tables, and other furnishings suggest the later Christian influence.

Because of the location of this parador in Merida, it is very popular with travelers en route to and from Portugal.

A special surprise awaits the traveler stopping here. Besides the appealing plaza at the entrance, the inn has its own private gardens in the rear with carefully trained hedges about twelve feet high forming a series of Moorish arches around a fountain bedecked with pots of carnations.

PARADOR VIA DE LA PLATA, Merida (Badajoz). Tel.: Merida 31-38-00 or 31-38-11. A former convent, now reflecting regional influence in decor, at 61 km. from Badajoz, 343 from Madrid. RR. Rates: See Index.

PARADOR COSTA DE LA LUZ
Ayamonte (Huelva)

"Right now we are looking down on a place where history has been made for thousands of years." I was standing on the terrace of a beautiful parador, located at the estuary of the Guadiana River which separates southern Spain and Portugal. My host, the director of the parador, was discussing the history of the region.

"First, the Phoenicians came here and then the Romans," he continued. "This area was taken over by the kings of Portugal, who then gave it to the Spanish knightly Order of Santiago. On two occasions it was the dowry of Spanish princesses who were to become the queens of Portugal. In fact, we might say that Ayamonte is a link between the two nations of the Iberian peninsula.

"For a short time it was the capital of Spain during the Napoleonic Wars," he added, "but with all of the conflicts in Europe, this particular place has never known the ravages of an invading army."

We watched the ferry boat crossing the river to Portugal. We were within sight of about three small villages on the other side of the river, and I could see the long rows of olive trees and rich green fields.

We went back inside and passed through the lobby, where there was an art exhibition featuring the work of local painters. The director explained that the combination of bright sunlight plus the water and the landscape make this a very popular location for artists. The parador was especially designed for this site, and each room overlooks either the town or the estuary. The long hallway was accented with huge pots of ivy whose green tendrils reached to the floor. It is a single-story building designed to blend with the skyline.

As we turned toward the dining room, the director explained that because of the proximity to the sea the typical Ayamonte cuisine tends to center on fish and crustaceans. "We have a continual change of specialties," he said. "Sometimes we have marine stews and now and then we have fresh sardines, which are caught at dawn. There are lobsters, prawns, crayfish, and clams available, and we try to keep our menu exciting by having as many of these regional specialties as possible."

The village of Ayamonte has received numerous national and provincial prizes in recent years for the beauty and cleanliness of its streets, gardens, and parks. After visiting this attractive fishing port, I can certainly see why.

PARADOR COSTA DE LA LUZ, Ayamonte (Huelva). Tel.: Huelva 32-07-00. A beautiful parador on the Guadiana River near the border of Portugal. At 60 km. from Huelva, 696 from Madrid. RR., swimming pool. Rates: See Index.

PARADOR CRISTOBAL COLON
Mazagon (Huelva)

I visited this parador on a stormy day and it still looked beautiful. It is located on the Costa de la Luz, south of the city of Huelva, overlooking the Gulf of Cadiz.

I toured the grounds after borrowing an umbrella from the concierge. From the cliffs, where the parador is located, I could see the whitecaps tossing about in the Gulf. This is one of the older paradores, especially constructed by the Ministry of Tourism for the purpose of accommodating travelers and holiday-seekers. There is a swimming pool and a beach, both of which are very popular during the summer months. In fact, the concierge informed me that reservations for the warm-weather months must be made a year in advance.

The interior design reflected the colors of the landscape and sea, with a great many yellows, light greens, blues, and light browns. The dining room had picture windows with a fantastic view of the gardens, cliffs, and the ocean beyond. As far as I could see, every room had its own patio, overlooking either the garden or the ocean.

As we were leaving this parador, the sun was breaking through and the afternoon promised to answer the wishes of all of those children and their parents who were hoping for the good weather. I, too, would have liked to remain for two or three days at this delightful parador on the Costa de la Luz.

PARADOR CRISTOBAL COLON, Mazagon (Huelva). Tel.: 37-60-00. A beachside parador, 42 km. from Huelva, 640 from Madrid. Beach, swimming pool. Rates: See Index.

HOTEL DOÑA MARIA
Seville

We had to ask directions to the Doña Maria only because the location seemed too perfect to be believed. It is just across the plaza from La Giralda, the famous 12th-century Moorish tower in the quiet heart of Seville.

Every room is different—full of antiques and personal mementos from the late Contessa de Albalat, who turned her ancient palace into a hotel some twenty years ago. We had room 310, which has a white canopied bed, a rose tile bathroom, and a view of the Giralda that would have been the envy of all those people trying to get the right angle for their cameras from the square below.

However, every guest can enjoy the spectacular sight from the rooftop terrace, with its unexpected swimming pool (so welcome after a day of touring) and white iron furniture.

The guest rooms are not very large at the Doña Maria, but all have private baths, radios, piped-in music, and direct-dial telephones. You can also arrange for your own TV set, though there is television in the first-floor lounge and in the cozy bar.

Continental breakfast of juice, assorted rolls with butter and jam, and tea, coffee, or chocolate may be ordered either in the room or in the blue and white breakfast room. No other meals are served, but there are so many restaurants nearby that the only problem is which one to choose each evening.

It's hard to beat an after-dinner walk in the gardens of the Alcazar.

HOTEL DOÑA MARIA, Don Remondo 19, Seville 41004. Tel.: 954-22-49-90. A 61-guestroom (private baths) friendly hotel in a one-time palace a few steps from Plaza de los Reyes, opposite the Giralda and the cathedral in the true heart of Old Seville. Open year-round. Swimming pool on premises. Manuel Rodriguez Andrade, Manager. Rates: See Index.

Directions: Plaza de los Reyes is on the other side of the Giralda from the main Avenida de la Constitución. You can see the Giralda from anyplace in town.

PARADOR DEL ALCAZAR DEL REY DON PEDRO
Carmona (Seville)

We were on the road from Seville to the mountain village of Carmona, a distance of only thirty-five kilometers. The torrential rain that had drenched the city and cancelled the Holy Week procession the night before was now replaced by brilliant Andalusian sunshine. Even from some distance we could see the white village and the Alcazar on top of a precipitous hill.

Upon our arrival we stopped for a few moments to do some shopping and then proceeded through a huge stone gate to another world—the world of Don Pedro the Cruel, for this magnificent parador was once his castle.

The completely walled courtyard was big enough for six football fields. In one corner, the unrestored crumbling remnants of the castle still stood as mute reminders of another epoch. Before going through the front door of the inn, we turned aside and walked through a colonnade of Moorish arches to a precipice overlooking the countryside. The vista was idyllic. It was Spain in springtime. Stretched out farther than

the eye could see was a series of small farms whose tilled grounds were bursting forth into life in the warm sun. It was a panorama of countless shades of green gathering new strength every day.

We passed through a large, two-story living room with walls decorated with armor and swords. These bellicose artifacts were balanced by the serenity of the open courtyard, where the fountains sent melodious sounds into the atmosphere. The sun was now shining directly overhead into this gentle haven and I appreciated once again the Moorish affinity for the musical sounds of water.

We walked through still another handsome living room and out onto a *terraza,* which I understand is the correct term for the outside larger balcony. Here we had another view of the countryside, including the swimming pool of the parador, a blue oval shape directly below us.

The director suggested that we might enjoy a tour of some of the guest rooms of the inn. We walked through a courtyard with a fountain and up two flights of stairs to the top floor. An elevator was also available.

He ushered us into an attractively designed bedroom and explained that all of the rooms had balconies. As is true in most of the paradores, the bedspreads, curtains, and rugs have designs that are identified with the local region.

"It took six years to build this parador," he explained. As I stepped out onto the balcony, I leaned over to look at the walls below, and I could see that restoration of this magnificent building was an engineering feat. Some of the skilled workmen must have been able to fly.

Other interior touches were handsome carved doors and carefully designed windows with multicolored panes.

As we returned to the main floor, I asked him about the swords hanging on the walls and he explained that these were copies of weapons belonging to Don Pedro and his brother, Henrique. "They had a duel," he said. "Henrique killed Don Pedro and became king. That was long ago."

PARADOR DEL ALCAZAR DEL REY DON PEDRO, Carmona (Seville). Tel.: 14-10-10; 14-10-60. A magnificent castle-parador high on a hill, 35 km. from Seville. Rates: See Index.

PARADOR CASA DEL CORREGIDOR
Arcos de la Frontera (Cadiz)

Arcos de la Frontera, one of the "white villages" of Spain, is a community that commands the traveler's attention. Sitting high on a promontory above the Guadelete River, the white walls of its houses and the gay colors of its patios have been likened to a staircase of light that compels the visitor to scale the heights. Many of the houses hang precariously over the edge of a ravine.

The road through the village to the plaza at the top led through narrow streets, where there seemed to be barely enough room for a single car.

However, the crest is a prize well worth the effort of negotiating the narrow streets because the beautiful church, the exceptional parador, and the plaza all share a vista that reminded me of the beautiful panorama at Carmona.

The parador is built in a restored stately home with many of the guest rooms and dining rooms sharing the impressive view. The comparative austerity of the white-walled exterior calls attention to the Gothic facade of the church.

Each of the twin-bedded rooms has attractive furniture and the entire atmosphere would encourage me to remain for a long visit.

The director of the parador was a most pleasant and accommodating man. We sat on the terraza and talked of innkeeping in Spain and America. "One of the things I enjoy most about being here is that many people return each year because they find it such a restful and inspiring experience," he said.

Even as we were talking, a schoolteacher from Connecticut, who was on a year's sabbatical in Spain, introduced himself and said that he had visited this parador three times during the past two years. "I have been to many," he said, "but this is by far my favorite."

PARADOR CASA DEL CORREGIDOR, Arcos de la Frontera (Cadiz). Tel.: 70-05-00. A restored stately home, at 85 km. from Cadiz, 666 from Madrid. Rates: See Index.

HOTEL DOS MARES
Tarifa (Cadiz)

Miguel and I were on the road from Cadiz to Algeciras, driving along next to the ocean, when I saw a sign for Hotel Dos Mares. It directed us through a grove of trees to a group of buildings on the beach.

That's how I met Robbert Jan van Looy, the innkeeper and owner of the Hotel of the Two Seas. Robbert (two b's are correct) and I hit it off immediately. He is a Dutchman, who has had wide experience in the hotel business in various parts of Europe. We settled down for a chat in the lounge of the inn, which enjoys a most impressive view of the ocean.

"We call this the Hotel Dos Mares because we are at the point where the Atlantic Ocean and the Mediterranean Sea almost come together," he said.

Robbert suggested a tour of the inn, so we started out by walking downstairs by way of a circular staircase that sweeps into a dining room overlooking the sea. The atmosphere was bright and gay with blue tablecloths and nautical decorations. We walked out through the adjoining stone-arched terrace to a grassy part of the beach, and I looked at some of the little bungalows in which most of the guest rooms are located. The cottages are separated by sufficient distance to give a feeling of privacy, and all of them overlook the dunes and the rolling surf. The rooms have twin beds and are very clean, and somewhat austere.

We returned to the inn and talked about the food. "Our menu is international because our guests come from all over the world. Of course, we always have Spanish dishes as part of the choice, but a

typical dinner menu has a choice of four first courses and two middle courses. Generally, we have a choice of either ice cream or fresh fruit for dessert.

I was very glad to find this intimate little fourteen-room inn on the water. From now on I will more frequently follow my intuition.

HOTEL DOS MARES, Apartado ao Tarifa (Cadiz). Tel.: (956) 68-40-35. A 14-guestroom privately owned seaside inn, 25 km. from Algeciras. Open April 1 to Nov. 1. It is necessary to reserve well in advance. Send first night's room charge as deposit. Rates: See Index.

RONDA, THE DELIGHTFUL AND UNEXPECTED

The road from San Pedro on the coast to Ronda in the mountains is unbelievable. It is one of the most twisting, turning, exciting scenic roads I have ever been on in my life. It is a steady climb for forty of the fifty-four kilometers, with views of the mountains, whose beauty is in their starkness. There is a moonscape quality about everything, with different strata of rock revealing surprisingly brilliant streaks of color. Sometimes on the distant ridges, I could see a cluster of houses clinging precariously to the sides of the mountains.

There were sweeping views of valleys and range after range of moun-

tains, some of them snowcapped. As we neared the end of the trip, the terrain softened somewhat, and there were pine and oak trees and flocks of sheep and goats being tended by a lone shepherd.

I never expected to find a town of such dimensions at the end of this narrow, twisty road. The biggest surprise about Ronda is that this small city has an extraordinary setting of almost unequaled grandeur on the lip of a gorge, which the guidebook says is 1,000 feet deep. Ronda makes a wonderful side trip.

PARADOR DEL GOLF
Torremolinos (Málaga)

I must confess that when I left New York I never expected to be playing golf at a country inn in Spain, but here I was at the Parador del Golf in Torremolinos playing nine holes.

I had heard about the Parador del Golf from Marilyn and Dan Sullivan, who live almost next door to me in the Berkshires. She and Dan are enthusiastic golfers and travelers, and it so happened that they went to Spain about three weeks ahead of me. They stayed ten days at this parador. In her letter to me from Spain, these are some of the things she had to say about her stay at this inn in Torremolinos:

"I know you will like it here. The beach is only about 100 steps away. We spend most of our time walking on the beach or on the golf course or enjoying the swimming pool built in the center of a three-sided square that is formed by the buildings of the inn. Our room is lovely with walls of pine board, and drapes and bedspreads of a finished burlap material with a Spanish design. And I have never seen such beautiful, enormous bathrooms.

"The golf course is great. You know how Dan is—it has to be just right to please him, and he is ready to come back to Spain anytime. One thing we can't get over is the food. I think we could put on ten pounds apiece if we aren't careful.

"Be sure you visit Marbella, it's an attractive seacoast town—there are many Americans who have condominiums there. I am enclosing a postcard showing all of the sailboats. I have to go now because Dan says we are teeing off in about three minutes. By the way, you can rent golf clubs here, so don't bother to bring yours."

Well, Marilyn, thank you so much. I think we have seen the Parador del Golf from your eyes. The only thing you didn't send me were instructions on how to correct my American hook while in Spain.

PARADOR DEL GOLF, Torremolinos (Málaga). Tel.: (952) 38-12-55. This parador is on the road between Torremolinos and Málaga. It is modern in design, with the beach nearby, a swimming pool, and a Robert Trent Jones golf course. Convenient to airport. Rates: See Index.

ITINERARY 2

This itinerary starts from Madrid, goes south to Toledo, northwest to Galicia, and crosses the top of Spain to the French border at San Sebastian. It returns to Madrid via Santo Domingo de la Calzada, Burgos, and Segovia.

TOLEDO

"Seventy kilometers from Madrid, the city of Toledo rises heavenwards, immersed in an atmosphere of violent light. It sprawls over an enormous crag that seems to be challenging space, while the fast-flowing River Tagus on its way to Portugal surrounds the city in a tight curve as though the ancient walls were anchored in this natural moat. The silhouette of the city stands out in sharp relief against a background formed by the crest of the encircling hills and the more distant ranges of hills and mountains.

"Toledo is the city which presents the most complete and characteristic ensemble of all that the genuinely Spanish land and civilization have ever been. It is the most perfect epitome, the most brilliant and evocative summary, of Spain's history. So, a traveler who can only

spend a single day in Spain ought, without hesitation, to spend it seeing Toledo." I wish I could say that I was the first person to write those impressive words, but somebody else wrote them first. They are from the brochure published by the Spanish Tourist Office.

Toledo—the Michelin Green Guide gives six-and-a-half pages to its churches, ancient palaces and houses, cobbled alleys, beautiful court-yards, lovely cloisters, synagogues, hidden chapels, museums, bridges, and the numerous excursions into the nearby countryside where Miguel Cervantes wandered and Don Quixote rode. It is a land of windmills and silhouettes of castles against blue skies.

El Greco, one of the great figures in Spanish painting, made his home in Toledo and bequeathed his best works to the city. His finest paintings are still in the city and its province, which have become a virtual museum for his works. Very near to the spot where the painter actually lived, there stands the El Greco House and Museum housing an important collection of his canvases, particularly the View of To-ledo.

There are so many periods of history involving Toledo that I shall suggest the reader turn to Michelin and other guidebooks for a more substantial account.

PARADOR CONDE DE ORGAZ
Toledo

In the waning sun of a Saturday afternoon, I arrived for what I thought would be perhaps a two- or three-hour stay in Toledo. Following the signs for the parador on the road around the walled city, I realized that this would be more than a mere hasty visit.

Guest rooms have balconies and the public rooms are decorated with gorgeous ceramic tiles and crafts typical of the region.

Conde de Orgaz has the most desirable view of this jewellike city, both day and night, and this view is eminently paintable—the earth colors of ocher and terra cotta are thrilling in their harmonious blending. As I stood admiring this panorama, the bells of Toledo began to toll the faithful to an early evening mass.

PARADOR CONDE DE ORGAZ, Toledo. Tel.: 925-22-18-50. A very pleasant well-designed inn with an exceptional view of the city of Toledo. Seventy km. from Madrid; 106 km. from Oropesa. Rates: See Index.

Directions: From Madrid, N-401 leads directly to Toledo.

PARADOR DEL VIRREY TOLEDO
Oropesa (Toledo)

Even though this 15th-century castle-cum-palace is auspiciously situated in the Alcazar of Oropesa, one of the things I remember most vividly is the huge stork's nest on the top of the town clock, in itself worth several photographs. The clock tower is on the top of an arch that provides a passageway for automobiles. Storks' nests are considered good luck in all of Europe.

Oropesa stands in the eastern foothills of the Sierra de Gredos and is one of those little Castilian towns that have somehow managed to preserve not only their character throughout the centuries, but also the historical and artistic traditions that testify to their past splendors.

On the crest of a small hill crowning the town is the castle that was once the palatial home of various dukes and other notables of Castile. In spite of wars and rumors of wars, the fortress was kept in a magnificent state of repair until the arrival of Napoleon's armies, who destroyed it.

The incredible thing about so many of these castles is that they are so *ancient!* The famed Isabella of Spain figures prominently in the history of this one, which was already old in her time.

Well, enough of history, except to say that the various owners would

53

certainly be pleased to see what has happened to their little home in the country, because in 1930 it was converted into a national parador, and that makes it one of the earliest in Spain.

Basically, it is built around three sides of a square; the fourth side is made up of some ancient ruins and a rather well-restored keep, or tower.

The view stretches across the plains to the snowcapped mountains that seem to rise suddenly from the floor of the plain. With the sun on the peaks, they looked as if they were moving closer and closer all the time. In fact, I would be moving towards them in a few days.

The inner balconies had been hung with dozens and dozens of plants, all in beautiful flowery profusion during my visit. The feeling is truly of old Spain and everything has been done in the tradition of the paradors.

The guest rooms are a tribute to the late King Alfonso, who initiated the construction of the paradors, and the bathrooms are a symphony of tile and convenience. Wandering from one end of the castle to the other, one cannot help but be impressed with the collection of old furniture and tapestries.

The Parador del Virrey Toledo in Oropesa is at or near important crossroads for the traveler in Spain. If he chooses, he can go north into the mountains to Jarandilla and Avila, or east to Lisbon by way of Merida, Badajoz, and then to Estremoz in Portugal.

PARADOR DEL VIRREY TOLEDO, Oropesa (Toledo). Tel.: (925) 43-00-00. A 44-guestroom hotel in an elegantly restored feudal castle, within a short distance of the mountains. Rates: See Index.

Directions: There are two Oropesas in Spain. This one is in the province of Toledo about 148 km. from Madrid. The other is by the sea about 440 km. from Madrid. This is on the N-V (E-4), one of the main roads west and southwest from Madrid. Parador signs lead through the village and to the castle on the top of the hill.

PARADOR CARLOS V
Jarandilla de la Vera (Cáceres)

It had been an interesting day, mixing the old Spain with the new, and now on the well-worn steps of this 15th-century castle here on the slopes of the Sierra de Jarandilla Mountains, the mix was becoming rather cacophonous.

A traveling carnival had set up shop just a few hundred yards from the parador. The portable Ferris wheel with its bright lights and the other rides that delight children of all ages were in full operation, accompanied by a public address system playing rock and roll. Apparently, carnivals are the same in all parts of the world.

I couldn't help but wonder what Carlos V would have thought of all of this activity. In 1555, he gave up his life as the reigning monarch and began the construction of a monastery at Yuste, about eight miles southwest of Jarandilla, where he spent the last two years of his life in quiet and solitude.

Carlos lived here at this castle for a few months while the monastery was being completed, and it appears to be much the same as it was during his time. There is a large courtyard, many towers and ramparts, and even a drawbridge. It was verily an almost impenetrable fortress.

The interior looks like a castle—stone walls, winding stairs, and tapestries. The guest rooms, combining old and new, are impeccably designed and the bathrooms are a joy. This is the case in all the Spanish paradors.

Eventually, even the Ferris wheel and the public address system grew weary and the carnival packed up, leaving Jarandilla to its four-hundred centuries of quiet and Carlos V could sleep in peace. However, I'm only kidding because, although this is a mountain town, it is really quite modern and there are many new buildings being built—quite in the spirit of what I found was going on throughout Spain.

PARADOR CARLOS V, Jarandilla de la Vera (Cáceres). Tel.: 56-01-17. A 16-guestroom hotel in an impressive feudal castle in the Sierra de Gredos mountains. The village itself is well worth the visit and the Yuste Monastery is nearby. Rates: See Index.

Directions: For the traveler between Madrid and Portugal on N-V (E-4), there is a choice of staying overnight at the parador in Oropesa or driving another 60 km. into the mountains to Jarandilla. Either could be an excellent choice. Jarandilla is on C-501 between Plasencia and Arenas de San Pedro. Curiously enough, C-501 actually starts on the outskirts of Madrid and I would suggest using this country road from Madrid to Jarandilla, instead of following the motorways. See map for verification.

PARADOR DE GREDOS
Gredos (Avila)

Now, here's one I almost missed and I'm certainly glad I didn't.

Having departed the parador at Jarandilla, I was traveling on a lovely mountain road (C-501) through several colorful villages, which even though remote all had modern facilities. The ever-ascending road winds around mountains and finally emerges above the treeline. It's just the kind of road I enjoy the most.

About thirty kilometers from Arenas de San Pedro, I saw a parador sign pointing to the left. Consulting my watch and realizing that I was already two hours behind schedule, I felt I might as well go the whole way. This road led up into the mountains about ten kilometers, arriving at what I later learned was the first of the Spanish paradores. Alfonso XIII was responsible for creating these wonderful Spanish national inns and he attended the opening of this one in 1928. It is located at an altitude of 6,200 feet and the entire aspect is one of complete mountain remoteness, although the parador is furnished with modern conveniences throughout.

I enjoyed a very good lunch and a short conversation with one or two of the other patrons. This would be a wonderful place to spend a few days on a quiet holiday. It might even be a good place to work on a travel book.

PARADOR DE GREDOS, Gredos (Avila). Tel.: (918) 34-80-48. A 79-guestroom mountain hotel, especially noted for its quiet atmosphere. Spectacular views of the Sierra de Gredos. Rates: See Index.

Directions: Gredos is on C-500 between El Barco de Avila (N-110) and C-501. It is about 57 km. from Avila.

PARADOR RAIMUNDO DE BORGONA
Avila

To someone who has never seen a completely walled city, Avila gives the impression of something fantastic and unreal—it is like a giant

stage set for the Middle Ages. The walls of Avila, the oldest and best preserved in Spain, if not in all of Europe, are of a most impressive size, forming a rectangle with a perimeter of 7,500 feet. Access to the city is through nine entrance gates.

When the sun shines on the towers and battlements, it gives the golden stones a coral blush, making the sight of this martial and monastic city even more dreamlike.

The history of Avila goes back to 2000 B.C. and there are still many sculptures representing bulls and pigs that bear witness to the existence of an ancient Iberian civilization that continued into the 1st century A.D. when the city was Christianized. Avila has seen Visigoths and Moors, as well as the great reconquest under Ferdinand and Isabella. All of this and much more, including the pervading influence of Santa Teresa, can be found in the palaces, museums, cathedrals, churches, and convents of this city. I would suggest contacting the Spanish Tourist Office in a major city in North America for a small booklet entitled *Avila,* available in English, that gives a wonderful background.

All of this doesn't leave very much space for me to discuss the parador, which has the full complement of amenities found in all the government-owned inns, and is reached by walking through a very handsome garden. Fortunately, if this parador is fully booked, the *Michelin Red Guide* for Spain and Portugal shows a 73-room luxury hotel, as well as two others that are rated "comfortable," in Avila.

Avila is 108 kilometers from Madrid and is also at a crossroads for the traveler who may be headed for either northern or northwestern Spain. Plan on spending the best part of the day, and enjoy lunch at the parador. Just seeing the walls of the city makes it a memorable experience.

Walled city of Avila

PARADOR RAIMUNDO DE BORGONA, Avila. Tel.: 21-13-40. A 27-guestroom hotel in one of the most impressive walled cities of Spain, 108 km. from Madrid, 65 km. from Segovia. Rates: See Index.

Directions: Avila is on N-501 between Madrid and Salamanca. Circle the walls of the city and follow the parador signs.

PARADOR TORDESILLAS
Tordesillas (Valladolid)

Not every Spanish parador is in an ancient castle, convent, monastery, or palatial mansion. Many of them have been newly built and provide excellent accommodations. This one is a rather sprawling edifice with modern appointments. The dining room has a very impressive tapestry showing the adventures of Christopher Columbus. The guest rooms all have the usual admirable amenities and are decorated in a contemporary mode.

The parador is located in a very quiet section of the city in an almost parklike atmosphere. It is one of the few in this section of Spain with a swimming pool.

Tordesillas is just a few kilometers to the southwest of Valladolid, a much larger city with several attractions for the architecture and history buff. Among other historical events, the marriage of Ferdinand and Isabella took place here in 1469.

Valladolid contains some excellent examples of the Isabelline style of architecture, as well as the Renaissance and the Herreran influence. The house where Miguel Cervantes spent the last years of his life is little changed, and it was my understanding that some of the present furnishings were belongings of this eminent Spanish author. The house where Christopher Columbus died is also in Valladolid. The church of Santiago has three works by Goya.

PARADOR TORDESILLAS, Tordesillas (Valladolid). Tel.: (983) 77-00-51. A 73-guestroom modern hotel tastefully decorated and located in a small city, 180 km. from Madrid and 30 km. from Valladolid. Swimming pool. Rates: See Index.

Directions: Tordesillas is located on N-VI, northwest of Madrid.

PARADOR CONDES DE ALBA Y ALISTE
Zamora

I went to Zamora from Tordesillas because I noticed on my excellent Michelin map of Spain (990) that a parador was located there, and it turned out to be a very pleasant Spanish city of about 50,000 people. Although there are no great tourist attractions, Zamora has a most natural and comfortable feeling.

I arrived to find people from the offices and stores filling the streets at noontime, and I was delighted to join the happy jostling crowd.

The parador is a rather austere 15th-century palace, with a well in the middle of the courtyard and double-decked galleries on both floors, as well as some rather intricate stonework decorating the pillars.

There is an impressive and majestic staircase to the second-floor gallery, off of which is the dining room. Overlooking the courtyard are excellent visitors' lounges with comfortable sofas and walls decorated with traditional Spanish prints.

Literature from the Zamora office of the Tourist Bureau indicated that the cuisine of the province has its own individual character. Included are some veal *presas* and other succulent roasts. There's also cod *à la tranca,* octopus *à la Sanabresa,* spiced with strong, tasty sauces, and the famous chickpeas and asparagus. Trout is well known further in the mountains.

PARADOR CONDES DE ALBA Y ALISTE, Zamora. Tel.: 51-44-97. A 19-guestroom elegant hotel in a former ancient palace. Zamora is a quiet city and this would make a pleasant overnight stop, 245 km. from Madrid. Rates: See Index.

Directions: Zamora is on N-630, which runs due north from Salamanca to Oviedo. The parador is on the Plaza de Canovas and takes a bit of persistence and patience to locate. I'd suggest hiring and following a taxi, since the distance is not too far.

PARADOR REY FERNANDO II DE LEON
Benavente (Zamora)

The main road from Madrid to northwestern Spain is the N-VI and the traveler is likely to share it with heavy traffic, including quite a few trucks. I looked in vain at my excellent map of Spain and Portugal (990) for secondary parallel roads, but unfortunately N-VI seems to be the only way.

However, the Parador Rey Fernando II de Leon is well worth the trip and is one of the most attractive accommodations in all of Spain.

This is another case of the Spanish government recognizing that one of the most attractive ways to present Spain in the best light is to create a blend of the old and the new. Jan Lindstrom's drawing of this parador shows clearly the tower of this castle-palace, all that remained after the soldiers of Napoleon devastated it. An enlarged photograph taken in 1880 is on display in the foyer of the castle and it underscores the remarkable restoration.

Two massive wooden doors form the entryway, and the new part of the parador has been designed around the old tower. A stairway of modern design leads up to the first level, where the beautifully designed

dining room with graceful arched windows looks out over the country-side.

A very handsome lounge on the second floor extends to two-and-a-half stories with a balcony and a beautiful hand-painted, vaulted ceiling. Adorned with impressive tapestries and some painted cloth, it is one of the most memorable rooms of this nature that I have seen in a parador. The textures of the fabrics combined ideally with the rough walls and beautifully finished wood.

The guest rooms, too, were most inviting, many of which had their own private balconies with rocking chairs—invitations for quiet contemplation or reading.

I enjoyed a very pleasant luncheon at this parador with the attractive woman director who spoke no English, and although I do very poorly at Spanish, each of us managed to make ourselves understood. She even took me on a tour of the kitchen. We laughed a great deal.

It's obvious that much of the stone rubble of the main portion of the castle had been used to construct the parador, and someone with an eye toward contemporary art has blended old pieces with new in a way that enhances each.

PARADOR REY FERNANDO II DE LEON, Benavente (Zamora). Tel.: 63-03-00. A 30-guestroom hotel in an impressively restored fortress, 259 km. from Madrid, 242 km. from Orense. Rates: See Index.

Directions: Benavente is located at the junction of several different main roads leading north or northwest. From Madrid take N-VI. From Oviedo, Leon, and other points north take N-630. The parador is on N-VI, northwest of the city.

PARADOR MONTERREY
Verín (Orense)

The road (N-525) from Benavente to Verín now assumed a character that was more to my liking. Apparently, a great deal of the truck traffic on N-VI continues north, and N-525 leads northwest through some very high mountains. I saw snowcapped peaks in the distance. A great deal of this road reminded me of northern New Hampshire.

Verín was the first stop in the northwest section of Spain, called Galicia. Many rivers filled with salmon flow through fruitful valleys. The courses of the rivers widen progressively until they lose themselves in the immensity of the Atlantic through *rías,* or estuaries. However, Verín has none of this bucolic, agricultural euphoria. Its location at some distance from the sea makes it a sort of country cousin to the rest of the province.

From the south, the first glimpse of the Castillo Monterrey with its high walls and turrets is impressive. Coming closer, I followed the parador signs, winding around the hill.

The panorama from both the parador and from the nearby Castillo Monterrey is magnificent. The parador is set on a high hill and has a very arresting view of the castle, which played an important part during the Spanish-Portuguese wars. Within the castle walls had been a town with a monastery and a hospital. It was abandoned during the 19th century; however, it is maintained by the government today and is open to travelers. I spent at least two hours wandering around the walls and old buildings and it reminded me very much of a hotel located in a castle-fortress at Trigance in the Alpes-Maritimes of France.

The parador is a modern building, tastefully decorated with furniture and decorations that fit in well with the design of the building. It has a swimming pool that would make it very pleasant for warm-weather visiting. Some guest rooms are small but comfortable.

It was here that I was introduced to a number of Galician dishes on the parador menu, which were fortunately translated into English.

A good reason to stay overnight or even longer at Verín is the opportunity to sit quietly for hours and look out over the truly magnificent panorama and to spend some time within the walls of the ancient castle. Even on a cloudy day you can see into Portugal.

PARADOR MONTERREY, Verín (Orense). Tel.: 41-00-75. A 23-guest-room mountaintop hotel, 6 km. from a most impressive preserved ancient castle. Swimming pool on grounds; 430 km. from Madrid. Rates: See Index.

Directions: Verín is at the junction of N-525 and C-532, 17 km. from the border of Spain and Portugal. It is on the road between Benavente and Orense.

PARADOR SAN TELMO
Tuy (Pontevedra)

There are actually two ways to go from Verín to Tuy. One is to follow N-525, the main road (colored red on the 990 Michelin map of Spain) to Orense, and then left on N-120 and proceed to the Galician coast.

The road I took through the mountains (colored yellow) was C-531 from Ginzo de Limia. (I almost always prefer the yellow roads to the red ones because they are less traveled.) Most of the mountains were covered with heather, and as far as the eye could see there were carpets of flowers stretching out to the horizon. The villages are rather remote and some of the old ways still persist. One can see women working in the fields and carrying bundles of grass on their heads. There are many burros.

A few kilometers beyond the turnoff, at the northern end of Ginzo, I came to the town of Celanova, certainly one of the bright spots of the trip. It was very clean and the central square was extremely attractive. Because it was not on the main road, it had a relaxed and natural feeling about it. It's just a few miles from the Portuguese border.

Tuy was a bit of a surprise. It is one of the oldest and most characteristic cities in Galicia, lying on the Mino River opposite the Portuguese city of Valenca. The *Michelin Green Guide* lists a cathedral, the San Telmo chapel, and the San Bartolome Church, as well as some gardens.

The Parador San Telmo was laid out along almost the same lines as the more modern hotel in Verín, the big difference being that this is next to the river, rather than on top of a mountain. It has a very pleasant aspect with a swimming pool and a garden, and from the parador you can look across the hill to the cathedral-fortress. There is a bridge across the river, making Tuy one of the gateways to Portugal.

PARADOR SAN TELMO, Avenue de Portugal, Tuy (Pontevedra). Tel.: 60-03-09. A 16-guestroom hotel of relatively modern design in a town on the Spanish-Portuguese border, 606 km. from Madrid. Swimming pool on grounds. Rates: See Index.

Directions: Locate Tuy, south of Vigo. It is accessible from the Portuguese coastal road N-13.

PARADOR DEL ALBARINO
Cambados (Pontevedra)

The town of Cambados is located geographically almost in the middle of one of the great series of estuaries on the Galician west coast, called Rías Bajas. Coming by way of the sea, it is but a short distance from Bayona and the city of Pontevedra; however, great care should be taken to avoid going to the other seaside city, Vigo, particularly during the morning and afternoon heavy traffic hours. There are alternate roads available.

Of particular interest in Cambados is the magnificent square. In a country where every village, hamlet, town, and city has a plaza, this one stands out.

I was particularly taken with this parador and impressed by the fact that this one was likely to be more quiet at night than the one in Pontevedra. It is located off the main street, almost directly on the tidal basin and set in a grove of swaying sycamore trees. Oddly enough, even though Cambados is in northwestern Spain, some distance from the Mediterranean, the basic foliage is semitropical because of the sun and presence of the Gulf Stream.

The tide was out during my visit and there were several fishing boats propped upright between posts on the wet sand. The wind was coming off the ocean and was most aromatic. Sea birds were having a noontime snack at the expense of the various shellfish.

The parador is in a contemporary building, apparently built for that purpose at least twenty years ago. The brilliant spring sunshine flooded the inner courtyard, where I enjoyed an early morning cup of hot chocolate and carried on an animated conversation with the parador director, who spoke little English and was as amiable a fellow as one could hope to find. Even with my very inadequate Spanish, we were able to have a very pleasant conversation.

It occurs to me that while no mention of Santiago de Compostela has been made thus far in this book (to be discussed in some detail in the following pages), many of these Galician paradors would be excellent places to stay while on a visit to that unusual city. Besides those that I visited, there are other paradors at La Coruña and Puertomarin. These would all be suitable for day visits to Santiago.

PARADOR DEL ALBARINO, Cambados (Pontevedra). Tel.: (986) 54-22-50. A 63-guestroom hotel in a relatively modern building on a river estuary and tidal basin. It is the only hotel listed in Cambados; 640 km. from Madrid, 53 km. from Santiago. Rates: See Index.

Directions: From Pontevedra take C-550, which leads out into a small peninsula and is about 1 hr. from Cambados. From Santiago follow N-550 to Puentecesures and then C-550 to Cambados.

PARADOR CONDE DE GONDOMAR
Bayona (Pontevedra)

With my arrival in Bayona, a relatively short distance from Tuy, I realized that I was experiencing the typical terrain of Galicia. Bayona was the first of the towns and villages on the estuaries of several rivers that I would visit in Northwest Spain.

It was to Bayona that the *Pinta* returned in 1493 with the exciting information that Columbus had indeed discovered the New World. Bayona was also the port to which many ships returned during the next few centuries with precious jewels and gold from the Spanish colonies in the New World.

By far the most impressive edifice in this part of Spain is the fortress Monte Real, within whose ramparts is located the spacious Parador Conde de Gondomar, with its 128 guest rooms, swimming pool, tennis courts, and beautiful gardens.

This is a luxurious hotel of a contemporary design. The furnishings, including beautiful carpets, tapestries, watercolors, oils, sketches, and a courtyard fountain, are in themselves worth a visit. In one room I saw what I'm sure is one of the world's most immense oil paintings. It portrayed sailors pulling away from a foundering ship during a storm. Of course, the guest rooms overlooking the sea are particularly desirable.

An exciting diversion is a walk on the walls, which extend for more than three kilometers to a point where the water from the Atlantic comes boiling in and crashing up against the rocks. The sound of the surf can be deafening. At the farthest point stands an old watchtower and a couple of old cannons pointing out to sea. One could sit here for hours imagining the stories that Monte Real could tell of the invasions of the Romans, Visigoths, Saracens, and even of John of Gaunt, the Duke of Lancaster, who lived here for a short time. Drake tried unsuccessfully to land in 1585, and Napoleon succeeded in holding this fortress for only a month.

PARADOR CONDE DE GONDOMAR, Bayona (Pontevedra). Tel.: 35-50-00. A 128-guestroom hotel in a reproduction of a typical stately palace from Spain's romantic past, within the ramparts of a famous fortress. Tennis, swimming pool; 618 km. from Madrid. A little too far to commute to Santiago. Rates: See Index.

Directions: Bayona is on the northwest coast of Spain between the Portuguese border and the city of Vigo, which should be avoided because of traffic problems. Bayona is a long drive from Madrid. I would suggest staying overnight at the parador at Benavente or the other at Verín, and then proceeding to N-120, and turning off at Ginzo de Limia on C-531 via Celanova.

PARADOR CASA DEL BARON
Pontevedra

This is an in-town parador in one of the busiest towns in Northeast Spain. In fact, Pontevedra and the city of La Coruña have the highest population density in Spain.

In a former palatial mansion, this parador, in its interior design and decoration, still looks much like the very expensive house of a nobleman or a merchant prince. The entrance and reception hall, with its broad, carved baronial staircase, would make an ideal setting for one of Shakespeare's plays. It would be excellent for romantic interludes and exciting swordplay.

The parador menu is well supplied from both the countryside and the sea. Salmon, trout, eels, hake, scallops, octopus, bass, and other fish grace the menu, as well as excellent oysters, crabs, clams, lobsters, king crabs, and others.

Be sure to order sardines (*redenidas*) and potatoes boiled in their jackets with spiced oil. Galician cuisine can be found in all the regional paradores, but I would encourage many adventurous forays into small local restaurants, especially for the lobsters.

The handicrafts of the area include laces, pottery, ceramics, basket jars, vases, platters, wicker work, gold, wood and stone carving, necklaces, small boxes made from tiny shells, wooden pails and buckets. The wooden shoes are most interesting, and some are small enough to be carried back home.

The celebration of festivals and pilgrimages is accompanied by ancient melodies played on the bagpipe and tambourines. A fascinating project might be to trace the arrival and influence of the Celts on the Iberian peninsula.

PARADOR CASA DEL BARON, Pontevedra. Tel.: 85-58-00. A 47-guestroom hotel in an ancient stately home. Suitable for commuting to Santiago; 607 km. from Madrid, 57 km. from Santiago. Rates: See Index.

Directions: If you are driving from Madrid, I would suggest an overnight stay at the parador at Benavente or Verín, both situated on N-VI and N-525. Pontevedra is located on N-550 between Santiago and Vigo on the northwest Spanish coast.

SANTIAGO DE COMPOSTELA

Had it not been for the apostolic zeal of James the Greater, the small city of Santiago de Compostela would never have become a powerful center of ecumenical faith, history, and culture, nor the great spiritual springboard that made possible the reconquest of Iberia from the Moors.

Built on legend, faith, and some astounding history during the Middle Ages, Santiago has attracted pilgrims from all parts of Europe, and today is one of the most sought-out tourist objectives in the world.

The pilgrimages to Santiago brought the peoples of all of Europe together and laid foundations for future intercommunication. These pilgrimages had important repercussions on medieval thought, literature, art, sociology, and economy, and without them it's very possible the western world would be quite different today.

The view of Santiago from a distance is most striking, and as evening draws on, the towers, churches, hospitals, monasteries, and palaces, with the light of the setting sun on their roofs, look like an immense stone bonfire ablaze in the midst of the lush, delicate, and varied greens of the woods, meadows, and cultivated fields.

Santiago is not just a city of monuments; the city itself is a monument. Its grace and charm can be appreciated at any time or in any weather. At night it is particularly enchanting, when the silence (except during the feast days) is broken only by the church bells.

The Santiago pilgrimages culminated at the cathedral, which has acquired its present appearance over the course of many centuries.

*Without my going into architectural details, I should note it is domi-
nantly Romanesque with many Gothic overtones.*

*Today, Santiago contains many places of great architectural interest,
particularly in the Old Town, with its buildings of great antiquity. I
personally found the tourists and travelers who filled the streets to be
of even greater interest, and I enjoyed the shops and stores that were
filled with all manner of attractive items.*

HOTEL DE LOS REYES CATÓLICOS
Santiago de Compostela

The *Michelin Red Guide to Spain* lists this hotel and about a half
dozen more that would be basically suitable for one or two nights in
Santiago. There are several paradores within pleasant drives of the city,
making them also very suitable for overnight accommodations.

Originally, the building in which this hotel is located was founded
by Isabel and Ferdinand as a pilgrim inn and hospital and is located on
one side of the great square that also contains the present cathedral. It
is built in the form of a cross, with a hollowed square that has four
patios. Even if one is not a guest, it is possible to visit the public rooms

between 10 a.m. and 2 p.m. and between 4 p.m. and 7 p.m. by applying at the hotel reception desk.

This 157-room, five-star hotel, palatial in the true sense of the word, is also part of the parador network in Spain, and reservations may be made through Marketing Ahead in New York City. I suggest requesting a room that does not face the plaza—rooms 101–105 and 205–209, for example, are on the noisy side.

It is like staying in a ducal palace, and all of the guest rooms have high ceilings and highly ornamented furniture. The public rooms are equally ornately appointed. The sophisticated menu and service are as close to Paris as is possible in a small city in northwestern Spain.

I skipped breakfast at the hotel and found a side-street bakery shop where I enjoyed a warm croissant and a cup of hot chocolate, while sitting in one of the smaller, more quiet squares of the town.

Where one stays when visiting Santiago, or *whether* one stays overnight is not important, since there are other accommodations available in nearby towns and villages. The important thing is to go.

HOTEL DE LOS REYES CATÓLICOS, Santiago de Compostela. Tel.: 58-22-00. U.S. reservations: 212-686-9213. A 157-guestroom palatial hotel, originally built in the 16th century, on the square with the famous cathedral and several other imposing and historic buildings. This is one of the showplaces of Spain. However, Santiago may be visited on day trips from several paradores within a short drive. There are six other hotels in Santiago according to the Michelin Red Guide; *610 km. from Madrid. Rates: See Index.*

Directions: All roads in Northwest Spain lead to Santiago. There is also a major airport. The hotel is immediately adjacent to the cathedral, which dominates the entire town and is easy to find. Parking for hotel patrons is in the plaza directly in front. This can be explained to the policeman, who will attempt to divert you to another street.

PARADOR CONDES DE VILLALBA
Villalba (Lugo)

I arrived in Villalba and found the 14th-century tower I had heard about—it's located in the middle of the town. Amazingly, it has actually been standing all these years. In a conversation with the parador director, I learned that it might even be of Moorish origin, possibly dating back to the 11th century.

The entrance is over a drawbridge and then into a three-story-high reception hall, adorned with fascinating paintings, murals, tapestries, and medieval artifacts. There is a big fireplace and a stairway leading to the floors above.

A very pleasant young man, the *conserje,* took me all the way to the top floor, and I saw most of the six guest rooms that had recently been redecorated. There were two rooms on the top floor and then one more flight up took us outside to the very top of the tower, where I looked out over the crenelated ramparts to the roofs of the town.

The narrow windows, which had once accommodated crossbowmen, were in walls nine feet thick. The staircase and the chimney that ran through the tower were modern additions.

The restaurant is on a floor actually below ground level and has a vaulted ceiling with rafters and overhead beams. It looked very comfortable. The menu, with many Galician entrées, was printed in three languages.

PARADOR CONDES DE VILLALBA, Villalba (Lugo). Tel.: (982) 51-00-11. A 6-guestroom rather attractive inn situated in an ancient medieval castle, 115 km. from Santiago; 70 km. from Ribadeo on the northern coast. Rates: See Index.

Directions: Locate Lugo on Michelin *map 990. Villalba is due north on N-634, one of the principal roads from Santander to La Coruña.*

CANTABRICA CORNISA

The Cantabrian Corniche stretches from the easternmost borders of Spain to the Ribadeo River in the province of Lugo. The whole shoreline is washed by the Cantabrian Sea and is broken by the Cantabrian Mountains that parallel the sea. The northern part of Spain is characterized by two geographic features: the sea and the mountains. The atmosphere of this region includes fertile meadows, rich pastures, and solitary steep-cliffed beaches. Behind the coast, the line of the mountains rises to the colossal heights of the Picos de Europa, a mountain mass impressive for the height of its peaks and for the magic labyrinth of valleys and incredible gorges carved in the rock by the rivers that cut through it.

However, not all of this area is bucolic in nature. La Coruña, El Ferrol, Gíjon, Oviedo, Santander, Bilbao, San Sebastian, and other cities are heavily populated and industrially oriented. The traveler should have patience until the return to the countryside. This northern shore is linked by coastal highways that for the most part are printed in red on the Michelin map (660) of Spain and Portugal.

PARADOR RIBADEO
Ribadeo (Lugo)

I was now at the top of Spain on the imaginary border line between Galicia and Asturias. Like a few other paradores that I would be visiting in the next two or three days, this one provides a respite for travelers along the road leading from west to east into France, Germany, and Britain, as well as for those visitors from northern countries who are enjoying an excursion into Spain. In fact, there was a bus tour from Germany having lunch at this parador during my visit.

Overlooking a river leading to the Cantabrian Sea, each of this parador's rooms has a balcony from which to enjoy the bustling river traffic, the cultivated fields across the river, and several small villages that are also visible. The dining terrace also partakes of this excellent and interesting view.

Below the terrace, indeed a very pleasant place, I discovered a small, welcome swimming pool.

The big living room is one of the most comfortable that I've seen yet, with a fireplace almost within a fireplace. There was a big reproduction of King Alfonso, the original of which I should imagine was painted in the 1920s. He's the man who started the parador movement and all of us who love Spain owe him a deep debt of gratitude.

PARADOR RIBADEO, Ribadeo (Lugo). Tel.: (982) 11-08-25. A 47-guestroom seaside inn with a very pleasant view of the river estuary; 592 km. from Madrid; 350 from Santander; 158 sometimes difficult km. from Gijon. Rates: See Index.

Directions: Ribadeo is on the principal east-west road across the top of Spain (N-632).

PARADOR EL MOLINO VIEJO
Gijón (Oviedo)

Because I'm an early riser, once again I literally was up with the birds. However, at this small six-room parador in a delightful park near the northeastern edge of Gijón, I was convinced some of the birds never had gone to sleep. Early morning joggers (ubiquitous lot, these joggers) passed by, raising a hand in greeting, and the ducks were already foraging for an early morning meal.

I reflected that this might also be called the parador of the ducks because there were so many ducks here in the park and on the millstream that runs under the hotel.

The previous afternoon's drive was one of the most interesting and rewarding in Spain. Often along the seashore and sometimes through beautiful ravines with towering mountains and terraced hillsides, it is a main road that requires much patience should the traveler get behind a truck. It alternately hugs the sides of the mountains, cresting at the top, and then plunges down into the river valleys below. Because it was spring, the fruit trees were beautifully in blossom and there were hues of green in the haying pastures. I'm sure that only a team of oxen could be used to plow such precipitous fields.

This is not the Spain of the south, although women work in the fields here and the wash is hung out to dry every day. There aren't as many castles on the skylines, and there's a brisk air of industry, even among the small farms. This is the area where there are barns and houses (*horreo*) built in a rather picturesque fashion on stilts, creating a somewhat Japanese effect. Also, this is one of the few areas in Spain where I ran across bagpipes, and if the traveler is lucky enough to be in a small village during one of the feast or celebration days, he's bound to have the experience of seeing native dancers being urged on by pipers.

Until I made this trip to northern Spain, I wasn't quite aware of the wide Celtic influences, and these are, so I'm told, the same Celts that Caesar called Gauls, who also lived in northern England, Scotland, and Ireland. Perhaps this is an explanation for the bagpipes.

My morning walk over, I returned to my very pleasant room and began to pack. The windows opened out onto the park and I was tempted to linger for a few extra minutes to enjoy the songs of the birds.

The previous evening I enjoyed a very good meal of baked pork and a good mixed salad. There were several dishes on the menu that indicated some originality in the kitchen. Dessert was oranges served in kirsch.

This little parador is listed as a restaurant with six bedrooms, all located on the second floor, off a bright, white-washed hallway, where the polished wood is an interesting contrast.

PARADOR EL MOLINO VIEJO, Gijón (Oviedo). Tel.: 37-05-11. A simple 6-guestroom inn adjacent to Parque de Isabel in a quieter part of a surprisingly large city; 465 km. from Madrid; 292 from Bilbao, 322 km. to La Coruña. Rates: See Index.

Directions: Traveling from west to east following N-632, take the motorway bypass from Avilés (A-68) to Gijón. Proceed east through the heavy traffic of the town, making inquiries for the Plaza de Toros. Then make inquiries for the Parque de Isabel. The parador is on the edge of the park. Coming west, be certain that you take N-632, a yellow line on Michelin *660, and once near Gijón inquire for Plaza de Toros.*

PARADOR GIL BLAS
Santillana del Mar (Santander)

There are twenty-four bedrooms in this parador, and I hope that every one of our readers who is planning a trip to Spain will reserve sufficiently in advance to be able to stay overnight in one of them. There are really two reasons to be here. First is the village itself, rich in history and literature, and the second is the nearby Caves of Altamira, where gifted artists who lived in this region 15,000 years ago painted bison, wild boar, deer, and horses on the ceilings and walls.

Right from the start I could feel that this village and its parador were different. It was off the beaten track, but still attracted tourist trade that

seems to be kept in control. There is an absence of the usual hurly-burly.

The placing of a parador here was a true inspiration, because both the parador and the village belong together. There's a very pleasant air of accommodation about both of them. The parador is one of the main stops on a journey across the top of Spain and the clientele is quite sophisticated, with many French, Americans, Germans, and Britons filling the rooms almost every night.

The parador is an ancient mansion of the family Barreda, and its name is a sentimental reminder of that notorious rogue, Gil Blas, who was the protagonist of Lesage's famous picaresque novel.

I wandered through the square in front of the parador on a sunny Sunday morning. A few of the housewives were straightening out the flower pots on many of the sun-drenched balconies, and even on a Sunday the ever-present laundry was on the line. The wonderful beige tint in the old stone buildings could have been acquired only by centuries of sun and weather.

Even as I wandered about the town on that morning, I began once again to feel the two contrasts of Spain. For example, I passed a music bar, where the night before I had heard the pervasive sounds of electronic instruments raising the patrons to a high-decibel Saturday-night fever. Certainly, the night belonged to the Spain of today, but with the sun on the ancient buildings, grass growing out of the tiled roofs, birds flying from gallery to gallery, and the tolling of the church bells, this morning belonged to the past.

PARADOR GIL BLAS, Santillana del Mar (Santander). Tel.: 81-80-00. A 24-guestroom inn pleasantly located in an ancient stately home near the Caves of Altamira; 392 km. from Madrid; 130 km. from Bilbao; 30 km. from Santander. Rates: See Index.

Directions: Santillana del Mar is on a road that cuts off a portion of the main road west of Santander. It is noted as C-6316 on the map.

THE CAVES OF ALTAMIRA

The caves themselves were not accessible to the public on my last visit; but it was possible for a limited number of people to sit in an informal theater and, leaning back in the seat, look overhead to see colored photographic reproductions of the paintings projected on the ceiling. Even in this somewhat restricted manner this is really an impressive experience, and I think it's most interesting because the prehistoric artists who lived in this section so many thousands of years earlier were the predecessors of the talented and sensitive artists, de-signers, and architects among the Romans, the Visigoths, and, of course, the Moors who were to follow.

These unknown cave dwellers expressed a freedom of spirit that is found in the works of such great Spanish painters as Goya, Velázquez, Gris, Miró, Picasso, and Dali. The simple statements on the walls of the Caves of Altamira are no less eloquent than the paintings on the walls of the Prado in Madrid.

Bookings can be made through the Tourist Office in Santillana del Mar. There are other caves open to the public not far from Santillana.

HOTEL DE LONDRES Y DE INGLATERRA
San Sebastian (Guipúzcoa)

There is always something of special note at the inns and small hotels mentioned in this book. This hotel near the border crossing between France and Spain has many memorable features; however, the one that really impressed me is the view on the ocean side facing La Concha Beach. Be sure to ask for this view as your first choice.

In addition to the beach itself, which stretches out on a wide arc, there is also a band of greenery between the hotel and the beach, with a wide promenade where residents and visitors seem to parade endlessly to and fro. This promenade must be at least five miles long, and it is possible to walk its length without crossing a single street.

As hotels go, this is of small-to-moderate size with 130 guest rooms, all of them with complete bathrooms, central heating, air conditioning, telephones, and televisions.

Although the cuisine of the hotel has an excellent reputation, I would suggest an additional visit to one of the many smaller restaurants in Old Town, an easy walk from the hotel.

Incidentally, the hotel is managed by a remarkable English-speaking woman, Begoña Andonegui, who has been with the hotel for thirty years, advancing through a chain of responsibilities to become one of the few women managers in Spain. I do hope you will have a chance to meet her.

My car was safely placed in a private garage, but there is also an underground public garage directly in front of the hotel.

If you are traveling for the first time from France to Spain, this hotel or the parador in nearby Fuenterrabia will give you a wonderful first impression of the country.

The city of San Sebastian has many museums, parks, and historic monuments. There are excursions and a funicular to the top of a mountain, providing a panoramic view of the open sea and the islands.

HOTEL DE LONDRES Y DE INGLATERRA, Zubieta 2, San Sebastian (Guipúzcoa). Tel. (943) 42-69-89. (U.S. reservations: 212-686-9213). A 4-star beach hotel with 130 guest rooms, 54 km. from Bayonne, 94 km. from Bilbao. Rates: See Index.

Directions: From France, continue through the border crossing. After reaching San Sebastian, check your map in either the Michelin red or green guides for Zubieta, the street on which the hotel is located. It borders the Playa de la Concha. Make a sharp right at the hotel's entrance, which faces away from the beach.

SAN SEBASTIAN AND FUENTERRABIA

The traveler from Bordeaux, Bayonne, and Biarritz in France is fortunate, indeed, to have N-10, an excellent highway. This becomes the A-1 when it crosses the border and proceeds on to San Sebastian. After the checkpoint, the A-1 passes near the small town of Fuenterrabia, where I had a chance to visit a parador. I also saw a beachside hotel in the city of San Sebastian. It intrigues me to realize that this road has for centuries been one of the most traveled in Spain, being one of the two ways used by the pilgrims. Eventually, it leads to Santiago de Compostela.

PARADOR EL EMPERADOR
Fuenterrabia (Guipúzcoa)

This parador is a castle fortress overlooking the town and the harbor. According to legend it was built in the 10th century as a key stronghold of the region. It was restored about 600 years later by Charles V, and served as a palace.

Its appearance is rather austere, with walls almost three meters thick. It is completely restored and the various guest rooms and public rooms are appropriately decorated, retaining a medieval atmosphere. For instance, it was explained to me that the neglected appearance of the patio was maintained on purpose, with vegetation growing between the age-old stones to stress its ancient character. The courtyard well was used to provide water for the garrison and the populace of the town during the numerous sieges suffered over the centuries.

For sheer atmosphere and a conviction of antiquity, I would rate this as one of the top paradores of Spain. There are sixteen guest rooms. All have baths and the contemporary amenities.

In contrast to the Hotel de Londres y de Inglaterra in nearby San

Sebastian, this parador is quiet and secluded. One can stay here and enjoy all of the advantages of San Sebastian and the nearby Basque region.

Parador El Emperador, Plaza de Armas del Castillo, Fuenterrabia (Guipúzcoa). Tel. (943) 64-21-40. This is a 3-star parador with 16 modern guest rooms. Rates: See Index.

Directions: Located at the Spanish-French frontier, approx. 30 km. from Bayonne and Biarritz.

PARADOR SANTO DOMINGO DE LA CALZADA
Santo Domingo de la Calzada (La Rioja)

Funny thing. I almost bypassed this parador in favor of continuing on closer to Madrid from San Sebastian. However, in looking at the map I realized it was on M-120, which, although it is a well-constructed road, is not really one of the Spanish main highways. I thought that perhaps I might find something that was a little less frequented by the average traveler to Spain.

Well, a number of things happened. First of all, as I was coming into the town you can imagine my delight at finding that a wedding was going on at the cathedral, which is on the same square with the parador. A very pretty Spanish girl bedecked in white, with many strings of pearls intricately woven in her hair, alighted from a shiny red car. Most of the onlookers were townspeople, and I joined them for a few moments.

My guest room facing the square was bright and cheerful, and while I thought about having lunch, noting that the parador served the noontime meal, the bride came out of the cathedral to the accompaniment of exploding firecrackers. Isn't this a most interesting custom!

There is a fascinating history connected with this town, which was built by Santo Domingo de la Calzada on the site of one of the ancient palaces of the kings of Navarre. Once again I came to another reference to the Pilgrims' Way to Santiago. According to the story, as the saint became aware of the pilgrims' sufferings, he devoted himself to relieving their pains by improving the roadways and building bridges.

The parador was originally built as a hospice and hospital in the 11th century, and has been redecorated according to modern standards of comfort, without losing its medieval atmosphere. The guest rooms have all the modern conveniences.

The town and the parador are good examples of a window on the "natural" view of Spain. From the square, the parador seems to be

rather unprepossessing, but once inside, its history is better appreciated. Passing through a small reception area, I was in a large room of stone arches. There are many tapestries, swords, and suits of armor to add to the atmosphere.

I believe that the traveler in Spain can make almost any visit to a Spanish town or village something special, and Santo Domingo de la Calzada is a good example.

One of the town's legends concerns the "roasted rooster that crowed again." Be sure that you make inquiries about it when you visit the parador. I hope you are there during a wedding.

PARADOR SANTO DOMINGO DE LA CALZADA, Plaza del Santo, 3, Santo Domingo de la Calzada. Tel.: (941) 34-03-00. A 27-guest-room, 3-star parador immediately adjacent to the famous cathedral of the town. Breakfast, lunch, and dinner served daily. Rates: See Index.

Directions: Once in the town, which is on M-120, drive toward the ever-visible cathedral, and you will find the parador.

PARADOR DEL RIO DEVA
Fuente De (Santander)

This parador was a surprise. It has seventy rooms furnished in a contemporary style. Its truly magnificent views are rivaled possibly only by the Parador Sierra Nevada near Granada in southern Spain.

The basic structure is stone, quarried locally; but in profile it looks like a European Alpine hotel. Built especially to accommodate the large numbers of Spaniards and other visitors who enjoy the wonderful mountain atmosphere, it is very popular over Easter, during Holy Week, and in July and August, when it's quite warm elsewhere in Spain.

PARADOR DEL RIO DEVA, Fuente De (Santander). Tel.: 73-00-01. A 78-guestroom modern hotel high in the Picos de Europa, with striking

views of valleys and mountains, immediately adjacent to an aerial tram-
way that ascends even higher; 426 km. from Madrid; 140 km. from
Santander. Rates: See Index.

Directions: Locate Santander on the map at the top of Spain, and then
look for N-621, which goes south from N-634 at Unquera. Follow this
wonderful mountain road approx. 40 km. to Potes. N-621 proceeds
even higher into the mountains and ends at Fuente De. From Madrid
and points south, take N-611 north and turn west on unmarked yellow
road on map between Aguilar and Cervera. Then follow C-627 to Potes
and follow above directions. The Michelin Green Guide shows several
itineraries among these mountains that have many gorges, defiles,
passes, and caves.

THE PEAKS OF EUROPE

I was asleep in the sunshine on the Picos de Europa. It was a
pleasant Saturday afternoon and after following N-261 from Unquera
to La Hermida and Potes, I had enjoyed an over-sumptuous lunch at
Parador del Rio Deva and decided to take the cable car trip to the
high mountains that tower behind it.

Even in mid-May there were snow fields on the very top and my
feeling of intimacy with the high peaks grew with every moment. As I
leaned back against some smooth rocks and closed my eyes, I felt that
the 8,000-foot peaks were closing in on me. I awakened to the sound
of laughter from a group of junior high school students who were
pelting their teachers with snowballs. There was much shouting and
horseplay, and one of the snowballs glanced off a rock near me. They
drifted away and for a moment all was quiet again.

The road from the sea to the mountains was unquestionably the most
spectacular I had experienced in Spain. Winding its way upward alongside a river in a deep gorge, with massive rocks towering at least a
thousand feet on each side, it passed through several small villages
and settlements, one S curve following another. The higher I climbed,
the more the air seemed to clear, leaving the sea mist below. Behind
me and ahead of me was a continual parade of vistas and panoramas,
and above all, the almost tortured statement made by the great bare
cliffs.

The jagged outline of the peaks was somber against the sky, and at
one point, I could actually see blue sky through windows in the rocks.
Sometimes the river was green and placid, and other times it rushed

down the falls between boulders in a white, frothy torrent. Where the soil had held, some farms clung to the precipitous hillsides.

The town of Potes was a very thriving mountain community, a sort of jumping-off place for skiers and travelers en route, somewhat reminiscent of Stowe and Aspen. It was obvious that it would be bent and stretched out of shape by the large number of international visitors who would come both in the summer and the winter. Today, on a Saturday in May, it was delightful.

SEGOVIA

It was 7:30 a.m. at the Parador de la Granja in Segovia. I surveyed the commanding view, not only of the small jewellike city of Segovia with its cathedral, Alcazar, and magnificent Roman aqueduct, but also of the snowcapped mountains that form a crescent of protection around the city.

This was my last morning on this trip in Spain and I mentally reviewed the previous day's events. Leaving Santillana on the northern coast in the morning, I had followed N-611 to Reinosa and C-6318 to N-623. North to Burgos, the road leads through an area of most impressive natural beauty. Over millions of years the river, similar to the Colorado in the Grand Canyon and the Genesee in western New York State, has carved its way through the earth, creating a tortuous and

twisting course and fashioning marvelous caves, rock cairns, and cas-
tles of limestone. I stopped for a brief midday picnic by the side of the
road overlooking the canyon and the river, and watched four or five
of the ever-present, ever-watchful eagles as they circled higher and
higher in the sky, caught by the updraft.

South of Burgos, I took the wrong turn for a "shortcut" and spent
at least an hour and a half wandering around on real Spanish country
roads, stopping at every village to get new directions for Segovia. It
was at the same time both irritating and humorous; however, I found
all of my informants cheerful, willing, and certainly verbal. Never had
so many things been said to me that I didn't understand. However,
basically, I was able to get the picture and I had the opportunity to
see rural Spain, which I would have otherwise missed.

Each of the little villages has its own stores and shops and is really
set apart from the others. From high places on the road it was possible
to see three or four villages at the same time. What I really desperately
needed was a compass. After some false starts and some retracing, I
did find the way to Segovia and to this unusual parador.

PARADOR DE SEGOVIA
Segovia

This must be the flagship of the fleet, because it is very modern and
yet retains a distinctive old Spanish flavor. This is more of the "new
Spain" that is conscientiously clinging to the best part of the past in
textures, materials, designs, and colors. The public rooms, dining room,
lounges, and numerous sitting areas have all been done in a tasteful
but highly contemporary manner. Very careful attention has been taken
to provide every lodging room with a contemporary Spanish flavor.

Every room has a view of the city and the mountains. From the
balconies I could look out over the countryside and see several small
villages, as well as many herds of sheep being tended by the traditional
sheepherders.

Late in the afternoon and early evening, I visited the great cathedral
and the fortress, but the most impressive thing to me about Segovia
was the marvelous Roman aqueduct running right across the center of
the city. With 118 arches it rises to the height of 96 feet. The exact
date of its construction is not known, although modern research places
it in the second half of the first century. It is a colossal piece of engineering and is an eloquent testimony to the architectural genius of
Rome. It still carries water, as it did when it was first built.

Oddly enough, as I was driving through Segovia to return to Madrid,
once again I witnessed a meeting of the old and new Spain—a herd of

sheep was being driven under the aqueduct through the middle of the town, and the police held up all the traffic as the animals came through.

Segovia, like Granada, Toledo, Merida, Fuenteovejuna, and the Alcazaba in Málaga, I shall never forget you.

PARADOR DE SEGOVIA, Segovia. Tel: 41-50-90. With more than 50 guestrooms and a 3,000-foot altitude, this is one of the newest paradores in Spain. Swimming pool, nearby skiing, excellent sightseeing in a rather quiet city. Spectacular views of the mountains; 91 km. to Madrid; 199 km. to Burgos; 860 km. to Santander. Rates: See Index.

Directions: Segovia is a relatively short distance from Madrid, the most difficult task being to find one's way out of the Madrid traffic and north on the N-VI. It leads through some dramatic mountain passes with snowcapped peaks.

CATALONIA: SPAIN'S NORTHEAST TRIANGLE

Catalonia is once again an autonomous region within the Spanish democracy, and the convenient way to get there is to fly directly to Barcelona. The international airport is new and efficient, with moving sidewalks to take you and your light luggage to the RENFE express buses that make the fifteen-minute trip to the center of Barcelona. There are also taxis and rental cars.

Several paradors and recommended hotels are within a two-hour drive of the airport or you can begin your visit with a transfer to Barcelona, renting a car there when you are ready to go on tour in the region and returning it to the airport at departure time.

The paradores and hotels in this section can be divided roughly between those on the Costa Brava—on the Mediterranean between Barcelona and the French border—and those in the mountains. The two different atmospheres provide an unusual opportunity to enjoy the best of both worlds.

The height and massiveness of the Pyrenees in Catalonia add further weight to the claim that after Switzerland, Spain is the most mountainous country in Europe.

Catalonia defines itself by language, an ancient romantic tongue with its roots in Provençal. Catalan was forbidden during the Franco years, but officially restored under King Juan Carlos. This would not overly concern the casual visitor except for the fact that maps and signs vary according to which language is used. For example, the city of Lérida is now Lleida; Vich is Vic. The directional road signs are sent out by Madrid and are in Castillian, though in some places they have been obliterated with spray paint and the Catalonian word scratched in. I found I had to consider the possibility that I was looking for a re-spelled turn-off, but it was really no problem.

By the way, Catalonia is also Catalunya.

HOTEL COLON
Barcelona (Barcelona)

Seldom are hotels more strategically located than the Hotel Colon. It faces the majestic Gothic cathedral, and if you have a room facing the Avenida de la Catedral as I did, you also have a box seat to enjoy the activity on the plaza below. I was fortunate that my stay included a Sunday, because on Sundays and holidays, the citizens of Barcelona dance the Sardana accompanied by fife and drum in the square.

This custom is observed throughout Catalonia. Parcels, pocketbooks, coats, and sometimes shoes are piled in the center of the circle and the dancers join hands and dance around them in measured steps. On holidays in the villages they would wear costumes, but street clothes are what I saw in Barcelona.

The Colon is a comfortable, well-furnished hotel convenient to many good restaurants, the Picasso Museum, and the narrow interesting streets of the Gothic Quarter. Nearby, too, is the famous pedestrian walk Las Ramblas, with its flower and bird market stalls. It is also just a pleasant stroll to Cuitadella Park, where there are many museums, the zoo, and an aquarium. Sunday afternoons the park is crowded with families enjoying the flower gardens and treating the children to ice cream and balloons.

The cathedral is illuminated at night, and the white birds darting in and out of the towers or wheeling against the darkening sky make a memorable picture.

HOTEL COLON, Avenida de la Catedral, 7, Barcelona-2. Tel.: 301-14-04. U.S. reservations: 212-686-9213. A 200-guestroom hotel in the Gothic Quarter facing the 13th-century cathedral. Restaurant, grill on premises, but many better restaurants in the immediate area. Rates: See Index.

HOTEL SANTA MARTA
Lloret de Mar (Gerona)

The Costa Brava begins at Blanes, and halfway between that town and Lloret de Mar is the Playa Santa Cristina and the pleasant resort hotel of Santa Marta. The first thing I noticed as I drove down the circuitous driveway is that no tour bus could make the grade. Obviously, the Santa Marta was making a point for solitude on this heavily trafficked coast. Even the swimming pool and tennis courts are away from the main buildings and down by the beach, where luncheon and snacks are served outdoors in the summer, and the children's playground is near the annex-in-the-woods, out of direct contact with the central house.

Its neighbors are private villas and a world-famous botanical garden, Pinya de Rosa. It has an excellent dining room, and in the morning I woke to the unmistakable aroma of baking bread. For the traveler who would like to dabble but not be submerged by the high-season activities of the coast, the Santa Marta is just about perfect.

One of the nicest ways to see the Costa Brava is by boat, so I took one of the small *cruceros* (cabin cruisers) from the beach below the hotel and commuted to the delightful villages, disembarking at will, then catching the next boat or perhaps the one after that to continue my journey of the day. It beats looking for parking spaces, and I returned midafternoon for late lunch and some rest and reading by the pool. At 6 p.m. I went to Blanes to see the fish auction, a daily event attended by all the restaurateurs in the area.

HOTEL SANTA MARTA (Relais et Chateaux: Iberia), Lloret de Mar (Gerona). Tel.: 972-36-49-04. U.S. reservations: 212-686-9213. A 70-guestroom, 8-suite family-owned hotel on seven wooded acres at Playa Santa Cristina between Blanes and Lloret de Mar, on the southern end of the Costa Brava. Closed Dec. 10 to Jan. 15. Swimming pool, tennis, water sports. Well located for visiting the area by car or by boat taxi service. Barcelona is 70 km. south; Gerona 42 km. northwest; the border of France, 101 km. north. Rates: See Index.

Directions: From the A-17 toll road take Exit 10 to Route N-2, then north, looking for posted signs to Santa Marta and Playa Santa Cristina. A slower way is the coast road A-19 from Barcelona, continuing on the N-2 after Mataro.

HOSTAL DE LA GAVINA
S'Agaró (Gerona)

When José Ensesa set out to create "the perfect resort" on his sea-swept point property on the Costa Brava, he spared no expense, and when I heard it was one of only seven five-star grand luxe–rated hotels in Spain, I had to stop by, if only for lunch. Will you be surprised if I tell you I stayed for three days or that only the press of time separated me then? Drop-in visitors aren't always so lucky, but it helps to be slightly ahead of high season. For value received, La Gavina was also less expensive than I would have guessed.

The public rooms are spacious, with palatial furnishings and many vases of cut flowers. My bedroom was also large and airy, with a deep balcony and a marble bath. The furniture appeared to have been borrowed from a museum, and the brocade on the walls matched the chairs. Clearly, this is no ordinary hotel. There are several places to eat lunch, outdoors and in; a candlelit dining room for the late evening meal.

In addition to the swimming pool and two beaches, tennis courts, the gardens and seaside walking paths, there are riding stables and water sports nearby, and a golf course three kilometers away.

HOSTAL DE LA GAVINA (Relais et Chateaux: Iberia), S'Agaró (Gerona). Tel.: 972-32-11-00. A 6-guestroom, 16-suite (family owned) luxury inn on the Costa Brava of deservedly high reputation with several restaurants. Closed Dec. 1 to March 30. Swimming pool, beaches, tennis on property; other sports available nearby. Barcelona is 110 km. south; 25 km. to Gerona.

Directions: From Barcelona on the A-7 or N-2 take the Vidreres exit (Salida 9) and go northeast to Llagostera, then due east to S'Agaró.

From Girona, southeast on the Cassa-Llagostera road, then east on Rte. 250 to S'Agaró.

PARADOR COSTA BRAVA
Aiguablava (Gerona)

When I reached the parador at Aiguablava I was at the northern end of the Corniche road that began at Blanes, and I was at the last parador before entering France at Port Bou. As a matter of fact, there were a number of guests who swore they could see the coast of France from their windows, though a glance at the map showed this was highly unlikely.

It is not necessary to come by the slow but beautiful Corniche. The quick trip is via the A-17 toll road to Gerona, then follow the signs east to Bagur. Parador Costa Brava is four kilometers south, high on a promontory overlooking the sea. It would have been a good spot for an eagle's nest or to watch for pirate ships in the days when corsairs found refuge in the coves of the region. The coves are now sought by swimmers and others who simply want solitude. Many of them can be reached only by boat.

There are plenty of golden beaches readily accessible, however, and villages straight out of the Middle Ages to explore. The 17th-century castle at Bagur was built on the site of one destroyed in 1465. With the parador as my headquarters I was also able to make a day trip to Ampurias and the Greco-Roman-Christian ruins there.

PARADOR COSTA BRAVA, Aiguablava-Bagur (Gerona). Tel.: 972-62-21-62. An 80-guestroom modern hotel overlooking the sea in an area of fine private villas. Beach below has playground equipment. Swimming pool on grounds. Located at Aiguablava above the road between Tamariu and Bagur; 4 km. from Bagur, 45 from Gerona, 134 from Barcelona on the northeastern coast. Rates: See Index.

Directions: Approaching from the south, follow signs to Palafrugell and Bagur. The parador road is posted at the junction, but if you miss it, go on to Bagur, then turn right and drive 4 km. south. If you take the A-17 to Gerona, you will want the main road east towards Bagur.

PARADOR CASTILLO DE LA ZUDA
Tortosa (Tarragona)

The dining room of the parador is huge, with a vaulted ceiling and Gothic windows, and although I was aware it is not the original struc-

ture, I was convinced from first glance that this is historic ground. The site held a Moorish fortress in the 8th century and was successively occupied by countless invaders.

The castle guarded the land bridge of the River Ebro, and its most appalling sight must have been in 1938 when Republicans and Nationalists clashed in one of the largest, most decisive struggles of the Spanish Civil War, the bloody Battle of the Ebro. Here and in the city of Tortosa, the story is retold and the lines redrawn for visitors.

By then, of course, the Zuda had already been a ruin for hundreds of years. In 1976, after total reconstruction, it was opened as a parador. A swimming pool was built on the rim of a Roman wall, and the guest rooms were decorated with regional furnishings and original art. Now it attracts a weekend luncheon crowd from Tarragona and even Barcelona, and is well located for those driving south along the Costa Daurada and the Costa del Azahar.

I was told a great variety of migrating birds stop to feed in the Ebro Delta; that the topsoil is responsible for notable fruit and vegetables; that I must not miss the patio of the Bishop's Palace in Tortosa.

PARADOR CASTILLO DE LA ZUDA, Tortosa (Tarragona). Tel.: 977-44-44-50. An 82-guestroom 4-star castle located outside Tortosa overlooking the River Ebro. A historic site for at least 12 centuries, the parador is a useful center for visiting the region or as a stopover between Barcelona and Valencia. Tarragona city, with its relics of Roman times, is a good day trip. Tortosa is 83 km. from Tarragona, 135 from Lérida, 524 from Madrid, 181 from Barcelona.

Directions: Coming from north or south along the coastal A-7 highway, exit at Tortosa and follow the right bank of the River Ebro.

PARADOR DE VICH
Vich (Barcelona)

It was easy to see why this has become a popular stop between Barcelona and the Pyrenees. The parador is not in town, but fourteen kilometers away in a beautiful mountain area overlooking a blue reservoir. Although technically a modern 4-star parador, it was built to the lines of a Catalan farmhouse and has the atmosphere of a fine resort.

There is a swimming pool, tennis court, and garden. The mountain views reminded me again that Spain is second only to Switzerland as the most mountainous country in Europe. Hiking trails are plentiful, and water sports are available on the reservoir. It seems an ideal spot to spend several days catching up from the exertions of travel or at least recovering from jet lag, being little more than an hour away from the Barcelona International Airport.

The town of Vich is ancient and notable for its cathedral and the Episcopal Museum next door. The murals in the cathedral by Catalan artist José Maria Sert y Badia have been compared with Michelangelo in power, if not precisely in subject matter. The original paintings were destroyed during the Civil War but were redone by the artist afterward. The Episcopal Museum contains many famous religious works dating from the Middle Ages. There are monasteries, sanctuaries, and the Castle of Sabanasa, all within an hour's drive from the parador.

PARADOR DE VICH, Vich (Barcelona). Tel.: 93-888-72-11. A 31-guestroom modern parador outside the city of Vich in a scenic mountain area. Swimming pool, tennis, hiking, and water sports as well as sightseeing. Good restful stopover from Barcelona 79 km. away; 14 km. to Vich, 141 to Port-Bou (frontier), 719 from Madrid. Rates: See Index.

Directions: Vich (or Vic) is on Rte. 152. From the Barcelona airport and city area, take Hwy. E-4 to the turn-off, north of Barcelona. The parador is 14 km. northeast.

PARADOR DUQUES DE CARDONA
Cardona (Barcelona)

From my window on the top floor of the castle I was able to see far across the Catalonian plain and speculate what it must have been like for those who commanded that volcanic plug in the 9th century. The fortress has been restored with all the 20th-century comforts, including an elevator, but in its center is a functioning Romanesque chapel, and one tower (called the "Minyona") dates from the 2nd century.

The small city of Cardona still has original walls with tributes to the citizens who followed the duke to the Battle of Lepanto and never returned. A bare and forbidding gray hill beside the town is a natural phenomenon—a mountain of rock salt. A small museum contains some geological information and a large selection of rock-salt sculpture by a local artist.

Early in September the festival called "Corre Bou," dating from the 16th century, attracts visitors from Barcelona and Madrid with its parades, feats of horsemanship, and costumes.

The dining room of the parador is especially fine, with a vaulted ceiling. I have almost decided that if I can't live like a king, I will settle for living like a duke.

PARADOR DUQUES DE CARDONA, Cardona (Barcelona). Tel.: 93-869-12-75. A 65-guestroom castle perched on a colonial hill overlooking the plain, the river, and the town of Cardona. This 4-star parador is about midway between Andorra and Barcelona, convenient for visiting the old city of Solsona with its museums and cathedral or the famous monastery at Montserrat. The parador is 97 km. from Barcelona, 99 from Andorra, 127 from Lérida, and 592 from Madrid. Rates: See Index.

Directions: From the north (Andorra), take the well-marked Route de Lérida south to Basella; then go east to Solsona and southeast on Rte. 1410 to Cardona. From Barcelona, take the Route de Montserrat to Montserrat, then northwest on Rte. 1410.

PARADOR SEO DE URGEL
Seo de Urgel (Lérida)

When I arrived in Seo de Urgel, I was only a fifteen-minute drive from the independent Principado de Andorra, and when I came to the parador, I was, in effect, the next-door neighbor of the bishop-prince of that country. For a full explanation of why the bishop lives in Spain, I was referred to the pulls of politics in the Middle Ages, which resulted in spheres being drawn with only passing regard for national borders.

The parador is on the site of an ancient church-convent in the heart of the Old Town, a choice spot available only to a government inn and within a few steps of the cathedral, the bishop's palace, and other Romanesque structures. Designing a modern building to blend with these surroundings was a challenge, and there is a continuing dispute in town as to its success. Parking is not only off-street, it is in an underground garage, which takes care of the space problem and also indicates the deep snow expected here in the winter.

Inside the parador, the 14th-century cloister has been preserved and its patio enclosed and hung with plants. There is an indoor swimming pool, too.

Seo de Urgel, an episcopal seat for fourteen centuries, appears today to be primarily a stopping place for those coming from or going to Andorra. However, it is also the market town for the region and on market days its narrow streets are crowded with vendors selling everything from live chickens to hand-thrown pots.

PARADOR SEO DE URGEL, Seo de Urgel (Lérida). Tel.: 973-35-20-00. A modern building with 85 guestrooms in the heart of the Old Town section of the city. Amenities include private telephones, dining room, indoor parking, and an indoor heated swimming pool. Convenient for all the ancient structures and adjacent to the Palace of the Bishop-Prince of Andorra and Urgellet, it is only 20 km. to the Principality of Andorra. The parador is 133 km. from Lérida, 214 from Barcelona, and 610 from Madrid. Rates: See Index.

Directions: Seo de Urgel (which also appears on maps and signs as La Seu d'Urgell) is on the bend where Rte. 1313 turns south towards Lérida (which may also be read as Lleida).

EL CASTELL
Seo de Urgel (Lérida)

A family-owned-and-run inn of high reputation and reasonable prices, El Castell is located on a hillside just below the ruins of a castle on the Lérida road. It is an exceptionally well-run hostelry with a dining room so fine that it caters banquets for the bishop as well as serving travelers. Luncheon on the terrace is memorable not only for the food, but the view of the valley, the city, and the Pyrenees.

Each guest room has a spectacular view, too. I had my choice of a balcony or a chalet-type room, and there are also two suites. A large outdoor swimming pool surrounded by comfortable lounge chairs and pots of bright flowers is set into the mountain just above the inn and below the castle.

The Tapies family sent their oldest son to the hotel school at Tulane University in New Orleans and have visited extensively in the United States. Ludi Tapies grew up in Andorra and can arrange private visits to the palace as well as give precise directions on avoiding the ticky-tacky main streets of Andorra and finding the beautiful high-mountain villages for which the principality is famous. She will also arrange fishing and hunting trips for her guests.

Jaume Tapies presides over the dining room and maintains the region's best wine cellar. The cuisine might be described as French-Catalan-Nouveau; the dessert trolley as the best of possible worlds.

EL CASTELL (Relais et Chateaux: Iberia), Seo de Urgel (Lérida). Tel.: 973-35-07-04. A 45-guestroom (family-owned) inn located on a mountainside below the castle on the Route de Lérida outside the town proper of Seo de Urgel. Excellent dining. Closed Jan. 15 to Feb. 15. Convenient for the area, especially Andorra, with personal attention by the owners to the special interests of the guests. Swimming pool open in summer. It is 20 km. from Andorra; 129 km. from Lérida, 210 from Barcelona, and 606 from Madrid. Rates: See Index.

Directions: The inn is well marked on the east side of Rte. 1313 (Route de Lérida) south of the town of Seo de Urgel.

PARADOR DON GASPAR DE PORTOLA
Artiés (Lérida)

The mountain driving required to reach this handsome lodge in the Pyrenees is no longer as difficult as I found it on my first trip. In fact, with the recently constructed new roads, the route is quite delightful.

There is still one road that leads through Aiguestortes National Park, a nature preserve and hunting ground (the words are not considered incompatible here) kept so primitive that those who enter some sections may do so only with authorized guides.

My visit was in early summer, and there were still patches of snow and evidence of the skiing season barely past. The parador is of striking architecture, not unlike mountain resorts in Yugoslavia, with rooms tucked cosily under the peaked roof.

Once I had rested I took a brisk walk along a trail leading from the parador grounds and soon found myself equally distracted by the spectacular mountain landscape about me and the tiny perfect wildflowers pushing up near my feet. I had hoped to confront a mountain goat from a reasonable distance, but found only other hikers coming and going. Most of them greeted me in French, a reminder that I was close to the border of that country.

Artiés is a popular but not overcrowded resort town with a number of good restaurants. The parador dining room is excellent, however, and the trout served was just as fresh and well prepared as the setting promised.

PARADOR DON GASPAR DE PORTOLA, Artiés (Lérida). Tel.: 973-64-08-01. A 40-guestroom 4-star mountain lodge high in the Pyrenees, only 24 km. from France. Skiing in the winter; hiking, canoeing, and fishing in the summer; adjacent to Aiguestortes National Park. The parador is only 8 km. from Viella, 170 from Lérida, 320 from Barcelona. Distances are deceptive, however, as the road is twisting. Rates: See Index.

Directions: Artiés is on Rte. 142, which may be reached by going west from Seo de Urgell to Rte. 147 at Sort, then north to Llavorsi and northwest on 142 through Port de la Bonaiqua (a mountain pass). From Lérida, it is north on Rte. 230 to Viella, then east to Artiés.

PARADOR VALLE DE ARÁN
Viella (Lérida)

Most paradors are situated either widely apart or at least on different routes, so I was surprised to find one high in the Pyrenees only eight kilometers from the other. Parador Valle de Arán is the older and larger of the two, a different style of architecture, and despite its mountain valley setting, it is part of Viella, the capital of the region.

Viella is not just a resort town either, though the skiing is understandably good. It was the home of prehistoric as well as Roman settlers, and there are many structures from its 17th-century heyday as well as a church dating from the 12th century.

The parador is named for the Valley of Arán, a place of rushing rivers, Alpine flowers, and mountain meadows. Again, I found French to be the second language of the parador and the town. As I strolled the narrow streets, the shops were doing a weekend business in sausage, cheese, and bread to fill the backpacks of the visitors. On a less culinary level, dolls in the colorful costume worn at local fiestas were being snapped up by collectors.

Back at the parador I was happy to see the balcony of my room bathed in sunlight. Not exactly hot, but warm enough and comfortable, I put up my feet and enjoyed the beauty of the countryside.

PARADOR VALLE DE ARÁN, Viella (Lérida). Tel.: 973-64-01-00. A 135-guestroom contemporary parador in the high valley of Arán, Spanish Pyrenees, with Alpine views from every room. Winter sports. Swimming pool and mountaineering in summer, hunting, fishing, canoeing. Near Aiguestortes National Park and France. Viella is 8 km. from Artiés, 18 from the frontier, 163 from Lérida, and 604 from Madrid.

Directions: From Artiés, continue due west for 8 km. and watch for signs to the parador. South on Rte. 230 to Lérida, where you can connect with the E-4 east to Barcelona or west to Madrid.

SOME IBERIAN OBSERVATIONS

Spain and Portugal are not the same, and Spanish words frequently are not the same as Portuguese words. Anyone making a trip to both countries would be well advised to purchase both Portuguese-English and Spanish-English dictionaries. Make certain that the food sections of these dictionaries are adequate, because this is an area that causes the most puzzlement.

Basically, the night and day porters (concierges and conserjes) at paradores and pousadas do not have any English at all. In such cases, it would be well to have one or two such phrases available as the translation for "I have a reservation for tonight" or "Have you a room for tonight?" It is well to recheck the following night's reservation, which will be done by the concierge and for which there will be a slight charge. Be certain that the concierge understands whether you are confirming a previous reservation or want a completely new reservation.

Breakfast at individual pousadas and paradores can vary widely, and in some cases they are extra. Completo breakfast *consists of simple buns or rolls and coffee. A good trick is to wander through the dining room and see what is being served. The alternative is to go to the nearest bar-restaurant for take-out coffee and to the grocery store for a picnic breakfast. I had a picnic at lunch about every day.*

Paradores do not supply Kleenex, but this, like practically anything else that the American or British traveler would find essential, can be purchased in stores throughout Spain and Portugal. The trick is to know how to ask for the proper item. In this case, it might be ''paper handkerchiefs.'' Remember, if all else fails, sign language will reign supreme.

The simple courtesies of life are necessary in both Spanish and Portuguese, including ''Please,'' ''Thank you,'' and ''I beg your pardon.''

Portugal

SPAIN

Sintra

LISBON
Cascais • Palmela   Estremoz •
• Setubal
• Evora

Serpa •

Armacão Santa Barbara
Sagres • de Pera de Nexe
FARO

INNS AND LOCATIONS

TRAVEL SUGGESTIONS FOR PORTUGAL

Pousadas, Palacios, and Other Portuguese Inns

It is possible and tempting to travel all over Portugal, spending every night in a government-owned inn, a pousada. Pousadas are similar to the paradores of Spain and are located in castles, convents, and so forth, though some have been built specifically to take advantage of a scenic spot. However, I have included other inns as they fit the criteria of good food, a friendly welcome, and providential location.

Pousadas are more than simple country inns, since each deliberately reflects the style and culture of the region in which it is located. Great open fireplaces, cool verandas, mosaics, and fine original art put the traveler in the mood to appreciate more fully the history and character of the country. Accommodations are good to excellent, with modern bathrooms and comfortable beds. Pousadas accept credit cards. MasterCard and Visa are the most widely used.

As the pousadas have relatively few rooms, reservations are necessary, especially during the high summer season. They may be made in advance through Marketing Ahead, 433 Fifth Avenue, New York, NY 10016; 212-686-9213. If you visit midweek and off-season, you can frequently find a room available, though not always the most choice. Try arriving midafternoon or asking your innkeeper of the night before to telephone ahead. Prices are reasonable, especially for the value received.

Pousadas serve three meals a day, with a continental breakfast included in the room price. Sandwiches, beverages, and snacks are available between meals. The regular meal is generally four courses with both a fish entrée and a meat entrée, each fully garnished with potatoes and vegetable. You can ask for three courses instead of four at a twenty-five percent reduction in price. Regional dishes are served as well as English-style grills with boiled or fried potatoes. Several hundred years of British tourism have left their mark on the cookery. The influence of France is seen in other inns.

Portuguese Menus

Small or large, Portuguese restaurants are likely to be very clean and serve same-day fresh food. As you would expect in a seafaring nation, fish is very good and served in a variety of ways. Caldeirada, a fish and shellfish stew similar to French bouillabaisse, is delicious. Grilled fresh tunny *(tuna) or* salmonete *(red mullet) and a green salad with plenty of chewy Portuguese bread and sweet butter are hard to surpass. The national dish is* bacalhau *(dried codfish), reshaped into an infinite number of dishes and worth sampling.*

Caldo verde *is a soup made with potatoes and kale that appears on many menus.* Porco à alentajana *is pork and clams, popular in the south-central Alentejo region, the farm belt of Portugal.* Bife no frigideira *is steak with mustard sauce. Desserts are often served from a cart and include almond cake, caramel custard, fruit tarts, and fresh fruit in season.*

Touring

"Praia" is the sign for a beach, and there are plenty of them. As the main roads do not hug the shore, you watch for a sign then proceed down an access road a few miles to the beach. Along the shoreline, there are spectacular cliffs with lovely golden beaches in coves as well as sweeps of open sand. Midweek, you will often have the beach to yourself, though weekends can be crowded especially in the areas nearest Lisbon. South-facing beaches are calm and good for swimming, but those that front directly on the Atlantic have booming breakers and treacherous undertows.

The Michelin Green Tourist Guide to Portugal *contains very good accounts of historic sites, buildings, churches, and local history. I found it indispensable. The Michelin map for Spain and Portugal (990) also guided me well. Contact the Portuguese Tourist Office (548 Fifth Avenue, New York, NY 10036) for information on the areas you intend to visit.*

My trip to Portugal began at Lisbon, then proceeded by rental car, first to the coastal area northwest of Lisbon, then south to the Algarve, east and north again touching the Spanish border before circling back to Lisbon. In this region I visited all the pousadas, though there are others in the north of Portugal that I will include in a future edition.

Lisbon and the Lisbon Coast

The areas just northwest of Lisbon attracted a good many of Europe's displaced monarchs a few decades ago, and so have an international style as well as many foreign visitors. The beach resorts of Estoril and Cascais are famous and crowded; the mountain town of Sintra is more of a retreat.

Sintra, one of the most beautiful and restful places in Portugal, is less than an hour's drive from the airport and is an oasis of tranquility. Byron called it a "glorious Eden," and it is still a place where gardens flourish, horse-drawn carts take leisurely drives, and hiking trails lead to great vistas as well as somewhat bizarre royal residences. It is convenient for touring the beach towns, but it is not the place to stay if you want to be in the center of the action.

There are no pousadas in Sintra, though its five-star hotel was originally restored by the government. I also sampled life in a private manor house that takes bed-and-breakfast guests.

PALACIO DE SETEAIS
Sintra

The name translates to "Palace of the Seven Sighs" for a reason more political than romantic. When the treaty ending the Peninsular War was signed on the premises, the Portuguese correctly guessed it was not going to send the French home as soon as promised. The diplomats adjusted to the realities with sighs. It is a beautiful building set back from the road in its own park with eighteen large antique-filled guest rooms and a dining room that attracts a Lisbon as well as a local clientele.

The palace was built in the eighteenth century as a private residence by a Dutch diamond merchant, became a hotel under government supervision, and is now owned by the Tivoli chain. Service and amenities are what you would expect for five stars, that is to say, first rate. The public rooms are exceptionally beautiful with hand-painted walls and museum-quality furniture. The carpets are hand-woven, needlepoint style, from the town of Arraiolos, in patterns designed especially for the hotel. There is a swimming pool and, of course, there are gardens. For all its elegance, Palacio dos Seteais is not prohibitively expensive, though reservations must often be made far in advance.

If you can't get a room, try to go for a meal or afternoon tea. It is only three kilometers outside Sintra.

PALACIO DE SETEAIS, 2710 Sintra. Tel.: 923-3200/25/50. Telex: 14410 HOPASE P. An 18-guestroom luxury hotel in a beautiful setting, with a fine restaurant, gardens, and views as well as historical and cultural associations. Open all year. Reservations important. Rates: See Index.

Directions: From the center of Sintra (outside the Royal Palace), take the road to Monserrate, technically the Rua Barbosa du Bocage. The Palacio is 1.5 km. north of Sintra on your right, set well back from the road.

QUINTA DE SÃO THIAGO
Sintra

One of the latest in the government's plan to make things comfortable and authentic for travelers is the encouragement of stately homes to open their doors to overnight guests. There are now a number of these throughout Portugal, and one of the most charming is just four and a half kilometers farther than the Palacio on the Monserrate road. At least that is where the turn-off is and the sign "Quinta de São Thiago." I proceeded down a dirt road that became increasingly narrow and rocky, and just when I decided I could go no farther, I was there. The *quinta,* a noble hacienda built in 1535, is behind huge green gates in a rock wall. Parking is across the road.

This has been the home of the English Braddell family for fifty years and has been open to guests only since 1981. There are ten rooms with private baths and two family suites with shared baths. Public rooms include sitting rooms, a library, a game room, a chapel, and a large dining room where breakfast is served at the guests' convenience and evening meals are served on request.

The grounds of the estate are well tended and lovely—flowers from the extensive gardens appear throughout the house as well. Mrs. Braddell not only gives helpful hints for touring, but will arrange for horse-

back riding and anything else her guests desire, including attendance at special events and *festas* generally not open to the public.

Inside the thick walls of the hacienda, you experience the way of life that has made the Sintra area so attractive to Europe's displaced royalty as well as to retired ambassadors and British merchant princes. This is country house lodging at its best.

QUINTA DE SÃO THIAGO, 2710 Sintra. Tel.: 923-2923. A 10-guest-room (private baths) privately owned 16th-century manor house on a country estate; also 2-family suites. Bed-and-breakfast rates, but evening meal available on request. Swimming pool, tennis court, gardens. Open all year. Reservations advised. Contact Mrs. R.N.L. Braddell. Discounts off-season. Rates: See Index.

Directions: Take the Monserrate road out of Sintra, past the Palacio dos Seteais (3 km.) for another 1.5 km. Turn right at the first and only right turn (there is a green sign indicating Quinta S. Thiago). Continue 900 m. to large green gates on left. Park across road.

A DAY IN LISBON

One interesting way to solve the problem of visiting a big city without taking the car into the Centro *is to leave the car at a recognizable point outside the city and take a bus into the center. In Lisbon I parked my car at the Santa Maria Hospital, checked the bus numbers that I would need to find my way back, and left the driving to the bus line.*

I congratulated myself every block of the way, because Lisbon has unbelievable traffic. It is a beautiful, sophisticated city with modern apartment buildings and wide boulevards bordered by attractive mosaic sidewalks. And yet a turn of the corner can be a journey into yesterday as one discovers the narrow, winding cobblestone streets that climb up and down the famous seven hills. But it also has heavy traffic.

I arrived in the center of the city and took bus 37, which follows a route from the downtown area (where there is always a long queue) through some of the more narrow streets of the Alfama (the old Moorish quarter) to the ruins of the Saint Jorge Castle crowning one of Lisbon's hills.

From the vantage point of the highest place on the castle grounds there is a very good view of the Tagus River and the great bridge and also of the majestic statue of Jesus. Also at the top in a little park there is the ever-present game of soccer that is a universal language here in Portugal. As soon as you have two small boys and a soccer ball, the game is on.

According to the Michelin Green Guide *on Portugal (don't leave home without it), the castle was constructed by the Visigoths in the 5th century and then strengthened by the Moors in the 9th century. It boasts ten towers linked by massive battlemented walls. Michelin doesn't say anything about the millions of birds nesting in the live oaks, whose calls are sometimes shrill and piercing and oftentimes soothing.*

On my way back to the bus, I saw an ancient, four-door, leather-seated, convertible Oldsmobile of 1922 vintage being used as a taxi—it was really sensational. At the bus stop outside the castle gates were old three- and four-storied buildings with people leaning out of the windows, looking down through the ubiquitous lines of laundry.

Lisbon has lots of outdoor cafes, and the passing show can be viewed also from the benches in the parks, gardens, and squares. The Portuguese version of the Good Humor men take their carts of ice cream up and down the cobbled hills.

Music, generally in melancholy strains, floats out from the taverns, restaurants, and houses, sometimes getting fierce competition from roosters, ducks, turkeys, and dogs. Street musicians play the lighter folk tunes.

One of Lisbon's great treats is the Gulbenkian Museum, which has one of the world's greatest private art collections, including two Rembrandts, a Rubens, and a rich collection of silver made for Catherine the Great by Thomas Germain. There are several small galleries exhibiting Roman, Greek, European, Egyptian, Mesopotamian, Islamic, and Oriental art treasures, as well as Persian tapestries, silver, ancient Greek and Egyptian pottery, jewelry, Turkish textiles, and delicately carved ivories and woodcuts from the Orient. The museum is located in an art complex that includes three auditoriums; one for music, a second is a theater, and a third for meetings. Around the corner from the entrance to the Gulbenkian, still on the property, is the Center of Modern Art. Opened in 1983, it contains over 500 works and was presented to Lisbon by the Gulbenkian Foundation.

YORK HOUSE/RESIDENCIA INGLESA
Lisbon

As soon as I stepped through the gates of York House, I left the city behind me. There are stone steps, flowering trees, a courtyard full of greenery, and a very old stone building. York House was a convent in the 16th century, restored from ruin in the 20th and converted into a pension by a French woman, who only recently retired from active management. As a pension it has sheltered not only travelers, but British and American foreign service personnel awaiting permanent housing, as well as any number of famous writers who stayed for months at a time.

This year when I returned, the pepper trees were still weeping over

the mosaics, but inside York House, new things were going on. A spate of handsome new rooms and suites have been added in another wing, but they fit in so perfectly with the old, you need not fear encroaching modernization. My favorite was suite 307 with its bank of small-paned windows, a bath done in Portuguese blue and white tiles, and a bed canopy made from the cover of an old well.

A few years ago, a handsome 19th-century town house, once owned by a British diplomat as well as the late Portuguese novelist Eca de Queiros and located just up the street, was renovated as an annex, adding more rooms and a touch of late Victorian style. The dining room is still in the original York House, though breakfast is served to guests either in their rooms or before the fireplace in the parlor of the Residencia Inglesa as well.

Food is prepared in a provincial French-Portuguese manner that has delicious results. There is usually a choice for the entrée, but otherwise it is a set three-course meal, both at luncheon and dinner. Lighter fare is available in the bar. York House, no longer strictly a pension, works on a bed-and-breakfast basis. In summer, however, you may be asked to take demipension; that is, one main meal either midday or evening.

Guest rooms are slightly larger in the Residencia Inglesa annex, while views are considered superior at York House, where your room will face either the courtyard or the river. All rooms are furnished with antiques and are immaculate. Although you are not in the center of town, you are on a convenient streetcar line, and the Museum of Ancient Art is close at hand. There is some limited parking next to Residencia Inglesa. Incidentally, the street name translates to "the street of the green window shutters."

YORK HOUSE/RESIDENCIA INGLESA, 32, 47 Rua das Janelas Verdes, Lisbon 1200. Tel.: 66-81-44 or 66-24-35. A 66-guestroom (private and shared baths) inn in the southwestern part of the city, not far from the 25 de Abril bridge, the longest suspension bridge in Europe, and the museum attractions of Belem. Rates: See Index.

Directions: Rua das Janelas Verdes is a short length of a street that changes its name with confusing frequency. It parallels the main avenue off the Rio Tejo waterfront, Av. 24 de Julho., and intersects with Av. Dom Carlos I. If you require instant directions, ask how to get to the Museu de Arte Antiga, just up the street. York House is on the north side of Janelas Verdes and Residencia Inglesa is on the south side.

HOTEL PRINCIPE REAL
Lisbon

After twenty-two years as a family-owned-and-run hotel, the four-star Principe Real has been acquired by the small Aldeia group as their only Lisbon property. I spoke with the friendly and enthusiastic new manager, who told me a "home-style" restaurant was being added and a few more amenities, but the hotel's many returning guests would find their long-time Lisbon favorite much the same.

So, be assured, the wall of blue and white tiles as you enter the front door will be left in place, and the tiny, elegant elevator will continue to carry you up the five floors. Rooms are still small and pleasant, with private baths and individual furnishings from various periods.

In addition to all of the conveniences of a large, modern hotel, rooms now include evening bed turn-down. Daily newspapers like the *Wall Street Journal* and *U.S.A. Today* are at your door, and when you arrive, you will find fresh fruit and flowers.

The buffet breakfast included in the tariff is American-style, with eggs, bacon, yogurt, fresh-squeezed juice, cereal and two breads, and coffee, tea, or chocolate.

The Principe Real doesn't look like much from the street, which is, by the way, a back one at the entrance to the Botanical Garden and just uphill from Avenida da Liberdade, the main shopping street of Lisbon. As you know, it's what is inside that counts.

HOTEL PRINCIPE REAL, Rua da Alegria 53, 1200 Lisbon. Tel.: 36-01-16/7/8. A 24-guestroom (private baths) in-town hotel in central Lisbon. Full American breakfast included. Open all year. Radios, tele-

phones, TV, plus many amenities. Near the Botanical Gardens and main shopping area. Rates: See Index.

Directions: From Avenida da Liberdade, turn west (uphill) at corner posted to Praca da Alegria and follow Rua da Alegria. Hotel is immediately on your left. Usually plenty of parking outside the door.

HOTEL DO GUINCHO
Cascais

The winds on this headland literally took my breath away, so I retreated through the inner courtyard of the Hotel do Guincho, a five-star notable small inn built in the Moorish style on the site of an ancient fortress.

Today, Guincho is the northern outpost of the "Coast of Kings," where so many displaced royals came in the aftermath of World War II. Now, celebrities who want to avoid the crowds leave the towns of Cascais and Estoril, with their large hotels, casinos, and golf courses, for this quiet inn where they can enjoy all the comforts, knowing their privacy will be respected.

Although Hotel do Guincho is not far from the beaches, markets, and excitement of the towns, it is best to have a car at your disposal (taxis can be summoned as well). While distances are not great for any dedicated walker, it is nearly always too windy.

Inside the inn, the guest rooms are handsomely and individually done, with arched doorways, brick ceilings, tile floors, alcoves, and antiques. All guest rooms have their own balcony overlooking the sea. Public rooms have a medieval ambience, while the dining room serves the finest French-Portuguese cuisine.

The views of the sea are vast, and when a storm is brewing or beating against the windows, it is easy to imagine yourself on the prow of a caravel heading for the New World. Incidentally, the next major promontory up the Estoril coast is Cabo da Roca, the westernmost point of Europe.

HOTEL DO GUINCHO, #5 Praia do Guincho, 2750 Cascais, Portugal. Tel.: 285-0491. U.S. reservations: Robert Warner, 711 3rd Ave., New York, NY 10017, 212-557-3400. A 36-guestroom (private baths) 5-star hotel on a promontory of the Estoril coast, 18 mi. from downtown Lisbon. European plan. Breakfast, lunch, and dinner. Open year-round. Swimming pool and golf privileges at Hotel Estoril Sol. Casino and nightly entertainment. Water sports, fishing, horseback riding, tennis, sailing, as well as Sintra, Mafra, and Queluz nearby. Rates: See Index.

Directions: From Lisbon, take the coastal road west toward Estoril. Continue past Estoril and Cascais going north. Hotel is on your left at Praia do Guincho.

POUSADA DO CASTELO PALMELA
Palmela

Here I was above the clouds in my own castle in Portugal, master of all that I surveyed—ready to send my ships to the New World and my traders to the Far East!

Sitting in the bedroom window of the Pousada do Palmela, just a few miles south of Lisbon, I was a hundred million miles away from the real world. High above the fields and the city, I was actually above the flocks of gulls that keep their constant winged vigil around the walls of this truly incredible fortress-cum-hotel.

The great walls that tower so menacingly above the countryside were built more than a thousand years ago by the Moors, as was a mosque transformed later into a church, only the ruins of which remain. Another line of fortifications was erected later, and nearby are what seem to be Roman ruins.

The pousada guest rooms, as in most cases, are modern with all the conveniences that travelers have come to appreciate, including private bathrooms, hot water, plenty of walking around space, and comfortable beds. This pousada should be on every traveler's Portuguese itinerary. In fact, when visiting Lisbon I would prefer to stay here or at the Pousada de São Filipe at Setubal, just a few miles away, but more about that in just a moment.

I spent at least a morning wandering about the grounds, all within

the massive walls. There were millions of beautiful yellow field daisies growing up among the ruins and in the crevices of many ancient buildings.

Here was a surprise—a swimming pool on the edge of the battlements; certainly one of the very sunniest spots, and from it one could look across the countryside or down through the steep fields, where goats seem to wander unattended.

The roofs of the town with their variegated patterns and planes cried out to be photographed or painted, and from that height the villagers below looked like vigorous ants busily going about the duties of the day. From the top of the walls, the view to the west is towards the mountains, and to the south there is a line of windmills. Taken all in all, it is one of the most impressive views in Portugal.

Ah, Palmela, how I wish I could press a magic button and return to your vaulted windows and exotic panorama again.

POUSADA DO CASTELO PALMELA, Palmela. Tel.: 235-1226. A 27-guestroom fortress-castle inn with large, pleasant rooms. Swimming pool. Forty km. from Lisbon, 200 km. from the Spanish border at Badajoz. Rates: See Index.

Directions: Leave the E-4 Motorway from Lisbon at Palmela exit and follow pousada signs straight up the hill.

POUSADA DE SÃO FILIPE
Setubal

It seems unfair that there should be two such magnificent pousadas within a short distance of each other. Besides the Pousada do Palmela,

Castelo Palmela

standing high on the top of a commanding hill overlooking miles and miles of the Portuguese countryside, there is this magnificently placed pousada on the cliffs, overlooking the estuary of the Rio Sado, the sea, and the Tróia Peninsula, leading to the sunny land of the Algarve. It's a joy to walk about the rocky ramparts and take in the entire panorama. Occasionally, I cast a furtive look over my left shoulder toward the walls of the other pousada, more pleasant than menacing at such a distance.

From Lisbon I had taken the second Setubal entrance from E-4 and followed the roads and signs to the Centro. From that point, the pousada signs directed me through the main part of town and up a steep hill where there was a certain ambivalence regarding the correct road (I subsequently learned to stay on a paved road and watch for a sign indicating the castle was to the left).

Passing through an ancient archway, I was in the moat of the castle, now being used as a parking area. I went through a huge door into a cavernlike entranceway, at that time being reconstructed. To my right was a long set of stairs leading through a tunnel at the end of which I could see a light. (There may now be an elevator.) I walked to the top and found a terrace overlooking the estuary and the sea.

The terrace was furnished with many small round tables with white umbrellas, and I learned from my own experience that it is possible to sit for hours just looking out over the fascinating panorama of the seaport town with its little ferries plying the estuary and literally dozens of dory fishermen out on the water almost at first light. At night the lights of the town create a yellow crescent of pearls stretching out as far as the eye can see.

A dissonant symphony of sounds drifts up from the town—fire sirens, police car signals, barking dogs, crowing roosters, and the ubiquitous moped.

That evening I joined the regular diners in the dining room, which also enjoys the spectacular view, and was invited to join a squadron of British Navy mine sweepers who were taking a holiday evening. We were a most jovial gathering.

The guest rooms, some of which were on the small side, were comfortable. Request a sea view.

I suggest the traveler book one night at the pousada at Palmela and the other night here at Setubal to enjoy the best of all possible pousada-castle worlds. Be sure to arrange reservations well in advance.

POUSADA DE SÃO FILIPE, Setubal. Tel.: 238-44. A 15-guestroom inn established in an ancient fortress, 50 km. from Lisbon; 200 km. from the Spanish border at Badajoz. Originally built in 1590 to subdue the inhabitants of the town below. There is a very pleasant chapel on the castle grounds. Rates: See Index.

Directions: From the center of Setubal follow pousada signs up the high hill to the castle walls.

POUSADA DO INFANTE
Sagres

For many visitors to Portugal, Sagres is where the Algarve begins. The Pousada do Infante is one of two pousadas on the southern coast, the other being in São Brás de Alportel, several kilometers to the east. I did find two other modest hotels in the Algarve, described in the following pages.

The Pousada do Infante turned out to be beautifully accommodating, as are so many of the other Portuguese government-owned inns. For one thing, it's set apart from the town, which is beginning to lose its native charm and succumbing to more highly touristic interests.

One of the thrilling things for me about this inn was its location at a geographical point that is rich in history. This is the point of land

111

around which the ancient Phoenicians sailed in their quest for further trade in the Atlantic Ocean. Here, too, the Norsemen and Vikings came from the north and swung east into the Mediterranean.

Today, ships from many nations are within sighting distance as they continue their journey to Africa around the Cape of Good Hope to the Indian Ocean, or perhaps around Cape Horn into the Pacific. The Portuguese thought so highly of it as a strategic location that they built the fortress of Prince Henry the Navigator.

Amidst all of this interesting history, I was surprised to discover that the decorative theme of the Pousada do Infante is Art Deco, which blends very well with the unusual marble in the hallways, arches, and floors. It is a two-story beige building, faintly reminiscent of the architecture of Florida in the early 1920s, before the great land boom. There is a feeling of respectability and restraint about it. Each of the bedrooms has a small balcony overlooking the patio, the cliffs, and the sea beyond.

The main lobby has a beautiful big marble fireplace with a vast semicircular couch in front of it and many, many comfortable chairs. The terrace off the main dining room is a very pleasant place to spend the afternoon. An overhead chandelier lends a sort of formal quality to the dining room.

I learned that during the high season the occupancy by American visitors was as high as sixty or seventy percent.

Instead of having dinner at the pousada, I went to a local restaurant, A Tasca, which overlooks the clear waters of the bay. Before going in I stood awhile and watched the fresh fish being unloaded in the cove and prepared for their next destination in a big, well-lighted shed. There was much shouting and singing as the men went about their work.

A Tasca's specialty is fresh fish, naturally. The catches of the day are posted on a blackboard, and everything is cooked to order. When ready for dessert, I made my selection from a refrigerated glass case where there were many cakes, tarts, and puddings, settling at last for a creamy vanilla custard and fresh berries.

POUSADA DO INFANTE, Sagres (Algarve). Tel.: 642-22. A 21-guestroom very comfortable seaside inn on the extreme western end of the Algarve, 286 km. from Lisbon. Would advise reservations as far in advance as possible. Near several of the famous Portuguese beaches. Rates: See Index.

Directions: From Lisbon follow the coastal road, which begins across the Rio Sado estuary at Setubal and continues to the southwest corner at Sagres. The pousada is well signposted.

THE ALGARVE

The Algarve is the entire southern section of Portugal, extending from Sagres at the westernmost point to the borders of Spain in the east. It is very much like the Costa del Sol in Spain and, in fact, each is an extension of the other. The word comes from the Arabic el gharb, which means the west of the "land beyond." Like the rest of the southern Iberian peninsula, it bears the unmistakable marks left by 500 years

of Moorish domination. *Not only in place names, but in architecture and in the characteristics of the people. Historically, it has always been a very important place, and the Phoenicians and Carthaginians, as well as the Greeks, Romans, Visigoths, and, of course, the Moors, have left vestiges of their tenures.*

Today, it is important as an international holiday objective. The winter temperature ranges between 50° and 68° Fahrenheit, and the summer, between 68° and 86°. The Algarve boasts of having over 3,000 hours of sunshine a year (California has 1,000 to 2,000). Early spring is supposed to be one of the best times to visit, when there is an abundance of flowers and blossoms and, I might add, relatively uncrowded conditions.

In the Algarve the beach is one of the main preoccupations, and there are all kinds of beaches available. There's also lots of golf, fishing, sailing, water skiing, night life, and shopping, not only for the crafts of the region, but in the chic shops in the larger cities.

There are several large cities in the Algarve—Faro, Lagos, Portimao, Albufeira, and Tavira. It's possible to fly to Faro from any point in Europe.

There are two pousadas in the Algarve: the one at Sagres is very popular and should be booked well in advance, and the other at São Brás de Alportel is located almost midway between Spain and the Atlantic Ocean. I also found two excellent small hotels. I think it would be possible to stay at any of these and enjoy some day trips to other parts of the Algarve.

I think the Algarve would be a very happy experience between November and April. The almond trees are in glorious bloom in February.

HOTEL DO LEVANTE
Armacão de Pera (Algarve)

Oh boy, that sun felt good. I burrowed into the warm sand, cradled my head in my arms, adjusted my sunglasses, and looked out towards the sea, where there were several small fishing boats and a large freighter dancing on the blue waters. Behind me and ninety steps up the cliff was the Hotel do Levante, a wonderful find for me.

I had spent the previous night in an unsatisfactory hotel in Albufeira, and because I was sure there was something along the road between Sagres and São Brás de Alportel, I doubled back on the beach road from Albufeira and stumbled into the somewhat modern village of Armacão de Pera. There were a few modern-looking, designed-to-accommodate-as-many-tourists-as-possible hotels, and then I caught a glimpse of Hotel do Levante, which had obviously been built a few years ago and had the pleasant white buildings and red roof that characterize Mediterranean design.

I liked it immediately and, after introducing myself to the management, I was taken on a short tour of some of the forty-one rooms, some of which have terraces and balconies. All have telephones, music, bathrooms, heating, and a sea view. I decided to take an hour on the beach in the sun and reflect upon my adventures in the Algarve.

I passed the inviting swimming pool, made my way down the wooden steps, and soon found just the right spot. At low tide the beaches extend for miles and miles in both directions. I was treated to the sight of parading beach strollers complete with broad hats against the already sizzling sun. It was fun.

My brief tour of this very attractive small hotel also included an explanation of the menu, which, because of the international nature of the guests, was printed in several languages. There are several different plans available, including a full three meals a day, if desired.

HOTEL DO LEVANTE, Armacão de Pera (Algarve). Tel.: 32322. Telex: 57478 Levant P. A very pleasant, quiet, seaside hotel just east of Albufeira and 47 km. from the Faro airport. (Not listed in Michelin.*) May be booked through a travel agent and various plans are available throughout the year with a considerable range in rates. Swimming pool, gardens, mini-golf, and quiet accommodations for children. Rates: See Index.*

Directions: Armacão de Pera is just 3 km. south of Route N-125. Follow signs to the south.

HOTEL LA RESERVE
Santa Barbara de Nexe (Algarve)

Many visitors think the Algarve is endless waterfront, but there are also back roads that lead to country inns and small villages. One of these inns is La Reserve, a Swiss-managed hostelry that began as a fine French restaurant in an old manor house. Its location is northwest of Faro, almost dead center in the Algarve.

Following signs, I found myself on a back road between the villages of Santa Barbara de Nexe and Esteval. La Reserve is surrounded by citrus trees and a whitewashed wall with wrought iron gates. I announced myself, and the gates swung open so I could proceed to the hotel, a handsome white Moorish structure set in gardens around a swimming pool. There are five acres of grounds with seventeen varieties of fruit trees and a large vegetable garden that supplies the restaurant.

La Reserve has twenty suites, including twelve studio-style and eight duplexes. The latter are two stories with living room downstairs, bedroom upstairs, and two verandas. All the suites have small kitchen facilities for light meals. Breakfast is served in the room or on the veranda. Lunch is available at the snack bar at poolside. Evening meals (which require firm reservations) are in the restaurant across the garden.

HOTEL LA RESERVE (Relais et Chateaux, Romantik Hotels), Santa Barbara de Nexe (Algarve). Tel.: (089) 90234 or 90474 or 90472. Telex: 56790 (Fuchs). An outstanding country house hotel and restaurant, 10 km. from Faro airport on a pretty back road between the coast and the foothills, not far from the Roman ruins of Milreu and the palace at Estoi or the market town of Loulé. Tennis courts, two swimming pools; horseback riding and golf can be arranged. Rates: See Index.

Directions: The main highway through the Algarve is Rte. 125. If you are driving west to east, after passing through Almancil watch for a road on your left leading north to Esteval. Turn left and follow signs to La Reserve. Coming from the airport or Faro and going east to west, the turn is at Patacão, towards Santa Barbara de Nexe. Again, there are signs to guide you all the way.

NORTH FROM THE ALGARVE

Leaving the Algarve and crossing the mountains, I found myself in the rolling farm country of Portugal. Donkeys wearing flowered hats still pull carts to market here, and the villages are crowned with centuries-old hilltop castles. It did not surprise me to find the best lodging available is in the pousadas.

POUSADA DE SÃO GENS
Serpa

The sun was setting and the shadows were getting longer as I sat on the spacious balcony of this pousada in central southeastern Portugal, about a pleasant afternoon's ride from the Algarve. Stretched out before me was a marvelously endless sea of corn and groves of cork oak. The sound of the birds singing their twilight song was reassurance that whatever else might be happening in the world, here in this portion of Portugal life was still sweet and anticipatory.

This pousada is in a building of relatively recent construction, but one that has maintained the memories of the Moorish occupation, which are found throughout the Iberian peninsula. The walls are chalk white and the balconies have the traditional elegant Moorish arches. The interior, with its elegant, spacious public rooms, high ceilings, and surprising fountains, provides a restful haven from what can be insistent sun.

Leaving São Brás de Alportel just before noon and heading north on N-2, I was delighted to find that the road ascended to considerable heights, passing through some most interesting villages and towns, including Barranco do Velho, Ameixial, and Almodóvar. This was the time of year that acres and acres of spring flowers bloomed in rampant purples and yellows across the high plains like a delightful, colored blanket. The landscape was playfully punctuated with the large umbrella cork trees that look as if they were painted in place.

Portugal has many storks and almost all of the towns and villages had steeples and roofs, where they could be seen nesting.

Dinner was enlivened by the presence of the vivacious woman director of the pousada, who made several interesting and helpful suggestions from the menu. I particularly remember a plate of sweets that she said were typical of the area.

A glance at the map would show that Serpa is on the main road from Lisbon to Seville, Spain, and would make an excellent overnight stop. I was headed north from the Algarve to the mountains of western Spain and found it made an ideal break.

POUSADA DE SÃO GENS, Serpa. Tel.: 523-27. A 17-guestroom extremely quiet and comfortable inn on the rolling plains of southeastern Portugal, approx. 221 km. from Lisbon. Characterized by splendid views of the countryside. Swimming pool under construction. Rates: See Index.

Directions: Serpa is on N-260 about 30 km. from the Spanish border at Rosal de la Frontera. The pousada signs are much in evidence.

POUSADA DOS LOIOS
Evora

It was raining in Evora, but I joined in grateful rejoicing with the inhabitants, many of whose ancestors have lived in this walled town since Roman times. In the courtyard of the Pousada dos Loios the

flowers of early May were grateful for the moisture, and small birds were flitting from bush to bush shaking the droplets from the leaves. Perhaps the spirit of the morning was best expressed by two of the maids of the pousada, who were on their knees scraping, brushing, and cleaning the stone steps and offering a gratuitous duet of Portuguese songs.

I had digressed from my usual picnic lunch, partly because of the rain, and also because the dining room atmosphere with the gleaming white napery and beautiful surroundings persuaded me to enjoy an indoor lunch. It consisted of cream of pea soup, followed by two small white fish, sautéed in butter and served with fresh spinach, a slice of very tasty tomato, and three small white potatoes.

The design of the arches and the delicate coloring and tints in the dining room were in the Manueline style, characterized by delicacy of design, beauty, and accuracy of color.

This pousada is a former 15th-century monastery with 20th-century conveniences, and the bedrooms, while extremely neat and furnished with cautious good taste, are a tad on the small side. As the brochure notes, "Over the years it has been embellished and enlarged with donations and legacies without losing any of its sobriety and dignity. The monks, whose habit was as blue as the skies of Alentejo, practiced charity, offered hospitality, and studied."

The town of Evora is well worth a visit and the traveler can park the car right next to the pousada and have the pleasure of an at least three-hour tour of many churches, palaces, museums, and stately mansions. I was most fascinated by the surviving columns of a Corinthian-style Roman temple, erected in the second century. The capitals and bases were of Estremoz marble and the columns of shaft granite.

I'll confess to having never heard of Evora until I started making plans for this trip, but my visit proved most interesting and rewarding. I could see why at one time it was the preferred capital of the kings of Portugal and the center of humanism, attracting scholars, sculptors, painters, and architects.

The pousada at Estremoz and this one in Evora are only a few kilometers apart and the traveler bent on using his time wisely could stay at either one and visit the other for lunch the following day. Both pousadas and towns have much to offer by way of supplying a feeling of Portugal, of both the past and the present.

POUSADA DOS LOIOS, Evora. Tel.: 06-240-51. A 32-guestroom elegant pousada in a former 16th-century monastery, decorated in the grand style. See Michelin Green Guide *for historic sites nearby; 142 km. from Lisbon; 108 km. from Badajoz, Spain. Rates: See Index.*

Directions: From the west leave N-4 at Montemor-O-Novo and follow N-114 to Evora. From the east leave N-4 just west of Estremoz and follow N-18, an enjoyable road. The pousada is located in the center of the walled town in the historic district.

POUSADA DA RAINHA SANTA ISABEL
Estremoz

Unlike the pousadas at Setubal and Palmela, really fortifications with many characteristics of castles, the Pousada da Rainha Santa Isabel is a bona fide live-in castle that also has a keep, a tower that thrusts its way even higher into the blue Portuguese sky.

This pousada is named for a queen saint—Isabel of Aragon, the wife of King Dinis, who was known as the poet king and the farmer king, and was an enormously active person who founded the university at Coimbra and established Portuguese, a dialect from the Oporto region, as the official language.

Both the pousada and its keep are on the top of a hill that dominates not only the town of Estremoz, but the entire countryside for miles around. Going up through the very narrow streets of the town with even the smallest model of automobile involves almost scraping the rough walls of houses on both sides.

However, the effort is well rewarded, not only by the inn's fabulous view, but also the excellent accommodations, furnishings, service, and food.

The pousada was built around a central courtyard, and the hallway that traversed three sides contained mirrors, sculpture, paintings, rugs, and very impressively decorated lamps. At each turn there was a delightful surprise—an old oil painting, an arrangement of painted furniture, or a delicate piece of porcelain.

I have visited many castle-hotels in many different countries of Europe, but I have never been in one that was so *well preserved*. I am not sufficiently well acquainted with periods of Spanish furniture design to vouch for its authenticity, but I can attest to the fact that every one of the guest rooms was furnished with opulent period furniture and richly embroidered or painted decorations, many in beautiful hand-tooled leather.

The dining room had a high, vaulted ceiling with several very substantial solid marble columns and very heavy wooden chandeliers. The high-backed chairs were covered in red velours with brass nail stubs, creating a highly decorative effect.

The *Michelin Green Guide* devotes an entire page to Estremoz, pointing out its famous potteries and the rural museum. There are several churches, including the chapel with wall murals depicting the life of Queen Saint Isabel. One depicts a particularly charming legend about the king and queen called the Miracle of the Roses. I will not spoil it for you.

There is a vast square in the center of the lower town with several interesting ancient buildings and a very lively Saturday market, as well.

POUSADA DA RAINHA SANTA ISABEL, Estremoz. Tel.: 226-18. A 23-guestroom luxurious hotel in a former medieval castle; 179 km. from Lisbon, 62 km. from Badajoz on the Spanish border, 46 km. to Evora. See Michelin Green Guide *for historic sites nearby. Rates: See Index.*

Directions: Estremoz is on the M-4. The pousada, on the top of the hill above the town, can be seen at some distance. Once in the center of the town, follow the pousada signs that lead up the hill.

Eastern France

ITINERARY 1 (PAGE 129)

GERMANY

• PARIS
• Barbizon
• Les Bezards
• ORLEANS
Loire Valley
• Chambord
Montrichard
BLOIS
Chenonceaux
• AVALLON

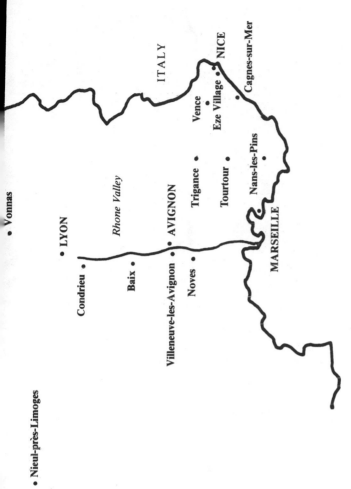

- Vonnas

- Nieul-près-Limoges

LYON
Condrieu •
Baix •
Rhone Valley
Villeneuve-les-Avignon •
• AVIGNON
Noves •
Trigance •
Tourtour •
Nans-les-Pins •
MARSEILLE
ITALY
Vence •
Eze Village •
NICE
Cagnes-sur-Mer

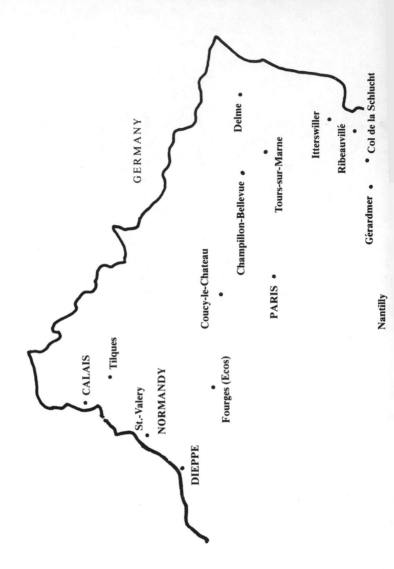

Eastern France

ITINERARY 2 (PAGE 163)

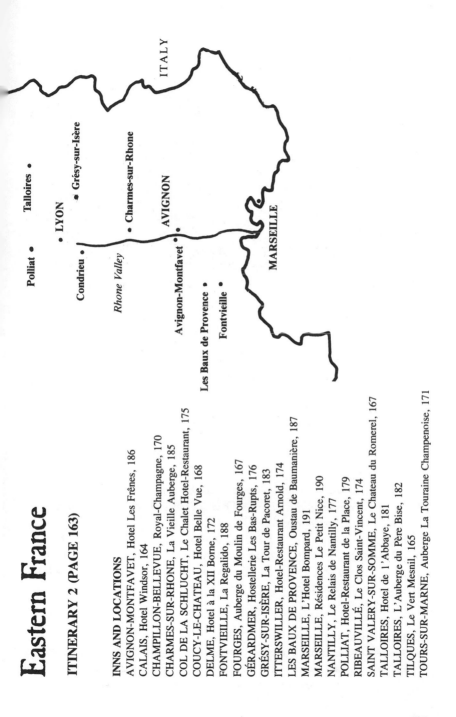

INNS AND LOCATIONS

TRAVEL SUGGESTIONS FOR FRANCE

How to Get There

Pan Am, Air France, and many other airlines fly directly from North America to Paris. Your travel agent is your best source for expert opinion about the many different packages and constantly changing special fares offered by many airlines. A Eurailpass is good in France.

French Visas

The French government requires visas from all visitors to France. Visas may be obtained through the French consulate or embassy offices or through most travel agencies.

Applicants must present a passport and two additional passport photos. The cost is $9.00. If application is made by mail, $2.00 for return certified postage should be added. It is best to allow at least two weeks for processing. The visa is good for three months.

Country Inns in France

The accommodations I visited are as diversified and complex as the country itself. They are located in ancient castles, chateaux, country houses, priories, conventional small and large hotels, and private homes. The price range is also very wide. In some cases, I splurged one night and became very economical the following night. There is a long tradition of personal innkeeping in France; in most cases, the proprietors themselves make their guests feel very much at home.

Bed and breakfast has never been very popular in France, but the idea was picked up recently by two different organizations. It is now possible to find accommodations both with farmers and castle owners (who are sometimes farmers themselves). For rooms on a farm, ask the Syndicat d'Initiative (local tourist bureau); for rooms at private chateaux, contact Bertrand Laffilé at the Demeures Club, 5 Place du Marché Sainte Catherine, 75004 Paris, France. For a further description of this venture see the section on Normandy.

Reservations

You and your travel agent can contact by telephone, either from North America or from France, every one of the accommodations mentioned in this book. You can travel either by a set itinerary or take it from night to night. I've done both and I don't speak acceptable French. I encourage adventuresome North Americans to travel to France in the off-season and try a few days of unscheduled travel. Every French tourist office in every city can make reservations, not only for local lodgings but also for those in other localities, through all other tourist offices in France.

Regardless of price, most of the accommodations I visited were clean and basically acceptable. I took quite a few sight-unseen. A traveler can have an absolutely marvelous experience in France by staying at accommodations that are members of the Relais et Chateaux, an organization dedicated to the highest innkeeping standards. I have noted several in this book in both of my major itineraries as well as in Paris. These accommodations are in castles, chateaux, country houses, and the like, and you can make reservations by contacting: David Mitchell & Company, (212) 696-1323. Reservations and confirmation can be made very easily for all of the member hotels, including those in other countries. Incidentally, at most hotels in France, breakfast is additional and in some cases a service charge is added. The rates that are included in the Index are for two people for one night.

For Itinerary 1 (Paris south to the Riviera), I had everything reserved in advance. For Itinerary 2 (Calais across northern France to the Rhine River and back through the French Alps; on to the Rhone River and south to Bordeaux), I made reservations a day in advance. Both systems worked beautifully.

Car Rentals

You can rent a car at almost every railroad station and airport in France. You can also make arrangements for your car to be picked up at one point and dropped at another, anywhere in France or Europe. See the section "Renting a Car for Europe" near the front of this book.

Driving in France

Let's begin with Paris. Like all of the principal cities of Europe and America, Paris has lots of traffic—but not as bad as I expected. While driving my rented car, I discovered that the drivers on the whole were quite courteous and the problem looks a lot worse than it is. You simply have to plunge in to discover that the traffic through the Arc de Triomphe is quite manageable. I hit it on my very first day in Paris and it was raining cats and dogs.

The beltway around Paris, called the Periphique, *has roads leading from it in all directions. The best thing to do when leaving Paris is to identify carefully both the number and the names of the principal cities on your route, such as Orléans, Chartres, or Lyon. Study the Michelin map in advance and exit the Periphique at roads leading to the main city on your route.*

Country driving in France is like country driving anywhere else. You'll probably discover that the French drive a great deal faster than the U.S.A.'s 55-m.p.h. speed limit. If they give you a dirty look as they whiz by just give them a friendly wave.

French Menus

I am not a gourmet in any sense of the word, and I don't consider myself an expert on food. Furthermore, my perusal of guides to French cuisine with the star ratings made me quite apprehensive about displaying my ignorance to French waiters and headwaiters. To top it all off, I really don't know anything about wines, except it is red wine for meat and white wine for fish. However, in all of the restaurants, brasseries, auberges, snack bars, bistros, and cafes I visited, I was treated with courtesy and consideration. I was surprised at how quickly I picked up "menu French."

In the French restaurants there are usually three fixed-price (prix fixe) menus. The higher the price, the wider the choice of the main dishes.

The à la carte menu has several advantages; for one thing, it is possible to skip a course or two and concentrate on something special. I quickly learned that ordering only soup (potage), bread (pain), salads, desserts, or cheese would not evoke any raised eyebrows or disdainful glances. There are over 400 different varieties of cheese in France, made from goat's, cow's, and ewe's milk. Sometimes several cheeses are served from a large tray and the diner can make a choice.

I encourage everyone going to France to put aside preconceived notions about French cuisine and service. It is a delightful education and, if approached with an open mind and a carefree heart, can be a delightful experience. Enjoy.

Itineraries in France

This section is made up of two itineraries. One starts in Paris and goes south through the edge of Burgundy and continues on to the wine country at Beaune, following the Rhone River to Avignon, and then swings east to Provence and the Riviera. The second itinerary begins in Calais and pretty much wanders across northern France to the Rhine valley and then continues somewhat hit or miss back toward the center of France, but also includes a touch of the French Alps. We have also included a side trip to the Loire valley and another to Limoges.

ITINERARY 1—PARIS-NICE

As I mentioned earlier, this is the first of two itineraries, and most countryside accommodations are members of the Relais et Chateaux and reservations can be made through David Mitchell, (212) 696-1323. Call the Paris hotels directly.

Paris: Some Tips

The first important thing to know about Paris is that it is divided by the Seine River into two essentially distinct parts: the Right Bank to the north, and the Left Bank to the south. The Right Bank is conservative; the Left Bank swings. This distinction dates back to the old days. At the beginning of the century the "in" crowd, consisting as always of artists and writers, used to hang around Montmartre. But, in the thirties, this changed when everybody moved down to Montparnasse. Then, in the forties, the crowd settled in the area of Saint Germain, named after the church of Saint Germain des Prés, and the existentialists gathered around Jean-Paul Sartre at the Rhumerie, one of the cafés on the Boulevard Saint Germain. At night, everyone went

into the caves *(cellars) or the* boites *(boxes), two French names for nightclubs, and danced to the sound of jazz. Ever since, the Left Bank is "in" and the Right Bank, "out."*

Most of the interesting sights, though, are in a very central area, easy to get to on the subway. The Parisian "metro" is reliable, comfortable, and fast; it is also simple to use. The bus system is also very convenient and clear route maps are posted at each bus stop.

The R.A.T.P. (this is the name of the public company that runs the bus and subway systems in Paris) offers special tourist tickets: two-, four-, and seven-day packages. With these tickets you can ride endlessly on the bus or the metro (in first class). And if you like to plan ahead, you may purchase these special tickets from the offices of S.N.C.F. (the French railroad system) in New York, San Francisco, Chicago, Los Angeles, and Miami.

Any problem concerning your trip in France (tours, visits, hotels) can probably be solved by the Office du Tourisme de Paris. Go to the head office on the Champs Elysées, number 127, or to the other offices in the railway stations or at the Tour Eiffel. They are open Monday through Saturday from 9 a.m. to 10 p.m., and on Sundays and public holidays from 9 a.m. to 8 p.m.

Paris on the Bus

If you don't feel like taking a guided bus tour you can easily get a first contact with the city on your own on the public bus. Start at the Place de l'Opéra. At the top of the Avenue de l'Opéra, which goes south from the bottom of the Opéra Square in front of the Opéra itself, is a bus stop. Climb into number 81, 27, or 21 to Chatelet. Tell the driver to let you know your stop. It is a pretty route, down the avenue and then alongside the Louvre Museum and the Seine River.

At Chatelet, the name of one of the two theaters facing each other on this square, cross the river on foot to the Ile de la Cité. You may choose to walk to the cathedral of Notre Dame through the flower market; it is a five-minute walk. You can also visit the Sainte Chapelle in the Palace of Justice, the church of Saint Louis.

In front of the Palace of Justice, take any bus and get off at Les Ecoles. This is the heart of the Latin Quarter and you are in front of Musée de Cluny. At the corner of Rue des Ecoles and Boulevard Saint Michel, take bus number 63. It goes to Saint Germain des Près, an interesting church, and also the name of the neighborhood where the existentialists gathered around Jean-Paul Sartre after the war. Then on to the Invalides on the same bus, where you may choose to see Napoleon's grave.

Behind the Invalides compound on Avenue de Tourville is the stop for bus 82, which will take you to the Tour Eiffel. Then, crossing the river and the gardens of Trocadero, arrive at the start of Avenue Kleber, where you will find bus number 30 to take you to the Arc de Triomphe (Etoile).

From there you can either walk down the Champs Elysées to the Place de la Concorde or take bus number 73.

If you visit only one place thoroughly and don't linger too long elsewhere, this being only a reconnoitering trip, you may arrive at Concorde in time for lunch at Maxim's.

HOTEL DE CRILLON
Paris

I daresay that most North American travelers to France will fly directly to Paris. With this in mind, I have included some small Parisian hotels of varying price ranges and locations. Since there are at least three hotels in the luxury class in Paris, I thought it would be fun to include one of them, just as I have done with the Ritz in Madrid.

I chose the Hotel de Crillon, centrally located in a most desirable location overlooking Place de la Concorde, with the Tuileries and the Louvre to the left, and the U.S. Embassy and the Champs Elysées to the right.

For one thing, it doesn't look like a hotel. It resembles one of the elegant public buildings of Paris, many of which were former palaces, as is the case here; 1758 is one of the dates that sticks in my mind. It's been a hotel more than a hundred years.

Today, affluent guests can enjoy the 180 guest rooms and 30 suites, as well as the cuisine.

I have visited the Hotel de Crillon on two occasions, separated by a year, and each time I was shown about by the voluble and attractive Michele de la Clergerie, who is in charge of public relations for the hotel. On the occasion of the first visit, the central courtyard was being completely rehabilitated, plans were made for redecorating and redesigning many of the famous *salons* and many of the guest rooms and apartments were undergoing great changes.

A year later, most of this work had been completed and, in fact, on the day of my visit the newly decorated and designed center courtyard was the scene of a photographic session with the chef and members of his staff, arrayed in brilliant white uniforms and hats.

Michele de la Clergerie explained that all the accommodations had been furnished with new bathrooms and many had soundproofing, air conditioning, radio, and TV sets. "We have made a great deal of progress," she said, "and we have accomplished a few more things, including the creation of the gallery-sitting room that links the lobby and the restaurant."

The experience at Hotel de Crillon is one of Continental luxury. The facade is relatively conservative, but the lobby and public rooms are sumptuously decorated as only the French can do it, with elaborate and detailed paintings on walls and ceilings and polished marble floors.

HOTEL DE CRILLON (Relais et Chateaux), 10 Place de la Concorde, 75008 Paris. Tel.: 42-65-24-24 (U.S.A. reservations: 800-223-6800.) (New York State: 212-838-3110 collect.) Rates: See Index.

Directions: Take a cab or the airport bus from either Orly or De Gaulle airports.

LA RÉSIDENCE DU BOIS
Paris

There I was, spread out at my own circular table with a red table-cloth, enjoying the perfect lunch at La Résidence du Bois. Momentarily alone in the garden of this exquisite little hotel, I really felt as if I had discovered one of the few quiet places of Paris, even though some of the adjacent buildings looked down upon this tiny enclave. The birds fluttered down to seek some crumbs and other tidbits from other tables, and the trees, now in full leaf, acted as a protection against the midday sun.

The waiter materialized from the miniature forest with a wonderful platter of meats and cheeses, a heaping bowl of salad greens with just the right mustard dressing, two fresh hard rolls, and a delicious glass of Perrier with lemon.

A morning in Paris walking along the Seine or touring the Louvre, or even venturing into the many gardens, can leave the traveler a little breathless and, during the warm season, not a little overheated. Having spent such a morning, I was now raising a glass in the direction of Oklahoma to Linda Lee Tharp for recommending this lovely little hotel. She assured me that it was exactly what I was trying to find in Paris: "The right touch of elegance, the right kind of attention and service without any obsequiousness."

I had already seen quite a few of the twenty guest rooms, all of which were notable for a restrained elegance and blessed quietness.

One of the pleasing features of La Résidence du Bois has to be the wonderful concierge, who is a woman of great charm and limitless information. She explained that although breakfast is served to all houseguests, a simple lunch and dinner can also be obtained with a

modest amount of notice. It's just the kind of service that I can appreciate because, although Paris can be a gastronomic adventure, there are times when all that is needed is a simple, quiet meal.

LA RÉSIDENCE DU BOIS (Relais et Chateaux), 16 Rue Chalgrin, 75116 Paris. Tel.: 4500-50-59. A 20-guestroom very quiet, comfortable, calm hotel in the 16th Arrondissement. Open year-round. Breakfast included in price of room. Simple lunches and dinners available on request to houseguests only. A few blocks from the Arc de Triomphe. A garage adjacent. Rates: See Index.

Directions: From Orly or De Gaulle airports, I suggest the airport bus and a taxi.

HOTEL DUC DE SAINT-SIMON
Paris

Turning off Boulevard Saint Germain and leaving behind the noise and tumult of pedestrian and automobile traffic, one finds Rue Saint-Simon, a haven of provincial peace. Located in the heart of the Latin Quarter on the chic west side, the Hotel Duc de Saint-Simon has a longstanding reputation for comfort and old-time elegance. In 1977, it passed into the hands of a very refined Swedish gentleman, Göran Lindqvist, who wanted to elevate the hotel to the four-star class. He cast a new spell on the establishment, adding an elevator, a breakfast room, a bar, and common room. He also redecorated all the rooms, using very pretty fabrics and putting handmade tiles from the south of France in most bathrooms.

"But everything is simple, no chi-chis," he stresses. "One should feel in a friend's country home right here in the heart of Paris." He has achieved his goal admirably, especially since many of the rooms overlook a string of private gardens. Some even have their own terraces with flowers, a welcome addition in the summer.

Mme. Lalisse, the director of the hotel, explained that she gives special attention to breakfast, the most important meal in the day. Fresh orange juice is served (a real rarity anywhere), excellent coffee, and real *croissants au beurre*.

HOTEL DUC DE SAINT-SIMON, 14 Rue de Saint-Simon, 75007 Paris. Tel.: 4548-35-66. A 34-guestroom, very comfortable hotel on a quiet street on the Left Bank. Place de la Concorde and the Louvre are within walking distance. No restaurant. Open all year. Rates: See Index.

Directions: From the airport or bus terminal, use a cab. During your stay, the metro station Rue du Bac is very convenient.

L'HOTEL
Paris

Staying at L'Hotel is like wearing an oversized gem. This explains why Liz Taylor likes it. But she's not the only one—most of the other show business people coming to Paris stay there, too.

It's the place to go when one is bored with the Crillon or the Plaza Athénée, the two very best hotels in Paris. L'Hotel is the third "very best." A four-star deluxe hotel, it is really a grand hotel in miniature, offering everything a larger hotel of the same category can offer and one thing more: flair. This is a quality shared both by the creators of this extraordinary place and its guests.

Each room has its own decor and is furnished with genuine antiques. Some are really very special, like the room of Oscar Wilde, who died in the hotel in 1900, and the room of Mistinguett, who never stayed here, but whose private bedroom was reinstalled in a very authentic setting.

L'Hotel is located on the Rue des Beaux Arts, a typical Left Bank street, especially on the days when the students of the nearby School of Architecture march out with their band and start a ball.

The day I visited there the owner, Guy Louis Duboucheron, was taking part in an antique airplane rally from Paris to Cannes. Don't expect to meet him, he's never there. But the staff is perfect. Staying at L'Hotel is better than being a guest in a friend's mansion—it's like making yourself at home while the host is away.

L'HOTEL, 13 Rue des Beaux Arts, 75006 Paris. Tel.: 4325-27-22. Telex 270-870. A 27-guestroom deluxe hotel on the Left Bank. Open all year. Rates vary with the size of the rooms, some of which are quite small and only have a shower (made of solid marble, of course). Rates: See Index.

Directions: Taxi from the airport or bus terminal. During your stay you may use bus number 95, which stops around the corner and goes toward Montparnasse in one direction and the Louvre and the Opéra in the other.

HOTELLERIE DU BAS-BREAU
Barbizon

I was having my first dinner in a French country inn, and to make it even more exciting, I was having my first genuine French soufflé. Its golden crust rose from the traditional white soufflé dish, proclaiming with a magnificent Gallic insouciance that it was, indeed, master of all it surveyed. For one breathless moment I was allowed to dwell on this model of perfection. Such style! Such grace! Such nobility! Such a divine fragrance!

The last, alas, was to be its undoing—I could wait no longer. And even while administering the *coup de grâce*, I realized that this *chef d'oeuvre* had withheld its crowning achievement to the very last moment. Closing my eyes to savor that first heavenly morsel, my senses thrilled to the indescribable taste of—praline soufflé!! I lost all touch with time and space . . . I was, indeed, on Olympus and this was ambrosia of the gods.

"You are, perhaps, enjoying your soufflé?" It was Jean-Pierre Fava, the innkeeper of du Bas-Breau, who stood beside my table with a twinkle in his eye. For a moment I could only nod vigorously, and then I regained my voice. "It is unlike anything I have ever tasted," I said.

"You are very kind," he replied. "And I am happy to say we receive many compliments for our praline soufflé."

One hundred and fifty years ago this inn on the edge of the Barbizon Forest carried on its signboard the name of its proprietor, M. Siron, and its best-known guest was Robert Louis Stevenson. The name was changed in 1867 to Hotel de l'Exposition, because it was being used as an exhibition hall for the Barbizon painters, including Carot, Rousseau, and Millet, all of whom painted in the forest. It became du Bas-Breau in 1937, when M. and Mme. Fava arrived, and its tradition, elegance, comfort, and gastronomy have since become well known. Jean-Pierre, the present innkeeper, is continuing the ideals of his parents.

The entrance to the inn is through an arch into a small courtyard with cobblestones and two big pots of geraniums and ivy. There are flowers everywhere, even in little flowerpots on the roof. An ancient French lamp hangs from the arch, and a stairway leads up to some guest rooms with window boxes full of flowers.

The next entrance is into the main reception hall and bar, where *petit déjeuner* is served each morning. Through the windows I could see the dining courtyard and other buildings containing more guest rooms. In the evening, the scene is lit with discreet lanterns, and the tables are occupied by happy diners.

All of the bedrooms have triple sheets, handsome bedspreads, and show pillows; many of them overlook a terrace, and others provide a generous glimpse of the gardens of the village. During my visit, the fruit trees and lilacs were in vivid blossom.

As Jean-Pierre said, "Our guests enjoy walking in the Fontainebleau Forest, driving through the countryside, and spending hours in the local shops."

I will also add that I am sure they enjoy the praline soufflés.

HOTELLERIE DU BAS-BREAU (Relais et Chateaux), 77630 Barbizon. Tel.: (6) 066-40-05. A 19-guestroom exceptionally comfortable inn with first-class service on the edge of the Fontainebleau Forest, approx. 1½ hrs. south of Paris. Breakfast, lunch, dinner. Closed from Jan. 1 to Feb. 15. Rates: See Index.

Directions: Follow Autoroute A-6 (Michelin sect. map 61) marked Lyon to Fontainebleau. Use exit (sortie) for Barbizon.

AUBERGE DES TEMPLIERS
Les Bezards

Following Jean-Pierre Fava's directions, I left du Bas-Breau and Barbizon, and within a pleasant hour-and-a-half drive I pulled up at the great gates of the Auberge des Templiers. This is on the road southwest to the chateaux country.

I stepped through a heavy front door into the reception area and found a two-story room with a very impressive tapestry on the far wall.

I moved into still another vaulted room, with a replica of a Crusader's cross over the massive mantel.

An extremely attractive Frenchwoman with short, blond hair, wearing a very chic striped gray and charcoal pantsuit, introduced herself, and she and I set out on a short tour of the many buildings and grounds. We walked across the garden, past the swimming pool and the barbecue lunch area. The tennis courts were just beyond. There were many trees and attractively landscaped lawns. We looked at several guest rooms and I found them beautifully furnished. "We are just a short, pleasant drive from Paris, so many of our Parisian guests come and stay a few days at a time," she said. "There is much to be seen and done, all within automobiling distance."

At lunch I learned that this particular region of France sent many knights to the Crusades, and that this building at one time must have been an abbey and a meeting place for the men-at-arms who set off on the great adventure. The word "Templiers" actually refers to a certain order of Crusaders. I found many references to this historical event throughout southern France.

A beautiful inn, a congenial innkeeping family, tranquility and graciousness. I found these at Auberge des Templiers. It was like an American country inn with a French accent.

AUBERGE DES TEMPLIERS (Relais et Chateaux), 45290 Les Bezards. Tel.: (38) 31-80-01. A 25-guestroom exceptionally comfortable chateau-inn with first-class service, 135 km. south of Paris. Breakfast, lunch, dinner. This is a resort accommodation with a swimming pool, two tennis courts, horseback riding, and golf nearby. Closed Jan. 15 to Feb. 15. Rates: See Index.

Directions: See Michelin sect. map 65. Exit A-6 at Dordives. Follow N-7 south to Les Bezards. If continuing into chateaux country (southwest), I advise Michelin 64, 68, and 72. (My line of direction in this book is almost due south.)

SIDE TRIP TO THE LOIRE VALLEY

In this edition, I have included three hotels in the Loire Valley. Between Orléans and Angers is a region rich in history and architecture, often called the "Garden of France." Our stops are at or near Chenonceaux, Montrichard, and Chambord. However, you should rely on the tourist offices and continue on at least to Angers, making a leisurely trip of it, exploring the back roads, seeing as many of the chateaux and palaces as possible, and partaking of the gastronomy of

the region. By all means, obtain a copy of Michelin Green Guide's
Chateaux of the Loire.

HOTEL DU BON LABOUREUR ET DU CHATEAU
Chenonceaux

Simplicity and excellence are rare anywhere and all the more unexpected on the touristic high road. This is why the owners of this
small hotel deserve to be praised.

Everything is pleasing here—the friendly welcome, the buildings,
picturesque and obviously unchanged for the past twenty years, the
food in the restaurant, the rooms, and, last but not least, the prices.

I personally would choose to stay in what they call the Annex Rousseau, a tiny house next door, preceded by a courtyard garden, with six
bright, cheery rooms, very quiet and overlooking a flower garden or
slanting roofs.

Monsieur et Madame Jeudi ("Thursday" in French) obviously put
their pride into keeping up the French provincial tradition of quality.

When I arrived it was already a bit late for lunch, and I had made
no reservations, a sin for many a French restaurant owner. The dining
rooms were already buzzing with animated conversation and the click-
ing of busy knives and forks. But an efficient and smiling maître d'hotel
soon arrived and found a table for me. I was promptly provided with
a bottle of the light wine of the region and some excellent paté as an
hors d'oeuvre.

After lunch, I walked to the chateau of Chenonceaux and strolled in
the gardens before actually going into the chateau for an interesting
visit.

HOTEL DU BON LABOUREUR ET DU CHATEAU, 37150 Chenon-
ceaux. Tel.: (47) 23-90-02. A small, village hotel, 35 km. east of Tours
in the Loire Valley, 224 km. from Paris. Wheelchair access. Open late
Mar. to early Nov. Famille Jeudi, Innkeepers. Rates: See Index.

Directions: The village of Chenonceaux is on N-76 between Montri-
chard and Tours.

THE LOIRE VALLEY CHATEAUX

A chateau is like a dream come true, rising alone, unique.
My favorite is Chenonceaux! . . . but then, chateaux are a very
personal matter. Come to think of it, they are much closer to Paris

than one would imagine, with Orléans just an hour and a half away on the Autoroute. Of course, the Loire Valley really is one of the magic areas in the world: imagine a lazy river under a pale blue sky meandering through gentle hills and sloping vineyards alternating with dark, deep forests and gay townlets, the perfect shrine for so many marvelous chateaux of the Renaissance.

Driving south, it is easy to pick up a few on your way, especially if one has a day or two to spend. I wanted to try to stay in a chateau, not just in a chateau hotel, but in a real chateau.

I found one, and I loved it, even though I must warn some of you that it may be less comfortable than a Relais et Chateaux hotel.

LE CHATEAU DE GUÉ-PÉAN
Montrichard

Gué-Péan is the largest of the smaller chateaux-hotels of the Loire Valley. Its white structure rises in the midst of green fields and woodland, appearing unexpectedly around the last bend in the road. The elegant buildings enclose a large rectangular courtyard with four towers, one on each corner. If you are very lucky, maybe you'll get a round room in one of the towers and dream, perhaps, of Mary of England and the French King Louis XII, who fell in love here in 1514.

Some people will care more for the architecture, austere yet elegant, typical of the 16th century; some will prefer the museum-arranged

rooms with historical furniture and paintings. To me, Gué-Péan is, more than anything else, the home of a particularly interesting man, Marquis de Keguelin, an elegant, Old World gentleman with the understanding of a true aristocrat.

We had a chat at breakfast in the big dining room, and he told me about the days of his youth in Montparnasse during the French Roaring Twenties and about the numerous famous writers and musicians, like Jean Cocteau and Boris Vian, who were his friends.

CHATEAU DE GUÉ-PÉAN, Monthou sur Cher, 41400 Montrichard. Tel.: (54) 71-43-01. A 20-guestroom 16th-century chateau in a tiny village between Montrichard and St. Aignan, near Chenonceaux, in the center of chateaux country. Open all year. Marquis de Keguelin, Owner. Rates: See Index.

Directions: The chateau is on a tiny road starting in the village of Monthou sur Cher. You'll find it just off N-76, after Montrichard, on D-176.

HOTEL ST. MICHEL
Chambord

Just outside the forest I was struck by the sign that said "Bucks—Does—Wild Boars Roam Wild." The image of royal hunting parties, with courtiers, trumpets, and prancing horses, rose before me, and when the breathtakingly grand Chateau of Chambord came into view, I would not have been surprised to see such a party trooping across the moat.

Actually, there *were* some equestrians cantering down the country road toward the forest, past the picturesque Hotel St. Michel, which is just a stone's throw away from, and facing, the great chateau.

I arrived late in the afternoon, just in time to enjoy, with the other guests, an aperitif at the hotel's outdoor cafe, which affords a magnificent view of the chateau. As the moon and one star rose in the sky we felt that we were experiencing the best of France in one of the most beautiful spots in the world.

Many years ago the hotel began its life as a drinking place for returning hunters. Since then, the Le Meur family, which has owned the hotel for at least seventy years, added rooms and set the standard of service and comfort that befitted the company it was keeping, across the way.

My room was comfortable and attractive, with a very clean bathroom. The geraniums on the windowsill were cheery companions as I enjoyed breakfast in bed the next morning, although I was still sated by the delicious dinner I had eaten in the hotel restaurant the night before, served by discreet and attentive personnel. Wines of the Touraine were featured, as well as quail and pheasant.

Some wonderful photographs of the wild animals in the forest have been taken by the owner, and made into postcards. They capture for a moment in time these beautiful animals in their own natural setting.

HOTEL ST. MICHEL, 41250 Bracieux, Chambord. Tel.: (54) 20-31-31. A 38-guestroom quiet graceful hotel in a tiny village, 49 km. from Orléans. Dinner reservation required with overnight stay. Open year-round except mid-Nov. to late Dec. Tennis on grounds. Facing the 16th-century Chateau de Chambord. Famille Le Meur, Innkeepers. Rates: See Index.

Directions: Chambord is 18 km. from Blois on D-33.

FRENCH VILLAGES

I fell in love with the French villages . . . the old stone houses sometimes covered with stucco of all colors, depending upon local soil . . . the trees that had been there for centuries, shading the squares and their outdoor tables and chairs . . . the churches, the small shops, and the ever-present fountain in the center of each village.

After a first trip to France, everyone has a favorite village, and it is great fun to go back and see if it has changed. Basically, of course, it never does. In the spring and fall, many villages are inundated with flowers . . . flowers in windows, in front yards, and in the square. Lucky, indeed, the traveler who arrives in the village on market day or even better when there is a carnival or a festival. It is a wonderful opportunity to see the villages in a holiday mood.

HOTEL LE CEP
Beaune

Hotel Le Cep is located in the heart of the town of Beaune, and I learned from the owner that it is one of the richest wine towns in France. "People come from everywhere," he said, "to sample the Burgundy wines at Beaune and many of them return to the hotel year after year."

Although breakfast is the only meal offered here, there are many good restaurants nearby.

On my last visit, I noticed that guests in the sitting room were reading at the table or carrying on a conversation. It was quite informal—different from the more formal atmosphere that I found in other places. I unfolded my copy of the *Paris Herald Tribune* and caught up on things in the U.S.A.

The rooms in Le Cep are each decorated in the style of a different century of French architecture. Mine was in Louis XV.

HOTEL LE CEP, 27 Rue Maufoux, 21200 Beaune. Tel.: (80) 22-35-48. Telex: 351256 CEPHOTL. A 46-guestroom in-town, comfortable but simple hotel in the Burgundy wine district, 37 km. south of Dijon. Beaune is an extremely interesting and prosperous town with a great deal of emphasis on the surrounding vineyards. Rates: See Index.

Directions: Michelin sect. map 65. Follow one-way road circling the inside of the city about ³/₄ of the way around. Look for hotel sign on left. There is an exit at Beaune from Autoroute A-6.

CHATEAU D'IGE
Ige

"We are," said Monsieur Jadot, "very quiet." I was visiting another chateau hotel and I liked it immediately. This was enhanced by the smiling M. Jadot, who was the very personification of innkeeping joviality. It was obvious that he, too, was much attached to this 13th-century fortified home in the Burgundian countryside that seemed so far away from the demands of the 20th century.

First, we walked around the outside of the chateau, where the massive walls are overgrown with a green cloak of ivy. In the gardens a deep pool had been created by the waters of the brook, which was shared by playful ducks and unusually large trout. "The trout are too large for the ducks," said M. Jadot. There was a little outdoor dining terrace, which, he explained, was used for dinner in the warm weather. His German shepherd, Puff, walked ahead of us. Overhead, the sky was blue, the spring birds were singing, and some of the flowers were in bloom. It was, to say the least, idyllic. In one corner of the garden there was a tower with a most pleasant apartment. "Very popular with honeymooners," he said. The bedroom window on the top floor had a beautiful view of the village and the valley.

Inside the main building were several apartments, many of them also in the towers, reached by well-worn stone steps twisting around a center pole. Guest rooms were varied in size and looked comfortable.

This chateau had many, many old tapestries, which relieved the rough texture of the gray-yellow stone walls. The furniture in the living and dining rooms was massive in style, and appropriate to the scale of the rooms.

Throughout my entire tour, Monsieur Jadot was smiling and laughing. We found several words in French and English that we shared in common.

Dinner is served only to houseguests and there is a choice of five main dishes. "We have a very good chef," he promised.

Chateau d'Ige was small in comparison to other castles I have visited, but it had an undeniable warmth. I am sure its quiet atmosphere brings joy and happiness to many guests.

CHATEAU D'IGE (Relais et Chateaux), 71960 Ige. Tel.: (85) 33-33-99. A 9-guestroom, very comfortable 13th-century fortified chateau enhanced with modern conveniences. Approx. 80 km. north of Lyon. Breakfast and dinner served to houseguests only. Romantic countryside, golf, horseback riding, and sailing nearby. Closed Nov. 5 to Feb. 1. Rates: See Index.

Directions: Michelin sect. map 69, 73. Exit A-6 at Mâcon Nord and from Mâcon follow road marked Charolles. A few km. out of Mâcon turn right at the village of Vineuse (D-85). Follow road to Ige and inquire for inn.

LA MÈRE BLANC
Vonnas

It was high noon in Vonnas. The atmosphere and general spirit at La Mère Blanc was busy and cheerful. Waiters and waitresses were hustling and bustling back and forth, serving a large luncheon party in one dining room. My table next to the window overlooked a small stream.

The proprietors are Jacqueline and Georges Blanc, third-generation innkeepers.

Monsieur Blanc explained that most of the items on the menu were regional specialties, with some nouvelle cuisine, and that the menu included six courses. This was the meal that the French eat once a day, either at noon or night.

At his suggestion I ordered the creamed chicken with crêpes that, as he said, "enjoys a local reputation." I've had chicken in various garb all over the world, but I am sure that any chicken would consider it a noble sacrifice to be placed on the table at La Mère Blanc, bathed in that truly marvelous cream sauce.

It was, however, the cream cheese that made this visit outstanding. I have never tasted such delicious, creamy, honestly-melt-in-the-mouth *fromage.* I ate every bit of it and as a result had to pass up the selection of six desserts.

All of the guest rooms are exceptionally well furnished and many with some rather startling color schemes, including lavender. Some of them had a kind of Spanish feeling about them.

Since my first visit, La Mère Blanc has become one of the most prestigious restaurants in France, the recipient of many accolades—more reason to take the short drive from the main autoroute at Mâcon.

LA MÈRE BLANC (Relais et Chateaux), 01540 Vonnas. Tel.: (74) 50-00-10. A 30-guestroom very comfortable hotel with an excellent reputation for food. Breakfast, lunch, dinner. Swimming pool on grounds. Tennis, golf, horseback riding, fishing nearby. Closed Dec. and Jan. Famille Blanc, Innkeepers. Rates: See Index.

Directions: From the north, leave the motorway at Mâcon Nord, follow N-79 approx. 10 km. on road to Bourg. Turn right at sign for Vonnas. La Mère Blanc is near the town square. From the south, leave motor-

way at Villefranche-sur-Saone and follow D-936 toward Bourg, watching for sign to Vonnas.

SIDE TRIP TO LIMOGES

Limoges, of course, is renowned for its fine porcelain and enamel work, and many workshops are open to visitors. There is much of historical interest, with the great Saint Stephen's Cathedral, begun in 1273, the museums, and the old quarter, dating back to the 10th century. For a stay in the countryside, just a short distance from the city, I found Le Chapelle Saint Martin most pleasant.

LA CHAPELLE SAINT MARTIN
Nieul-près-Limoges

Once upon a time there was a Frenchman named Henri Dudognon. He had a son, Jacques, then a young man of twenty. One day they were traveling in their car through the Limousin countryside, and what should they see among the trees but an old mysterious house. Its walls were completely covered with ivy and red vines; on one side was a deep forest and in front a small antique chapel. In the back were immense, flowing grounds and a lake. Henri and Jacques fell in love with it and bought it as a country house.

Many years later, Jacques and *his* son, Gilles, faced with the alternative of selling the house in order to open a restaurant in Paris, chose to stay and transform it into a perfect hotel.

This is one of the Relais et Chateaux in which you feel completely at home. The food is superb and has even improved since Gilles himself assumed full responsibility in the kitchen. Everything on the menu is imaginative and refined, perfectly fresh and beautifully served.

This is the way they like it for themselves and want it for everybody else. It's worth trying.

LA CHAPELLE SAINT MARTIN (Relais et Chateaux), 87510 Haute Vienne, Nieul-près-Limoges. Tel.: (55) 75-80-17. A 10-guestroom very comfortable 19th-century house in a parklike setting, with a lake, 4 km. from Limoges. Closed Mondays and between Jan. 1 and Mar. 1. M. Jacques Dudognon, Innkeeper. Rates: See Index.

Directions: Driving south on N-147, take D-35 before Limoges.

HOTELLERIE BEAU RIVAGE
ET L'HERMITAGE DU RHONE
Condrieu

I had been in France a few days and was feeling quite comfortable with my growing list of French verbs and nouns, when I arrived at Beau Rivage and immediately met another American couple who were on a combination business and pleasure trip. Since they were experienced travelers in France, I asked the husband for his opinion of French innkeeping. This is part of what he said:

"I have traveled in France several times and I have always found the French hotel keepers and their staff extremely accommodating and pleasant, and willing to go to any length to make their guests as comfortable as possible. For example, here, Madame Castaing has been the principal chef for many years, as well as being the owner, and you can see for yourself that she comes out of the kitchen frequently, exchanges a few words of conversation with her guests, and radiates the feeling of hospitality."

Beau Rivage is right on the banks of the fast-flowing Rhone River as it makes its way south toward the Mediterranean. In the summertime, guests are served on patios overlooking the river and many of the guest rooms have a river view.

In addition to the extensive à la carte menu, there are also three set menus. I chose the middle one that included a delicious freshwater fish served in a very tasty sauce, succulent fresh French beans, and a choice of three main dishes—steak, guinea hen, and lamb chops. There were also scalloped potatoes discreetly seasoned with garlic.

The headwaiter held a lively discussion with my friends about the features that lovers of good wine seem to hold so dear: the year, the fragrance, the length of time in the bottle, and even the name of the wine grower. "Yes, we French really do get down to the fine points of wine," he said. "The length of time the sun shines on the grapes during the day can play an important role, so that the exposure of the vineyards could be a factor." It was explained to me that wine grapes are gathered in late September because they cannot be picked in the rain.

I learned that many people stayed at Beau Rivage for several days at a time, because there is good fishing, horseback riding, tennis, golf, and the beautiful back roads of the incomparable countryside.

The evening was a marvelous success. Madame paid us a short visit and we toasted her dinner and her beautiful inn. Then we all resolved to sell our stocks and bonds and move to the Rhone valley of France, where we could meet frequently for dinner at Beau Rivage.

HOTELLERIE BEAU RIVAGE ET L'HERMITAGE DU RHONE (Relais et Chateaux), 69420 Condrieu. Tel.: (74) 59-52-24. A 25-guestroom very comfortable inn on the bank of the Rhone River, 60 km. south of Lyon. Breakfast, lunch, dinner. Tennis, swimming, golf, outdoor sports nearby. Closed early Jan. to mid-Feb. Rates: See Index.

Directions: Michelin regional map 246. As nearly as I can determine A-6 goes into A-7 at Lyon. Follow the road clearly marked Marseille and use the exit (sortie) marked Condrieu. Proceed south on N-86 about 10 km. The inn is on the left between the road and the river.

SOUTH FROM CONDRIEU

It was Saturday morning along the Rhone. All the people from the little riverside villages were making a holiday of it, visiting the shops and stopping in the town square to exchange some tidbits of conversation with their friends. There were long loaves of delicious French bread carried under arms and colorful shopping bags loaded to the brim.

The towns and cities on the opposite side of the river were a picturebook sight with green vineyards and flower-laden orchards blending into the red roofs.

Following N-86 I could occasionally see the remains of an old tower or castle in the distance.

I turned off at Saint Paray, en route to Saint-Romain-de-Lerps, and had my first experience with high hills in France. As the road swung back and forth across little valleys and up into the higher ground, there were increasingly interesting panoramic views of the Rhone valley. Since it was a promising May day with a warm sun, the industrious French farmers and their families were already working in the fields. To the south and east it was sunny, but the clouds and fog still had to burn off to the west.

Now, I had reached the village located at the crest of the hills and followed the signs over the rolling Burgundy countryside to the Chateau du Besset.

HOSTELLERIE LA CARDINALE
Baix (Ardèche)

I was now back for the second time in the riverside village of Baix, and would be revisiting one of the places that I had seen on my first trip to France a few years ago. I was anxious to meet the relatively new owners, with whom I had been in correspondence. Route N-86 became the village street and sure enough there was a signpost pointing to the left toward the river, indicating that La Cardinale was a short but welcome distance from the main road.

As with a few other accommodations in this book, the Hostellerie La Cardinale is a member of the Relais et Chateaux group, but is distinguished by the fact that its original proprietor, M. Tillot, conceived the idea of forming Relais et Chateaux, an organization of small hotels of culinary distinction, with the purpose of promoting one another.

Of course, the building had not changed; it probably hasn't changed since August of 1642, when Cardinal Richelieu apparently remained there overnight on a journey from Paris. On the day of my visit the very attractive terrace with colorful umbrellas had a few other Sunday patrons, and the flowers of late May were in interesting contrast to the texture of the ancient brickwork.

The new proprietors are all members of the Motte family, and fortunately they speak excellent conversational English. They were kind enough to invite me for lunch on the terrace and I must admit that I was charmed by the attractive mother and daughter, as well as by the pleasant fish served in a light wine sauce with tiny onions and a side dish of rice. My notes indicate the mashed potatoes were so light and fluffy they must have been run through the blender more than once.

I was extremely curious to know whether or not they had received many guests as a result of being included in the earlier edition of this book, and they were delighted to draw my attention to their guest register, where many Americans had mentioned *CIBR, Europe* in their comments. Incidentally, nothing pleases me quite so much as receiving letters from travelers who have stayed at places I have recommended. I feel as if we all belong to a very special little club, and I love to receive notes about your adventures.

La Cardinale is not as grand as some of the other Relais members, but quality and taste are certainly evident in the sitting and dining rooms and guest rooms. All have been furnished in beautiful French antiques, as well as with several contemporary paintings, and the atmosphere is easy and comfortable.

Just a few minutes away there are other guest rooms and sitting rooms in another building, La Résidence, located on a height of land with a broader view of the river and a definite feeling of luxury in the country.

HOSTELLERIE LA CARDINALE (Relais et Chateaux), 07210 Baix. Tel.: (75) 62-85-88. A 15-guestroom village inn overlooking the Rhone River, approx. 130 km. south of Lyon. Besides lodgings in the main inn, there are rooms in La Résidence on a hillside outside the village. Breakfast, lunch, and dinner. Private swimming pool. Tennis and horseback riding nearby. Open mid-Mar. to early Jan. Rates: See Index.

Directions: Baix is on N-86 south of Le Pouzin. If on A-7 or N-6, you can cross the river at Le Pouzin or Montelinar. Baix is actually part of Rochenaure.

HOSTELLERIE LE PRIEURÉ
Villeneuve-les-Avignon

Avignon is one of the showplaces of southeastern France. It is rich in history, tradition, scenery. The countryside is dotted with names that are rich in meaning—Arles, where van Gogh painted some of his sunlit landscapes; Aix-en-Provence, the capital that has been a great artistic center for centuries; Grenoble, surrounded by clifflike mountains; Marseille, filled with art museums and ancient monuments; and Avignon, itself the seat of the Papacy in the 14th century, dominated by the Pope's palace, a fortress sometimes austere and sometimes luxurious, complete with watchtowers and frescoes.

Such historic and artistic wealth makes Le Prieuré, located as it is at the double gateway to both Spain and the Riviera, one of the most sought-after accommodations in the south of France.

Located in Villeneuve-les-Avignon, a small town across the Rhone River from the much larger city of Avignon, it is much more quiet and less tourist-oriented than its larger neighbor.

With guests from all parts of the world gathered on the terrace and beside the swimming pool, Le Prieuré's atmosphere is decidedly cosmopolitan. Conversations flow in German, English, French, and Japanese, with everyone quite willing to share their travel adventures.

For hundreds of years the inn was a priory; more recently it has become a hotel of the first class presided over by a most pleasant, urbane innkeeper, Jacques Mille, who, like a good many innkeepers, has learned to be affable in any language.

The hotel and gardens reminded me very much of the gardens in the Alhambra in Granada, with their carefully tended irises and roses, small evergreen hedges, and conical-shaped evergreens, which seem to grow everywhere in the Mediterranean countries. In the morning, the bees were buzzing among the ivy in the breathtakingly bright sunshine of Provence. The walk to the parking area is through a long, arched rose trellis.

Guest rooms for the most part are contemporary in design, and my room, with its one glass wall and sliding door leading out to a balcony that overlooked the swimming pool and tennis courts, had bright modern furniture and draperies. Meals are served in the gardens under the trees.

I made a return visit to see Jacques Mille, who is the most Americanized Frenchman I have ever met. It was a wonderful pleasure to sit in the new dining room with him and listen to his bubbling enthusiasm about the changes that have been made. "The chimney and fireplace were moved, stone by stone, and replaced here in the new part," he pointed out. Several new guest rooms have also been added.

"Of course, our guests still continue to use this as a touring base

151

for visiting Avignon, and we have our own group of ancient buildings, called La Chartreuse, which at one time was an abbey.''

HOSTELLERIE LE PRIEURÉ (Relais et Chateaux), 7 Place du Chapitre, 30400 Villeneuve-les-Avignon, Tel.: (90) 25-18-20. A 38-guestroom very comfortable inn in the center of one of France's most popular historic and cultural regions. Breakfast, lunch, and dinner. Swimming pool, two tennis courts on grounds. Wheelchair access. Within a very short distance of the town of Avignon. Closed Nov. 1 to Mar. 1. Rates: See Index.

Directions: Michelin sect. map 81 and regional map 246. From the north via the Autoroute: note that at Orange, about 10 km. north of Avignon, A-7, the main autoroute from Paris to Nice, has a junction for A-9, which goes to northern Spain. Use the Avignon exit on either of these two autoroutes and Villeneuve is on the west side of the Rhone River. If using N-86 from the north, turn east at Bagnols and follow N-580 into Villeneuve.

AUBERGE DE NOVES
Noves

Monsieur Lalleman, enjoying a respite from his duties as host of this delightful inn just south of Avignon, joined me on the terrace, where I was having lunch.

When I remarked about the leisurely service, he responded, ''Here at Auberge de Noves there is no hurrying the meal. Even our salads are made specially. They are not waiting in the refrigerator to be served. All of this takes time.''

In the meantime, I noticed him keeping a watchful eye on the waiter who was making this selfsame salad of fresh watercress, chopped shallots, and greens, all mixed in a handsome silver bowl. Carrots, mushrooms, onions, lettuce, and sliced tomatoes were added. When I remarked that the salad would seem to be a meal in itself, he shrugged and said, ''This is only a side dish.''

It was a beautiful day in the south of France. The birds in the garden were everywhere, chirping, singing, whistling, and fighting. The flowers were already in full bloom. Butterflies were flitting from table to table, and guests, having completed their meal, were going for leisurely walks through the quite extensive gardens.

The arrival of some freshly made sliced paté launched M. Lalleman into a short dissertation. ''We have many kinds of paté,'' he said. ''In fact, the chef in any good French restaurant is able to make his own particular creation. Ours does wonders with rabbit, duck, and goose

liver, but a good paté can be made from many combinations of ingredients.'' He excused himself for just a moment, while I watched the waiter at the next table deftly carve and debone two delicious-looking roast ducklings. Seeing my interest, the guests at the table offered me a succulent morsel. It was delicious.

Following lunch, my host showed me through many of the guest rooms of the inn, all gaily decorated, and he pointed with pride to the swimming pool in the garden which, during less clement days, has a plastic bubble placed over it. There was a view across the meadow to ancient towers in the distance.

AUBERGE DE NOVES (Relais et Chateaux), 13550 Noves. Tel.: (90) 94-19-21. A 22-guestroom very comfortable Provence manor house a few km. south of Avignon. Breakfast, lunch, and dinner. Tennis and swimming pool on grounds. Golf and fishing nearby. Closed Jan. to mid-Feb. Rates: See Index.

Directions: Michelin sect. map 81 and regional map 246. Autoroute A-7; use the Avignon Sud exit. Follow N-7 across the river, take first right and the next main right. Go about 1 km. and look for sign on left.

DOMAINE DE CHATEAUNEUF
Nans-les-Pins

A traveler from Paris to Nice or Cannes on the autoroutes would do well to stop his headlong flight and remain here for a few days just to let the serenity and tranquility of southern France envelop him.

The Chateauneuf is in the center of thickly wooded parkland, surrounded by 250 acres of vineyards and forests. On the day of my visit, the chestnut trees were in bloom, the birds were singing, and there were white doves restlessly circling the chateau. The courtyard was flooded with sunlight filtering through the leaves, and a warm, spring breeze gently wafted its way among the flowers. I could have remained a week.

As my hostess explained, this is an 18th-century chateau that has seen the passing of royalty in France, the horrors of the Terror, and the glories of the Empire. "It is still here now," she said, "as peaceful and as calm as ever."

"Elegant but informal" are the words that occur to me. The lodgings are all very pleasant, with comfortable chateau furniture and many oils and watercolors. The dining room overlooks the park, and in warm weather meals are taken outside.

Of particular interest to me was a corner room on the main floor with a collection of local crafts: scarves, handkerchiefs, dolls, jewelry, and similar items all presented in a most attractive way.

The three tennis courts were in use while I was there, and the pool had some midday swimmers. My hostess told me that, unlike conditions in Saint Tropez, 80 kilometers to the east, there are separate sunning areas for ladies and gentlemen in this chateau.

The Domaine de Chateauneuf indeed is quiet and tranquil. It is the south of France the way I hoped to find it.

DOMAINE DE CHATEAUNEUF (Relais et Chateaux), 83860 Nans-les-Pins. Tel.: (94) 78-90-06. A 34-guestroom, including 4 suites and 2 villas, comfortable but simple 18th-century manor house with its own beautiful park, 150 km. west of Cannes and 45 km. east of Marseille. Breakfast, lunch, and dinner. Swimming pool, tennis courts, and 18-hole golf course on grounds. Horseback riding, fishing, and other recreation nearby. Closed Dec. to mid-Apr. Rates: See Index.

Directions: Michelin sect. map 84. Exit Autoroute A-8 at St. Maximin. Follow N-560 south and watch for D-80, which leads to the village of Nans-les-Pins.

LA BASTIDE DE TOURTOUR
Tourtour

For postal purposes this castle-hotel is located in Salernes, one of the villages near the larger city of Draguignan. As far as I am concerned, it is located in the extremely scenic village of Tourtour, which, I learned, is pronounced "too-too" (the "r" being silent).

La Bastide de Tourtour is situated in one of the most picturesque and attractive landscapes in Provence—on a promontory almost 2,000 feet above sea level with a very impressive view of the countryside. The inn is set in the middle of a great pine forest.

While sitting at the pool I learned just how convenient the inn is to all the scenic attractions in this section of Provence. I struck up an acquaintance with a couple from Atlanta, Georgia, who had come for two days and were now extending their stay for a week. "I can't imagine a better place to enjoy the south of France" was one of the most frequently repeated comments. "It's only about an hour and a half to Cannes, Nice, and Saint Tropez, and we took a day trip to the Verdon Gorges and went over to Monte Carlo. We stopped and had lunch at the Chevre d'Or. I hope you will go there." (I did.)

This inn is in a most imposing restored castle, whose austere beige-colored walls and towers of native stone belie the luxurious interiors. The heavy stone arches and beamed ceilings in the reception hall and living and dining rooms have all been gracefully accented with golden upholstery and draperies. It is a memorable scene, particularly in the evening, when candles are lit on every table.

It is obvious that the owners and innkeepers have taken a personal pride in the guest rooms, all of which are furnished most luxuriously. Many of them have their own balconies with a panoramic view that stretches for over 100 kilometers.

My friends from Georgia were most enthusiastic about the food, emphasizing the fact that they had already had three dinners, each with a different specialty. "We like to drive around in the daytime and get a lunch of bread and cheese," they said, "but it is such a joy to return here in the late afternoon, go for a swim, and then rest until dinnertime. I hope you won't tell too many people about it."

LA BASTIDE DE TOURTOUR (Relais et Chateaux), 83690 Tourtour. Tel.: (94) 70-57-30. A 26-guestroom very comfortable restored castle in the high hills of Var (Provence), 100 km. from Nice. Breakfast, lunch, and dinner. Wheelchair access. Swimming pool and tennis courts on grounds. Beautiful walks, back roads, and gorgeous views nearby. Closed Oct. 3 to Apr. 28. Rates: See Index.

Directions: Michelin sect. map 84. Draguignan; follow D-49 (spectacular road) to Ampus. Turn left on the road to St. Pierre de Tourtour and Tourtour. Alternate road is D-557 out of Draguignan to a point outside of Villecroze. Turn right on D-51 to Tourtour.

THE MARKETPLACE AT DRAGUIGNAN

It was ten o'clock in the morning and the entire plaza at Draguignan was now the weekly farmers' market. Earlier in the day, the farm trucks had chugged into the square with loads of carrots, cauliflowers, potatoes, beans, enormous green peppers, artichokes, bananas, oranges, strawberries, eggplants, pineapples, and dozens of fresh fruits and vegetables. Stalls and tables appeared almost miraculously, offering cheeses in every flavor and style, poultry, meats, fish, flowers, pastries, and even pet hamsters and rabbits.

It was a gorgeous, sunny day, and to protect the tables, canopies and umbrellas were quickly put up. Some musicians were holding forth in one corner.

I bought a sweet roll in the bakery and some milk in the butcher shop and sat down on the bench to enjoy the scene. A little French girl in a beautiful blue dress that matched her eyes came and sat down next to me and solemnly offered me a bite of her delicious chocolate ice cream cone. It was too much to resist; chocolate has always been my favorite.

CHATEAU DE TRIGANCE
Trigance

It distresses me to realize that a great many people are going to visit Provence, the Cote d'Azur, and the Riviera, but will not find their way to these magnificent mountains and the truly breathtaking beauty of the Verdon Gorges. A day trip from Cannes or Nice would be enhanced by a stop at Trigance for lunch.

Not that Chateau de Trigance is undiscovered. Far from it. In looking at the guest list I found that very many well-known people from all over the world had apparently studied the road maps and found their way to this wild, wonderful country and its 11th-century fortress-castle.

First of all, there is the walk up the steps. The castle was built on the top of the hill to prevent besiegers from reaching it, and there is no way of avoiding the climb. However, once you have reached the battlements at the top, the feeling of exhilaration is so great that the ascent is soon forgotten. Here I was, surrounded by a ring of mountains and I could just imagine what dramas had been enacted on this site for a thousand years.

There are only eight guest rooms in this fortress; however, all of the conveniences have been added and everything is very comfortable. The main dining room is carved out of the rock, and the atmosphere is definitely medieval.

While meandering around the castle, I came upon something that still raises the hair on the back of my head. I walked through the dining room and down some stone steps into a very dark and somewhat gloomy tower. Seeing the sunlight filtering through a narrow window, I stepped into a room, and there in front of me was a woman with gray hair dressed in medieval costume. A very fierce-looking man was standing next to her. They looked so real I was frightened. Then I laughed as I realized they were only papier mâché figures.

Two of my closest neighbors, Ruth and George Ripley, made a stop at Chateau de Trigance a few years ago. "Absolutely spectacular" is the way Ruth Ripley describes it.

CHATEAU DE TRIGANCE (Relais et Chateau), 83840 Trigance. Tel.: (94) 76-91-18. An 8-guestroom comfortable but simple inn located in an ancient 11th-century castle near the entrance to the Verdon Gorges. Breakfast, lunch, and dinner. Closed Nov. to Easter. Rates: See Index.

Directions: This will take some persistence, but it is well worth it. Locate Draguignan on Michelin map 84. Follow D-955 north through Montferrat, through the military reservation, north to Riblaquon. Trigance is about 4 km. to the northeast on D-90. This is about 10 km. from the Verdon Gorges. Leave the car in the parking space, and your luggage will be brought up to the hotel in a lift. Walk the 75 steps up the side of the precipice and along the path to the reception desk.

LES GORGES DU VERDON

As incredible as it seemed, just a few hours earlier I had been sunning myself on a Riviera beach under a blue Mediterranean sky. Now, I was standing on the rim of a high cliff, looking down into the depth of the Verdon Gorges in the northern part of Provence. This is an area of absolutely breathtaking views, with bridges soaring over the deep chasms, and villages so precariously perched on the top of rocky precipices that they seem almost ready to topple over into oblivion.

This is a place where even the widest-angle lens does not capture the view. The road leads through several tunnels plunging down next to the river and then twisting up treacherously, clinging to the sides of the cliff to the very top of the rim. It reminded me of the volcanic crater on the island of La Palma in the Canary Islands.

HOTEL LE CAGNARD
Cagnes-sur-Mer

Talk to anyone who has been to Le Cagnard and invariably they will roll their eyes to heaven and say, "Unbelievable." Looking back on it I am not sure that it ever happened. Le Cagnard is part of a medieval fortress called Haut de Cagnes, overlooking the city of Cagnes and a considerable expanse of the Mediterranean. Viewed from a distance, the permutations of towers, bridges, walls, and crenelated battlements exist in a bluish, purplish haze. The amazing thing is that inside this walled promontory are churches, nightclubs, restaurants, art galleries, jazz clubs, hundreds of apartments, an outdoor park, narrow streets in which it is very easy to get lost, hundreds of steps (all of which seem to go up), and a definite shortage of parking spaces.

The hotel is perched precariously, but safely, on the outer walls. My room was on the very top of one of the towers, and its somewhat monastic air was relieved by a white ceiling, blue walls, reproductions of van Gogh paintings, and red furniture with blue flowers. My casement windows had a glorious view looking down into the town and out across the sea. I sat cross-legged in one window, watching early-morning Cagnes come to life.

The dining room looks as if it has been carved right out of granite, with a vaulted ceiling and a small balcony; when the long Riviera twilight descends and the candles are lit, it is indeed very romantic. The specialties on the menu are *carré d'agneaux aux herbes de Provence,* and *daurade flambée au pastis.* They also serve an impressive bouillabaisse.

Off the dining room there is an absolutely glorious little balcony decorated with geraniums, which I shared with several other guests who fell into two categories—people who were visiting for the first time, whose conversation was based on their adventures in locating Le Cagnard, and those blasé many-timers who by now knew their way

around and had their favorite little shops and small streets. It is very popular with Americans. We all agreed that if you liked it, you liked it a lot.

HOTEL LE CAGNARD (Relais et Chateaux), 06800 Cagnes-sur-Mer. Tel.: (93) 20-73-21. A 14-guestroom comfortable but simple inn located in a castle high above the town of Cagnes-sur-Mer in the Alpes-Maritimes. It is situated about midway between Cannes and Nice. Breakfast, lunch, and dinner served daily. Within a short drive of the Riviera beaches. Closed from Nov. 1 to mid-Dec. Rates: See Index.

Directions: Michelin sect. map 84. From Autoroute A-8 (the main road to Cannes and Nice) use Cagnes Sortie (exit). Bear to the right at sign for Cagnes-Vence. Do not take the first left that goes up the hill, nor the road to left marked Grasse, but continue on to a roundabout (traffic circle) and follow the road to Vence. This leads through the town of Cagnes. The key words are "Haut de Cagnes." Start looking for this sign on the right when the road to Vence leads up a hill. Turn right and follow a twisting road to the top. There are a few signs for the hotel. Take road as far as you can and walk the rest of the way to the reception. I had a comically exasperating time locating this place.

LE CHATEAU DU DOMAINE ST.-MARTIN
Vence

It was a beautiful, warm day on the French Riviera. I had taken the road from Cagnes to Vence and, following the signs to Coursegoules, could see the Chateau St.-Martin high in the hills above me. It looked most impressive. The road wound upward, and I found myself at the entrance, which was the well-restored ruins of an ancient drawbridge, now permanently open.

Even before the construction of the original castle and drawbridge by the Knights Templars after their return from the Crusades in the 12th century, St.-Martin already had a history, since it was named for a bishop of Tours and an evangelist to the Gauls who had lived here as early as A.D. 350.

I walked through the courtyard and through the doors leading into the entryway. Inside, I found an elegant, formal atmosphere with many tapestries, arched windows, rich-looking furniture, and many oils and prints. There were several guests enjoying luncheon in the dining room and on the balcony, which had an awesome view from its 1,500-foot elevation.

When Harry Truman visited many years ago, he told the owners that they really needed a swimming pool, so they built one and called it the

Truman Swimming Pool. There are tennis courts on the estate and the golf course is not far away.

In the main building of the Chateau Saint-Martin are fifteen *très élégantes* guest rooms, most of them reached by climbing the richly carved marble staircase to the second floor. Many of them have views of the town, countryside, and the Mediterranean from their balconies. There are additional guest rooms in small, individual Provençal country houses on the estate.

The atmosphere was extraordinarily light, peaceful, and quiet. Fresh summer nights and sunny days make it ideal for a tranquil vacation experience. It is just fifteen minutes from the Mediterranean, and within a short drive of the old medieval town of Vence, with its art gallery with works by Dufy, Carzou, and Chagall. The Matisse Chapel in Vence is world famous.

LE CHATEAU DU DOMAINE ST.-MARTIN (Relais et Chateaux), 06140 Vence. Tel.: (93) 58-02-02. A 25-guestroom exceptionally comfortable hotel with first-class service on the heights overlooking Vence and the Riviera in the Alpes-Maritimes; 30 km. from Cannes, and 16 km. from Nice. Breakfast, lunch, dinner. Swimming pool and tennis courts on grounds. Golf nearby. Short distance from Matisse Chapel in Vence. Closed Dec., Jan., and Feb. Rates: See Index.

Directions: Michelin section map 84. Follow the road D-36 from Cagnes to Vence. In Vence look for signs for Coursegoules and then Chateau St.-Martin.

CHATEAU DE LA CHEVRE D'OR
Eze Village

"This may be the most beautiful view on the Cote d'Azur." It was twilight. Three of us were seated on the patio of the Chevre d'Or, overlooking the Mediterranean, quietly absorbing the delicate shadings of color as daylight turned to darkness. These sentiments were expressed by Judy, who with her husband, Alvin, had been traveling up the Italian Riviera into France, visiting several attractive hotels en route. "Perhaps it is the night, the company, and our beautiful day all coming together, but I have never seen anything like this before and probably never will again." We all nodded in silent agreement.

La Chevre d'Or is at the top of the highest point of Eze Village, which can be seen from some distance away traveling up the Moyenne Corniche. It is, according to the *Michelin Green Guide* for the French Riviera, "A prime example of a perched village clinging like an eagle's nest to a rock spike towering 1,550 feet overlooking the sea." Caution. There are two communities named Eze. One is Eze Mer, on the edge of the Mediterranean Sea, and the other is Eze Village, some distance above. Artists and craftsmen had set up stalls and shops in the village, and I purchased a very handsome watercolor of Eze.

The innkeeper is Monsieur Bruno Ingold, a sophisticated, cordial Swiss gentleman. His staff is headed by the headwaiter, Claude, who works deftly from table to table, preparing the many French specialties, overseeing the service, and conversing expertly in many different languages.

The few guest rooms are in a romantic style and, incredible as it may seem, innkeeper Ingold has created a very small swimming pool on the tiny terrace. It is most welcome for a quick plunge during the sunny season.

La Chevre d'Or is always booked considerably in advance for July and August, but between the 20th of August and the 10th of October it might be possible to call the day before and reserve a room. This is an excellent time to be on the Riviera; the sun is still high, the water is still warm, and most important, the crowds are far thinner.

While we were talking, night had fallen completely and the deep blackness was punctuated by the pearl-like pinpoints of moving lights as cars traversed the roadway below. It is all really much beyond my meager powers of description.

CHATEAU DE LA CHEVRE D'OR (Relais et Chateaux), 06360 Eze Village. Tel.: (93) 41-12-12. A 14-guestroom very comfortable inn, clinging by its fingernails to the cliffs high over the Mediterranean, about 12 km. from Nice. Breakfast, lunch, and dinner. Small swimming pool on grounds. Tennis nearby. This is an excellent place to stay (as are all of the others in this section of France) to enjoy the recreation on the Riviera. Closed Dec. to Mar. Bruno Ingold, Innkeeper. Rates: See Index.

Directions: Michelin sect. map 84. Eze Village is located on the Moyenne (Middle) Corniche (N-7). After reaching Eze Village turn right at the first road after the bus park at a sign that says "Tourist Information." Follow this road to the parking area for the village. Lock your car, don't take your bags, walk up the ancient stone steps through an alley to a sign with a goat's head on it. Bear left through a narrow ancient street that winds around the outside and persist until you reach the front door of the inn. They will send someone back for your bags and tell you how to solve the parking problem.

ITINERARY 2—DOVER, CALAIS, NORMANDY, THE MARNE, THE WINE ROUTE, SAVOIE, AVIGNON-MONTFAVET, LES BAUX DE PROVENCE, ARLES, MARSEILLE

Most of the reservations on this itinerary were made on a day-by-day basis. There is some overlap with Itinerary 1; however, it is not significant.

HOTEL WINDSOR
Calais

For many visitors to France who do not go directly to Paris, Calais is one of the principal ports of entry, the others being Boulogne, Dieppe, and Le Havre.

As you leave France, Calais is an open gateway to England, thanks to the large number of ships and Hovercraft routes. It is an excursion center for travel to Kent and the towns and seaside resorts of Folkestone, Dover, Deal, Sandwich, Ramsgate, Margate, and Canterbury.

After taking the train from Victoria Station in London to Dover, I experienced some delays because of labor problems and eventually took a Hovercraft across the channel, an interesting adventure lasting only thirty minutes.

I picked up my AutoEurope car and, after making a decision to stay in Calais for one night before continuing, I decided to do what many other Americans and Britons have done—I asked the advice of the attendant in the auto rental office about a medium-priced hotel in the town. It's interesting how decisions that seem rather small at first can play such an important role in certain aspects of a traveler's adventures.

The Hotel Windsor was a very pleasant, medium-priced hotel, about fifteen minutes by car from the port of entry. Let me further say that the particular area in which it is located seemed to be highly tourist-oriented, and there are several restaurants and other hotels as well. However, I discovered the next morning as I was leaving Calais that there is a whole second city that presents quite a different aspect. Had the car rental man suggested a hotel in the larger, less tourist-oriented area I would have had an entirely different experience. The line between these two sections is marked by an impressive Rodin sculpture of the six Calais burghers who offered to sacrifice their lives in exchange for the lifting of the siege against the city at that time.

The Windsor is typical of other medium-priced hotels in the same class. The price included a *douche,* the French word for shower bath. The toilet facilities are down the hall. The room was very comfortable, quite large, had two beds, and the shower and washbowl were in a separate little room. There was one lamp over each bed, one central overhead lamp, and no other lamps on the tables. It was clean, and the wallpaper was very pleasant. The cost included *petit déjeuner* (breakfast), which consisted of French bread, a croissant or two, some jellies and jams, and either hot coffee or hot chocolate. These are served in a small separate room, which seemed to be the custom throughout the country. There were no restaurant facilities at the hotel.

French, English, and Italian were spoken, and the innkeeper was very agreeable.

My stay at the Windsor gives rise to the advice that it is a good idea to take a room on what might be called the "quiet side" of a hotel, and to make sure there are no neon lights shining in the window after dark. When choosing a hotel in a town or a small city, try to avoid one located on a main thoroughfare.

HOTEL WINDSOR, 2 Rue du Commandant Bonningue, 62100 Calais. Tel.: (21) 34-59-40. A typical, medium-sized hotel in the more tourist-oriented section of Calais, about 15 min. from port of entry. Clean, comfortable rooms with the wc down the hall. Continental breakfast included in price of room. English is spoken. Open all year. Rates: See Index.

Directions: Calais, like other French ports, has ferry and/or hovercraft connections with England. Get a good map of northern France (Michelin 998 will do very nicely, also Michelin 51).

LE VERT MESNIL
Tilques

I departed Calais in the rain but with high hopes, and driving along the N-43 I saw a sign for this chateau and decided to take a look. I was to do this several times on this trip to France, with varying results.

This time, however, it proved to be a fortuitous move because the chateau was set back in a quiet park and had many very attractive features, including some gardens, tennis courts, and pleasant walks in the forest.

I was greeted in French by a somewhat austere concierge, who put me in the charge of a young chambermaid wearing red toenail polish and open-toed sandals. The two of us continued on a tour of many of the guest rooms, most of which had high ceilings and very pleasing views of the lawns and park. Some of the rooms had been decorated recently, and some of the bathrooms were particularly impressive.

The restaurant had a marble floor and rather formal covered chairs and an intimate view of a stable-courtyard on one side and beautiful front gardens and lawn on the other. The prices and menu appeared to be a good value.

This would be an excellent stop for a traveler arriving in or departing from Calais. It is only about forty kilometers from the port and, I think, creates a very pleasant, lasting impression of French hospitality. There was little English spoken here, but lots of understanding of English, if you get my drift.

LE VERT MESNIL, Tilques, 62500 St.-Omer. Tel.: (21) 93-28-99. A 70-guestroom chateau-hotel with restaurant, 40 km. from Calais, in a park setting. All of the rooms have private bathrooms, telephones, and TV. Tennis, volleyball, gardens, and forest walks. Wheelchair access. English spoken. Rates: See Index.

Directions: Tilques is a small village on the N-43 between Ardres and St.-Omer. Michelin 51 shows details.

NORMANDY

This is the country of cream, cider, and calvados. One of the ways to see it is to stay at private chateaux. The idea is not new to France, but the spirit in which Bertrand Laffilé organized his association is new. One must be an accepted member of his club, the Demeures Club, in order to be welcomed as a guest in the thirty-five chateaux in his organization, most of which are in western France. There is a membership fee of 800 francs per family, but it is well worth it if one plans to visit more than two places, because the prices of rooms are very low (150 to 300 francs) compared to other, more commercial, accommodations.

In each chateau, there are no more than two guest rooms, and the chatelains have pledged to receive no more than one party at a time, therefore providing a really personal welcome for their guests. It is an interesting arrangement because the chateau owners enjoy the opportunity to meet new people, and they are usually people who are in love with their chateau, who have made some sacrifice to keep it going. Conversely, guests have the opportunity to experience life in a French home and to enjoy these very beautiful chateaux at a most reasonable price.

For further information, write to Bertrand Laffilé, Demeures Club, 5 Place du Marché Sainte Catherine, 75004 Paris, France.

LE CHATEAU DU ROMEREL
Saint Valery-sur-Somme

A number of French landlords are opening their doors to the traveler these days. Some keep their distance and remain unavailable to their guests. But most of them actually enjoy playing the bed-and-breakfast game and take their role as host very seriously.

Such is the case of M. and Mme. F. Knecht, who live in a big white house on high ground alongside the harbor of Saint Valery sur Somme. The large, wooded park hides a swimming pool open to guests on sunny days.

I had a large, nicely furnished room, and thoroughly enjoyed my stay, especially breakfast. I am very fond of breakfast. Mme. Knecht had laid a beautiful table in her lovely dining room. The lace-covered table was generously laden with croissants, homemade jams, and tea, served on delicate china.

I felt particularly warm and happy, starting off for a day's walk in the national park of Marquenterre, one of the biggest bird sanctuaries in Europe. And the fact that it rained all day didn't alter my good mood one bit.

LE CHATEAU DU ROMEREL, 15 Quai du Romerel, 80230 St. Valery sur Somme. Tel.: (22) 26-93-23. A large, stately bed-and-breakfast home with a few rooms, on the harbor. Private baths. M. and Mme. F. Knecht, Owners. Rates: See Index.

Directions: St. Valery is on the coast near Abbeville.

AUBERGE DU MOULIN DE FOURGES
Fourges

Sleeping Beauty's house. I felt I was having a very convincing dream. Turning off the main road into a smaller road, I went through a little village, taking a narrower road into a thick forest of beautiful tall oaks and chestnuts that suddenly opened up to reveal a river, the Epte. On the river was the most perfect millhouse anyone could imagine. The location was green and quiet, the building was right out of a storybook, complete with a large waterwheel, mossy roof, and welcoming cat. When I arrived it was raining, but everything was bright and shiny inside.

Lunch is served in a narrow dining room with windows on the water, looking out beyond the forest. You can try all the typical dishes of Normandy, including a fish soup made with cider, tripe, and anything made from or with apples, the Norman fruit. Don't forget to ask for a *trou normand,* a little glass of calvados (liquor of apples), in between the different dishes.

This, in all respects, is a typical French place, for its qualities and its shortcomings. The service, especially on weekends, is a little slow, and the downstairs bathrooms are not the brightest I have seen. But the rooms are nice and the whole place is so amazingly pleasant and simple that I think it's worth it.

Reader Comment: ". . . a charming setting, most convenient to Giverny, and offers outstanding French provincial cuisine, but we fear the rooms are a bit rudimentary."

AUBERGE DU MOULIN DE FOURGES, Fourges, 27630 Ecos. Tel.: (32) 52-12-12. A simple, picturesque millhouse inn with a good restaurant; some rooms with showers. Closed Mon. and Tues. Rates: See Index.

Directions: Take the Autoroute de l'Ouest from Paris; exit Mantes Est toward Vetheuil, La Roche Guyon, and then north to Amenucourt (pretty view of the Seine valley). Take road D-37 from there.

HOTEL BELLE VUE
Coucy-le-Chateau (Aisne)

I was enjoying a post-dinner constitutional around the small village of Coucy-le-Chateau, which sits on a height of land and has great fortifications on all four sides. I passed through a triangular-shaped village square and noted quite a few buildings of Dutch design. I understand that Flemish architectural influence is quite extensive in this part of France. It's really not very far from the Belgian border.

The day had started in Calais, and in midafternoon, after visiting a few accommodations, I decided to telephone ahead to the Hotel Belle Vue to make a room reservation for the evening. I soon discovered that no English was spoken here and after resorting to a few halting French idioms (I'd suggest you have such phrases and others available at all times), I was sufficiently assured in French that I would be welcome.

I'm going to elaborate a bit because as I subsequently discovered this was a typical middle-range accommodation, and I found many of the same features and drawbacks in other similar places.

For one thing, this was my first overnight visit in a place where not

even a modicum of English was spoken. I was glad to have a simple phrase book, including some translations of French menu items. Later on, I didn't need it, but at the start of the trip I had to become adjusted once again.

First, the bedrooms. They were pleasant and comfortable, although two people would have found my room with two beds rather cramped. There was only one light in the room and that was between the two beds. The bedroom had a washbowl and a bidet. There was pleasant blue wallpaper and the beds were reasonably comfortable, although there was a certain austere quality in that not all of the beds had cotton sheets.

The greatest emphasis here was on the dining room, and I later learned that the evening meal was typical of many I would have—reasonably priced and delicious. The starter course was either a very good house paté or a pancake filled with onions and mushrooms and other delightful local vegetables. Being on the edge of the Champagne area they served a little aperitif wine called *ratifia,* which is a stage in the refinement of what finally becomes champagne.

There were several choices for the main dish and I must admit my notes are a bit hazy, but apparently it was very good.

The dining room had round and square tables with white undercloths and brown overcloths, recorded classical music, and quite a few interesting photographs and pewter plates and mugs decorating the walls. The photographs were of various views of the castle, which I could see right outside the window. Dinner is served at seven o'clock.

During my walk I found my way up on the walls of the fortifications, where there was a fantastic view of the valley. On my way back to the hotel I dicovered a discothèque with lots of colored lights and young people arriving in cars and on motorscooters. So the old France meets the new France.

HOTEL BELLE VUE, Porte de Laon-Ville Haute, 02380 Coucy-le-Chateau (Aisne). Tel.: 23 52-70-12. A castle-hotel set in a small fortified village. Excellent dining room, reasonably priced. Closed Tues. Comfortable, somewhat austere guestrooms with washbowl and bidet. No English spoken. Rates: See Index.

Directions: Locate Soissons, northeast of Paris. Coucy-le-Chateau is on the D-1 between Soissons and Chauny. Michelin detailed map 56.

CHANTILLY

Chantilly is forty-nine kilometers northeast of Paris. It is a city famous for its castle, museum, and beautiful forest, but most of all, for its culinary spécialité: la crème Chantilly. *It is sold at every street corner and lavishly spread on all desserts, so I shall say no more about it. The name of Chantilly is also synonymous with horses: 3,000 horses train here every year and the racetrack is one of the first in France. This equine activity gave birth to another tasty* spécialité: le crottin *(literally means horse manure), a goodie made from chocolate, walnuts, and almonds, to be found only at Chez M. Richet, maître-patissier, a pastry shop at 45 Rue du Connétable. Just ask for it.*

For a description of the castle, better turn to your Michelin Green Guide. *Suffice to say here that its collections make it one of the major museums in France. It is open every day from 10:30 a.m. to 5:00 p.m. except Tuesday. Many other marvels of nature and art are nearby: the ponds of Commelles, the Abbaye de Royaumont—the most beautiful abbey of the Cistercians in this region. The castle grounds, too, are remarkable.*

ROYAL-CHAMPAGNE
Champillon-Bellevue (Marne)

The signposts directed me to Arras, Cambrai, Amiens, Soissons, and Reims, and although I was not to realize it until later, the next two days had a quality of almost *déjà vu*, a feeling as if I had been there before. This might be explained by the fact that as a boy I had grown up with the literature and motion pictures dealing with World War I.

I was certainly far removed from any of the vicissitudes of conflict as I sat on the terrace of one of the bedrooms of this luxury hotel that is a member of the Relais et Chateaux.

I toured many of the guest rooms and there was a definite decorator feeling or a kind of studied elegance in each; although the color schemes and patterns were different, all had wallpaper, draperies, and bedspreads to match. Each room had telephone service and a radio—quite a difference from my accommodations at another Belle Vue in Coucy-le-Chateau the previous night. The price was also considerably different.

The Relais et Chateaux book classifies this particular accommodation as "comfortable, but simple." To me it seemed a cut or two higher than that. The reception area is quite grand and is decorated with many classic prints of nobility on horseback. The dining room is also designed to overlook the impressive sweep of the valley.

The Royal-Champagne is located near the autoroute between Paris and Metz. It is a very short distance from the great cathedral city of Reims.

ROYAL-CHAMPAGNE, (Relais et Chateaux), Champillon-Bellevue (Marne). Tel.: (26) 51-11-51. New as of Sept. 1989: (26) 52-87-11. A luxury hotel in the heart of the Champagne country between Paris and Metz, 15 km. from Reims. Guestrooms are elegant, with telephones and radios and panoramic views. Wheelchair access. Rates: See Index.

Directions: Located on N-51 south of Reims en route to Epernay. Michelin detailed map 56.

AUBERGE LA TOURAINE CHAMPENOISE
Tours-sur-Marne (Marne)

Although I may have mentioned it before, one of the most helpful books for emergency purposes that a visitor in France can possess is called *Logis et Auberges de France*, a guide to a group of small, medium-priced hotels, usually family run. Not all of them are acceptable. When we come right down to it, one of the reasons I'm writing this book is to provide information on acceptable accommodations in all price ranges for a trip to part of France.

Such an accommodation is La Touraine Champenoise, run by the Schosseler family.

I had waited until midafternoon before starting to telephone for accommodations that evening, feeling that May was definitely not the height of the season and that I would have no trouble. Well, I found that even in May it's best to start telephoning earlier, and I did see a couple of lodgings in the town of Epernay, which were not at all acceptable. By 5 p.m., I finally made a telephone connection with Madame Schosseler and was delighted to learn that indeed there was a room for me.

This little hotel is typical, but at the same time above standard, of other places I was to see, and has a very pleasant dining room with some good original oils and watercolors. The guest rooms are not very large, but large enough, and some have wc facilities as well as showers.

It is situated on the edge of the Marne Canal, and there always seemed to be a barge or boat of some kind in sight. Just a hundred yards on the other side of the canal is the famous river associated with many of the conflicts in this part of France.

As is typical, there were three menus. There was a simple one at the lowest price; the second had three choices; and the third, the most expensive, had six courses.

Madame had fairly good English and with my fairly atrocious French we managed to communicate quite satisfactorily. This would be an excellent stopover for a visit to the Champagne country and also the city of Reims.

AUBERGE LA TOURAINE CHAMPENOISE, 51150 Tours-sur-Marne (Marne). Tel: (26) 58-91-93. A small, typical hotel on the edge of the Marne Canal and close to the Marne River in a calm, peaceful setting. Pleasant dining room and adequate guest rooms, some with private bathrooms. Some English spoken. Closed Jan. 1 to 15. Rates: See Index.

Directions: This is a good place to mention that, because of various changes, French maps do not always have the correct road numbers. However, this little village just across the Marne River is located off the Epernay-Chalons road, shown as RD-3 on Michelin map of northern France 998 and detailed map 56. Look for signs on the north side.

Enter now a new character in the dramatis personae—the French Tourist Offices. These offices are located in about fifteen principal cities, and if you're lucky enough to find an office where someone speaks English (if you don't speak adequate French), they can make reservations for you in all parts of France.

HOTEL À LA XII BORNE
Delme (Moselle)

I spent most of the day traveling from near Epernay to Nancy. Part of the trip was alongside the Marne Canal and River, with the road leading to several towns of different size, and I realized that the journey was taking much longer than I had anticipated. It had turned quite warm by midafternoon when I arrived in Nancy at the tourist office and discovered that even though it was the beginning of the week and although there was no festival or holiday being celebrated, two of the *logis* I was going to visit could not accommodate me. I threw myself on the mercy of the young woman at the tourist office to see if she could make other arrangements. She made several phone calls and found that everything in the immediate vicinity of Nancy was filled. I finally took the *Logis* book and began to choose places at random; we telephoned and, between the two of us, we located this place, just a pleasant drive to the east and north of Nancy.

I arrived at Delme about six o'clock in the evening. The hotel was located on a main street and a busy road to Metz (try to avoid accommodations on the main street or at least get a room in the back of the house).

The town is not located in a particularly scenic area. There are some hills and valleys, but it is not all that exciting.

However, dinner was exceptional. The first dish that caught my eye was the frogs' legs prepared in a Lorraine sauce, the base of which is Riesling wine, reduced to about a tenth of its original volume, and herbs and cream. The result is a real feast—the small frogs' legs were unusually tender and the sauce was good enough to eat with a spoon. I learned that the base of most Lorraine cooking is butter, whereas in some parts of France it is oil, or goose or pork fat. The menu ran to three or four price levels. Among other dishes, there were escargots served in a Champagne sauce, coq au vin, and duck l'orange. There was a great deal more to this little hotel than was evident from the exterior, including an extensive dining room and kitchen, and apparently its reputation has spread to several of the nearby urban areas.

Incidentally, it was here that I learned that the French phrase for "doggie bag" is *pique-nique demain,* translating literally to "picnic tomorrow." On most days I did not stop for lunch at a formal restaurant, there being only so much of this rich, wonderful French food that can be absorbed in a day, so I stopped at various shops, buying cheeses, breads, and fruit, or I asked for a *pique-nique demain* from the meal the night before.

HOTEL À LA XII BORNE, 57 Delme (Moselle). Tel.: (8) 701-30-18. A 20-guestroom (private and shared baths) hotel on the main route to Metz, northeast of Nancy, with just adequate guestrooms. The pleasant dining room is superior with an extensive menu. Open all year. Rates: See Index.

Directions: Locate Nancy and then follow N-74 to the junction with D-955 at Chateau-Salins. Delme is on the road between Chateau-Salins and Metz. Michelin detailed map 57.

HOTEL-RESTAURANT ARNOLD
Itterswiller

Itterswiller is one of the many lovely villages on the Wine Route, which winds its way through the eastern slopes of the Vosges Mountains.

I was originally attracted to the Arnold because it was situated in a vineyard with a lovely view of the valley and the mountains beyond. It turned out to be a three-star hotel with a little more sophistication than I had found elsewhere.

The rooms were most comfortable, and fifteen of them had their own balconies overlooking the view of the vineyards and mountains.

The menu included some of the specialties of the region, such as wild boar. If you're staying elsewhere in the vicinity this might be a good place to have dinner, which, at the time of my visit, started at 100 francs.

HOTEL-RESTAURANT ARNOLD, 67140 Itterswiller. Tel.: (88) 85-50-58. Telex: Arnold 870550F. A 28-guestroom Wine Route hotel-restaurant (3 stars) with most impressive views and comfortable bedrooms. Conveniently located for longer stay in the Alsatian wine region. Somewhat sophisticated international flavor. Listed in the Michelin *and* Logis et Auberges de France *guides. Rates: See Index.*

Directions: Itterswiller is in the center of the Alsatian wine country, 446 km. from Paris and 41 km. from Strasbourg. Obtain special Wine Route map from any tourist office. Also on Michelin detailed maps 62 and 87.

LE CLOS SAINT-VINCENT
Ribeauvillé

This very impressive accommodation is one of three included in the Relais et Chateaux group located in the Vosges Mountains and Rhine valley area. Because Relais et Chateaux are usually excellent places to stop, I was doubly regretful at not being able to visit the other two. One is located in Colroy-la-Roche and the other in Rouffach. Information about them can be found in the Relais et Chateaux publication.

I'll always remember this place because of spending two mornings enjoying a breakfast of hot chocolate and fresh croissants on the balcony of my room overlooking the vineyards in the foreground and the sweep of the Rhine valley in the background.

Guest rooms were furnished and decorated with a thought toward creating an atmosphere that would blend well with the beautiful views of the vineyards and the Rhine valley.

Unfortunately, during the time of my visit the restaurant was closed, although I did find excellent evening meals nearby. *Michelin* has awarded Chef Bertrand Chapotin, who is also the owner, one rosette and lists among the house specialties *ris et rognons de veau aux petites legumes* (veal sweetbreads and kidney with vegetables) as well as *filet de turbot à l'oseille.*

LE CLOS SAINT-VINCENT (Relais et Chateaux), 68150 Ribeauvillé (Haut-Rhine). Tel.: (89) 73-67-65. A 9-guestroom and 3-suite luxury accommodation on a hillside overlooking the Alsatian vineyards and the Rhine River at a distance. Restaurant closed Tues. and Wed. Accommodations available at all times. Open early Mar. to mid-Nov. Paris, 429 km.; Colmar, 15 km. Rates: See Index.

Directions: Ribeauvillé is on the section of the Wine Route which skirts the base of the Vosges Mountains between Sélestat and Colmar. Michelin detailed maps 62 and 87.

LE CHALET HOTEL-RESTAURANT
Col de la Schlucht

One of the most interesting and contrasting experiences in the east of France is to take one of the very good roads from the Route du Vin over the Vosges Mountains. Following D-417, I stopped at the crest of the mountain in a small village that had a decidedly tourist air, meaning that there was a big parking lot and several restaurants.

I picked one place just on the basis of appearance and because it occurred to me that a traveler coming through there in May might find it a lot of fun to stop and look over the outlook to the east, down a rather precipitous valley toward the Rhine River.

It turned out to be a very pleasant surprise. The innkeeper is a young Frenchman, M. Bouet, who married a Scottish lass, Hazel Bouet, and I chatted with her long enough to find that May is indeed a good time to come there. You can phone from anywhere in France and make the reservation. It has a sizable restaurant and it is obvious that they do a great many off-the-highway meals.

The somewhat plain bedrooms were quite clean and I would suggest that the rooms facing the east would be preferable.

Hazel Bouet, who came originally from Edinburgh, explained that we were about 4,500 feet in altitude and that there were several ski lifts nearby for both downhill and cross-country skiing.

The menu had an emphasis on Alsatian dishes.

The place had a rather bustling but natural feeling, although it could be very busy at certain times of the year. The rates were most appealing (see Index).

LE CHALET HOTEL-RESTAURANT, Col de la Schlucht, 68140 Munster. Tel.: (89) 77-36-44. A hotel-restaurant in a small village at the crest of a mountain, 4,500 feet high, in the Vosges in a tourist area. Clean, plain bedrooms—those facing east recommended. Open year-round. Downhill and xc skiing nearby. English spoken. Rates: See Index.

Directions: Col de la Schlucht is on D-417, one of several roads that cross the Vosges Mountains, which act as a natural shelter for the Rhine River valley. The area is crisscrossed with many delightful back roads. There are dozens of ways to go from point to point. See Michelin detailed maps 62 and 87.

HOSTELLERIE LES BAS-RUPTS
Gérardmer

You just never know what you're going to find in France. At first I thought this hotel was a Bavarian nightmare with a sort of pseudocontemporary facade. At least ten badges of acceptance were at the front door and it is also listed in the *Logis de France*. It's one of the few members of Relais du Silence, an organization devoted to the maintenance of tranquil accommodations. I cannot on such a short visit judge its tranquility.

In the reception area I saw a handsome man in a chef's outfit who turned out to be Michel Philippe, who could very well be a star of television and cinema. Furthermore, he was quite versed in English and I happened to catch him at a time when the kitchen was not that busy.

I toured almost all of the guest rooms and most of them were furnished in contemporary Scandinavian, one or two had classic furnishings. The rooms in the back have a very close view of the mountains and those in the front are larger with a more pleasant view.

At lunch, I had my first taste of noisettes of wild boar, which was served with two different sauces. Also, on a most attractively arranged plate was a small mashed-potato ball, which had been dipped in egg, rolled in slivered almonds, and either baked or fried. These are called *pommes amandes* and they are served with very thin french-cut green beans and baby carrots with their tops on. Lunch was completed with some Muenster cheese. I agree that Monsieur Philippe deserves all of the honors and diplomas that are hanging in the reception area.

I would also give this place the Berkshire Traveller four-star rating for having the most elegant public toilets I have ever seen. There was carpeting on the floor and a sort of common wash-up room shared by men and women—the theme is Art Deco all the way.

Michelin lists Bas-Rupts as a top-class restaurant with one rosette. Since this is a resort area, there are also several places nearby.

HOSTELLERIE LES BAS-RUPTS (Relais du Silence), 88400 Gérardmer (Vosges). Tel.: (29) 63-09-25; Telex: 960-992. A 19-guestroom (private baths) mountain hotel-restaurant with many citations and memberships. Additional rooms in Chalet Fleuri, adjacent. Tennis, school for xc skiing close by; downhill ski area 2 km. Rates: See Index.

Directions: Gérardmer is also on D-489, which runs across the Vosges Mountains, beginning I believe at Chaumont and ending in Colmar. Michelin detailed maps 62 and 87.

LE RELAIS DE NANTILLY
Nantilly

It had been a very interesting day that started at Le Clos Saint Vincent in Ribeauville in the valley of the Rhine. The road had taken me across the crest of the Vosges Mountains to Gérardmer and into Luxeuil, the city of the baths. I deliberately chose to follow the yellow roads on my

Michelin map of northern France (998) instead of following the usually more traveled roads printed in red.

The trip was well worth the trouble as it led through a somewhat unspoiled and natural part of France with beautiful views of the countryside. It was so unspoiled that I looked in vain for signs of small hotels or inns that I might include in this book, but to my dismay I found none. It just wasn't a road that an ordinary tourist would choose.

I had made reservations at Le Relais de Nantilly, so I felt fairly safe in arriving about six o'clock in the evening, knowing that my reservation had been confirmed and that I would have a good dinner and a comfortable bedroom.

This is a lovely chateau surrounded by generous fields and parklands. It's quite typical of some of the middle-sized chateaux that I saw during my trips to France. The original use was probably by a well-to-do family of the 19th century, and most of the guest rooms were quite large with excellent views of the countryside, and all had modern bathroom facilities.

The dining room here was surprisingly small, which I think made it more cozy. Several interesting watercolors adorned the walls. The service was very agreeable and quite informal. A man whom I took to be the manager and the proprietor was also the headwaiter, and the rather attractive woman at the front desk turned out to be his wife, who also assisted in the dining room service. The atmosphere was like that of many American country inns owned by husband-and-wife teams.

The dinner was most enjoyable. I had some fresh fish in a creamy sauce that was so delicious I surreptitiously dipped my bread in to soak up all of it. The remainder of the menu had typical French dishes. I chose an enticing dessert from a center table.

The morning was very pleasant, with guests enjoying a cup of coffee and warm croissants at the bar. I think we were all relieved to find that the all-night rain had stopped and we had a fresh, sunshiny morning in which to start another day.

This little chateau was very pleasant and had one quality that I found quite indispensable—it was very quiet.

LE RELAIS DE NANTILLY (Relais et Chateaux), Nantilly, 70100 Gray. Tel.: (84) 65-20-12. A 26-guestroom chateau-hotel surrounded by park and woods in a quiet, unspoiled countryside. A small and informal but excellent dining room. Large bedrooms with modern baths and telephones. Rates: See Index.

Directions: You'll definitely need Michelin 998 (northern France) to locate this place. Locate Dijon and follow D-70 toward Gray. Note

D-2, a secondary road leading to Autrey. The Relais is on D-2. Michelin detailed map 66.

HOTEL-RESTAURANT DE LA PLACE
Polliat

At Mâcon I left the N-6 and headed east on N-79 toward Bourg and the French Alps at Annecy. However, en route I stopped at this very pleasant little town and decided to include this hotel and restaurant as typical of many of its type available in France. It is listed in the *Logis* book, and *Michelin* gives it a rather humble rating: "plain, but adequate hotel." I found it to be tremendously interesting and particularly enjoyed myself. It is not very likely that you'll run into very many other Americans or Europeans, either at dinner or as overnight guests. It is a place where, in the words of James Thurber, "truck drivers stop."

Located about 400 yards off the main road on a small parking plaza, it is far enough away from the truck traffic to be relatively undisturbed at night.

The first floor of the building contains a busy restaurant, a busy bar, and a reception/TV room. I had to make a few halting explanations in English to convey the idea that I wanted to see the bedrooms.

The receptionist led me through the back of the dining room to an outside back stairway that led up to a pleasant little guest balcony, and on to several different bedrooms, which were plain but serviceable and, above all, clean.

I would encourage the reader to feel free to seek accommodations of this type as well as those of a more elegant nature. I think travelers to France discover early on that the cost of the meal does not necessarily indicate the amount of enjoyment to be derived from it. For instance, this is far from an elegant restaurant, but there were tablecloths and the least expensive menu included a soufflé as well as selections of eels, trout amandine, grilled lamb chops, and a quarter of roast chicken. There were eleven main dishes along with vegetables, cheese, and dessert. It was one of the best values for the money I found in France and it was certainly a great deal better than some that would cost three or four times as much. At the far side of the dining room was a group of posters advertising motocross and shooting contests.

I was given a tour of the very busy kitchen and it was the equal of many that I visited where the menus were far more expensive.

This is a good place for me to explode the myth about Americans not being accepted in France or that the French always refuse to speak English, resenting visitors. I received very affable nods and greetings from truck drivers and motorcyclists of both genders and nobody thought it strange that I was talking into my tape recorder all the time.

So if I arrived here about eight o'clock at night, I'd welcome the opportunity for a quiet bedroom and a reasonably priced meal; if I were traveling with children, I'd think that it was exceptional.

It's interesting to note that this village is just a few minutes from one of the great restaurants in France, La Mère Blanc, praised elsewhere in this book. I might say that Monsieur George Blanc, who has the coveted three stars from *Michelin,* is himself a very humble man and I wouldn't have been surprised to find him partaking of the noon meal at the Hotel de la Place. La Mère Blanc enjoys a deserved reputation in France, but the Hotel de la Place has its own little niche.

HOTEL-RESTAURANT DE LA PLACE, Rte. Nationale 79, 01310 Polliat. Tel.: (74) 30-40-19. A 10-guestroom small but busy, typically French hotel-restaurant just off the main highway in a pleasant town. Bedrooms are clean and adequate. Restaurant offers a good selection at very reasonable prices. Closed 1 wk. and 3 wks. in Oct. Rates: See Index.

Directions: Polliat is just another wide place in the road on N-79, about 10 km. west of Bourg-en-Bresse.

FURTHER NOTES ON FRENCH CUISINE

I've always considered myself more a chronicler of people and ambience than an expert on cuisine. I prefer to leave food critiques to my peers in the travel-writing world, and as I have remarked several times in this and other books, I am by choice an almost-teetotaller. Oh, I've sampled the wines in various sections of Europe with what I call a "sacrificial sip," but you'll find no knowledgeable, gustatory phrases flowing from my pen. By the way, it's possible to travel all over Europe and not feel that it is necessary to drink the wine if you would prefer to abstain. The bottled mineral water is very satisfactory and does not interfere with relishing the truly unusual and excellent food. For years an old wives' tale has been circulated (by the vintners) that the water in certain European countries is literally undrinkable and it is necessary to drink wine everywhere in self-defense. It is also untrue that headwaiters in great French restaurants are offended if wine is not ordered with the meal. The fact is a great many Europeans do not take wine with their meals. I encourage the reader to follow whatever course of action pleases him or her, and not to be concerned about the so-called customs of the country. No one really cares.

Having disavowed myself of any expertise in the food and wine de-
partment, I will say that I have been tremendously pleased at all cat-
egories of European restaurants, from the simple to the three-star. I
think there is a generous sampling of various levels of cuisine in this
book and I approach the subject with a typical American palate and
admiration for a good meal.

HOTEL DE L'ABBAYE
Talloires (Haut Savoie)

As one of the guests who joined me briefly at the table on the terrace
in front of the Hotel de l'Abbaye said, *"Il fait beau."* Even if I had
forgotten that this French phrase means "It's a beautiful day," I would
certainly have gotten his meaning, because the gorgeous sunlight was
sparkling on the lake waters, not more than twenty yards in front of
us, against the green backdrop of mountains that seemed to plunge into
the lakeside. Fluffy clouds overhead played hide and seek.

It was the calm end of a day that had started north of Dijon and
involved a very spectacular ride over the mountains from Bourg to
Nantua and beyond. I was feeling particularly fortunate that I had stumbled into this section of France. Although it is located on the edge of
the French Alps (Mount Blanc, as well as the ski resorts, is just a few
miles away) it is not on the general route of the first-time traveler to
France.

Hotel de l'Abbaye, a member of the Relais group, had much to
recommend it. For one thing it has a most interesting history that
became evident as soon as I walked through the rather austere front
entrance. The building was built as a priory in the 11th century and
for six centuries was very rich, thanks to gifts from the bishops and
counts of Genève and the dukes of Savoie. In 1674 it became a royal
abbey but fell into disrepair because the monks, who were really feudal
lords of the time, were more interested in the delights of the flesh than
in spiritual atonement. The French Revolution saw the Benedictine
abbey destroyed.

Today, it is a very pleasant and modern hotel enjoying an unsur-
passed view of Lake Annecy and the mountains. Above all, it is beautifully calm and quiet.

Another attractive feature for me personally is the fact that it is run
by a family, and part of my information was gathered during an interesting talk with the father of the present innkeeper, who beguiled me
with some fascinating facts, not only about the hotel but also about the
surrounding area.

I remained at the Hotel de l'Abbaye for two nights, partly because it was one of the most enchanting of all holiday experiences and partly because the village also is the location of one of the very few three-star restaurants in France: L'Auberge du Père Bise, about which I will report directly.

HOTEL DE L'ABBAYE (Relais et Chateaux), Route de Port, 74290 Talloires (Haut Savoie). Tel.: (50) 60-77-33. A 33-guestroom hotel (private baths), originally an 11th-century priory on the shore of Lake Annecy in the scenic Savoie district. Closed mid-Dec. to mid-Jan. À la carte menu. Tennis, golf, boating, beautiful walks, and backroading. Rates: See Index.

Directions: I drove from Mâcon east to Bourg and then followed D-979 to Nantua and Bellegarde (N-84). This section is part of the truck route from Lyon to Genève. The trucks go on to Switzerland at Bellegarde and the road becomes driveable into Annecy (N-508). An alternate road would be to continue to pick up the main Autoroute from Lyon to Annecy. At Annecy follow the roads to Genève, but keep your eye peeled to the right for the road to Thones. This road passes down the east side of the lake and there will be an arrow pointing toward Talloires. It is the only way to get there. Once in the village point your car toward the lakeshore. Good luck. Michelin detailed map 92.

L'AUBERGE DU PÈRE BISE
Talloires (Haut Savoie)

A visitor to Talloires ought to spend at least two night there, of which one would be spent dining at Père Bise. I might add that I had my other evening meal at Hotel de l'Abbaye and found it to be excellent.

Because of its reputation as one of the twenty-one or so *Michelin* three-star restaurants in France, it would be quite easy to be intimidated by Père Bise before ever entering its door. It is located on one of the points of land that jut out into Lake Annecy, and it has a beautiful terrace that is especially inviting on warm afternoons and evenings, although dinner is actually served inside the restaurant.

The menu, which has several courses, really is dedicated to quite simple preparations of regional produce and is further enhanced by the fresh-water fish from the lake. The fruits and berries as well as the cheeses of the region are excellent. It is well to inquire about the local cheeses, as some of them are different and very satisfying. The cuisine is in the classic French style and the choices should include *l'omble chevalier*, the fish from the lake.

The dinner menu runs about $120 and allows a choice of several different dishes. It's also possible to order à la carte, but as nearly as I can determine it is still an expensive experience. The menu is changed almost daily and I would suggest that almost anything would be satisfactory. Remember to save some space for a selection from the dessert cart. A superb dessert is the *marjolaine,* a seven-layered chocolate dessert, which makes me almost perish with joy when I think of it.

Oddly enough, the same lake fish is also served at the rather simple restaurants in the village.

There are a few rooms here also, which I have not seen but understand are elegant.

L'AUBERGE DU PÈRE BISE (Relais et Chateaux), 74290 Talloires (Haut Savoie). Tel.: (50) 60-72-01. Michelin 3-star restaurant with rooms on the shores of Lake Annecy. Wheelchair access. Classic French cuisine, with both full-course and à la carte menus. Closed mid-Dec. to mid-Feb. Rates: See Index.

Directions: Follow directions as given for Hotel de l'Abbaye. Michelin detailed map 92.

LA TOUR DE PACORET
Grésy-sur-Isère (Savoie)

What a wonderful day! I reluctantly left the Hotel de l'Abbaye in Talloires on the shore of Lake Annecy and headed in a southerly di-

rection on N-90 between Albertville and Chambèry. To the east the towering snowcaps of the French Alps soared into the blue sky. The road ran beside a rushing river with small farms on both sides of the valley. Ahead was a sign for an auberge, and out of some sixth sense I decided to turn off, wishfully thinking perhaps I might find that ideal, out-of-the-way French inn that no one had ever visited before, run by bilingual, gracious French people who couldn't do enough for their guests.

Would you believe that La Tour de Pacoret was almost perfect.

In the first place, the setting in the mountains of Savoie is breathtaking. It is a 14th-century watchtower that was the former residence of the counts of Pacoret. The tower has had later additions to it and I'm sure the original counts lived in simple luxury.

The views from all of the guest rooms are impressive. All of the rooms have carved beds, armoires, original oils, and private wc's. The rooms are named after flowers, of which the area has an abundance.

One of the focal points is a delightful terrace that enjoys a panoramic view of the mountains. This beautiful view is also shared by the dining room.

The longer I stayed, the more enchanted I became, and I was also delighted to learn that a very pleasant lunch was served as well as dinner. This is one of the wine regions of France, and the countryside, as in Alsace, also has a typical Route du Vin.

This little gem is also in *Michelin,* and, as a Relais du Silence, has received very good marks, particularly for being quiet and secluded. The owner is a sophisticated Frenchwoman and it is obvious that her taste is the dominant influence in the furnishings and decor.

Now don't tell anybody I told you about this place. It will be our secret. (I did tell two dear friends, Janet and Ruth Pinkham. They adored it.)

LA TOUR DE PACORET, Grésy-sur-Isère, 73460 Frontenex (Savoie). Tel.: (79) 37-91-59. A secluded former 14th-century watchtower, now a 2-star hotel-restaurant in the midst of breathtaking scenery in the Savoie district. All bedrooms have private baths and impressive views. Closed Dec., Jan., and Feb. Dining room offers lunch as well as dinner. Rates: See Index.

Directions: The main road between Albertville and Chambéry has two designations: N-90, which leads on into the high mountains and the St. Bernard pass, and N-6. Grésy is a small village on D-201, about 4 km. to the northwest, running parallel to the main road. La Tour de Pacoret is well signposted. Michelin detailed map 92.

LA VIEILLE AUBERGE
Charmes-sur-Rhone

After an interval of a few years I once again drove down the N-86 from Lyon toward Avignon. The sun was shining, the day was fair, and after the success of finding such an exceptional restaurant on the previous night, I fully expected to discover some outstanding inns and small hotels that day.

As I passed by a small village on the west bank of the Rhone, I noted a sign indicating that La Vieille Auberge, the village inn, was located just a short distance from the highway. I turned into the village and after negotiating some rather pleasant but narrow streets, spotted the front entrance to the inn and pulled into a convenient parking space, sometimes a problem in European towns.

What a delight this inn proved to be! It has a very attractive tiny reception area and was flanked on the right by a dining room with a low vaulted ceiling. Since it was late May, an ancient fireplace was filled with fresh flowers. The rough walls were adorned with tapestries, and I've never seen tablecloths any whiter.

Although the staff was in the midst of scrubbing down the hallways and cleaning the rooms, one young man who seemed to be more or less in charge was delighted to show me a few of the bedrooms and explain the items on the menu.

I was very pleased with the bedrooms. They all had wc's and, even though this was a building dating back to the 16th century that had probably seen several different uses, they were of a very comfortable size. Some of the rooms looked out into a little courtyard and others had a view of the colorful roofs of the village.

The menu had several local specialties, and I learned that the chef was also the owner of this little village inn, which would have been quite in place in many parts of North America.

This would be an ideal stop for anyone traveling north or south from Avignon or Marseille. Prices (see Index) are relatively modest and I would imagine that the rooms are quiet. If the cuisine is half as palatable as the appearance of the dining room, all should be well. It was only after I left that I discovered that it was listed in both *Michelin,* which rated it as a "comfortable restaurant," and the *Logis* guide to hotels.

LA VIEILLE AUBERGE, 07800 Charmes-sur-Rhone, Ardèche. Tel.: (75) 60-80-10. A chef-owned small village inn-restaurant in a 16th-century building in the Ardèche area near the Rhone River. Guestrooms have private baths and telephones. Restaurant offers breakfast, lunch, and dinner; closed Wed. and Sun. eves. Rates: See Index.

Directions: This village is not shown on Michelin 999 (southern France); however, it is just a few km. south of Valence on N-86, which parallels the Rhone River on the west side. The N-7 and A-7 run parallel to the river on the east side and there are convenient exits and a bridge crossing opposite Charmes.

HOTEL LES FRÊNES
Avignon-Montfavet

It was very quiet in Avignon-Montfavet. Only the sounds of birds interrupted this sublime quietude as I stretched on a deck chair beside a swimming pool at Les Frênes Hotel. The warm afternoon sun of Provence was lulling me into a delicious lassitude and I realized that this was one of the few times on my second excursion through France that I had actually taken the time to act like a vacationer.

I leafed through a small guidebook outlining the historic and cultural sites and palaces of the city, preparatory to a visit in the early evening. I had barely had time a few years earlier to see the Papal Palace and other truly impressive landmarks within this walled city.

Les Frênes was a perfect setting for a few hours in the sunshine. It's an elegant small hotel, built in the early part of the 19th century and artfully located in a park with expansive lawns, very beautiful gardens, and swaying trees that in May were in full leaf. There were two swimming pools, one for children and one for adults.

Guest rooms are for the most part in small individual apartments and, in addition to being very tastefully decorated, all have private bathrooms, color television, and directly connected telephones.

The dining room and a most comfortable parlor are in the main building. It's the kind of atmosphere that invites the traveler to enjoy the rather sumptuous surroundings, including some good, original, palette-knife paintings. The proprietress, Mme. Biancone, takes the orders, and the guests are seated when the first course is ready. The dining room looks out over the park past the swimming pools.

There are three menus of varying prices and an à la carte menu. As I have remarked several times, it is sometimes easier in France to choose from the à la carte menu. Since I had eaten rather handsomely at noon, I decided to have a single course and perhaps a dessert— French desserts are very difficult to refuse.

It's quite easy to reach the center of Avignon, and I'm happy to say I enjoyed a most agreeable evening in the moonlight of Provence.

HOTEL LES FRÊNES (Relais et Chateaux), Avenue des Vertes Rives, 84140 Avignon-Montfavet. Tel.: (90)31-17-93. A 15-guestroom 19th-century hotel set in a park, 7 min. from Avignon. All bedrooms have private bathrooms, telephones, and TV. Swimming pool. Rates: See Index.

Directions: Follow the ring road around Avignon and take the turn-off for Montfavet, on the right after the turn-off for Marseille.

OUSTAU DE BAUMANIÈRE
Les Baux de Provence

This is one of the great places to eat in France. *Michelin* has awarded it five red crossed spoons and forks and three rosettes. I understand there are only five or six other restaurants in France to receive this highly desirable rating.

At the time of my visit, bookings for the evening meal were closed, but since I've never considered myself a particularly astute critic of food to begin with, I felt the only loss was the opportunity to enjoy what I'm sure would have been an exceptional meal. Incidentally, the menu is à la carte.

The location is most unusual because it enjoys a full view of some more of the rocky fortifications of the village of Les Baux de Provence and it is surrounded by beautiful formal gardens and a lovely reflecting pool. Oustau de Baumanière is set in its own box canyon, surrounded by pinnacles of limestone that have eroded over countless centuries. I hadn't really planned to stop here, and I arrived much too late in the day to feel comfortable about asking the assistant manager at the reception area to take time from a busy checking-in session with newly arrived guests to show me any of the rooms. Actually, I was booked for the night a few kilometers away, but this was a surprise discovery.

However, let me hasten to add that I feel very good about including it in this book. Even without my having a meal or staying overnight, I recognized the unmistakable signs of good taste and discrimination. It might be a bit pricey for some travelers, but there are many who will undoubtedly agree that it's worth it. The parking lot was filled with Mercedes-Benzes and Peugeots. There were also a couple of vintage Rolls-Royces.

OUSTAU DE BAUMANIÈRE, (Relais et Chateaux), Les Baux de Provence, 13520 Maussane les Alpilles. Tel.: (90) 54-33-07. Telex: 420203 Baucabro. A luxury hotel-restaurant set in a small canyon at the foot of limestone cliffs. Bedrooms are in several buildings and have private bathrooms and telephones. Tennis, swimming pool, horseback riding on grounds. Rates: See Index.

Directions: Locate Les Baux in the area south of Avignon and north of Arles. I recommend following the roads printed in yellow on Michelin 999 (southern France). Detailed map 83.

LA REGALIDO
Fontvieille

Chef-owner Jean-Pierre Michel had just returned from the fish market and he whipped the cover off his market basket like a magician to show us some big, beautiful sea bass. "I prepare like a filet of sole and then slice the way you would a smoked salmon," he said. "It is one of our most popular main dishes."

The invitation to come into the kitchen of this lovely little inn a few miles outside of Arles was an indication of its genuinely friendly spirit. I don't believe I've been invited to visit more than three other French kitchens and certainly never a kitchen by a member of the Relais et Chateaux, where there is sometimes a distance between the guest and the chef.

But La Regalido was different right from the start. The entrance is through a vine-covered arch into a tiny but exquisite garden with just enough lawn to provide an accompaniment for roses and other seasonal flowers. The swallows were busy chasing each other from tree to bush, and there were a few bright umbrellas against the Arles sun.

Inside the reception area there was an immediate feeling of acceptance. Behind the small reception desk there was a bright-eyed, black-haired woman who proved to be the wife of the innkeeper, and in a welcome fireplace was a small fire. It so happened that there were occasional rain showers during the time I was there and the brightness and warmth of the fire were extremely welcome. There were bright flowers around this reception-lobby area and many brightly shining copper utensils on the walls, along with scenes from the local country-side, all original oils and watercolors.

Jean-Pierre spoke excellent English and we had a very lively conversation about the cuisine of the house. When I asked him whether it was classic or nouveau cuisine, he replied, "Fifty-fifty—I learned from my father who had a restaurant in Toulouse and grew up in the business."

I've seen it this way in American country inns so frequently. Two people working hard and raising a family and loving their work. I wish that everyone could have seen this kitchen; it's much larger than a kitchen in an American inn and has a splendid array of pots and pans, knives, cleavers, herbs and spices, wines, and all the essentials. But so very clean. I can still remember the scent of fresh asparagus, strawberries, onions, and wonderful green lettuce with droplets of water.

The guest rooms are quite "cottagey" and have beautiful bright colors. It's really a wonderful place to wake up in the morning with the windows open to the garden; I could lie abed and look at the swooping swallows.

Distances in this part of France are not very great and it would be possible to enjoy a two- or three-night stay here at this lovely little inn and tour the nearby scenic areas such as the Camargue, the city of Arles, where van Gogh found the kind of light and atmosphere that inspired him, and even venture a day trip to Avignon and possibly Marseille.

LA REGALIDO (Relais et Chateaux), 13990 Fontvieille. Tel.: (90) 97-62-01. A 14-guestroom very comfortable village inn in a pleasant town, 717 km. from Paris. Exceptional gardens. Wheelchair access. Van Gogh country. A very short drive to the nearby city of Arles. Closed late Nov. to mid-Jan. Lunch and dinner served. Rates: See Index.

Directions: Fontvieille is just north of Arles. La Regalido is on the main street. Detailed map 83.

RÉSIDENCES LE PETIT NICE
Marseille

I would take it that this hotel, being a member of Relais et Chateaux, is one of the deluxe accommodations in Marseille. I have included another in the same basic area, but probably a little less pricey.

As shown in the sketch, it sits right on the rocky shore of the Mediterranean, looking out over the harbor past a Roman lighthouse.

Le Petit Nice has the same very elegant air and atmosphere in its public rooms that I've seen in the grand hotels in Nice. The dining room has a sweeping view of the harbor and every table is placed so that diners may enjoy the sunset and the view of the harbor lights. There are marble floors, handsome chandeliers, elegant furniture, and extremely coordinated panels of wallpaper. The lounge that precedes it is furnished ornately in a turn-of-the-century manner with a little Art Nouveau added.

I can't speak for all the guest rooms, but mine was not particularly well decorated and it had none of the extras that I had come to expect of members of the Relais et Chateaux. It was quite a contrast, for example, to La Regalido in Fontvieille, where I had spent the previous night—but that was something exceptional. (The hotel brochure, on the other hand, shows very elegant bedchambers. Perhaps I got the one that needed decorating. Unfortunately, I left too early in the morning to see others.)

The location of this hotel is indeed special and it is possible to gaze out over the sea literally for hours, watching the fascinating harbor traffic in this extremely busy French port. There are many transatlantic and Mediterranean cruise ships, fishing boats, oil tankers, almost, it seems, within touching distance.

As far as I can determine there is no other hotel in Marseille that has such an intimacy with the water.

For dinner I enjoyed the bouillabaisse, although I have learned that bouillabaisse can be exceptional in even the most humble of waterfront restaurants. I had portions of two desserts; the chocolate mousse, a specialty of the house, was delicious to say the least, and the black currant sorbet had just the right touch of tartness about it. After dinner I wandered for a moment through the garden, which was dramatically lit by strategically placed floodlights, and stood a long time on the parapet, looking out past the lighthouse to the sea.

RÉSIDENCES LE PETIT NICE et Marina Maldormé (Relais et Chateaux), off Corniche J. F. Kennedy, 13007 Marseille. Tel.: (91) 52-14-39. A quiet, secluded seaside luxury hotel. Closed Jan. Conveniently located for all of the attractions, gardens, cathedrals, galleries, parks, and other Marseille attractions. Rates: See Index.

Directions: These directions also serve basically to get to Résidence Bompard, which follows. I came into Marseille on the A-7 and left it at the exit for Vieux Port. Continue to a fork in the road and follow the one on the left marked "Juliet." This leads through the tunnel and emerges on the Corniche J. F. Kennedy. Follow this road, which eventually leads into the business district, and after about a mile, during which time the sea is on the right and frustration on the left, there will be a small sign for Le Petit Nice on the right, down an alley. Turn down to the end of the alley and you'll see parking for Le Petit Nice. My suggestion is that you leave your car in the parking space and use a cab for any further driving.

L'HOTEL BOMPARD
Marseille

This was another good find. It was recommended to me by some people I met during the two weeks I had been traveling in France, and along with Le Petit Nice it has the symbol in *Michelin* that means "very quiet and secluded." On a hill in a pleasant little park in the residential section of the city, L'Hotel Bompard has a small garden and a very attractive terrace where one can enjoy the flowering plants and trees and singing birds. The guest rooms are pleasant and appropriately furnished.

Breakfast is offered, but there is no lunch or dinner. I think it would be an agreeable and less expensive alternative to Le Petit Nice, and apparently there is no parking problem. There are bungalows on the grounds that have fully equipped kitchens.

The manager recommended a bouillabaisse restaurant that has a spectacular view of the harbor and, although I did not have an evening meal there, I was quite impressed with the general atmosphere. The name of this restaurant is Le Rhul and it is located at the turning point on the Corniche J. F. Kennedy.

L'HOTEL BOMPARD, 2 Rue des Flots Bleus, 13007 Marseille. Tel.: (91) 52-10-93. A 47-guestroom very quiet hotel, about 5 min. from the hustle and bustle of the Corniche J. F. Kennedy. Convenient to all of the Marseille attractions and activities. Rates: See Index.

Directions: Follow directions already given for Le Petit Nice but, instead of turning right at sign for Le Petit Nice on Corniche J. F. Kennedy, go just a short distance farther and look on the left for Le Rhul restaurant. Turn left and proceed up the hill; do not be dismayed because it is a very narrow street. If you get lost at the top of the hill ask a friendly passant *and you will discover how close you are to La Résidence Bompard.*

YOU ARE ARRIVING IN PARIS . . .

The traveler to Paris will find it most useful to know which of the two Paris airports, Charles de Gaulle or Orly, is his or her destination.

Charles de Gaulle

There are two terminals: Aerogare I is used for foreign airlines and Aerogare II is for Air France. Aeorgare I has seven satellite buildings and passengers use moving walkways. Aeorgare II, with typical Gallic practicality, is much simpler with only a short walk between the gates and passport control.

There are no porters at French airports, but carts are available at both airports. If it is necessary to deplane at Charles de Gaulle and go to one of the two Orly terminals, Air France buses leave every thirty minutes from Gate 36. One should allow at least an hour and a half. There are free shuttle buses between the two Charles de Gaulle terminals.

Getting to the city: Air France buses leave every twenty minutes for Porte Maillot. Other buses (350) go to Gare de L'Est, and bus (351) goes to Nation. These leave every thirty minutes, and the trip takes about an hour.

A taxi ride takes about half an hour and will run between fifteen and twenty dollars. It can be worth it if it's your first trip.

There is also a train from the Roissy-Rail Station, reached by bus from Charles de Gaulle, and it goes to Gare du Nord and the Chatelet,

Luxembourg, Port Royal, and Denfert-Rochereau stations. The fare is about four dollars.

Be sure to take notice of the landmarks at the terminals so that you will recognize them upon your departure. Air France coaches leave every twenty minutes for Charles de Gaulle I and every fifteen minutes for Charles de Gaulle II. The bus terminal is in the basement of the Palais de Congrès at Porte Maillot. Allow an hour to be on the safe side.

Orly

There are two terminals at Orly: Orly Sud (south) and Orly Ouest (west). These are connected by shuttle buses. The west terminal is used for French domestic flights; the south terminal for everything else. Use the green-light line if you have nothing to declare.

Carts, but no porters, at Orly.

Air France buses leave from Orly Sud to the Invalides Terminal every twelve minutes from Exit I. The cost is about four dollars. Bus 215 at Exit D goes to Place Denfert-Rochereau, on the south side of Paris, and costs about a dollar.

It's O.K. to take the rides that are being hawked by the free-lance taxis, but vehicles in the well-organized taxi line are supervised by the police. The cab to the Opéra from Orly Sud will run about sixteen dollars. You should figure on a ten percent tip plus the luggage cost, which is nominal.

Air France coaches to Orly Sud and Orly Ouest leave Les Invalides every ten minutes. It's a short ride by comparison, but still allow an hour.

North Sea

NETHERLANDS

• ANTWERP

BRUGES
• Keerbergen

GENT   BRUSSELS
• Hasselt-Stevoort

Maarkedal

LIEGE
Fraineux • •
Villers-le-Temple •   Spa •

Comblain-la-Tour
• Durbuy

Lisogne •
• DINANT   • La Roche-
en-Ardenne

Couvin •

Noirefontaine

FRANCE   Corbion •
• Herbeumont
• Martué-Florenville

LUXEMBOURG

Belgium

INNS AND LOCATIONS
BRUGES, Hotel de Orangerie, 206
BRUGES, Hotel de Tuilerieen, 208
BRUGES, Hotel Prinsenhof, 205
COMBLAIN-LA-TOUR, Hostellerie St. Roch, 228
CORBION, Hotel des Ardennes, 217
COUVIN, Au Petit Chef, 212
DURBUY, Le Sanglier des Ardennes, 225
FRAINEUX, Domaine du Chateau de Fraineux, 229
HASSELT-STEVOORT, Scholteshof, 234
HERBEUMONT, Hostellerie du Prieuré de Conques, 219
KEERBERGEN, Hostellerie Berkenhof, 201
LA ROCHE-EN-ARDENNE, Le Vieux Chateau, 223
LISOGNE, Le Moulin de Lisogne, 221
MAARKEDAL, Hostellerie Shamrock, 210
MARTUÉ FLORENVILLE, Hostellerie du Vieux Moulin, 218
NOIREFONTAINE, Moulin Hideux, 215
SPA, Manoir de Lebioles, 232
VILLERS-LE-TEMPLE, La Commanderie, 230

TRAVEL SUGGESTIONS FOR BELGIUM

How to Get There

Sabena Airlines and Pan Am, as well as most major airlines, fly from North America to Brussels, most with a stopover en route. Eurailpass is good in Belgium.

Introduction to Belgium

For such a small country (about the size of Maryland), Belgium is amazingly diverse. The two main languages, French and Dutch, are divided fairly equally, with Dutch spoken in the north (Flanders) and French in the south (Wallonia).

In the tourist areas, English is widely spoken. I had a few encounters where my fractured French and some serious sign language had to be employed. My exchanges with Dutch-speaking inhabitants were confined, of necessity, to repeating names of towns or streets or pointing to my map. A smattering of French or a French phrase book will usually get you by in most of the country. Belgians are a friendly people and I always found them eager to be helpful.

Belgium is a land of flowers, castles, museums, festivals, processions, fascinating art cities, quaint country villages, and ever-changing scenery. It is especially known for its handmade lace and tapestries, and let us not forget its chocolate. A peculiarly Flemish phenomenon are the beguinages. *They are tiny communities begun in the Middle Ages for women who wanted to retreat from the world but were unwilling to take full vows as nuns. They are still occupied by women, many of whom make Belgium's beautiful handmade lace.*

I was particularly struck by the vast panoramas with almost 360-degree vistas of rolling countryside, green fields interrupted here and there by strips of forest, and little villages in the distance with church spires rising on the horizon. There are always clouds of some kind and they make the sunsets incredibly theatrical. More than once I simply had to stop and watch the magnificent show.

On this trip I concentrated on the Ardennes, with a few stops in the areas around Brussels and in Bruges. The Ardennes (a familiar name to those acquainted with World War II), is one of the loveliest forest regions in the world. Brussels, with its resplendent 12th-century Grand Place and magnificent architecture, is not only the capital of Belgium, but is considered the capital of Europe, containing the headquarters of the European Economic Community. Bruges is an enchanting, tiny, centuries-old city that in some respects seems to have been frozen in time but is actually experiencing an interesting renaissance. Belgium is very much of the 20th century; however, I have chosen to emphasize the historical and art treasures rather than its many and varied modern accomplishments.

If you would like to be on hand for the many festivals, processions, fairs, and other events that take place throughout the year, write to the Belgium Tourist Office, 745 Fifth Avenue, New York, NY 10151, telephone: 212-758-8130, or visit the tourist offices in the towns. They are called Syndicats d'Initiative.

The climate in Belgium is comparatively mild, if unpredictable. Even summers can be somewhat cool, so it is wise for the ladies to have a sweater or wrap.

Country Inns in Belgium

Wherever I went in Belgium I found a dedication to hospitality and service of the highest order. In some places, the tradition of innkeeping had been carried on by the same family for generations.

There are myriad small and inviting hotels throughout the country, and the ones I visited were sometimes in busy towns or small, quiet villages or tucked away in the remote countryside. I found them in converted mills, castles, abbeys, mansions, and farmhouses, as well as in inns that had been dispensing hospitality for centuries.

Although they all have individual touches and some are more European than others, the comforts and conveniences they offer are quite standardized. Nearly all guest rooms contain telephones and color television along with the omnipresent small amenities. Some have the added luxuries of well-stocked minibars, remote TV controls, clock radios, magnifying mirrors, hair dryers, and the like.

The attention and care given to dining room decor is universal—I saw some superb dining rooms. Chefs have become very important in Belgium; in fact, there are several books listing the premier chefs of Belgium and seven of those renowned chefs are included in this book. They are nearly all owner-chefs, and as such, have little time to spend with their guests, although most of them have several assistant chefs.

Myriad walking trails thread most of the country and nearly every hotel has maps outlining the trails in their area. I found a much greater tolerance for children than in their American counterparts. I was also a bit surprised to find that many places accept pets also.

Reservations

Your travel agent can help you with making reservations, or you can call directly if you want to discuss your accommodations in detail. It is also possible to reserve rooms through the Belgian Tourist Office. Call 011-32-223-05029.

According to government regulations a list of room rates must be displayed in each room. Rates in Belgium include taxes and gratuities (service) and no additional tipping is necessary, although extra services might warrant some small remuneration.

In nearly all the inns and hotels included here, dinner is obligatory with an overnight stay, although you are politely asked if you would like to make a reservation for dinner. This should pose no hardship, since an important reason for staying at these places is the superb meals.

Dinners without wine range roughly between $25 and $65, with adjustments for fluctuation in the exchange rates. When making reservations, remember that the quoted rate at the time you make your reservation may be less or more than at the time it is billed, because of fluctuations in the currency. Something else to consider in planning your itinerary is many small hotels' practice of being closed sometimes two or three days during the week.

Car Rentals

See the section "Renting a Car for Europe" in the front of the book. Car rentals are available everywhere.

Driving is probably the best way to see the country, although the railway system is the densest in the world and there is frequent and efficient rail service to almost all parts of the country.

Driving Tips

The roads are excellent and well signposted; however, most traffic signs are in symbols, and some are a little obscure as to their meaning. I was glad to have a map that included an explanation of them. One of the etiquettes of driving in Belgium, indeed in all of Europe, is to stay in the right lane, except to pass, and always to signal when you move from one lane to another. Americans are very lax about this, a fact that is of some annoyance to Europeans.

Because of the two languages, towns and streets often have both

Dutch and French names. It is well not only to have a bilingual map, but also to be aware of both names of towns you are headed for, particularly in the northern part of Belgium. Here are some of the double names:

Brussels—Bruxelles, Brussel
Bruges—Brugge
Antwerp—Antwerpen, Anvers
Liege—Luik, Luttich
Ghent—Gent, Gand
Mons—Bergen
Tournai—Doornik

It is interesting to see the number of English words that are used in various businesses: "dancing," "camping," "shopping center," "car wash," "self-service." Nearly all gas stations are self-service, and they are often run by women. On secondary roads and highways, it is not always easy to find a gas station open on the weekends. Remember that gas is sold by the liter, which is little more than a quart.

I find the secondary routes and back roads more interesting than the main highways. If you're not in a hurry, driving through the little villages and towns can be a lot of fun, and the countryside is lovely. Sometimes it is necessary to stop and ask directions. This is a wonderful way to practice your French or, in the north, your Dutch.

Dining in Belgium

The dining rooms and restaurants of the hotels and inns I visited mainly offered haute, or basically French, cuisine. There were usually two or three set menus of varying price, along with a wide range of à la carte offerings.

While I was there in the fall, every restaurant featured gibiers, or game, and the menus offered all sorts of treatments of cheuvreuil (venison), canard sauvage (wild duck), pigeonneau (pigeon), lièvre (hare), and other game dishes, along with a wide variety of appetizers, fish, lobster, beef, veal, and lamb.

As previously mentioned, some Belgian chefs have gained national prominence, and their menus reflect great pride in the quality and distinction of the food. I have not tried to duplicate the rather lengthy descriptions of various dishes and would suggest, if you have the opportunity, that you look up the French words for fruits and vegetables and herbs and seasonings.

I found the presentation of food always artistic, and the service, whether presided over by a maitre d'hotel with a squad of waiters or *by the proprietor and one waitress, was always impeccably professional and somewhat dramatic. I was particularly impressed by the sense of style displayed by even the youngest busboys, who, interestingly enough, all seemed to assist with serving, too.*

I was a little surprised that in nearly all of these very beautiful and elegant rooms, some of them in a former abbey or castle, where the decor was of a rather sober, conservative nature, the background music was invariably the sort of innocuous forties American pop usually referred to as elevator music.

Although the cuisine seemed to me to be French, the Belgians assured me that they have developed their own distinctive gastronomy.

In order to find the truly Belgian specialties, I think it is necessary to go to restaurants patronized by the local inhabitants. There you will find a variety of beer-based dishes (Belgium is famous for its beers), such as sea pike cooked in Gueuze, eel or mussels cooked à la Breughel, or potage aux garçons brasseurs (a soup made with beer, ham, bacon, turnips, lentils, leeks, and tomatoes). Some other specialties are canard des maraichers (caramelized roast duck served with fresh spring vegetables), goose liver paté à la Namuroise, trileye (a cold soup with a gingerbread crumb base), or veal à la Liègeoise, made with juniper berries. Waterzooi is a Flemish kind of soup made with fish, chicken, or eel, along with leeks and oysters.

Everywhere in Belgium you will see the sign "Fritures" or "Frites"—it appears that Belgians are very fond of french fries. Desserts, especially the chocolate confections, are tantalizing. Do try the tarts and waffles, as well as the wonderful fancy breads. And there are many delicious local fromages (cheeses).

BRUSSELS

Any description of Brussels starts with the Grand Place, or Grote Markt, which is certainly the most splendid town square I've ever seen.

It was my good fortune to meet a very pleasant young fellow who decided to go with me to see that I didn't lose my way. I had actually been asking for directions to a bookstore with English books, and in the process, he guided me to the Grand Place. He was clearly very proud of his city. This great cobblestoned square is bordered by 17th-century guild houses, the town hall, and the Maison du Roi, with stunningly carved and gilded facades. The square was filled with colorful flowers being offered by myriad vendors, and there were outdoor cafes on the edge of the square, where a happy crowd was sipping coffee or beer and enjoying the view.

There are handsome palaces and cathedrals, French-style boulevards, majestic state buildings, and heroic statuary. The most famous statue, however, is the small **Manneken Pis**, of a cherubic boy who sends a thin stream of water into the fountain. He's known as the "oldest citizen of Brussels." Among the seventy museums is the Museum of Fine Arts, which contains one of the finest collections of old masters in the world.

For complete information on Brussels, including a schedule of the festivals, theater, dance performances, music concerts, and opera, ask the Belgium tourist office for brochures, particularly one titled "Key to Brussels."

Grand Place, Brussels

HOSTELLERIE BERKENHOF
Keerbergen

Jean-Pierre Koch has a buoyant, lively manner and talking with him is a lot of fun. When you combine such a positive attitude with great energy, drive, and perseverance, you have an unbeatable combination.

When Jean-Pierre and his wife, Jacqueline, built their small restaurant with a couple of rooms in what was then a woods, little did they know that in less than twenty years Hostellerie Berkenhof would become one of the top hotel-restaurants of Belgium. M. Koch is now president of the prestigious international organization Relais et Chateaux and has been one of Belgium's master chefs for many years.

In a very interesting conversation with me he described how recognition of the importance of chefs evolved. "Up until the 1960s," he said, "the maitres d'hotel were always the stars. The chefs worked back in the kitchen, and nobody knew who they were or paid any attention to them. Paul Bocuse was the first chef to gain recognition, and he brought attention to other chefs."

It's true that today Belgium's top chefs are the stars; in fact, I've seen several books listing as many as eighty chefs who are considered the best in the country. As to M. Koch's prowess in the kitchen, I will simply say that my roast lamb was done to pink perfection with a piquant mustard sauce, accompanied by a selection of broccoli, snow peas, string beans, and carrots.

I had made a simple choice from a long and sophisticated menu that featured oysters in champagne, escalope of salmon, roast pheasant, and several other tantalizing dishes.

Hostellerie Berkenhof looks very similar to the other affluent homes in the residential area surrounding it, with parklike grounds and pretty gardens. The salons and sitting rooms have a fairy-tale elegance, decorated by Jacqueline Koch in soft mauves and pale pinks, with ceiling and window draperies of crinkly silk taffeta and Louis XV furnishings. A small fire was glowing in the carved marble fireplace of one cozy sitting room and large windows looked out on a garden. M. Koch pointed out several original oil paintings done in the style of the old masters.

The lounge has a more masculine feeling, with cocoa velour upholstery on the easy chairs and a massive antique bar that the Kochs found in an ancient cafe.

The guest rooms are perfectly charming, with pretty floral fabrics and white-painted, French-style furnishings and paintings. Rooms are aptly named Cyclamen, Camellia, and Forsythia, and they all have a flowery, light, and airy quality.

I was impressed by the number of American signatures and comments I found in the guest book; there were many from California.

Monsieur Guido, the manager, greets guests at the door, taking their coats and generally making them feel very much at home. He was extremely helpful in explaining the best road to take into Brussels, which turned out to be a straight shot into the city.

Hostellerie Berkenhof, only a few miles from the airport, makes an excellent first or last stop in Belgium, and it is strategically located for easy trips to Brussels, Antwerp, and several special towns, like Mechelen, Lier, and Louvain.

HOSTELLERIE BERKENHOF (Relais et Chateaux), 5 Valkeniersdreef, 2850 Keerbergen. Tel.: 015-23-48-03 or 23-48-47. Telex: 25703 Berhof. An 8-guestroom with 2 suites (private bathrooms) luxurious and homelike hotel-restaurant in an affluent residential area, equidistant from Brussels and Antwerp, approx. 10 km. southeast of Mechelen. European plan. Dinner served to travelers. Closed 3rd week of Nov.; Dec. 20 to Feb. 9; Sun., Mon., and Tues. weekly. Tennis, golf, horseback riding, nature walks, and an abundance of historical and cultural attractions in Brussels, Antwerp, and other towns nearby. Jacqueline and Jean-Pierre Koch, Proprietors.

Directions: From Brussels, take the road to Haacht and watch for signs to Keerbergen and the hotel.

ANTWERP, LOUVAIN, MECHELEN, AND LIER

In addition to Brussels, Keerbergen is within an easy drive of Antwerp, Louvain, and Mechelen, all of which have many points of historical and cultural interest. Antwerp is a flourishing modern metropolis and world port with a rich heritage of art. It has all the attractions of a large city, including a huge zoo, museum, famous puppet theater, and many magnificent historic buildings. Several of the paintings of Rubens, a native son, can be seen in the great Notre Dame cathedral and the Church of St. Jacques.

Louvain has particular interest as the home of the oldest university (1425) in the Low Countries and the library, destroyed in wars and reconstructed twice, where Erasmus studied and lectured and Sir Thomas More printed his classic Utopia. *The wonderful ornate stone lacework of the Town Hall is adorned with 236 statues.*

Thousand-year-old Mechelen is famous for its chiming bells and its tapestry weaving mill. There are also some Rubens works in the Church of St. John and the Church of Our Lady. The splendid main square is surrounded by 13th-century buildings and a Gothic cathedral. Mechelen hosts an international folklore festival, which I understand is quite spectacular.

Don't overlook Lier and its enchanting Beguinage, with colorful little picture-book houses lining narrow cobbled streets. A curiosity is the astronomical clock on the Zimmer Tower.

BRUGES

Here is a jewel of a city in which the student of history or architecture or romance can revel. From the 11th to the 17th centuries, Bruges was the richest, mightiest, and loveliest city in northern Europe. Then the gradual silting of the Zwin River, caused by storms and currents in the North Sea, brought the prosperous ocean trade from all corners of the world to a stop. Bruges became a forgotten city.

Great Flemish artists, artisans, and craftsmen flourished in Bruges, as their many magnificent guildhouses testify. Today, Bruges is practically a museum of historic buildings, with wonderful examples of Romanesque, Gothic, Renaissance, and Baroque architecture. The Gruuthuse Museum is considered the finest medieval palace in Belgium.

There were sightseers galore in and around the old town square, and I was among the many who roamed about, map in hand. Walking through the narrow, winding, cobbled streets of the old section is fascinating. The great market square (Markt) is the center of activity, and everyone uses the 13th-century belfry as a reference point. Soaring over 250 feet above the town, its forty-nine bells have been tolling messages for the Brugeois for centuries and still perform carillon concerts to this day. If you're up to the climb, the view from the parapet is breathtaking.

I can't begin to mention all the beauties of Bruges, but perhaps most famous are the six miniature paintings by Hans Memling, along with his exquisite Ursula shrine in the Memling Museum in the Hospital of St. John and Michelangelo's white marble Madonna in the Church of Our Lady. But there are many examples in the several museums of the great Flemish masters, such as Breughel, Van Eyck, and Van der Goes, along with stunning examples of the art of sculptors, goldsmiths, tapestry makers, lacemakers, potters, cabinetmakers and others.

One of the most beautiful of Belgium's beguinages is here in Bruges. Encircled and criss-crossed by canals, Bruges has been called the "Venice of the north." A very nice way to see the sights is by boat, and there are all sorts of boat tours.

There are various festivals and processions throughout the year, not the least of which is the important Flanders Music Festival. This international festival is held in other Flemish cities, and continues from spring through the fall.

Restaurants in Bruges

After a packed Sunday of sightseeing and looking at hotels, I found that the restaurants I wanted to try were closed on Sunday night, and I made an unfortunate choice of a small, nearby place that didn't please

*me. However, although I have not eaten at the following places, they
have been highly recommended.*

De Snippe, 53 Nieuwe Gentweg; 050-33-70-70
In an ancient mansion, extremely elegant—haute cuisine

Vasquez, 38 Zilverstraat; 050-34-08-45
*A 1468 house built by a steward of Isabella of Portugal—haute
cuisine*

Restaurant 't Begijntje, 11 Walstraat; 050-33-00-89
A small restaurant with interesting regional specialties

Sint-Amandskelder, Sint-Amandsstrat 11; 050-33-50-06
Specializing in fish and game in season

*Cafe Restaurant Breydel-de Coninck, 24 Breidelstraat;
050-33-97-46*
The place to eat mussels

Eglantier, 120 Ezelstraat; 050-33-29-46
Small, personal restaurant

't Pandreitje, Pandreitje 6; 050-33-11-90
Specialties: lobster with caviar, chicken with truffles and morels

HOTEL PRINSENHOF
Bruges

It was just dumb luck that I stumbled onto the right street in that
tumultuous traffic on the tortuously crooked and narrow streets of
Bruges. (But never fear, I obtained explicit directions for finding the
Prinsenhof.) I left my car in front of the small canopied entrance and
walked into the foyer, with its inviting and homey, very European little
sitting room on one side and registration counter on the other.

Katrien Soenen greeted me with a friendly smile and called a young
man, Thierry Lemahieu, to come and help with my bags. They both
came out to the car with me, and Thierry (''Call me Jerry,'' he said)
drove it to a parking place in back of the hotel. Parking is a major
problem in Bruges. I found these young people extremely accommodating in providing all kinds of advice on how to find my way around
this fascinating city.

I learned later that Katrien and Thierry are soon to be married, and
they will be managing the hotel, as Katrien's father, Franz Soenen,
spends less time there.

Franz is usually on the scene at breakfast, greeting guests and keeping an eye on things. He's a jovial, congenial fellow and it was fun exchanging a few jokes with him over breakfast, which includes ham and cheeses, along with cereals, fruit juice, assorted breads and rolls, and coffee, tea, or chocolate.

The cheerful dining room is done in pale peach, with a display of French Strasbourg porcelain in a gorgeous antique Dutch breakfront that belongs to Katrien's mother. A wonderful old Flemish tapestry on the wall depicts Bruges in the 15th century, with knights on prancing horses, a castle on a hill, and the famous belfry, which is still standing.

The Prinsenhof was a private house until 1985, when the Soenen family turned it into a hotel. The guest rooms are very nicely decorated and the modern bathrooms are immaculately clean and complete in every respect, even to towel warmers.

On the hotel's quiet side street there is no traffic noise, which partially accounts for its listing in the Relais du Silence.

Friendliness and comfort are some other reasons for its inclusion in this special organization. I think the Prinsenhof has all three attributes in abundance, and I would add yet another: a very European atmosphere.

HOTEL PRINSENHOF (Relais du Silence), Ontvangersstraat 9, 8000 Bruges 1. Tel.: 050-34-26-90. Telex: 81315 Prins B. A 16-guestroom (private baths) in-town hotel on a quiet side street a few blocks from the center of historic Bruges. Breakfast only meal served. Familie Soenen-Vandeputte, Innkeepers. Rates: See Index.

Directions: In Bruges, follow signs to Center; just before the tunnel, turn right (do not go in tunnel) and continue to large square with fountain in middle. Turn right at Zuidzandstraat and continue to St. Salvator's Cathedral on the right. Take first street on left (Zilverstraat) passing Restaurant Vasquez. Continue to end of street, making a left turn, and another left turn onto Noordzandstraat. Take first street on right (Prinsenhof) which brings you to the old residence of the Dukes of Burgundy. Turn left and continue to the end of the street, turning right on Ontvangersstraat to the front entrance of the hotel. (Your car will be parked for you in the back of the hotel.)

HOTEL DE ORANGERIE
Bruges

What could be more romantic than a room overlooking the Dyver, one of Bruges's loveliest canals? Well, possibly one overlooking a charming, pocket-sized inner courtyard garden. Both alternatives are possible at the Orangerie, once a 16th-century monastery and later an aristocratic private residence.

Beatrice Strubbe-Geeraert, blond and vivacious, sat with me at a little table in the reception area, which looked out through a plate glass window at the courtyard garden. A palm tree gave the tiny garden a tropical air. A metal spiral staircase swirled around to the first and second balconies, where planters filled with greenery, white plaster walls, a red-tiled roof, and tall windows with louvered shutters emphasized the tropical effect. It was a surprising discovery in this city of cobblestone streets and tightly packed medieval buildings.

Beatrice told me that she, her sister, Christine Geeraert, and her husband, Dirk Strubbe, had converted this private house into a hotel in 1984. They remodeled it, keeping the Flemish architecture in the public rooms, installing an elevator, and completely modernizing the guest rooms and bathrooms. Some of the guest rooms have the original exposed beams in the ceilings, and one room I saw had a raised-hearth brick fireplace. They are all nicely furnished and replete with all the modern conveniences.

The dining room and salon overlook the canal through high mullioned windows. The tall black marble fireplace in the dining room is a replica of the one in Rubens's house in Antwerp, and the fireplace in the salon is equally interesting, with heavy, twisted wood pillars. I thought I detected some Spanish influence in the wrought iron chandeliers and beamed ceilings, but Beatrice assured me that the decor was entirely Flemish. Antique Flemish tapestries decorate the paneled walls, along with some striking surrealist paintings by Delvaux. The mixture of antique and modern furnishings gives the rooms a pleasing eclectic feeling.

Breakfast is usually served in the dining room, but you can have it in your room if you like, or on fine days between June and September, on the terrace, watching the ducks paddling about and the boats puttputting by.

Breakfast usually includes slices of ham and cheese, along with orange juice, croissants, and coffee.

This ivy-covered building on the Dyver canal is right in the center of town, just two blocks from the historic Market Square.

HOTEL DE ORANGERIE, Kartuizerinnestraat 10, B-8000 Bruges. Tel.: 050-34-16-49. Fax: 050-33-30-16-16. Telex: Orange 82443. A 20-guestroom (private baths) in-town hotel on the Dyver canal in the center of historic Bruges. Breakfast only meal served. Open year-round. Swimming, sauna, and solarium available at Tuilerieen. Inquire about off-street parking. Beatrice Strubbe-Geeraert, Manager. Rates: See Index.

Directions: Entering Bruges, follow signs to Markt (the market square). On the square, take the Wollestraat, on the right of the belfry tower, and continue 2 blocks to Kartuizerinnenstraat on the right.

HOTEL DE TUILERIEEN
Bruges

When the Strubbe-Geeraert families realized that they were running out of rooms at the Orangerie and that they really had to do something about the parking problem, opening another hotel seemed the obvious thing to do. While Beatrice and I were looking out the window at the Orangerie, she pointed out the building across the canal, a 17th-century private residence that became available for sale just at the right moment. The Strubbe-Geeraerts bought it and converted it into a very elegant modern hotel. It had been open for only a month when I was there in October 1988.

Everything is brand new, and the guest rooms and tiled bathrooms all have that sparkling, right-out-of-the-bandbox look. The color scheme is shades of blue throughout. Carpeting, bedspreads, padded headboards, upholstery, and draperies are in serene, soft gray-blues. The furniture is contemporary and smart, with pretty ceramic lamps, nice watercolors, comfortable settees and easy chairs, and full-length mirrors. Rooms are all completely equipped; those on the third floor are interesting, with windows in the slanted ceilings. You can look out over the rooftops of the town.

The dining room is more traditional and very elegant, with marbleized pillars, a marble floor, a crystal chandelier, and a tall fireplace. This room is done in shades of peach and burnt orange, with cashmere draperies framing the tall windows. Breakfast is served here.

The large indoor pool can become more of an outdoor pool when the windows and ceiling are opened. There is also a Jacuzzi, a sauna, and a solarium. And I mustn't forget the off-street parking in back, which is so important in Bruges, and which really started the little seed that eventually blossomed into this fine hotel.

HOTEL DE TUILERIEEN, Dyver 7, 8000 Bruges. Tel.: 050-34-36-91. Fax: 050-34-04-00. Telex: Orange 82443. A 25-guestroom (private baths) in-town hotel on the Dyver canal in the center of historic Bruges. Breakfast only meal served. Open year-round. Swimming, sauna, Jacuzzi, solarium on premises. Off-street parking. Famille Strubbe, Innkeepers. Rates: See Index.

Directions: Entering Bruges, follow signs to Markt. At the market place, go on the right of the belfry tower to Wollestraat, continuing over the bridge to Dyver Street and turn right to No. 7.

GHENT, TOURNAI, AND OUDENAARDE

Although Ghent is an active industrial city with a modern port and the capital of Flanders, for architectural antiquities it has no equal in Belgium. In the old, or inner, town there is no match for the view from St. Michael's bridge, leading from the Grass Quay to the Wheat Quay, looking east. There is 1,000-year-old St. Nicholas, the forty-four-bell Gothic belfry, the flamboyant Town Hall, a row of 17th-century guild houses, and St. Bavo, where one of the half-dozen greatest master-pieces of the world resides: the polyptych The Adoration of the Mystic Lamb *by the Van Eyck brothers. The largest of the beguinages in Belgium is found in Ghent.*

A certain amount of hunting is necessary to track down all of the riches in this historic art city.

Flower markets, the Flanders Festival, puppet theaters, open-air dramas, and boat tours on the canals are a few of the possibilities for entertainment.

A procession commemorating those who died in a plague has been held every September since 1090 in Tournai. It was an important industrial center in Roman times and is the cradle of the Frankish kings. As the second oldest town in Belgium (after Tongeren) it has some of the oldest townhouses in Europe. The 12th-century Cathedral of Notre

Castle of the Counts

Dame has been called the most remarkable example of Romanesque architecture in the Western world. It contains a spectacular collection of paintings. A little southeast of Tournai is the beautiful Beloeil castle, with its 300 acres of formal gardens and Neptune fountain decorating the great Neptune pool.

Oudenaarde, as the birthplace of tapestry making, is another art city of considerable importance. Be sure to see the tapestries in the council chamber of the splendid Town Hall and the tapestry museum in the Cloth Hall.

HOSTELLERIE SHAMROCK
Maarkedal

I felt as if I were sitting in the salon of some Indian or Persian potentate, but Claude DeBeyter, with his elfin grin and twinkling eyes, assured me that this in reality had been the home of an English baron. Of course, I thought, this little carved, painted, arched, and domed salon was a very British reference to the scope of their Empire. When this beautiful manor house was built in 1928, the empire was probably at the very meridian of its power.

The house was patterned after the style of the famous English architect Edwin Luytens, and Claude tells me that only recently they have been laying out the gardens in the manner of Gertrude Jekyll, a leading English landscape designer of the last century. Shamrock feels very much like an English country house hotel.

Livine DeBeyter, in her gracious way, showed me two perfectly

superb guest rooms that had not yet been occupied by incoming guests. The feeling here is eclectic and sophisticated. Draperies and matching bedspreads are of heavy fabrics in subdued floral prints and there are massive antique armoires and modern Scandinavian-style built-in cabinets in light woods. But everything goes well together. The rooms are spacious, with high ceilings and tall windows looking out over lawns and gardens. All the guest rooms are entered through two doors, an inner and an outer door, both lockable, and there are hidden safes in each room along with all manner of other conveniences.

The bathrooms are nothing short of fabulous—mine had a hardwood floor, a long marble counter with double sinks and a wide mirror over it, a floor-to-ceiling mirror on one wall, a telephone, and a bathtub with a body shower and an overhead shower. There was a tall, narrow window at one end looking out on the park. Lighting came from ceiling spotlights that created a dramatic effect. The bathrooms are totally modern and incredibly pristine. I'll have to confess, I was frankly in love with mine.

I very much liked the art throughout the house, which was mostly contemporary, with some fine pastels and gouaches, along with a group of interesting collages by Kelly in the little Persian salon and a couple of good reproductions of Miro.

Claude takes a very personal interest in his dinner guests, conferring with them over their menu choices. I was fascinated at the way he made several trips back and forth between the kitchen and the table of one couple who had evidently requested some rather complicated dish. Claude is listed as one of the master chefs of Belgium. I suppose I missed my chance for a delightful gastronomic adventure, but I limited myself to a lamb cutlet and asked him if I could have an extra helping of vegetables. The lamb was tender and flavorful, with a wonderful sauce, accompanied by a mixture of zucchini and tomatoes and a side dish of potatoes au gratin, which had just a hint of a golden, crispy crust and were delicious.

I regret that I wasn't able to sample more fully the arts of these master chefs of Belgium, but in my case, discretion is the watchword. If you want to have a conference with Claude, I suggest you get down to dinner shortly after seven, because it becomes very busy later and he doesn't have time to leave the kitchen.

My impression of Shamrock is that it is top drawer in every respect. Everything is done with great taste and style, and the feeling is of being a guest in a private home—there is practically no printed material in sight, other than a discreet folder on the bedside table with many suggestions for diversions. This is a place where you can relax and feel pampered.

HOSTELLERIE SHAMROCK (Relais et Chateaux), Ommegangstraat 148, Muziekbos, B-9681 Maarkedal. Tel.: 055-21-55-29. Telex: 86165. A 6-guestroom (private baths) luxurious country house hotel and restaurant in a residential/farming area in the Flemish Ardennes about 30 min. south of Ghent. European plan. Breakfast, lunch, and dinner served to travelers. Closed mid- to late July; Sun. eve. thru Tues. lunch weekly. Golf and tennis at Oudenaarde Country Club and sightseeing in the historic and fascinating art cities of Tournai, Ghent, Oudenaarde, and Beloeil nearby. Bruges is 45 min. and Brussels is 1 hr. away. No pets. Livine and Claude DeBeyter, Proprietors. Rates: See Index.

Directions: From Brussels, take N-8 to N-60 south. Do not turn at sign for Maarkedal, but continue until the turn-off for Muziekbos, to the left. Take this road for about 5 km. to Shamrock.

COUVIN

Couvin was built around and on top of rock cliffs, with a canal flowing through its center. Deep within those rocks are two impressive caves, the Caves of Neptune and the Caves of Abime. In the small, picturesque town of Chimay, nearby, is the Renaissance-style chateau of the Princes of Chimay. Paradoxically, Chimay is also on a car-racing circuit.

AU PETIT CHEF
Couvin

Suddenly, I was aware of a slight movement on the black velvet chair, and then I saw blazing yellow cat eyes looking at me. I realized that a black cat, nearly invisible on the black velvet chair, was washing itself. ''That's Mischka,'' laughed Nadine Dassy, a sleek, smartly dressed lady. I had been admiring the bar in the very sophisticated little lounge. Antoine Dassy explained that it was made of anodized aluminum. The highly polished, marbleized, tortoise-shell finish and the way it was lit gave it a most dramatic effect. It is the most spectacular bar I've seen and could easily be described as a piece of modern sculpture.

The lounge is small and intimate, with a round, raised-hearth fireplace, glass-topped tables with metal, bamboo-style legs, small black velvet chairs, and a medieval tapestry on the cream-colored wall.

There are several dramatic touches at Au Petit Chef. One wall of the dining room has a tall lavabo in a niche with vines and other

greenery, behind which is a three-sided amber-colored mirror. The soft trickle and splash of the water provides a pleasant background note. The bright colors of a striking arrangement of gladiola on the table at one end of the room were reflected in the amber-colored mirror, which covered an entire wall.

Antoine, who is renowned as one of Belgium's master chefs, is a dapper gentleman. His English, fortunately, was somewhat better than my French, and so we were able to communicate fairly well. I was surprised to learn that the house, formerly a private residence, was only about twenty years old. Several of the guest rooms have wonderful, ancient-looking hand-hewn beams and posts, and I had assumed it was a very old building.

The guest rooms have such romantic names as Tristan and Iseult, Romeo and Juliet, and Casanova. They are tucked away in corners and nooks and under the eaves and are romantically decorated in various floral wallpapers, with matching curtains and bedspreads. The bathrooms are just as varied as the rooms, some with carpeted, some with tiled, floors, and all are very nice.

M. Dassy offers a full menu, including a prix fixe dinner and à la carte dishes, and of course in the fall there are many game offerings. My sea bass with tomatoes and basil was delicious, and in response to my request for additional vegetables, I was served a side dish of nicely prepared string beans and spinach. Instead of the silver-plated dish covers under which hot dishes are usually served, Au Petit Chef has pretty porcelain domes. As I've described before, a bit of showmanship is involved in the lifting of these dish covers. It seems to be a universal rule that everyone's dish at one table must be revealed at precisely the same moment.

Au Petit Chef is on a hill above the town and has a small apple orchard in back and a patio on the side, where meals are served in nice weather. The windows of my room looked out across the front lawn to the roofs of the town and to the belfry with the clock tower. As I gazed out on this scene in the gathering dusk, the bells rang for vespers. They sounded wonderful.

AU PETIT CHEF (Relais et Chateaux), 6 Dessus la Ville, 6400 Couvin. Tel.: 060-34-41-75. A 7-guestroom (private baths) intimate chef-owned inn-restaurant on the edge of a small but busy town approx. 50 km. south of Charleroi, in the south of Belgium. European plan as well as other package plans. Dinner is obligatory with overnight stay. Lunch and dinner served to travelers. Closed Feb., Mar., 1 wk. in Sept., and Tues. and Wed. weekly. Tennis, nature walks, grottoes and caverns, horseback riding, Chimay castle nearby. Nadine and Antoine Dassy, Proprietors. Rates: See Index.

Directions: In the center of Couvin, look for sign to the inn.

BOUILLON AND THE SEMOIS VALLEY

The most direct route from Couvin to Bouillon, Noirefontaine, and the Semois Valley is via the N-5, across the French border and thence to Charleville-Mézières and Sedan and then back to Belgium and Bouillon. However, don't forget that you need a visa to enter France; I understand the French border guards are very strict about it.

The Castle of Godfrey de Bouillon, a great leader of the Crusades, is one of Belgium's marvels, one of its most important relics of the Middle Ages. This imposing medieval stronghold sits on a rocky ridge at a hairpin turn of the Semois River, a brooding presence over the ebullient holiday town below.

The Abbey of Orval, located about thirty kilometers southeast of Bouillon, was founded in 1131 by the Cistercians and became a chief center of religious learning in Europe. It has been rebuilt twice, but there remain some fascinating ruins, which are well worth a visit.

Saint Hubert is the patron saint of the Ardennes, having been converted upon seeing the sign of the cross on the antlers of a stag when he was hunting in the forest. A church and a monastery were founded in his honor in the village that bears his name, about forty kilometers northeast of Bouillon. The present Church of St. Giles is the third one erected on this exact site, and it has an impressive Basilica. Every year, in September, there is a hunting festival ceremony, with a fanfare of hunting horns, a mass, a blessing of the animals, and a parade in honor of St. Hubert.

Throughout the valley of the Semois, there is swimming and fishing and horseback riding. There are wonderful views, with many walking trails to follow through the woods and along rivers and streams— perfect spots to have a pique-nique.

MOULIN HIDEUX
Noirefontaine

I cocked a drowsy eye out my glass-paned door at the misty morning and, reluctant to leave my cozy, toasty nest, promised myself another half-hour in bed. A bit later, looking out the window at the woodsy hillside, where autumn leaves were laying down a golden carpet and birds were flitting among the branches, twittering and singing, I saw that the morning was rapidly clearing and I arose with a light heart.

When I turned on the light in the marble bathroom, the radio automatically switched on to some bouncy American big-band tunes, and then I was really wide awake.

From the door of my room, which opened out onto a little stone walk and thence onto the lawn where some pretty flowers bordered the hillside, I could see down the slope to beds of roses and other flowers. There were birch trees and a little bench for contemplating the gardens and the pond beyond, where two majestic white swans floated serenely, followed by a bevy of ducks quacking energetically.

The plantings were lovely. Even though an early frost had stricken some of the flowers, there were still many blossoms coloring the landscape in late October.

This is a really gorgeous setting. In fact, my first words when I drove across the tiny stone bridge into the grounds were "absolutely fabulous." And my next words were "Moulin Hideux—of course—'hidden mill.' " This beautiful old stone building is deep in the woods, albeit on a good paved road. A boisterous stream tumbles down the hill, creating little waterfalls alongside the hotel, and flows noisily into the pond in the front.

Until Charles Lahire's family turned the mill into a restaurant in 1946, villagers had been bringing their grain to be milled here for nearly 300 years. Charles pointed out a photograph taken in 1946, showing the dilapidated building with its thatched roof. As a boy in the 1950s Charles worked in the restaurant; he always knew he wanted to take it over some day. He and his wife, Martine, did just that in 1972.

Today, Moulin Hideux is one of the premier small hotels in Belgium, with a renowned chef and restaurant. The feeling of the old mill is still there in the dining room, with its low ceiling, heavy beams, stone walls, and deep windows with small panes, and some of the hallways and corridors remind one of the original character of the building.

Martine Lahire's decorative talent has created some luxurious and beautiful guest rooms, each with a personality all its own. One room she showed me was done in pretty pastels, while another had a bright, splashy, fabric wall covering. They all have interesting antique pieces, engaging bibelots, original paintings, and beautiful marble bathrooms. They are fully equipped with all the modern conveniences.

As is the European custom, I sat in the salon with other guests enjoying an aperitif before dinner and making my selections from the very interesting menu. My decision was easy since I confined myself to a fillet of sole à l'orange and some additional vegetables, but other guests required more involved conferences with the maitre d'.

The decor of the salon was striking. It was actually a long, enclosed porch lined with windows. The rosy hue of what had been a rough exterior wall was echoed in the sophisticated geometric print upholstery of the many lounge chairs and settees. Pink and white begonias filled the planters bordering the windows. The grounds and the waterfalls were dramatically lit to create an entrancing nighttime view.

The dining room was very vivid and gay at night, with orange and white tablecloths, candlelight, flowers, and sparkling table settings. And it was even brighter and more cheerful in the morning with sunlight streaming in the windows and a view of the pond and the trees

The little printed card that came with my breakfast suggested a game of tennis, a walk in the forest (for which there is a map showing several trails), various motor trips and sightseeing (for which there is also a map), or perhaps simply a quiet day in the sun in the garden with a leisurely lunch. Unfortunately, I could stay for none of the above, and I bid a regretful adieu to Charles (who sounds like Maurice Chevalier) and Martine Lahire, who is really delightful. They both make their guests feel very much at home.

Incidentally, I was all wrong about "hidden mill," but you'll have to ask the Lahires about that.

MOULIN HIDEUX (Relais et Chateaux), Rue de Dohan, 6831 Noirefontaine. Tel.: 061-46-70-15. Telex: 41-989. A 13-guestroom (private baths) secluded and luxurious hotel-restaurant in the Semois River valley in southeastern Belgium. European plan; dinner reservation required with overnight stay. Breakfast, lunch, and dinner served to travelers. Restaurant closed Tues. and Wed. Hotel closed Dec., Jan., and Feb. Tennis and nature walks on grounds. Hiking, swimming, horseback riding, picnicking, fishing, sightseeing nearby. Famille Lahire, Proprietors. Rates: See Index.

Directions: Noirefontaine is off Rte N-89, and the hotel is 3 km. from the town on the Rue de Dohan.

HOTEL DES ARDENNES
Corbion

The wide lawn around the side and back of the hotel sloped gently down to the wading pool and fountain, and Hedwige Maqua waved to her husband, who was hard at work cleaning the pool. "We also have a tennis court and two pétonque courts," she told me proudly. She explained that pétonque is played with heavy balls, so I'm guessing that it must be the Luxembourg version of lawn bowling.

Hedwige, her husband, and their three children are only part of the family team running this excellent village hotel. Hedwige's husband bakes the pastries and runs the restaurant, while his brother rules in the kitchen.

The day I visited, the hotel was fully occupied by hunters, and a long table, set aside for them in the very attractive dining room, was beautifully and formally arrayed with rows of wine glasses, china, silver, a snowy tablecloth, and fresh yellow roses. This was not the sort of rough and rugged setting one associates with hunters.

A glance at the menu told me that Chef Maqua followed the traditional French cuisine; however, Hedwige assured me that it was possible to ask for a more simple menu with, for instance, lamb cutlets with vegetables or a grilled steak.

This is a most pleasant and homey hotel in a small village perched on top of a steep hill. The road from Bouillon winds up through the forest, and at one lookout point near the top, the view stretches for miles across the trees to faraway hills. The guest rooms on the back of the hotel have much the same kind of panoramic view.

The guest rooms and bathrooms are all very clean and nicely furnished. There are some adjoining rooms that would work well for families.

Corbion has some claim to fame as the retreat of the French poet Paul Verlaine, who spent several months there writing in a small house beside a brook. I was intrigued by the very steep, winding streets, with houses and shops perched nonchalantly along their edges. An ancient spring in the middle of town must have been a gathering place for villagers in days of yore. The Syndicat d'Initiative of Corbion has produced an excellent brochure outlining many walks as well as motor trips to all kinds of interesting places within 100 kilometers.

HOTEL DES ARDENNES, B-6838 Corbion-sur-Semois. Tel.: 061-46-66-21 or 46-68-69. A 35-guestroom (private baths) hotel-restaurant in a picturesque hilltop village, 7 km. from Bouillon, close to the French border. European and other plans available. Breakfast, lunch, and dinner served to travelers. Closed Jan. 2 to Mar. 15. Tennis, wading pool, pétonque courts, snooker, maps for walks available on premises. Hunting, hiking, sightseeing nearby. Famille Maqua, Proprietors.

Directions: From Bouillon, follow signs to Corbion.

HOSTELLERIE DU VIEUX MOULIN
Martué Florenville

The pretty pink dining room was getting a complete cleaning, as were the sitting rooms, the day I stopped by. Chairs were stacked and pushed to one side, floors were being scrubbed, and windows polished. Nevertheless, I could see that the dining room was charming, with its low beamed ceiling and window boxes filled with flowers.

I was really pleased to find this cozy, homey little inn. It had been an 18th-century mill, and when Monsieur Filippucci led me down the stairs from the terrace, I saw that water from the Semois River rushed right by the steps into the flume of the old mill.

The green lawn and bright flowers provide a lovely setting, and tables are placed outside for guests to enjoy refreshments and the cool breezes, while listening to the low roar of the river and gazing at the bucolic view of distant fields and hills.

There are some wonderful antiques in the hallways, and the ancient tapestries, upholstery, and carpets have seen better days, but the guest rooms are bright and cheerful, with modern furniture, and the rooms I saw had modern, very clean bathrooms. All of the rooms on the back of the hotel have their own balconies overlooking the river. One room had a working fireplace, twin beds, and double basins in a marble tile counter.

The cuisine here, as everywhere, is French and includes game. I can't vouch for the food, but I would guess that it's good.

M. Filippucci doesn't speak English, so be prepared to practice your French.

HOSTELLERIE DU VIEUX MOULIN, 6821 Martué-Florenville. Tel.: 061-31-10-76. A 19-guestroom (private and shared baths) converted 18th-century mill on the Semois River in the ancient hamlet of Martué, 1 km. from Florenville on the fringe of the Ardennes. European plan and various packages available. Breakfast, lunch, and dinner served to travelers. Closed mid-Feb. to mid-March; Wed. during the week. Forest walks, fishing, riding, tennis, boating, and numerous historical and cultural attractions nearby. M. and Mme. Filippucci, Proprietors. Rates: See Index.

Directions: From Florenville, take the road to Martué and watch for sign.

HOSTELLERIE DU PRIEURÉ DE CONQUES
Herbeumont

Sitting on a rude log bench, taking in the rustle and rush of the Semois as it flowed by just a few feet down the grassy bank, looking across the water into the forest on the other side, I could well imagine some cowled monk meditating in this selfsame spot two or three centuries ago. Or, bringing me more to the present, a fisherman casting for trout, enjoying the peace and tranquillity of the moment.

I had just taken a stroll around the grounds in back of the Prieuré de Conques, past the flower beds and a very old apple orchard to one of several log benches placed along the bank of the river.

This had been a place of quiet and repose since the 7th century, when the first monastery was built here. Since then its fortunes had risen and fallen more than once. The present priory was built in 1732, abandoned for 100 years during the 1800s, and resurrected in the 1900s. Monsieur and Madame DeNaeyer bought it for their home in the 1940s and converted it into a hotel in 1963.

It's a rather odd, institutional-looking building—very long and narrow with a kind of mansard roof and a row of dormers across the front and back.

The DeNaeyers' grandchildren and some nieces and nephews were visiting the day I arrived, and walking into the reception area where there was a long table piled with a motley collection of papers and other articles, I had the impression it was a rather rumpled, informal place. Later, at tea and then at dinner, I realized that under the informality there was definitely a sense of order and organization.

Although the furnishings are formal, with velvet-covered sofas and chairs, bronze chandeliers, impressive fireplaces, and many oil paintings, Prieuré de Conques has a very lived-in quality, which also extends to the guest rooms.

A wide, winding staircase leads to the upper floors, and the halls are very wide, with handsome, heavy antique pieces. The hallway on the third floor (or second floor, as it is called), which is under the eaves, is rather spectacular, with a row of slanted spears holding the light fixtures. All of those rooms were occupied, so I was unable to see them, but I understand they are architecturally interesting, having slanted ceilings and exposed ancient posts and beams. Some of the guest rooms are brighter and more attractive than others. However, a new annex is being built in the garden a few steps from the main house, which will have six new suites. They should be in working order by the time this book is published, and everything will be brand new.

As one would expect in a Relais et Chateaux hotel, the restaurant is superior, and I enjoyed an excellent dinner. M. DeNaeyer was a cordial host, chatting with his guests and seeing to their wine glasses. I'm sorry we didn't have more time to talk; he is a very knowledgeable and interesting person. Mme. DeNaeyer, pert and petite, was friendly and helpful with suggestions about things to see and do in the area.

HOSTELLERIE DU PRIEURÉ DE CONQUES (Relais et Chateaux), 176 Rte de Florenville, B-6803 Herbeumont. Tel.: 061-41-14-17. An 11-guestroom and 6-suite (private bathrooms) converted ancient priory deep in the Semois River valley, approx. 20 km. from Bouillon. European plan; dinner obligatory. Breakfast, lunch, and dinner served to travelers. Closed Jan. and Feb. Although restaurant is usually closed on Tues. in early Mar., April, Dec., exc. Christmas and New Year's, call to confirm. Trout fishing in the Semois on grounds. Many lovely nature walks, boating, Abbaye d'Orval, July music festival at St. Hubert nearby. No pets. M. and Mme. DeNaeyer, Proprietors. Rates: See Index.

Directions: From Florenville, go through Chassepierre and Ste. Cecile, and continue on road to Herbeumont, approx. 10 km. to the hotel.

DINANT, NAMUR, AND ENVIRONS

Dinant is the pleasure capital of the River Meuse, with endless possibilities for recreation and sightseeing excursions. This delightful riverside town is nestled under the rock cliffs that dominate the town and seem to crowd it into the river. At the top of the cliffs is the Citadel, which can be reached by a cable car. There's a chairlift (télésiege) *to the Montfort Tower on another cliff, 400 feet above the town.*

Dinant is renowned for its engraved yellow copper, called dinanderie. *Perhaps not so renowned, but tasty morsels nevertheless, are the big brown cookies called* couques.

Namur is a quiet, peaceful town with several museums containing ancient artworks, particularly the Diocesan Museum of the Cathedral of St. Aubin, with a Merovingian shrine and a 14th-century crown. Namur, too, has a citadel on a cliff, not so striking as Dinant's, overlooking the point where the Meuse joins the smaller Sambre.

On the Philippeville road, just outside Dinant, is La Merveilleuse, a grotto with beautiful white stalactites. This is one of several eerie grottoes in Namur Province. Two others a few miles farther south are the Grotto of Rochefort and the Grotto of Han-sur-Lesse; both offer an exciting experience.

From nearby Anseremme, near the junction of the Lesse and the Meuse, you can embark on a number of activities: climbing at Freyr or visiting its castle, boat or kayak trips on the Lesse, excursions to the nature reserve at Furfooze with wonderful walks, or a visit to prehistoric caves, to a Roman camp, or to the feudal castle at Veves.

Between Dinant and Namur are the lovely gardens of the Chateau d'Annevoie, and on the way do look in on the tiny town of Bovignes, dating from the Middle Ages.

LE MOULIN DE LISOGNE
Lisogne (Dinant)

The tiny black burro came to the wall to greet me and nuzzled my hand when I petted his furry nose. I should have had a carrot. Four sheep in the little meadow munched thoughtfully, watching me. I was strolling around the grounds of this old stone mill, converted into a small hotel, deep in the countryside not far from the historic town of Dinant. (*Moulin* is French for "mill.") It's an idyllic spot, with the River Lesse, not much more than a stream at this point, flowing gently by the grassy banks. A little bridge leads across the river and into another meadow.

A German couple with their pretty teenage daughter were just returning from their morning constitutional as I came around the front of the building. We all admired the tubs of yellow daisies that decorated the terrace, where white garden furniture was set up for outdoor dining. They told me they like to find places like this, where they can go for walks and enjoy nature.

Alain Blondiaux, innkeeper and chef, is a very low-key young man, and his wife, Martine, is vivacious and extremely pretty with dark, laughing eyes. They are an enterprising young couple.

Their restaurant is altogether charming and rather romantic, with large, arched, plate-glass windows, hand-hewn beams, a pale peach color scheme, and soft, discreet lighting. In the center arch is a glass door leading to a porch for open-air dining. The room has a south-of-France, or Spanish, feeling. The lobby and sitting room are decorated in an interesting, cozy, and comfortable fashion, with soft, leather-covered chairs and sofa, country antiques, some good abstract expressionist paintings, and a tall arrangement of beautiful red roses.

They have a sophisticated French menu that offers oysters in a champagne sauce, lobster, poached salmon, trout, roast pheasant, venison, veal kidneys with wild mushrooms, and lamb. I was there in mid-October, which is the season for game (or *gibier*) dishes.

Although my room and the other guest rooms and bathrooms I saw were clean and had the necessary furnishings, including telephones, they were rather drab and poorly decorated. The hospitable innkeepers, the ambience of the downstairs, the excellent food, and the beautiful surrounding countryside overcame my doubts about recommending this place. I am doing so, but with reservations because of the guest rooms.

Readers who are not so concerned about room amenities will find this converted old mill in its sylvan setting an ideal and tranquil base from which to explore the fascinating cities of Dinant and Namur and the several castles in the area, especially the spectacular Walzin Castle and the one in Annevoie with its rare and beautiful gardens.

LE MOULIN DE LISOGNE (Relais du Silence), Rue de Lisonnette, B-5501 Lisogne (Dinant). Tel.: 082-22-63-80. A 9-guestroom (private baths) converted mill hotel-restaurant in a small sylvan valley on the Lesse River, about 5 min. from Dinant. European plan; dinner reservation required with overnight stay. Breakfast, lunch, and dinner served to travelers. Closed mid-Dec. to mid-Feb.; Mon. and Tues. weekly. Tennis court, trout fishing, children's swings on grounds. Dinant and Namur with excursions and guided tours, prehistoric caves, river rafting, nature walks and hikes, Annevoie chateau and gardens and other castles nearby. Alain Blondiaux and Martine Blondiaux-Legrain, Innkeepers. Rates: See Index.

Directions: From Dinant, take N-936 towards Ciney. Watch for the Moulin de Lisogne sign. The road winds through forest and hills for 3 or 4 mi.

THE ARDENNES FORESTS

The Belgian Ardennes is a vast region that encompasses nearly all of the eastern section of Belgium. It is a fascinating area of sylvan charm with great nature reserves, where lost river valleys slip into deep, mysterious woods, stands of sleek beeches and delicate larches alternate with thick evergreen forests and occasional clumps of holly trees, and rock ledges drop off 1,000 feet to a silver ribbon of river that winds towards the Meuse River. There are grottoes and caverns and prehistoric sites to explore. There's trout fishing, canoeing, and bathing in the many rivers, brooks, and cascades. And miles of nature walks and hikes, with maps outlining the scenic routes, or if you prefer, guides who will show you the best places to see a herd of deer or a wild boar.

In the Ardennes, you can drive on wonderful back roads, perhaps getting lost for a few moments in a deep forest or encountering a fine castle or a charming ancient village.

The Ardennes contain large and small towns of more than passing interest, some dating back to Roman times, others with marvelous artworks in their castles, churches, and museums. And folklore and tales of treachery and triumph abound. There are, too, traces of the ravages of war, including many mementos of world wars I and II, such as monuments to the American soldiers who fought there.

In this vast holiday region there are hundreds of hotels and restaurants of all kinds. I offer here a sampling of special small hotels throughout the Ardennes, which will provide you with a comfortable and pleasant base from which to explore the many delights of this fascinating area.

LE VIEUX CHATEAU
La Roche-en-Ardenne
One road leading to La Roche from N-4, called the Route des Forêts (N-888), is nineteen kilometers of forest and fields and tiny villages. There was still some color when I was there in late October, but I'm sure in early October the drive must be absolutely gorgeous and full of brilliance and color.

Once the feudal stronghold of the counts of La Roche, the ruins of the old castle, perched high on a great rock, loom darkly over the town. Before the counts came along, this site was successively a neolithic dwelling, an ancient settlement, a Roman fort, and the Roman house of the kings of France.

What makes Le Vieux Chateau especially interesting is its proximity to this spectacular ruin—you just walk up to the third floor and out the back door and cross a little elevated footbridge, from which you can see the rooftops of the village. Up some steep stone steps, past a little herb garden, and there are the great crumbling walls of the castle rising up before you. I would love to have seen the inside of the ancient citadel, but the tours were closed for the season.

Tucked into the center of this busy mountain town, Le Vieux Chateau is a bit deceptive on the outside—it is little more than a door in a row of shops. However, beyond that door are some charmingly decorated guest rooms on the upper floors and an excellent restaurant run by André Linchet, who is cited as one of the eighty finest chefs in Belgium.

With cheerful colors, dried flower arrangements, mirrors, and interesting paintings, the small guest rooms are bright and gay. I was quite taken with the ingenious architecture in the bathrooms, which makes maximum use of minimum space and still creates a pleasing effect with greenery and special lighting. Rooms on the back have a view of the castle on the steep cliff above.

There is much to do in this light-hearted, bustling town. I enjoyed just ogling the beautifully displayed meats in the *charcuteries* and the tempting windows of the *patisseries*. There are incomparable walks and hikes through beech woods, beside fast-flowing streams and rivers, down into mysterious grottoes and caverns, and there are always rocks of all shapes and sizes to clamber around. There are tours and guides for all of these activities, as well as festive events and the fascinating folklore of this region.

LE VIEUX CHATEAU, 6 rue Pesse, 6980 La Roche-en-Ardenne. Tel.: 084-41-13-27. A 9-guestroom (private baths) small in-town hotel-restaurant with a Belgian master chef in a mountain holiday region, approx. 30 km. north of Bastogne. European plan; dinner reservation required with overnight stay. Breakfast, lunch, and dinner served to travelers. Closed mid-Feb. to mid-March, and mid-June to mid-July; Tues. and Wed. during week. Shops, festivals, guided forest tours, walking, hiking, horseback riding, swimming, fishing, hunting, and canoeing nearby. No pets. André and Michele Linchet-Najman, Innkeepers.

Directions: La Roche is easily reached by a number of main routes.

The hotel is in the center of town. Parking is available in front of the hotel.

DURBUY

In order to get the most enjoyment out of this picturesque "smallest town in the world" on the Ourthe River, you need to know some of its history. A little booklet is available from the Syndicat d'Initiative (tourist office) in Durbuy that will acquaint you with some of the background of the ancient buildings, and especially the soaring castle that dominates the town. Several of the tiny cobbled streets are limited to pedestrian traffic. They are lined with shops, boutiques, dress shops, charcuteries, patisseries, parfumeries, *and busy sidewalk cafes. There are fifteen marked trails of varying length and difficulty through the surrounding hills, woods, and valleys, where the Ourthe River and rippling streams wend their way.*

The narrow streets are easily clotted with cars, but there are various parking areas around the town. I was lucky enough to find a parking place on the street close to the hotel; however, there are parking spaces behind the hotel.

LE SANGLIER DES ARDENNES
Durbuy

The wine cellar was beautifully organized—like a library—with row upon row of thousands of bottles, many coated with a venerable layer of dust, lying aslant in the tall stacks. Monsieur Cardinael pointed out some of the prestigious labels, Chateau la Tour, Mouton Rothschild, Romanée Conti, and, surprisingly in this rarefied company, a California winery, Opus One. M. Cardinael is a collector of wines; among his Mouton Rothschilds, he has a 1945 bottle worth 1,000 francs and an 1894 bottle which he does not put a price on and will never open. Not being knowledgeable about wines, I could only gaze in awe as he took me through his cellar. In a little anteroom, he showed me his wife's marvelous collection of 250 antique porcelain cheese dishes. If you can catch him when he's not busy in the kitchen, I'm sure he'll be glad to show you his wine cellar—he's a most unaffected and cordial gentleman.

Le Sanglier des Ardennes ("the boar of the Ardennes") is right in the center of Durbuy (pronounced dur-boo-ee), which calls itself the smallest town in the world. Even with the minuscule population of 350, it really seems larger than our small towns, where there may be a block or two of shops and businesses and then a few homes scattered over a wide area. Durbuy is densely concentrated within roughly less than a square mile. This is because Durbuy has been a walled town since 1331, when it was surrounded by a moat. Its existence was first recorded when its castle, the Castellum de Durbui, was mentioned in 1078. Many of the narrow, cobblestoned streets are off limits to cars, and there are little cul-de-sacs with shops and offices in ancient buildings. It's an absolutely fascinating tiny, busy, medieval town cradled in a pocket of hills and forests and protected by the castle and the great stone cliffs that rise up around its perimeter.

M. Cardinael, who is renowned as one of Belgium's master chefs and a connoisseur of wines, has expanded his hotel to include three ancient buildings in the town: Résidence Alexandre, across the main street; Le Vieux Durbuy, two blocks away in a little pedestrian cul-de-sac; and the Cardinal, which has fully equipped apartments in a former abbey. The rooms in the Alexandre and Le Vieux Durbuy are more typically European in style than those in Le Sanglier, which have just been remodeled and decorated and are quite luxurious, with state-of-the-art bathrooms.

One of my favorites in Le Sanglier was room 40, under the eaves, with hand-hewn beams in the ceiling and a skylight looking up at the trees across on the hill. The king-sized bed had a white corduroy bedspread figured with pastel flowers, and the furnishings were a nice mixture of antique and modern pieces. I would recommend rooms on the back of Le Sanglier and Alexandre, as the nightlife seems quite active and traffic on the street continues past midnight.

As M. Cardinael said, autumn is their busiest time and perhaps things are a little quieter in other seasons. This is the season for game in all the restaurants, and Le Sanglier was no exception. Their menu offered woodcock mousse, breast of wild duck, saddle of hare with chestnut pureé, wild pigeon paté, stuffed wild mushrooms with foie gras, pheasant, and farm chicken cooked in sea salt, green sauce, and boiled vegetables. The desserts are legion and delectable. I tried the poached trout with nettled butter and snails accompanied by tiny julienned potatoes and other vegetables, and it was, simply put, a taste treat. In the interest of maintaining my waistline I eschewed the cheeses and desserts, but of course with coffee came that little collection of delicacies known as *les après sucres*. Something I appreciated at Le Sanglier was their supplemental menu in English, which you should ask for if you're as uneasy with your French as I am.

LE SANGLIER DES ARDENNES (Relais du Silence), 100 rue Comte d'Ursel, 5480 Durbuy-sur-Ourthe. Tel.: 086-21-10-88. Telex: SANDUR 42240. A 14-guestroom (private baths) small, popular hotel and restaurant with suites and additional rooms in nearby buildings in a tiny, medieval, but very active town in the Ardennes, 50 km. south of Liège. European plan; other plans available, including a golf plan. Breakfast, lunch, and dinner served to travelers. Closed Jan. Maps for walking tours, golf, tennis, archery, shopping, bicycling, kayaking, horseback riding. Famille Cardinael-Alexandre, Innkeepers. Rates: See Index.

Directions: There are several routes south from Liège, N-63 being the most direct main highway to Durbuy; however, I suggest taking the more scenic and interesting back roads that follow the Ourthe River.

LIÈGE

One of the great commercial centers in the 1400s, Liège still has a great deal of heavy industry. It is known for its fine, precision-built firearms. The Liègeois have a tradition of heroism throughout a history rife with battles. A fascinating 17th-century monument erected to the spirit of freedom stands in the Place du Marche. It's too complicated to describe, but well worth a visit. A walking tour in the vicinity of Place St. Lambert, the main square and oldest part of the town, will lead you to many of the fine historic churches and museums of the town. The Citadel dominates Liège and can be reached by the 407 steps up the hill or by car for a splendid panoramic view. There are all of the shops, restaurants, parks, cultural events, and entertainments one

Liège

expects of a large town. *Composer César Franck and Georges Simenon, creator of Inspector Maigret, are two of Liège's native sons.*

The province of Liège is one of the chief portals to the Ardennes forest, with rolling hills, magnificent trees, rivers, brooks, and cascades.

Huy is on a bend of the Meuse, with the Citadel, site of a Roman castle built in A.D. 148, looming above the center of the town. The view of the Meuse Valley from the Citadel stretches twenty miles both upstream and downstream. Among Huy's treasures: one of Belgium's finest and purest Gothic churches, the Collegiale, with a celebrated rose window and many ancient works of art; the Old Bridge (1294), which has undergone several reconstructions after destruction in wars; and a delicate 15th-century bronze fountain, which graces the Grand Place.

HOSTELLERIE ST. ROCH
Comblain-la-Tour

As I drove up and parked in front of the hotel, Monsieur Dernouchamps was deep in conversation on the front steps with a couple of rather tweedy-looking gentlemen, who were obviously taking their leave after having had luncheon at the hotel. They were laughing over some *bon mot* one of them had made, and I thought M. Dernouchamp seemed like a very convivial fellow. Like many of the owner-chefs I've met who have been accorded top honors for their cuisine, he is completely natural and unaffected.

Only about twenty minutes from Liège, Hostellerie St. Roch sits on the bank of the Ourthe River at the edge of the quiet little town of Comblain la Tour. A hostellerie for over 100 years, it was taken over by the Cawet family in 1947, and in turn by their daughter and her husband, M. Dernouchamps, in 1973.

It has the air of a successful, well-patronized establishment. There's a great feeling of tradition in the paneled walls, the leaded pane windows, and the wonderful painted porcelain tap on the antique bar.

A little arcade leads from the foyer to the dining room, elegant with tapestry-covered chairs, sparkling table settings, beautiful flowers, and many windows overlooking the river. The arcade is lined with glassed-in arches that look out on a grassy courtyard and off to the terrace, where tables and chairs are set out for alfresco dining on the river bank.

Guest rooms are on the back of the building, with garden and river views. I saw several of them, and they are all decorated with personality and charm. Each room had something that caught my eye. Room 25 had a handsome black marble counter in the bathroom; room 36 had very pretty wallpaper and a matching bedspread on the queen-sized bed; room 10 looks out on the courtyard, and the light fixtures have little crystal teardrops.

I'm not sure whether any of the handsome antique pieces throughout the hotel are for sale, but M. Dernouchamps deals in antiques, along with everything else he does, so it's quite possible some pieces might be available for purchase.

HOSTELLERIE ST. ROCH (Relais et Chateaux), 4171 Comblain-la-Tour. Tel: 041-69-13-33 or 69-21-54. Fax: 041-69-31-31. A 13-guest-room (private baths) hotel with a Belgian master chef in a quiet town approx. 20 min. south of Liège, in the Ourthe River valley. European plan; dinner reservation required with overnight stay. Breakfast, lunch, and dinner served to travelers. Closed Jan. and Feb.; Mon. and Tues. during week. Tennis on grounds. Maps for walks available. Boating on river. Golf, athletic fitness center, and all the attractions of Liège and surrounding villages nearby. Famille Dernouchamps-Cawet, Proprietors. Rates: See Index.

Directions: From Liège take N-30 south to Harze and follow signs to Comblain-la-Tour. The hotel is just by the bridge over the river.

DOMAINE DU CHATEAU DE FRAINEUX
Fraineux (Nandrin)

This place was recommended so highly that I felt duty-bound to at least stop in for a look-see. The chateau, set in parklike grounds, was destroyed during the French Revolution and was rebuilt in the 1800s.

It remained a private residence until 1982, when part of it was made into a hotel.

Madame Pieteur, the director, spoke very little English; her son (I could hardly believe she had a grown son) spoke a bit more, but they put me in the hands of a young and pretty assistant, Nancy Boulanger, who spoke English quite well and gave me a complete tour.

"Elegance and style" would sum up my impression of the common rooms, which comprise the downstairs of the chateau. I understand that the second-floor rooms are private apartments. The spacious foyer, drawing room, and dining room, with their high ceilings, tall windows, parquet floors, and oriental rugs, are serenely and beautifully decorated.

As this is a member of Relais et Chateaux, I'm sure the cuisine is excellent. I looked over the menu and it seemed both interesting and extensive, with ten choices for the main course. Guest rooms are across the courtyard in the Pavillon, and they are most attractively decorated and outfitted for aesthetic pleasure and total comfort, with all possible amenities, including marble counters in the bathrooms.

The grounds cover sixteen acres, with woodland walks and a pond, which I glimpsed through the trees, where some swans and ducks paddled.

I would suggest a springtime visit, when the fruit trees, the magnolia tree, and the rosebushes and flowerbeds will make this place a symphony of color, and there will be ducklings in the pond and birds in the trees.

DOMAINE DU CHATEAU DE FRAINEUX (Relais et Chateaux), 20, Rue de la Chapelle, Fraineux, B4151 Nandrin. A 6-guestroom (private baths) elegant and luxurious chateau in the tiny village of Fraineux, about 20 km. south of Liège. European plan. Dinner reservation required with overnight stay. Lunch and dinner served to travelers. Closed Jan. and Feb.; Tues. eve. and Wed. weekly. Beautiful park for leisurely strolls. Many lovely back roads with ancient villages, thermal baths at Chaudfontaine, and golf, as well as all the other attractions in Liège and Huy nearby. Mme. Janine Pieteur, Director. Rates: See Index.

Directions: From Liège take N-63 south, watching for signs to Chateau de Fraineux.

LA COMMANDERIE
Villers-le-Temple

I am a little hesitant about recommending this place, and do so mainly because of its interest as a very ancient landmark. Comprised of a cluster of stone buildings around a large courtyard, this settlement was the command center of an order of the Knights Templars for several centuries.

Today there are guest rooms and an excellent restaurant. I found the room I stayed in quite drab and a bit threadbare for all its elegant velvets and velours. The housekeeping was also a little careless. However, there were other rooms in better condition, with pleasant tiled bathrooms. Some of the antiques were really remarkable. There is little English spoken here, so bring your French phrase book and a relaxed attitude.

The rates are modest, the cuisine is French and very good, with a wide selection, and there is much to see and do in the immediate vicinity. On a back road to the village of Huy is a wonderful, tiny forest, with a gorge and a stream running through it—perfect for a hike and a lovely picnic.

LA COMMANDERIE (Relais et Chateaux), 4155 Villers-le-Temple. Tel.: 085-51-17-01 or 51-19-09. Telex: 59674 COM. A 14-guestroom (private baths) hotel and restaurant in an ancient and historic complex, about 25 km. south of Liège. European plan. Breakfast, lunch, and dinner served to travelers. Closed Jan. and Feb.; Wed. weekly. Walking tours of historic sites of Knights Templars, including a museum, tennis, golf, fishing, swimming, and scenic backroading nearby. Famille Lorneau, Proprietors. Rates: See Index.

Directions: From Liège, take N-63 south. Watch for sign to Villers-le-Temple.

SPA

Spa was the first watering-place in history, and as such, gave its name to all subsequent watering-places. In the 18th and 19th centuries, European royalty and celebrities, including Peter the Great of Russia, flocked to Spa for both "the cure" and amusement. It is still a famous and popular holiday resort, with all sorts of curative baths and springs, along with the inevitable casino. The town is full of shops, restaurants, hotels, and banks, but there are dozens of lovely paths and roads radiating from the town for quiet rambles to surrounding villages. Some special places are Sauvenière, where there is a spring that was supposed to have helped childless women; the beautiful Roannay Valley; the Cascade de Coo, a thunderous waterfall on the Amblève River near the town of Stavelot; picturesque Malmedy, which holds an exciting carnival in February; Botrange, the highest point in the Ardennes; and Robertville, with the Reinhardstein castle. Not far from Spa is Fran-

corchamps, with a huge stadium and a racecourse where all sorts of races are held, including automobile and motorcycle races.

MANOIR DE LEBIOLES
Spa

Winding up the narrow, curving road into the hills above Spa, I was relieved to be getting away from the frenetic activity of this resort town. In a mile or two I passed through the ancient farming village of Creppe, finally reaching a plateau where the road was little more than a country lane that crossed a field and led into a small woods. As I came out of the woods, before me rose the towers and turrets of a fairy castle. That was my first exciting glimpse of Manoir de Lebioles.

I drove down through the impressive arched entrance gate into the courtyard, where a fountain splashed, surrounded by a manicured lawn, sculptured hedges, and flowers.

Madame Rita Cauwels-van Cauwenberg, a strikingly beautiful, impeccably groomed lady, welcomed me graciously in her charmingly accented English, and I was whisked up the wide staircase to a magnificent corner room the size of a tennis court. The twin beds were mahogany, the lovely little French desk held a vase of red rosebuds, and the windows looked out on gardens. A fire blazed cheerfully in the carved marble fireplace, and I gazed at my pleased reflection in the tall gilt mirror above it. I felt as if I'd stepped into a 19th-century play. However, there was nothing 19th century about the TV or stereo or telephone. I passed over the dish of wrapped candies, took an apple from the bowl of fruit, poured myself a glass of mineral water, and investigated the bathroom.

Tall windows with shutters looked out on the courtyard. The entire room was faced with white tile decorated with blue figures, and in

addition to an oversized bathtub, there was a stall shower. Soft, thick, white towels and a terry robe awaited me. I should have come with a couple of steamer trunks and a personal valet. Oh well, traveling in the grand manner isn't for the likes of me.

Mme. Cauwels showed me the other guest rooms the next morning, and each one was more exquisite than the last, done in lovely, subtle colors and furnished with great taste and style. The rooms on the back of the castle have a fabulous twenty-mile view of hills, forests, fields, and villages. It must be breathtaking in mid-October when the foliage is ablaze with color.

As one would expect in a castle, everything is on a grand scale; there are great, heavy, double doors, marble floors and massive fireplaces, huge windows with floor-to-ceiling draperies, wall-sized tapestries and paintings in the style of the old masters, and elegant antique furnishings. Although this was built in 1907 as a replica of an 18th-century castle, there are some unmistakable Victorian touches, such as the wooden pillars and the carved wooden cherubs in the Great Hall.

The dining room and sitting room are cozy but somewhat formal. Aperitifs are served in the Great Hall, where a perpetual fire seems to be blazing away in the walk-in fireplace and where one has a tendency to speak in hushed tones. The French cuisine offers set menus and an à la carte menu and is presented with an eye to aesthetics. The two pleasant and polite waitresses serve quietly and proficiently, while Mme. Cauwels moves around, chatting with her guests and pouring the wine.

A series of terraces in the back of the castle lead down into the surrounding woods, where there are trails for walks and cross-country skiing.

This is a perfect place to enjoy a touch of Old World luxury and country quiet within a few minutes of the bustling town of Spa. But make your reservations early—there are only four beautiful rooms available.

MANOIR DE LEBIOLES, 4880 Spa (Creppe). Tel.: 087-77-10-20 or 77-02-76 or 77-02-79. A 4-guestroom (private baths) luxurious castle-hotel in the countryside, 5 km. from Spa, at the northern edge of the Ardennes. European plan; dinner reservation required with overnight stay. Lunch and dinner served to travelers by reservation. Restaurant is closed Sun. eve. Hotel is closed Jan. Special weekend rates. Tennis, nature walks, xc skiing on grounds (ski rentals available). Diversions of all kinds in Spa. M. and Mme. Cauwels-van Cauwenberg, Proprietors. Rates: See Index.

Directions: In Spa, watch for hotel signs—they are easy to find.

HASSELT, DIEST, ZOUTLEEUW, AND TONGEREN

Hasselt is the county seat of the province of Luxenbourg, and is famous for its juniper berries and gin (genievre) and for having the earliest steam-based distillery (1880) in Europe. Worth seeing are the Church of Our Lady, St. Quentin's Cathedral, and the Genever (gin) Museum. Hasselt has a number of carnivals, festivals, and processions. Those intriguing communities known as beguinages, a peculiarly Flemish phenomenon, may be found in both Hasselt and Diest.

Diest is an ancient fortified town. Visit the interesting museum in the town hall's Gothic cellars and also the magnificent Church of St. Sulpice.

There are many Roman relics and medieval fortifications in Tongeren, founded in the 1st century and the oldest town in Belgium. The statue of Ambiorix in front of the impressive Basilica of Notre Dame commemorates the great chief who vanquished Roman legions in 54 B.C. More important is the Basilica, which is the chief glory of Tongeren, with a rich treasure of artworks.

Zoutleeuw has a charming main square with a Renaissance town hall and the grandiose St. Leonard, with its rare and curious double statue of the Virgin Mary and a striking array of artworks.

In Bokrijk there's an open-air museum with reconstructed 12th-century Flemish villages, including a small church.

SCHOLTESHOF
Hasselt-Stevoort

Even though I had arrived at the worst possible time for a tour of the hotel—1:30 on a Sunday afternoon with the dining room overflowing—Christian Souvereyns greeted me most cordially and brought his father, Roger Souvereyns, the owner and obviously very busy chef, to meet me. Roger insisted I have some lunch, and although I had intended only to stop here for a quick look around, I agreed to have just a taste of something. He suggested a langoustines salad. Before I was through I'd had quite a repast, beginning with a delightful paté maison on toast points, served to me in a salon with other guests, who were enjoying aperitifs and studying the menu. A group at the next table were having an animated discussion over the twenty-page wine list, which one gentleman was poring over with great concentration. Finally, one of the ladies got up and leaned over his shoulder to get a better look. After further study and discussion, the decision was finally made, and Christian took their order. Soon he came back with two very dusty-looking bottles, which, after he had shown them to the gentleman and

secured his approval, he took away to be prepared for service.

I was already feeling very good about this place. I liked the reception area, which could double as a solarium, with its glass roof, one wall of windows, and many plants. It looked out on a little courtyard of lawn, potted plants, and sculptured hedges, and across to an old brick building with a red-tiled roof. But then I was to discover all sorts of little niches and corners, where similar gardens were tucked away.

When Christian conducted me into the dining room, I was even more impressed. (I might say, in passing, that Christian is a very tall, very handsome young man, and I think he's doing his father proud. He is obviously very proud of the place, and I'd say he had good reason to be.)

The dining room really delighted me. It is the first one I'd seen in Belgium where the kitchen is in full view of the restaurant. This, along with the bright and cheerful decor of yellow tablecloths, creamy plaster walls, and rough-hewn blond wood beams, combined with the many interesting artifacts lining shelves and display cabinets, gave the room a lively ambience.

My small salad turned out to be a rather large one, with succulent morsels of shrimp bedded among curly endive, chicory, and watercress, some flavorful, chewy seeds, and a marvelously piquant dressing. I polished it off with great gusto, along with a hot, crusty, buttered roll and a glass of Riesling.

The guest rooms are all furnished in a most charming and imaginative manner with textured fabric wall coverings and different architectural features in each room. In one suite, with a Moroccan motif, the bed is in the loft. Another room has a more traditional look, with a canopied bed and elegant antiques. The bathrooms are all modern and well appointed.

Objets d'art are everywhere—I could have browsed for hours in the sitting room for the houseguests. Fascinating books are piled on the coffee table, the shelves overflow with books and magazines, pre-Columbian figures stand in corners, and beautiful orchid plants are placed here and there throughout the house.

Scholteshof was the 17th-century farm of the sheriff (*Scholt*) of the seigneurie of Stevoort. The stout brick buildings have withstood the ravages of time very well, and the Souvereyn family have surrounded them with medieval herb and rose gardens, orchards where chickens are free to roam, and pastures where cattle graze.

The words that immediately comes to mind when I think of Scholteshof is "panache." I was sorry I couldn't have stayed for several days.

SCHOLTESHOF (Relais et Chateaux), Kermtstraat 130, 3512 Hasselt-Stevoort. Tel.: 011-25-02-02. Telex: 39684 TESHOF. An 18-guestroom (private baths) elegant hotel-restaurant in the Flemish countryside, 6 km. from Hasselt; approx. 35 km. west of Maastricht. European plan; dinner reservation required with overnight stay. Breakfast, lunch, and dinner served to travelers. Closed Jan.; restaurant closed Wed. weekly. All of the cultural and historical attractions of Hasselt, Tongeren, and other picturesque towns nearby. Roger Souvereyns, Owner-Chef; Christian Souvereyns, Manager. Rates: See Index.

Directions: From Brussels, take the N-2 or A-2 to Exit 25 outside of Diest. Drive towards Hasselt and Kermt. Turn right at Kermt and watch for signs to hotel.

The Marianum in Zoutleeuw

Luxembourg

INNS AND LOCATIONS
BERDORF, Parc Hotel, 248
ECHTERNACH, Hotel Bel Air, 246
EISCHEN, La Gaichel, 242
LUXEMBOURG, Hostellerie du Grunewald, 250
MONDORF-LES-BAINS, Hotel du Grand Chef, 240
WELSCHEID, Hotel Reuter, 244

TRAVEL SUGGESTIONS FOR LUXEMBOURG

How to Get There

The Luxembourg airport offers as painless an entry to Europe as I can think of. It is small, uncrowded, and very manageable. However, the flight on Icelandair (the only airline from North America to Luxembourg) tends to be long and uncomfortable, with a stopover in Iceland. The discomfort can be somewhat alleviated by a seat in their business or Saga class, which offers something of a bargain. The stop-over in Iceland provides the opportunity to buy a number of duty-free items.

Eurailpass is good in Luxembourg.

Introduction to the Grand Duchy of Luxembourg

This tiny country (999 square miles) has been perhaps the most-wanted country in the world. In its 1,000-year history, it has been wanted by the Burgundians, French, Spaniards, Austrians, Prussians, and Germans. As a result, its fortress was the most powerful in the world for centuries, with a castle, built in 963, perched high on a rock bluff and an underground system of tunnels and fortifications (casemates). Today, remnants of the great walls and bastions exist cheek by jowl with futuristic towers of glass, steel, and stone in the city of Luxembourg. The cultures and influences of those who sought to conquer Luxembourg are still evident in its architecture and customs.

This is a softly beautiful country of rolling hills and hidden valleys. Romantic, picturesque villages cluster around ancient castles on the sides of hills or around ancient churches off on the horizon amid green fields.

Like Belgium, it offers many wonderful nature walks or rock climbing in the lovely forests of the Ardennes and the great Germano-Luxembourg park area, with their many rivers and streams. Everywhere, there are sights of historical interest, dating back to prehistoric and Roman times.

Americans will find traces of their own involvement in World War II here and there, in the military cemetery at Hamm, where 5,000 American soldiers, members of General Patton's 3rd Army, are buried, along with the general, and in monuments and plaques commemorating various battles.

There are dozens of fascinating festivals and processions throughout the year, as well as theatrical, musical, and cultural events, sports competitions, and folklore performances. The state museum has some fine examples of the Dutch and Flemish painters and a large collection of tapestries. There are great cathedrals, museums, and castles throughout the country.

Luxembourg is one of the seats of the European Economic Community and has an active role in the industrial, financial, and judicial life of modern Europe. However, rather than the modern aspects of Luxembourg, I have stressed the historical features of the places I've visited.

I recommend that you write for further information to the Luxembourg Tourist Office, 801 Second Avenue, New York, NY 10017; telephone: 212-370-9850, or visit the Syndicats d'Initiative in almost every town of any size for complete information about the region.

Luxembourg is bordered by Belgium, France, Germany, and the Netherlands. Although its main language is Luxembourgeois, French and German are widely spoken, and I found that English was in use nearly everywhere.

Country Inns in Luxembourg

Although I visited only a few of the small and interesting hotels of Luxembourg, I have the sense that many are carrying on traditions of innkeeping that have been handed down through generations. That is certainly true of several places I saw. As I remarked in Belgium, the chefs and their cuisine play an important part in Luxembourg hotels, and much attention is lavished on the dining rooms, in some cases more than on the guest rooms. However, I believe no matter where you stay you will find the hospitality warm and friendly and the rooms spotlessly clean.

Luxembourg Menus

The better hotels and restaurants adhere to a French-style cuisine, so, with some exceptions, for the more regional specialties, you must seek out neighborhood establishments.

Luxembourg produces its own wines in the southern Moselle valley. Some famous Luxembourg specialties are the Ardennes hams, quenelles (calf liver dumplings with sauerkraut and potatoes), fresh river fish, gras double (a variety of paté), jellied suckling pig, treipan (black pudding) with sausages, potatoes, and horseradish, a cooked Luxembourg cheese, and pastries and chocolates. During Carnival season (just before Lent) a pastry is made called les pensées brouillées *("puzzled thoughts").*

Reservations

In planning your itinerary, keep in mind that nearly all of the country hotels are closed on certain days during the week, usually Monday and Tuesday and sometimes Wednesday. Special arrangements are possible if your stay will overlap one of the closed days; however, it is wise to work this out in advance. Also, be aware of the holidays, since advance reservations are imperative in the resort and holiday areas at those times.

Driving in Luxembourg

Rental cars are available throughout Luxembourg. For further information, see the section "Renting a Car for Europe" in the front of this book. Roads and signs are excellent, and the back roads lead to all sorts of fascinating places. The rail and bus networks provide complete and comprehensive tours and are certainly convenient alternatives to driving.

HOTEL DU GRAND CHEF
Mondorf-les-Bains

I decided to make a slight detour on my way from Luxembourg to Eischen to have a look at this center for rest and relaxation, where Europeans have been coming since the mid-1800s to "take the waters." As a matter of fact, Victor Hugo was one of the illustrious personages who found respite and relief in the thermal baths and treatments. The thermal center is in a big, beautiful park with flower gardens, huge trees, and shrubs and plants of all kinds.

Mondorf-les-Bains is close to both the German and French borders. Actually, while Mme. Diderrich, the concierge for the Grand Chef, was showing me around the hotel, she pointed across the back lawn to a little river, beyond which she said was France.

The Grand Chef has an air of elegant, genteel shabbiness. Built in

1852 by a French nobleman, its main sitting room is furnished in Louis XV style, with tapestry-covered chairs and settee, a carved marble fireplace, a beautiful antique clock, tall windows, and a great gilt mirror over the fireplace.

I was able to look at only two rooms since the others were all occupied. They were simply furnished, but I was told all guest rooms contained telephones and television. The bathrooms seemed very clean, with all the necessary equipment.

The owner-chef, Paul Bosseler-Diderrich, wasn't there at the time of my visit, but I understand he has four chefs in the kitchen, and there are three pleasant and roomy dining rooms, which implies a good-sized clientele. I noticed partially full bottles of wine and mineral water on several tables, which Mme. Didderich explained were kept for their long-term guests.

Their menu is changed everyday and features such main dishes as coquilles St. Jacques au gratin, poached turbot with hollandaise, lobster cassoulet, duck à l'orange, and veal cutlets. Desserts might be chocolate mousse or mocha cake. The menu is à la carte and quite extensive.

This hotel is listed by the Relais du Silence, and it does seem to be a pleasant, tranquil spot, surrounded by a small park with 140-year-old gingko trees.

The tree-lined streets of Mondorf-les-Bains are narrow, and I imagine in the summer they are thronging with tourists who come not only for the thermal baths but for the summer concerts in the park, the casino, horse races, fencing and archery tournaments, and other festivities and entertainments.

HOTEL DU GRAND CHEF, 36, Ave. des Bains, P.O. Box 53, L-5601 Mondorf-les Bains. Tel.: 68122 or 68012. Telex: 1840 GACHEF LU. A 40-guestroom (private baths) hotel in a spa town close to the German and French borders. European plan. Other plans available. Breakfast, lunch, and dinner served to travelers. Open late April to mid-Oct. Adjacent to spa center with indoor and outdoor thermal swimming pool. Guided walks, bus tours, historic sites, golf, tennis, horseback riding, casino, shops and restaurants, concerts and festivals nearby. Famille Bosseler-Diderrich, Innkeepers. Rates: See Index.

Directions: Mondorf-les-Bains is 15 km. south of Luxembourg. Take N-3 to Frisange and turn east on N-13. Follow signs to Mondorf. Signs in town will direct you to the hotel.

ARLON AND EISCHEN

The hiking trail system around Eischen is called the Vale of Seven Castles. This is a rather fanciful title, but the scenery is delightful. I mention the Belgian town of Arlon here, since it is only a few miles from Gaichel.

Arlon is of particular interest to students of Roman archaeology for the many traces of Roman occupation in evidence in church walls and altars. The Institut Archéologique is a treasury of decorated Roman stones from the 1st and 2nd centuries A.D. Some of them record fascinating scenes of daily life. From the tower of the Church of St. Donat in the center of Arlon, you can see a panoramic view of the countryside that stretches for forty miles.

LA GAICHEL
Eischen

The fountain shimmered in the spotlight, and the birch trees and bushes surrounding the pond, caught in the gleam of the lights, seemed to float in the blackness of the night. Sitting in a comfortable lounge chair beside one of the floor-to-ceiling windows of the salon, I was able to enjoy this dramatic scene while I chatted with Monsieur Jacquemin.

He was telling me about the line of succession of the innkeepers of La Gaichel, which began as a farm and restaurant in 1852. He pointed out the genealogy chart on the wall with pictures of each of the owners. It seems that ownership of the hotel passed to the first innkeeper's daughter and her husband, who also had a daughter whose husband eventually became the next innkeeper. And so it has gone since 1852, with the owners having all girls and the hotel remaining in the same family through marriage. M. Jacquemin is planning to retire in the near future, passing the reins over to his daughter and her husband.

Although M. Jacquemin was very fluent in English, I found the rest of the staff a little uncertain, and with my fractured French it was difficult to get beyond the simplest conversation. However, I enjoyed a lovely dinner of poached salmon, served on a bed of finely julienned carrots with a delicate sauce, which made a very pretty picture on the plate.

The dining room was beautifully decorated, and the service was impeccable. The cuisine is French and as M. Jacquemin told me, the menu is changed weekly. It's an extensive menu and includes dishes that have been specialties for generations—crayfish, trout, Ardennes ham, hare, partridge, and homemade patés, as well as the more usual lamb and beef dishes.

Along with a certain sophistication in the decor and furnishings, there are little touches that give this place a homey quality. A basket of apples sits on a wooden bench in the little entryway, and there's a barrel full of umbrellas for a walk in the rain.

My room was quite pretty, with a little balcony overlooking the park. I was unable to see any of the other rooms as they were all occupied. M. Jacquemin told me all the rooms have balconies and fine views.

LA GAICHEL (Relais et Chateaux), Route de Mersch, Eischen. Tel.: 391-29 or 39-84-87. Telex: 60141 JAGAU-LU. A 13-guestroom hotel-restaurant with a Belgian master chef, on the border of Belgium, 4 km. from the town of Arlon. European plan. Breakfast, lunch, and dinner served to travelers. Dinner reservation required with overnight stay. Closed Sun. eve. and Mon. Open Feb. thru Dec. Tennis, sauna, 40 acres of park and forest with trails for walks on grounds. Maps for extensive walks in surrounding countryside, historic villages nearby. No pets. Famille Gaul-Jacquemin, Innkeepers. Rates: See Index.

Directions: From Luxembourg, take the E-9 to Steinfort, turning off on road to Eischen. Continue past Eischen to Gaichel.

BOURSCHEID, WILTZ, CLERVAUX, AND VIANDEN

Although Welscheid is within easy reach of all of these historic towns, I wouldn't try to see them all in a day. Close by is Bourscheid, on a high plateau, with the remains of an 11th-century fortified castle looking down from a rocky peak, 450 feet above the Sure River.

243

Castle in Vianden

Wiltz is a combination of the old and the new. The lower part of the town is purely commercial, and the upper part contains buildings of historical interest. The lofty 17th-century castle and its surrounding park host a theater festival in July and August. Wiltz is an international center for Boy Scouts.

Clervaux is a forest village that is of interest to Americans as the home of Philip de Lannoi, who came to Massachusetts in 1621. He was an ancestor of Franklin Roosevelt (whose middle name was Delano—de Lannoi). The medieval castle that belonged to the de Lannoi family had to be restored after World War II. This entire area bore the brunt of German occupation in that war.

Vianden, lying on the banks of the Our River, is one of the most charming villages in all the Ardennes. Its hilltop castle dating from the Middle Ages has been beautifully restored, and there are several other ancient buildings of interest. Victor Hugo spent his exile from France in Vianden, and his house and mementos have been preserved for public viewing.

HOTEL REUTER
Welscheid

Madame Marie-Anne Reuter, a pleasant, attractive lady, was telling me about a reciprocal walking tour package among ten hotels in the region. This sounds like a great idea for walking or hiking enthusiasts. Luggage is transported from one hotel to the next night's stop, while the guests continue their walk through the beautiful countryside.

Hotel Reuter is a busy village inn, tucked away at the end of a lovely road that winds through a narrow valley threaded by a silvery stream.

Monsieur Lucien Reuter explained that four generations of his family had owned this property, which was a farm originally. It had been turned into a hotel by the time he came along, and he grew up in the hotel. He has been the chef and owner since 1973. The buildings are grouped around what had been a farmyard and is now a parking area.

I arrived about 2:30 in the afternoon, and I was amazed to discover that the dining room was overflowing with diners, and both M. and Mme. Reuter were terribly busy. They were kind enough to take a few moments to talk to me and show me the hotel.

The new wing, which is very modern, has a large common room with wide windows. A number of people were reading or talking or just enjoying the view of the meadow and the goats and chickens. An elevator took M. Reuter and me to the second floor, where he showed me several very nicely furnished and completely equipped modern guest rooms with well-appointed, immaculate bathrooms. The rooms in the old section are not quite as desirable as the new rooms but are quite satisfactory and very clean.

I did not sample M. Reuter's cuisine, but judging from the obvious popularity of the restaurant, it must be good. He told me everything is made from scratch. The menu offers a wide selection of salads, hot and cold appetizers, and main courses that include meats, game, and fish. I also noted a special *Menu d'Enfant.*

This modest, unpretentious hotel, nestled in a lovely, unspoiled valley, offers an intimate experience of the life of a tiny country village, as well as a good base for exploration of other picturesque and historic villages, such as Bourscheid, Wiltz, Clervaux, and Vianden.

HOTEL REUTER (Relais du Silence), 2 Rue de la Wark, L-9191 Welscheid. Tel.: 829-17 or 819-138 or 817-399. An 18-guestroom (private and shared baths) village hotel-restaurant in a tiny farming village in the secluded Wark valley. European and other plans available. Breakfast, lunch, and dinner served to travelers with advance reservation. Closed mid-Nov. to mid-Dec. and late Jan. to mid-Feb.; also during carnival. Maps for walks available, games room, children's playground on premises. Several points of historical interest nearby. No pets. Marie-Anne and Lucien Reuter, Proprietors. Rates: See Index.

Directions: From Ettelbruck watch for signs to Welscheid.

ECHTERNACH

This wonderful medieval town is the oldest in the Grand Duchy of Luxembourg. The narrow, crooked, cobblestoned streets are lined with 15th-century buildings and ancient ramparts.

A dancing procession that originated in the 13th century and is the only one of its kind in the world is held here in May. Close to the border with Germany, which is delineated by the River Sure, this area, known as "Petit Suisse," or Little Switzerland, was inhabited by the Celts, the Gauls, and the Romans. Some of the existing ruins include parts of a large Roman palace and a Merovingian fort near the old parish church of St. Peter and St. Paul, the oldest Christian sanctuary in the country. Just twenty-two miles away in Germany is Trier, founded by the Romans in 16 B.C. Echternach, for all its medieval atmosphere, entertains many tourists, and the shops and restaurants and little outdoor cafes were bustling with activity the day I was there in mid-October.

HOTEL BEL AIR
Echternach

I stood on the balcony of my room and watched as a mist drifted in, settling into the dips and curves of the surrounding hills, giving the scene a dreamy quality. The yellow and golds of the birches and poplars seemed luminous in the gathering dusk.

Below me a fountain splashed in a large round pool encircled with rose bushes, and a little beyond the outer edges of the velvety green lawn, I could hear the rustling flow of the Sure River as it wound through the wooded ravine.

I had just returned from a stroll with Monsieur Schmitt, the manager, through the beautiful grounds of the Hotel Bel Air. As we walked past the terraced patios, where garden furniture was arranged for table service, he pointed out the tennis court and the little Roman-style pavilion farther down the slope that had once been used as a sort of beer garden. There were aggregate-stone paths that led beyond the terraced lawns with their sculptured hedges and flowerbeds into the surrounding woods. M. Schmitt, in his slightly accented English, explained that in addition to several different walks through the eight acres of hotel grounds, many footpaths were marked out in the adjoining woods, which were part of a great natural park area maintained jointly by the German and Luxembourg governments.

We commented on how the world has changed since a few decades ago, when this region had been nearly decimated by the Germans during the Battle of the Bulge. In fact, the hotel suffered heavy damage from bombs.

M. Schmitt is a most gracious gentleman, and his guests seem to enjoy chatting with him—I overheard various conversations in French and German. While no Americans were in evidence, during my visit I saw many glowing comments in the guest book by Americans from all parts of the United States. There were also signatures of such famous people as Willy Brandt, Pierre Trudeau, pianist Claude Arrau, and even Benny Goodman, along with a number of ambassadors; Charles, the Grand Duke of Luxembourg; and many European celebrities.

The Hotel Bel Air has a rather staid, conservative feeling, a quality of having been there for a long time. Guest rooms in the modern wing have large windows and sliding glass doors opening onto balconies. Although the decor is not particularly interesting, the rooms are outfitted with all the modern conveniences, including telephones, clock-radios, TV, and tiled bathrooms. The bathtubs have hand-held showers; the toilets are in a separate cubicle.

Large windows line two sides of the spacious dining room, where there is a parquetted floor, brass chandeliers, comfortable chairs at roomy tables set with snowy linen, crystal stemware, and gleaming silver.

The service is impeccable, with deft waiters moving quietly and expertly among the tables, eyes watchful for a glass to be refilled, more sauce to be offered, a dish to be removed. I had veal cutlets cooked to perfection and with the most delicious wild mushroom sauce I've ever tasted.

The Bel Air is considered to have one of the best restaurants in Luxembourg, with a French cuisine that is extensive and varied. Their menu depends on what is fresh at the market, but they *always* have fresh trout, which I saw jumping in the fresh-water pond below my window.

HOTEL BEL AIR (Relais et Chateaux), 1, Rte. de Berdorf, 6409 Echternach. Tel: 729383. Telex: 2640 BELAIR LU. A 33-guestroom (private baths) conservative, comfortable hotel and restaurant with a Belgian master chef outside a medieval walled town in the Petit Suisse region of Luxembourg. European plan and various pension plans available. Hotel is open year-round, but the restaurant is closed Jan. and Feb. Tennis on grounds. Small playground for children. Woodland walks and hikes in Germano-Luxembourg natural preservation area, and sightseeing in Echternach and nearby historic and ancient villages. No pets. Famille Schmitt-Alesch, Innkeepers. Rates: See Index.

Directions: From Luxembourg, take E-29, 34 km. to Echternach. Then watch for the road to Berdorf. The hotel is 1 km. from Echternach.

PETIT SUISSE

The road between Echternach and Berdorf runs through an amazing woods, where gigantic rock formations rise mysteriously among the trees and at times hang ominously over the road, with mosses and ferns growing out of the cracks. I found it exciting and brief, because this spectacular forest soon gave way to the more placid aspect of fields and meadows and a little village. Deep in the woods, however, are many more gorges, ravines, and caves where Stone Age tribes probably sought shelter. These bizarre rock formations, one of the geological curiosities of western Europe, are thought to have been formed after the Ice Age, when ice floes and torrents of water cut paths through the sandstone.

There are well-marked trails throughout the 3,000 acres of forest, and there is a rock-climbing school in the rocks of the Wanterbach.

The Berdorf plateau, overlooking the Black Ernz, the Sure, and the Aeshbach valleys, is an ancient settlement with important neolithic and Gallo-Roman finds. The nearby ancient villages of Beaufort and Haller also provide an opportunity for interesting exploration.

PARC HOTEL
Berdorf

The Petit Suisse region is a prime tourist destination, and there are many hotels in the area. I particularly liked the Parc Hotel for its homey, comfortable feeling and its beautiful gardens, with rare trees and shrubs in the midst of fields, just outside the picturesque little village of Berdorf.

Innkeeper Corneille Schwenninger, who built the hotel in 1935, is committed to preserving its original character as a family-style hotel.

The little sitting area near the reception counter, the parlor, the lounge, and the main dining room have a wonderful, old-fashioned European flavor. However, the guest rooms are all attractively modern in decor with telephones, color TV, and radios. The bathrooms are unusually large and well appointed. There is a modern circular dining room with a spectacular copper-hooded rotisserie in the center of the room, where charcoal-grilled dishes are served.

During a fateful week in December, 1944, the Parc Hotel played an important part in the Battle of the Bulge. F Company of the 12th Infantry was bivouacked in the hotel, resting up from months of bitter fighting, when the German Army launched a fierce offensive all along the western front. For a week the Americans held the line, and F Company defended the hotel, finally beating the enemy back. A reunion and ceremony on the fortieth anniversary of that week was held in Berdorf in 1984. A framed citation from the American Army hangs proudly on the wall of the entrance of the Parc Hotel.

I sat on the front porch at one of the tables under the grape arbor and tried to imagine what war must have been like in this peaceful little village. A bee droned over the flowers, and birds twittered in the trees, and only a tranquil silence answered my thoughts.

PARC HOTEL (Relais du Silence), 39, route de Grundhof, 6550 Berdorf. Tel.: 7-91-95. Telex: 2916 PARC BE. A 19-guestroom (private baths) very comfortable, family-style hotel in the fascinating and historic Petit Suisse region. Modified American plan; breakfast, lunch, and dinner served to travelers. Open from Easter to last week in Oct. Swimming pool, children's playground on grounds. Tennis, hiking, rock climbing, footpaths, historic ruins, and other touristic attractions nearby. Rates: See Index.

Directions: From Luxembourg, take E-29 to Echternach, watching for turn-off to Berdorf. In Berdorf, take the road to Diekirch and Grundhof for about ½ block to the hotel.

LUXEMBOURG

The city of Luxembourg is of surpassing beauty, one of the most satisfying and photogenic small cities in Europe. Coming into the center from almost any direction is an exciting experience, seen from any

angle, in any light, and most particularly at night, when it is illuminated.

Almost anything you want to look at in Luxembourg is diverting. The city itself is perched on a rock, oddly cut into an M by the very deep valleys, which are spanned by sixty impressive bridges. It is a city of ancient fortifications and battlements turned into parks, of ancient towers, palaces, cathedrals, and elaborate monuments, and of a rich and fascinating history. Cultural events of all sorts abound, and in the summer there are enough public concerts and folkloric performances to delight any visitor.

HOSTELLERIE DU GRUNEWALD
Luxembourg

I was extremely pleased to find the Grunewald. In a suburb just outside the center of the city, it offers personal, friendly, and quiet hospitality, while still being convenient to all the city attractions. It's an excellent first- or last-night stop in Luxembourg, just minutes away from the airport.

Pulling in to the parking area on the side and in the back of the hotel, I noticed the pleasant little courtyard, surrounded by plantings and a low stone wall, beyond which was a slope covered with trees and foliage.

The back entrance led into the small foyer, which looked very European with its Louis XIV, rose, velvet-covered, high-backed sofa and chairs, a tall armoire, a crystal chandelier, and the cheery fire burning in the raised hearth.

Madame Decker, the gracious owner of the Grunewald, entrusted me to the care of the pleasant young receptionist, who showed me some of the guest rooms.

They are distributed around winding corridors, up a few stairs and down a few others. The hallways are interesting, with little tables and lamps, paintings, and bibelots.

The guest rooms I saw were nicely furnished, with private bathrooms and all the modern comforts. Lace-curtained windows look out on the back garden or over the street in the front.

The adjoining restaurant is run by Madame Decker's niece, and I had an agreeable dinner there, along with the many others diners, who appeared to be enjoying themselves.

Madame Decker proudly showed me the guest book, which had been signed by many important and distinguished guests—even the king of Luxembourg. And more important—John Glenn!

Nothing could be more convenient than the ten-minute drive to the airport on a road that led through a beautiful woods and some residential streets, completely circumventing city traffic. It was a delightful end to my trip to Luxembourg.

HOSTELLERIE DU GRUNEWALD (Romantik Hotels), 10 Route d'Echternach, Dommeldange, L-1453 Luxembourg. Tel.: 43-18-82 or 43-60-62. A 28-guestroom (private baths) quiet and comfortable in-town hotel and restaurant on the outskirts of Luxembourg, 5 min. from downtown. European plan. Breakfast, lunch, and dinner served to travelers. Hotel is open year-round. Restaurant is closed 3 wks. in Jan.; Sat. noon and Sun. eve. All of the cultural, recreational, and historic attractions of Luxembourg nearby. No pets. Madame L. Decker, Proprietor. Rates: See Index.

Directions: Look for signs to Rte. d'Echternach either coming from the city or the airport.

AUSTR

SWITZERLAND

Merano •

Cernobbio   Lake Como
Pallanza •   Bellagio

Erba

• MILAN

Portofino

GENOA •

FLORENC

FRANCE

Massa Pisana   •

                Moggio

• PISA   Pop

San Gimignano •

SIENA •

Sinalunga

ROME
•

Sterzing-Vipeteno

Mauls

YUGOSLAVIA

Italy

VENICE

RAVENNA

Castel Rigone

INNS AND LOCATIONS

TRAVEL SUGGESTIONS FOR ITALY

How to Get There

Pan American Airlines and several others provide excellent service to Italy from North America. Your travel agent will advise. Your Eurailpass is good in Italy.

Country Inns in Italy

In addition to visiting a few of the so-called grand hotels and deluxe hotels in Italy, I found country inn hospitality in villas, country houses, and ancient castles. However, in only a small number did the proprietors actually become involved with the guests.

Reservations

Some of the inns I visited in Italy belong to the Relais et Chateaux. For full reservation information see "Travel Suggestions for France."

Reservations at other than Relais et Chateaux may be made directly or through toll-free New York booking offices, as indicated in the final facts paragraph for each inn.

Italian Menus

Italy has more regional cooking than any other country I visited in Europe. On the coast, fish and seafood dominate the menu; in the

Alpine section, it is cornmeal for polenta; farther south, it is rice; and in southern Italy, flour is the base for a great many dishes. Some areas of Italy have extensive grazing lands, so that beef becomes one of the main dishes; however, where there is less pasture, pork and lamb are seen more frequently on the menu.

Italy is a place where individualism plays a great role, and this individuality expresses itself most vividly in the preparation of pasta. With all due respect to several Italian-American restaurants I have visited, I never really tasted pasta until I got to Italy. For one thing, it is not a whole meal, it is one course—part of a carefully orchestrated meal. Pasta is the term applied to many different types of flour-based products such as macaroni, spaghetti, noodles, and ravioli, and comes in all shapes, forms, sizes, and names in various regions of Italy. I am sure that every Italian restaurant worth the name serves homemade pasta in all of its many permutations. The sauces alone would fill a cookbook.

As in every country I visited, in all types of food-serving establishments—the ristorante, the albergo, the trattoria, and, of course, the pizzeria—I was assisted by a collection of good-humored head-waiters, waiters, bartenders, and also other patrons. After all, isn't it true that there is a little Italian in all of us?

Car Rentals

Travelers for whom Italy is part of a continent-wide itinerary should see the section "Renting a Car for Europe" at the front of the book. The best way to see Italy is by car.

Driving Tips

First and most important, many gasoline stations in Italy close at 12 noon and open about 3 p.m. Special coins are needed to use the pay telephones.

For information about driving in Rome, see the directions for reaching the Lord Byron Hotel, Rome. The international road signs are described in the Michelin Green Guide to Italy.

MY ITINERARY IN ITALY

This itinerary begins in the Italian Lake District north of Milan, continues on to the Italian Alps, and then south to Venice. From there, following in order: Portofino, Pisa, Florence, Siena, and Rome.

ALBERGO VILLA AZALEA
Pallanza (Lake Maggiore)

Enrico Leccardi, his mother, and his sister, Carmen (when she is not working in Milan as a sociologist), are the innkeepers at this exceptionally warm and comfortable inn a short distance from Lake Maggiore in Pallanza.

The building is most unusual. It sits on top of a hill in a little forest overlooking an almost perfect park with orange, lemon, and sequoia trees that were in blossom when I was there, as well as evergreens and palms. There are flowers, shrubs, and bushes in great profusion. It has a wedding-cake feeling and the top story is really an oversized cupola that reminded me of the Mainstay in Cape May, New Jersey.

Breakfast is the only meal offered here; however, Enrico's mother is queen of all she surveys in the kitchen.

This is one of Italy's most sought-after vacation areas and the Villa Azalea offers an interesting alternative to staying in the more palatial hotels. In May, June, September, and October a room can usually be obtained without a reservation.

Reader Comment: "This beautiful place definitely lives up to its billing. . . . more than matches your description."

ALBERGO VILLA AZALEA, 28048 Verbania, Pallanza. Tel.: (0323) 506692. An 11-guestroom modest inn in the middle of a beautiful park about five min. from downtown Pallanza. Italian Lake District recreation available within a few moments' drive. Breakfast only. Closed end of Oct. to Easter. Famiglia Leccardi, Innkeepers. Rates: See Index.

Directions: Look for signs for Albergo Villa Azalea in downtown Pallanza.

PALLANZA

For hundreds of years, indeed, thousands, the lakes of northern Italy have meant a mild climate, natural beauty, and peaceful surroundings. They have a romantic, poetic aura. Poets, musicians, and painters like Dante, Stendhal, Manzoni, Ruskin, Toscanini, and Hemingway, among many others, found respite and inspiration there.

The Italian lakes have become synonymous not only with mild climate, beauty, and quiet, but with a rich variety of attractions, such as swimming, boating, sports, excursions, cultural and social life, folklore, and outstanding cuisine. The traditional boats, with their white awnings, are in themselves symbolic of some of the unchanging customs. The picturesque watercolor effects of the fishermen's villages are much the same as they were in the last century, and the lakes themselves, bordered by mountains, parks, and vineyards, are always beckoning the visitor to return.

Let us stop for a moment here and say the word "Maggiore" several times. It is pronounced with a soft "g" and the "a" is pronounced "ah." Just the sound of the word is soothing and relaxing, and Lake Maggiore is all of that and much, much more. Say it again: Maggiore . . . Maggiore.

CASTELLO DI POMERIO
Erba (Lake Como)

My tower bedroom at the Castello di Pomerio was in the oldest part of the castle, dating back to the 13th century. One of the windows was very narrow, just large enough to provide a view of the countryside, but presenting a very small target for arrows or musket balls by any besiegers. However, a large window overlooked a neighboring villa and lakes and mountains in the distance. The rough stone walls were partially covered with tapestries and there was a heavy table and chair next to the fireplace to complete the medieval atmosphere. The plumbing, however, was not medieval.

This castle-inn is built around a central courtyard, paved in small stones, in which there are two beautiful mulberry trees. There are wooden balconies around three sides of the square and the stone walls and red-tiled roofs create a quiet, tranquil place, quite unlike anything I had found thus far in Italy. There are flowers everywhere, both indoors and out.

The dining room had very high wood ceilings supported by heavy beams that contrasted remarkably with the stone walls. There was a large table with a great collection of salads and cheeses and desserts. I saw fresh strawberries, blueberries, grapes, and all kinds of confections.

Restoring and refurbishing this castle has been the work of its owner, signora Lita Donati. As she explained to me, "We have greatly emphasized the necessity for reproducing the naturalness of the past six or seven centuries. Where new windows and walls had to be created, we've tried to maintain the graceful arches of old. We uncovered some absolutely magnificent frescoes in the main dining room hall that had been hidden for many years. This is one of five ancient castles in this vicinity, all connected by tunnels."

Our conversation turned to the subject of accommodating today's sophisticated travelers. "I think people enjoy staying here very much," she said, "because this is one of the oldest castles in northern Italy and because we have added some of the recreational facilities that travelers have come to expect. There are two swimming pools, two sponge-surface tennis courts, an outdoor grill area, and a sauna.

"Many of our guests stay here for quite a few days and travel by car to all of the points of interest and beauty in the Lake District. We are just a few moments, literally, from the shores of Lake Como."

In the main lounge there was some electronic equipment, indicating that although this may be an old castle, there was very modern entertainment. That night, a young man played classical selections on the piano with great fervor and sincerity.

CASTELLO DI POMERIO, 22036 Erba, Como. Tel.: (031) 627516. Fax: (031) 628245. Telex: Pomeri 380463. A 58-guestroom restored ancient castle with modern conveniences in the middle of the Lake Como district. Breakfast, lunch, and dinner. Indoor and outdoor swimming pools, tennis courts, sauna on grounds. Golf, horseback riding, touring lake country all nearby. Open all year. Rates: See Index.

Directions: Erba is located on the road that runs from Como to Lecco. Look for sign for Castello di Pomerio on the north side of this road. It is well marked. Do not go into the town of Erba.

GRAND HOTEL VILLA SERBELLONI
Bellagio (Lake Como)

"You must go to Bellagio; even in the rain, it is beautiful." Lita Donati at the Castello di Pomerio was insistent. "It is a beautiful, unspoiled village and you definitely should see Villa Serbelloni!"

Signora Donati was right. Bellagio *is* beautiful in the rain and the Villa Serbelloni belongs to another world in another century. It is situated in one of the most romantic settings imaginable, almost at the point where the two arms of Lake Como join. There is a sandy beach, swimming pool, and beautiful gardens, all adjacent to the lake. The drawing rooms, dining rooms, and lounges have marvelously painted frescoes and ceilings and an airy openness that is unexpected in a building constructed over a hundred years ago.

I was told that Americans don't find their way to Bellagio very frequently, and that for many years it has been a favorite of the English. I am sure that Shelley and Byron walked these shores, and drew inspiration from the mountains, lake, and sky.

The Villa Serbelloni has been owned by Rudi Bucher and his family for many years. Although it was a busy day for him, he took a few moments to point out some of the more attractive aspects of both the hotel and the town. "There are many wonderful day tours here in the Lake District," he said. "We suggest that our guests take the demi-pension, which leaves them free to make the noontime meal optional. Most of the time they return in the middle of the afternoon to enjoy the tranquil view of the lake and the mountains and to walk in our gardens."

On beautiful Lake Como, the Grand Hotel Villa Serbelloni is a leisurely look backward into the 19th century.

GRAND HOTEL VILLA SERBELLONI, 22021 Bellagio, Lake Como. Tel.: (031) 950-216. An 85-guestroom luxury hotel, literally at the heart of Lake Como. Breakfast, lunch, and dinner. Heated swimming pool, private lake beach, tennis court, boating, water skiing on grounds. Golf nearby. Open April 10 to Oct. 10. (As with all hotels of this nature in Europe, there is a wide variety of rooms and eating plans. There are special reductions for children, rooms for servants and chauffeurs, rooms with a park view and a lake view. All of this sounds like the Serbelloni is unusually expensive, but actually there are some rooms without views of the lake that are quite reasonable.) Rates: See Index.

Directions: Lake Como is shaped like an inverted Y. *Bellagio is at the confluence of the two arms of the lake. It is also accessible from Varenna and Cabenabbia by ferry. About 1 hr. from Milan.*

GRAND HOTEL VILLA D'ESTE
Cernobbio (Lake Como)

Villa d'Este is one of the world's most famous hotels. With 180 rooms, I would not call it a country inn, but anyone who visits the Lake Como area should at least stop for lunch or dinner. This is exactly what I was doing when I met another American couple from Cleveland, who were making their first return visit after spending their honeymoon at Villa d'Este thirty years ago. We were seated on the terrace overlooking the lake, and naturally I asked them if it had changed very much.

"We were worried about that," they both responded. "We thought perhaps it might have been 'modernized,' as so many other things are, but it is almost exactly as we remembered it. We found our favorite spot in the garden and we were actually able to have our old room again—the food is still exceptional. We are planning to come back for our fiftieth!"

Villa d'Este has a most intriguing and unusual history. It was built in 1568 by one of the wealthy families of Italy. In the 18th century it was renovated by a former La Scala ballerina who married an Italian nobleman. During this period, the gardens were perfected, with an avenue of cypress trees bordering a cascade of fountains. This same lady made a second marriage, to a young, handsome, Napoleonic general, and since she feared he might suffer from military nostalgia, she had a series of simulated fortresses and towers built on the slopes overlooking the gardens, where he and his friends could play war games. They are still here.

Unquestionably, the most interesting chapter in the history of the Villa centers on Caroline of Brunswick-Wolfenbuttel, Princess of Wales and the future Queen of England. This unhappy lady discovered Lake Como in 1814 and devoted the next five years of her life to adorning and decorating Villa d'Este. All of this put a great strain on her resources and she returned to London in 1820, hopefully to take her place on the throne beside her husband, King George IV, but a scandalous divorce action filed against her by the king was thought to have caused her to die broken-hearted in 1821.

In 1873, the estate became a luxury hotel, providing hospitality for European nobility and wealthy guests from all over the world.

Today, Villa d'Este is indeed a swinging place. The parade of Rolls-Royces has been augmented by Fiats and Renaults. Things are still done in the grand manner, but it is not stiff or formal. Every imaginable resort facility is available, and there is both a discotheque and a night club. It is very popular with Americans.

Caroline of Brunswick-Wolfenbuttel, wherever you are, your beloved Villa d'Este is in good hands.

GRAND HOTEL VILLA D'ESTE, 22010 Cernobbio, Lake Como. Tel.: (031) 511-471. A 180-guestroom exceptionally comfortable resort-hotel with first-class service, on the western shore of Lake Como. This is a complete resort facility, including indoor and outdoor swimming pools, private beach, motor boating, sailing, water skiing, surfing, tennis, golf, squash, and night club. Rates: See Index.

Directions: Cernobbio is just 5 km. north of the town of Como, near the southern tip of the western arm of Lake Como.

This part of Italy is as much Austrian as it is Italian. When asking directions in the city of Merano, I was given answers almost entirely in German. I stopped in two places to determine the location of Castel Freiberg; in one, a waitress took me outside and pointed in the general direction, and in the other, the proprietor took me to one of his guests who spoke English and who, in turn, made a marvelous map with extremely good directions. To double-check myself before heading up the mountain, I stopped once more and asked directions from a lady who was selling cold drinks in the street. Before I knew it we had drawn a crowd of people with helpful suggestions. Everyone was extremely friendly and cooperative.

HOTEL CASTEL FREIBERG
Merano (Fragsburg)

I was strolling around the walls and grounds of what was, for the moment, my own castle, thrust high into the blue skies of northern Italy. Circling me on all sides was a ring of mountains, white-clad sentinels announcing the first snowfall of the season. The view from this side was of rolling green upland meadows, where a herd of cattle placidly grazed. I could hear the tinkling of the bells even at this distance. At the far end, farmers were taking the last hay crop of the season.

I left the crenelated battlements that might have protected the men-at-arms in earlier days, and passed a young gardener who had paused for his morning snack of round brown bread, some meat, and a bottle of wine. He was responsible for the gorgeous array of flowers that was sending forth a divine and fragrant message.

Now, I came to a grassy terrace with an outdoor swimming pool, tennis courts, and a few swings and slides for children. The view from here was of the city of Merano, and on this clear day everything in the valley seemed to be miniaturized, and I felt almost as if I could step into space.

The interior of Castel Freiberg is rather formal, with a series of drawing rooms, including a card room with color television, heavy castle-type furniture, and floors of mellowed terra cotta. The beige walls have been amply decorated with pieces of armor and other warlike reminders of earlier days. Everything is beautifully kept with great style and grace.

The castle dates back to the 14th century and has an extensive history that includes several noble Italian families. As is the case with many European castles, it fell into disrepute and disrepair; rescued by the present proprietor in the 1960s, it was opened as a hotel in 1973.

Since my last visit, several American readers have visited here and their accounts of the castle have pleased me very much. Getting there from Merano is half the fun (see directions).

HOTEL CASTEL FREIBERG (Relais et Chateaux), 39012 Merano. Tel.: (0473) 44196. A 40-guestroom very comfortable castle inn located at 2,400 ft. in the Italian Alps. Breakfast, lunch, and dinner. Swimming pool, tennis courts on grounds. Fishing, horseback riding, water skiing, mountain climbing nearby. Closed Nov. thru March. Rates: See Index.

Directions: Merano is located high in the Italian Alps, a relatively short distance from both Switzerland and Austria. First, get directions to the Scena (Schenna) section of the city. The inn is located in a small community called Fragsburg. Passing the Hotel Angelica, look for sign at bridge on the right that says Labers. This will also have the hotel and Fragsburg signs. Turn right over the bridge, head up the side of the mountain. There are street lamps and the road is very twisty. To the right will be a sensational view of Merano. If necessary, reassure yourself by stopping at a small restaurant on the right-hand side of the road. Persist, have faith, believe the signs. Once you have arrived at the top of the mountain, ignore the parking lot and drive to the left on a brick roadway that eventually will lead to the entrance. Park car, leave bags, check with concierge who is amazingly informed, and I will leave everyone in his hands.

A DAY IN THE ITALIAN ALPS

I was headed out of Merano in a northeasterly direction toward Passo di Giovo. The clouds gathered at the tops of the mountains, but the valley was quite sunny as the sun filtered through. There were many apple orchards in full fruit and apple sellers along the road.

The floor of the valley with its meadows and farms is as appealing as the upland meadows and pastures with small houses set high above. There are numerous single cable lifts, which valley farmers use to bring bales of hay down from the upper pastures. The architecture is Italian Tyrol, which means the top floors of the old houses are often wooden, with white-painted stone and plaster ground floors. Hundreds of flow-

erpots suspended from the overhanging roofs splash their bright colors against the beautiful, weathered wood and white walls. The overhanging roofs provide shelter against rain and snow. Some of the older houses have stones on the roofs.

Here, the cow is queen of all she surveys, as the road signs imply, and twice a day the traveler is apt to find cattle being driven across the main road. There is something about looking into the eyes of a Tyrolean brown cow that apprises one of the true order of things.

Now the road begins to hug the mountains with a series of linking S-turns, and there are many waterfalls coursing down from the very tops of the mountains, like silver ribbons tracing their way among the various shades of green trees. Jagged mountains cut into the skyline with their saw teeth, while occasional old barns and houses cling to their sides. It is a countryside that is verdant and challenging, with massive vastness of gentle meads, rushing rivers, and thousands of shades of green with an occasional accent of red or beige.

It is a place where small kittens sit sunning themselves on stone walls and cattle placidly munch their way through the meadows—a place where waterfalls seem to emerge from the sides of the mountains; where barnyards have fat roosters and goats; where the wash is hung out in the sunshine and the wind; and where birds lift the hearts and spirits of all who hear their full-throated, joyous songs.

HOTEL STAFLER
Mauls

The view looking south from the little balcony off my room at the Hotel Stafler was wonderful. It was a gorgeous, bright, sunshine-filled morning, and I could look straight up to the top of a snow-clad peak. The birds of spring were flitting about in the pine trees, almost within touching distance, and at this 'tween-seasons time, I knew the chilly atmosphere that called for a sweater at breakfast time would be replaced by the warmth of spring by noon.

All of this fresh air and a good night's sleep put me in a wonderful frame of mind for breakfast, and I left my room and walked downstairs through a couple of very attractively furnished parlors into a pretty dining room. It was brightened by the sunshine coming through the Brenner Pass. All of the furniture and decorations are traditional, and the many arrangements of cut flowers were very pleasing.

Hans Stafler, the innkeeper, joined me for a cup of coffee, and he commented that most people know the Stafler for a midday or a dinner stop, and do not realize what a comfortable hotel it is. "We have ample rooms, an indoor swimming pool, and all of the attention to cuisine and service that can make anyone's stay a real pleasure,'' he said.

The menu was a pleasant surprise for me, mostly because it had many Italian offerings. I had dined the previous evening in an adjacent smaller dining room, where a small group of men from the area was undoubtedly celebrating some special occasion. They were all dressed in Tyrolean garb, which made it even more of a party.

There are times in everyone's life when the only really satisfying dinner is a plate of spaghetti. The Stafler had spaghetti in various forms with various sauces, and I am happy to say that my spaghetti Bolognese was exactly what I wanted. There are also many non-Italian specialties on the menu.

Situated as it is on the Italian/Austrian border, the Stafler is a most interesting mix of two cultures. The menu is bi-, and sometimes tri-, lingual, and this mix was underscored even more by the fact that the men at the next table, inspired no doubt by the occasion, sang many songs in Italian and German and even one in English, with smiles toward me.

ROMANTIK HOTEL STAFLER, Brenner Strasse, 10, 39040 Mauls. Tel.: (04) 72-671360. A 35-guestroom (private baths) mountain-pass hotel in the Italian Alps, completely surrounded by great mountain peaks. Breakfast, lunch, and dinner served. Closed Nov. and Dec.

Directions: On the map Mauls is just south of the Brenner Pass and Innsbruck. (It is also known as Maules. The map in this section shows both the Austrian and Italian names for various towns.) The most convenient way to Mauls from Bolzano is to follow Rte. 12, off the Autobahn.

HOTEL KRONE
Sterzing-Vipiteno

This could well be the setting for a Mozart opera. It has many of the necessary elements, including a very beautiful and charming innkeeper. More about her later.

The hotel is a wonderful mixture of several different kinds of architecture and decoration, and is actually 850 years old. It became an inn in 1490, having, at some earlier time, been a monastery. A trace of that early use can be seen in the little chapel that remains intact within the hotel. Among the Tyrolean and Biedermeier furnishings is a variety of formal oil paintings, including some 18th-century personages.

The entranceway leads into a vaulted reception area, where there are many photographs of well-known contemporary patrons. A collection of old handmade keys, among the mementos of yesteryears, are very special, indeed. There is an original painting of the Hapsburg family tree almost cheek by jowl with photographs of Charlie Chaplin and Marlene Dietrich.

Innkeeper Renate Seeber, who has blond hair and sparkling blue eyes, proudly pointed out that the *Stube* (bar) is one of the oldest in this region. "It is about 450 years old. The famous Tyrolean patriot Andreas Hofer started the revolution when he spoke from this room." The wooden ceilings and walls displayed many mounted deer heads and great antlers, and the reminder of a very old custom is preserved in this room. In days of yore, the members of a particular trade union or guild all sat together at the same table. Each trade or craft had its own emblem to mark its table. Today, those emblems still designate the tables that were reserved for the blacksmiths, the shoemakers, the leatherworkers, the musicians, and so forth.

Venison is one of the specialties of the house and it is served in many different forms. Dumplings are also a specialty, and there is a dish that has samplings of three different kinds of dumplings. A menu in English has a detailed description of the special dishes.

Besides traditionally furnished guest rooms in the main house, additional rooms were being created in the Hotel Maria, a pensione right next door.

Of course I was completely captivated by Renate, and as I was leaving, she put a copy of Hotel Krone's special "recipe for happiness" in my hands, which I reproduce for you:

Take 12 months, clean them from bitterness, avarice, pedantry and fear.

Divide each month into 30 or 31 pieces, so that the stock will be sufficient for one year exactly.

Prepare each day separately with one part work and two parts humor and happiness.

Add 3 tablespoons optimism, 1 teaspoon tolerance, 1 pinch irony, and 1 pinch tact.

Then mix the whole with lots of love!

Decorate the dish with a bouquet of niceness, and serve it daily with cheer.

HOTEL KRONE, Alstadt 31, 39049 Sterzing-Vipiteno. Tel.: 0472-65210. A traditional village inn located in a busy resort community in the Italian Alps, just south of the Brenner Pass. Breakfast, lunch, and dinner. Closed Jan. 15 to Feb. 1, and Nov. 20 to 30. Sterzing is a center for many downhill and xc ski areas and is ideal for walking and touring in this section of Italy. Tennis, indoor swimming pool, and boating nearby. Renate Seeber, Innkeeper.

Directions: Sterzing-Vipiteno is located off the Autobahn, just a few minutes south of Innsbruck and the Italian/Austrian frontier. Follow Rte. 12.

TWILIGHT IN THE PIAZZA SAN MARCO

Idling away the hours in the San Marco piazza is a continuing preoccupation in Venice—the tables and chairs of the various cafes are filled from 10 a.m. until midnight. At noon, the orchestras appear in the cafes, and there ensues a battle of the bands, with at least three different groups playing at the same time; however, the result isn't cacophony, since they are some distance from each other. The orchestra for my cafe strikes up a medley, not of Vivaldi or Puccini, but of Oklahoma!, *for which they receive a smattering of applause. Shadows are getting long now, and the sun has dropped behind the palaces. Sweaters and coats are being put on and the sunny afternoon is chang-*

ing into a fall twilight. The huge metal figures on top of one of the buildings have drawn back their hammers to let the world know that it is, indeed, five-thirty. A toddler from a nearby table climbs up on the chair next to mine and dips a finger into my hot chocolate—what a look of instant pleasure comes across his little face as he tastes this heavenly concoction.

The pigeons, which enliven the piazza by day, have all but disappeared; maybe it's because the people selling corn have folded their little carts and traveled home for a Venetian dinner.

The first of the many artists have returned to the center of the piazza to set up their easels and show their work once again, and the crowds at the cafe become more numerous as twilight deepens into evening. Now, a man selling yo-yos with lights in them comes strolling by, followed by the usual group of young people. At the far end of the piazza, they are playing with Frisbees—but mostly the San Marco piazza is people; people walking arm-in-arm, solitary strollers, people visiting for the first time, and others who know exactly where they are going.

Ah, Piazza San Marco! One day I shall return with the pigeons, to hear your beautiful music and watch your wonderful people.

HOTEL LA FENICE ET DES ARTISTES
Venice

I am indebted to Lynn and Charlie Henry, whom I met on the Rialto bridge, for recommending this hotel to me—I think it was a great find. For one thing, it is just around the corner from the Teatro la Fenice, and the artists appearing there are quite likely to be booked at the hotel.

I browsed through several guest registers with fascinating signed photographs and compliments from singers, actors, and conductors. Like the Algonquin, it has that artistic ambience.

La Fenice consists of two buildings—the old section, which does not have a lift (there are bellmen to help with luggage), and a newer section with a lift. Both buildings are air-conditioned, and every room is furnished with great individuality in the "romantic style," and all have baths.

Because these are very old buildings, there are some interestingly shaped hallways and rooms, with views out of corners into hidden courtyards overlooking the canals. Seven rooms have their own terraces, and provide an ideal place to rest in the late sun after a lovely day in Venice.

I found it very easy to get information and assistance at the main desk here. The concierge is at home in several languages and has a good sense of humor in many of them.

Breakfast, the only meal served, is taken during clement weather in a secluded L-shaped garden, and at other times in a small dining room

located between the two buildings. There are two restaurants just a few steps away, both of which are highly recommended.

HOTEL LA FENICE ET DES ARTISTES, 1936 San Marco, Venice. Tel.: (26) 403-32-333. U.S. reservations: 212-477-1600. A 75-guest-room hotel of the second class, centrally located a short distance from the Piazza San Marco. Open all year. Rates: See Index.

Directions: From Grand Canal Station at parking garage, take either water taxi or ferry to Pier 15 (be certain to have a complete understanding in advance with the water taxi driver as to cost). Porters will be available at Pier 15 to carry luggage to hotel.

RISTORANTE AL TEATRO
Venice

I had several recommendations for this restaurant, just a short distance from the Hotel la Fenice. Lynn and Charlie Henry mentioned it first and their recommendation was backed up by the concierge and director of the hotel. The word was that this restaurant, in addition to being a regular family-style Italian restaurant, also had some of the best pizza in Venice.

There were different types of dining rooms. I ate in one where there were fish nets and other fishing gear hanging from the ceiling. Mounted securely on one wall was a Venetian gondola.

The headwaiter was very helpful. We settled on pizza with anchovies and a small salad. However, the rest of the extensive menu was most exciting. The dessert cart, wheeled around in most Italian restaurants for everybody to "ooh" and "aah" over, was particularly tempting.

There was also a more elegant dining room, La Mansard, on the top floor of the building, which started out as a club, but is now open to anyone. It is richly appointed with beautiful furnishings and paneled walls; in one corner a pianist was playing Gershwin.

Here was an opportunity for me to see Italians in a totally unself-conscious atmosphere. There were several families with children and it was a very gay, happy, inviting place. I enjoyed not only an unusually good pizza with fresh mozzarella cheese, but also the fun of watching people at other tables having a good time.

RISTORANTE AL TEATRO, Campo San Fantin 1917, Venice (located a few steps from Hotel la Fenice). Tel.: (041) 37-214-21-052. A good restaurant in the middle-price range located a short distance from the Piazza San Marco. No rooms available. Open every day.

PORTOFINO

One look at the brochure on Portofino and I was enchanted beyond measure. Portofino is an old fishing village at the end of a small peninsula that thrusts its way into the Mediterranean, and is reached from Santa Margherita by a magnificent winding coastal road, considered to be one of the most beautiful drives in the world. On a brilliant fall afternoon the sea was blue and the flowers and trees were in their final burst of glory. Best of all, because it was not the height of the season, the traffic on this road had been reduced to a minimum.

The village of Portofino is clustered around a natural harbor, and although it is a prime objective of tourists, the main business is fishing, an occupation that has persisted for several hundred years. The crescent-shaped harbor is surrounded by small cafes, restaurants, and curio shops that attract many sightseers. The brochure on Portofino can be obtained by writing the Tourist Office, 16034 Portofino.

ALBERGO SPLENDIDO
Portofino

I was savoring a lunch of fresh Gorgonzola cheese, Italian bread, grapes, and some small, very tart Italian oranges and luscious pears. The view from the terrace at Albergo Splendido, overlooking a portion of the harbor at Portofino and the Mediterranean Sea beyond, was so enchanting that it brought a lump to my throat.

Before me in the wonderful Riviera afternoon, boats were bobbing on a blue harbor, beyond which was an ice-cream-cone-shaped, green, forested hill, at the top of which was a most appealing villa. Here was a scene that had been enjoyed by Phoenicians, Roman nobles, and tourists from all parts of the world for many centuries.

The mid-October sun was so strong that I spent most of the afternoon at the pool, getting a light tan and alternating between reading a novel and looking at the hilltop skyline, replete with the wonderful silhouettes of the green trees against the blue horizon.

Later, I walked from the hotel down the hill into the narrow streets of the village and out into the harbor area. I arrived at five o'clock to the accompaniment of two different sets of church bells. On a bench by the water, I idled away an hour watching the fishing boats returning with the day's catch, and then I wandered back into town to enjoy a hot chocolate at one of the outdoor cafes.

My dinner at the hotel was enlivened by the company of two English people—we sat outside on the terrace and chatted until well past midnight. A piano played lightly in the background, and in the semidark-

ness, the soft voices and occasional laughter of other guests created a warm feeling of belonging.

Down in the harbor, the riding and cabin lights of the boats were bright punctuation points in the blue velvet of the night, and the street lights of the town seemed like an enchanted pearl necklace disappearing around the small hill.

In the bright sunshine the next morning, again there was breakfast on the terrace, a conversation with some tennis players, and a reluctant goodbye to my friends of the previous evening. They were on their way north and would stay near Nice that evening. "Oh, we stop here every year," they said, "sometimes for two or three days. It is on the road to Rome."

The Albergo Splendido was what I was looking for on the Italian Riviera. The rates are in the luxury class, but considering its comparatively small size and romantic setting, I think it is worth it.

ALBERGO SPLENDIDO, Salita Baratta 13, 16034 Portofino. Tel.: 0185-269551. Telex 28-10-57 Splend I. A 67-guestroom exceptionally comfortable inn with first-class service overlooking the exquisite harbor

273

of Portofino. About 1 hr. south of Genoa. Breakfast, lunch, and dinner. Swimming pool and tennis on grounds. Fishing, water skiing, golf, horseback riding, and exceptional Italian Riviera scenery. Closed late Oct. to late Mar. All rooms face the sea. Half and full pensions available. Rates: See Index.

Directions: Portofino is just off Autostrada (A-12). Using the exit for Rapallo, follow signs through Santa Margherita. Before reaching Portofino village, watch carefully for signs to Albergo Splendido, leading up a precipice road on the right.

VILLA LA PRINCIPESSA
Massa Pisana (near Pisa)

Dinner at Villa la Principessa was over; I returned to the living room, where there was a crackling fire sending out a welcome warmth against the mild chill of a Tuscany October evening.

A very attractive Italian couple invited me to share their delicious roasted chestnuts, and while we were getting acquainted, the last piece of wood was put on the fire, and we asked the porter to replenish the supply. He replied, "The wood is burning too fast." This started a series of jokes about fireplaces and wood and darkness that had us all laughing in both English and Italian. Another bundle of wood arrived and the laughter and good conversation continued well into the late hours of the evening. All of this played against the rather impressive background of the villa; the main living room has an extremely high ceiling and the walls are adorned with a large collection of oils from a variety of Italian periods, mostly portraits of noblemen. They all seemed to be gazing approvingly at an elaborate coat-of-arms over the fireplace.

Villa la Principessa is set in the midst of a very lovely park with a terrace on two sides. The view from the swimming pool offers a panorama of the Tuscany hills.

Guest rooms are quite luxurious; the furnishings more modern than traditional.

We all met for breakfast the next morning as the sun streamed in the windows of the dining room. The gardener was already preparing for the oncoming, relatively mild winter. This is a quiet part of Italy, although the city of Pisa, with its famous leaning tower, is just a short distance away.

VILLA LA PRINCIPESSA (Relais et Chateaux), 55050 Massa Pisana, Lucca. Tel.: (0583) 370-037. A 44-guestroom very comfortable inn in a beautiful villa approx. 25 min. north of the city of Pisa. Breakfast, lunch, and dinner. Swimming pool on grounds; tennis, golf, horseback riding, and Leaning Tower of Pisa nearby. Open mid-Feb. to late Nov. Rates: See Index.

Directions: Use Lucca exit from Autostrada (A11). Follow signs to Pisa. Villa la Principessa is on the right about 5 km. from Autostrada exit. Massa Pisana is not on many Italian maps. It is a wide place in the road on Rte. 12 between Lucca and Pisa.

FLORENCE (FIRENZE)

Florence, like Rome and Venice, is one of the main cultural tourist attractions in Italy. Between visits to several small hotels and inns, I did manage to see the Duomo—the great cathedral in the city, as well as the famous doors on the Baptistry created by Ghiberti. I walked across the Ponte Vecchio, the bridge over the Arno, traditionally the center of the gold and silversmith shops, and also visited the truly inspirational Uffizi Museum.

For full details on everything in Florence, I recommend the Michelin Green Guide to Italy, *which has devoted ten pages to Florence.*

HOTEL REGENCY
Florence

Florence is a busy, bustling city . . . one of the great tourist objectives in Italy. Naturally, with this kind of reputation and with so much to see and enjoy, finding peaceful and quiet accommodations (with a convenient place to park) can sometimes present a problem. The Regency answered all of these conditions.

The director is Arturo Secchi, a most accommodating and well-informed man, with lovely Florentine manners that put me immediately at ease. I have had an extensive correspondence with him ever since my first visit, and his latest letter says that the Regency has been officially classified as a deluxe hotel. They have thirty-eight rooms, but are probably going to have forty, since they have purchased a building immediately adjacent. All of the rooms have a bath or shower, a radio, air conditioning, and color television. Everyone enjoys the lovely private gardens.

There is a park in front of the Regency with dozens of beautiful sycamore trees and a place for children to play. It is in a very quiet section of Florence and provides quite a change from the busy downtown area.

My first impression, once inside the front door, was of hundreds of fresh flowers. They were placed everywhere—in the sitting rooms, lobby, and in the dining rooms.

Arturo took me on a brief tour, including guest rooms, most of which had high ceilings, harmonizing curtains and wallpaper; many overlooked the garden or the park.

Over lunch, he talked about the food on the Regency menu, which is "homemade and natural." One of the interesting house specialties is a T-bone steak that comes from the fat cattle in the Tuscan countryside.

The Regency is that quiet corner in Florence that many people will find delightful.

HOTEL REGENCY (formerly the Umbria) (Relais et Chateaux), Piazza M. d'Azeglio 3, 50121 Florence. Tel.: 587-655-602. New York reservation telephone: 800-223-5581. A deluxe, quiet, 38-guestroom conservative hotel, convenient to all the Florentine museums and beautiful churches. Parking facilities. Breakfast, lunch, and dinner served. Open year-round. Rates: See Index.

Directions: When you arrive by car in Florence, inquire for the Piazza d'Azeglio, a small park. The Regency is about six squares from the Duomo.

COUNTERPOINT ON THE PONTE VECCHIO

In the middle of the bridge called Ponte Vecchio, which spans the Arno between the Pitti Palace and the Uffizi Museum, there is a bronze bust of Benvenuto Cellini, the master craftsman of Florence.

Today, a few centuries after Cellini, the Ponte Vecchio is more than a bridge; it is actually the street of the gold sellers, where, in addition to the shops, there are young people who spread out on blankets their designs and crafts in leather, silver, jewelry, ceramics, and paintings.

In the very middle of the bridge on a Sunday afternoon, a group of young people can be found singing to guitars and bongo drums. From time to time, their friends drop by and "sit in," singing the choruses softly after the main singer and guitar player have done a few verses.

The passersby also create a good show . . . sightseers of all ages in all types of garb, conversing in many languages and accents . . . some of them, perhaps themselves Florentines, strolling in their Sunday best after the noontime meal . . . young ladies in knee-high white boots and black dresses . . . there are Germans and Scandinavians with long hair and blue jeans—sometimes it is impossible to tell the nationality.

I am not sure what Signor Cellini is thinking about all this. His bust faces the young people in the street, but his eyes seem to be raised to heaven. I think that's just perhaps an accident of design; I would think that Benvenuto appreciated this kind of a good time.

PENSIONE HERMITAGE
Florence

"The Hermitage is just like a private club." These are the words in which Jim Mellow of Saint Louis described this unusual accommodation in the center of Florence. "You don't even realize you are in a small hotel."

His recommendation was backed up by Malcolm Frager, my concert-pianist neighbor, who was also most glowing in his praise. Thank you, gentlemen.

The Hermitage is located literally a few steps from the Ponte Vecchio and is just around the corner from the Uffizi and Pitti museums and the Duomo.

An elevator carries guests to one reception room on the fifth floor, which also has the dining room with a rooftop view, and a living room with a very cozy fireplace. Just one flight above is a roof garden with many flowers, and even more inviting views of the town. Accommodations are in small but tidy rooms.

Breakfast, the only meal offered here, is served on the terrace in the summer, and there are many good restaurants nearby.

High season at the Hermitage is from March to October and fortunate, indeed, are the guests who are able to obtain accommodations here during this time. English, French, and German are spoken by two members of the staff.

PENSIONE HERMITAGE, 1, Vicolo Marzio, Piazza del Pesce (Ponte Vecchio), 50122 Florence. Tel.: 055-28-72-16 or 26-82-77 or 29-89-01. A 16-guestroom intimate inn in the heart of old Florence within walking distance of all of the main attractions. Breakfast is the only meal served. Probably closed during Nov. High season is from March to Oct., but anyone writing in advance will receive a room confirmation. Rates: See Index.

Directions: The Hermitage is about 20 steps to the famous Ponte Vecchio. Park as close to the Piazza del Pesce and the Ponte Vecchio as possible; proceed on foot until you find Vicolo Marzio. There is a brass plate on the side of the building. Take the elevator to the fifth floor, where the reception desk is located.

TRATTORIA CAMMILLO
Florence

Frederick and Christine Boes from Dusseldorf, with whom I became acquainted in Florence, suggested that I join them for dinner at the Trattoria Cammillo. "This is not a so-called exclusive restaurant," said Frederick. "It is a place where Florentines enjoy a family meal."

We took a taxi to the center of the city, walked over the famous Ponte Vecchio, and within a few moments were at the door.

The Trattoria Cammillo is not elegant in any sense of the word. Fortunate guests (those *with* reservations) stand inside the front door and wait for a table to become available. The waiters deftly carry the trays over their heads and good-naturedly work around the anxiously waiting, hungry, expectant, would-be diners. "Don't let all this bother you," said Frederick; "believe me, it is well worth it."

Finally, the owner informed us that our table was ready; we were unceremoniously seated, and the fun of choosing from the menu began. From my chair I could look right into the kitchen, where there were many shiny pots and pans and busy chefs exchanging badinage.

Briefly, the evening at the Trattoria Cammillo was a great success. We all sampled each other's choices and pronounced them delicious. My opening course was spinach with cheese and tomato sauce. For the main dish I had veal scaloppine—thinly sliced veal in a most marvelous sauce. Frederick had chicken breasts baked just right, topped with some cheese and basil.

Dinner moved on in what was now a leisurely pace, as there were no more diners waiting. At the cheese course, I had Bel Paese for the first time in Italy. It was a very delicate cheese, and I was to order it several times in the future. Another very good, inexpensive, local cheese is called Pecorino.

Dessert was baked pear, a house specialty. Other specialties on the menu were Scaloppine Capriccio, scampi with curry and wild rice, and Florentine tripe.

Frederick, Christine, and I resolved we would write a book on the small, little-heralded restaurants in Italy. It would take 1,000 years and begin with Trattoria Cammillo.

TRATTORIA CAMMILLO, Borgo San Jacopo 57, Florence. Tel.: 21-24-27. This is an excellent, moderately priced family restaurant. Not certain whether it is closed on any nights during the week. Telephone ahead for reservations and then be prepared to wait.

Directions: Trattoria Cammillo is located about two blocks from the Ponte Vecchio on the south side of the Arno River. It is a few squares from the Pitti Palace.

HOTEL PORTA ROSSA
Florence

The 13th-century tower of the Porta Rossa is a firm indication of the inn's claim to being the oldest in Florence. I was unable to visit the suite in the tower, which was occupied by honeymooners, but I accept unquestioningly the assurance that it has an incredible view in all directions.

The lobby is Old World, with high ceilings and a burnished reception counter. Rooms are large, many with fireplaces and frescoes. Things are a bit tatty, but you never doubt for a minute you are in Europe. In a day when hotels tend to strip down as they modernize, this is worth remembering.

Porta Rossa means "red gate," so you see where the lines were drawn in medieval Florence. Now the inn is in the center, convenient to all that has made the city on the Arno world-famous. The Ponte Vecchio is only a few blocks away.

The only meal served is breakfast, but the neighborhood is full of trattorias as well as ristorantes. If you are there in March, as I was, you will find artichokes are the specialty on every menu. I had an artichoke omelet with a glass of white wine and the chewy bread of

Tuscany that I will never forget. Unfortunately, I have lost the slip of paper on which I wrote the name of the place, but you will find its equivalent, I am sure.

HOTEL PORTA ROSSA, Via Porta Rossa 19, Florence. Tel: 287-551. A 71-guestroom hotel in the center of Florence. Breakfast the only meal served, but many restaurants and cafes nearby. Open all year. Rates: See Index.

Directions: From the train station, go straight on the Via Belle Donne to the Piazza da Strozzi then turn right on Via Monalda one block to Via Porta Rossa. Turn left. Hotel Porta Rossa is on the left side of the street.

PENSIONE CASENTINO
Poppi (Arezzo)

If you don't feel like driving all the way back into the touristic main street, head toward picturesque Poppi, another marvel handed down from the Middle Ages, a miniature city set on top of a hill with an imposing and graceful fortress. I liked the Pensione Casentino because it is an example of what a good and unpretentious hotel can be in Italy—everything is up to standard: rooms agreeable and quiet with comfortable furnishings, a garden, and a good location in the town. You'll find a cool and comfortable room at the Pensione Casentino facing the castle in a pretty garden.

Poppi itself is a little jewel of a city, one of the myriad well-polished, subtly gleaming gems adorning the hills of Tuscany and Umbria.

PENSIONE CASENTINO, 52014 Poppi (Arezzo). Tel.: 0575-52-90-90. A quiet, small hotel. Open from June to Oct. Lucca Gatteschi, Owner. Rates: See Index.

Directions: Poppi is 38 km. north of Arezzo.

IL CEDRO RISTORANTE
Moggiona (Arezzo)

On my way between two interesting monasteries, hidden away in the wild Apennines east of Florence, I made a refreshing detour into a thick forest of trees that covered hill after hill. I finally arrived at Moggiona, a little mountain village overlooking a valley, with a river flowing into the Arno. There was nothing in sight but green turning into blue in the distance. I stopped to have a bite, and sat down to a feast. From beginning to end the *cucina casalinga* (homemade) was a

delight, as was the *coniglio in porchetta,* roasted rabbit. Dinner is about 22,000 lire, wine included.

As in so many other small Italian restaurants, the cook is none other than the owner's wife. Brava, Franca Tassini.

IL CEDRO RISTORANTE, 52010 Moggiona (Arezzo). Tel.: 0575-556-080. A tiny but good restaurant in the mountains east of Florence. Closed Mon. except in summer. Italo Tassini, Owner.

Directions: From Poppi, go 10 km. into the mountains to Moggiona.

HOTEL LA CISTERNA, RISTORANTE LE TERRAZZE
San Gimignano

The most important piazza in any Italian village is the one with the well, and the historic walled town of San Gimignano is no exception. Despite the fact that running water is now the rule, local people still meet at the *cisterna* to visit. Even the teenagers hang out there.

Although I suggest you spend the night if you can in the delightful Hotel La Cisterna, I hope you will at least have lunch in its excellent restaurant, La Terrazze. Tuscan food is at its legendary best here in the hill towns, and I had one of my finest meals in Italy overlooking the beautiful valley in one direction and the red tile rooftops in the other.

The front of the hotel is narrow but vine covered, so you will see it at once when you reach the bare stone piazza. On the brightest day, the interior is cool and tranquil. The Salvestrini family has been running this mecca since 1919 and has made an art of hospitality as well as fine cookery.

Meats are cooked over an open fire, by the way, and the pasta is homemade. House specialties make good use of fresh herbs and local wines, including the fabled Vino Santo, the holy wine of the monks. A fine end to the meal is a glass of Vino Santo with small hard cookies to dip into it. I was particularly pleased to see printed on the menu which items had been previously frozen (three fish).

The guest rooms are large and comfortable with private baths and thick stone walls.

HOTEL LA CISTERNA AND RISTORANTE LE TERRAZZE, Piazza della Cisterna, 23, San Gimignano. Tel.: 0577-940328. A small inn on the piazza in the center of a historic hill town. Large rooms, all with baths/showers. Notable restaurant serves provincial Tuscan food and local wines. Closed Nov. 11 to Mar. 10. Famiglia Salvestrini, Proprietors. Rates: See Index.

Directions: When you enter the gate of the walled old town of San Gimignano, continue straight ahead, bearing right, to the Piazza della Cisterna. The inn is opposite the well and is vine covered.

HOTEL CERTOSA DI MAGGIANO
Siena

The serene and flower-filled cloister of the oldest Carthusian monastery in Tuscany is just the place to plan your day of visiting the sights of Siena, Italy's best-preserved medieval city. The stone tower, the

well, and the cloister are original, from 1313, and the main building is only a few centuries newer, but the monastery has been a hotel since 1975.

Today a dining terrace overlooks a large heated swimming pool. There is a tennis court and a private park for strolling. Restoration has been lovingly carried out, while at the same time guests are unquestionably pampered.

It is hard to pick a favorite guest room. The view of the ancient tower bathed in moonlight is unabashedly romantic, so perhaps I would ask next time for one facing the cloister. In the evening, everyone gathers downstairs in the handsome drawing room for aperitifs; after dinner, we play a friendly set of dominoes in the paneled game room and look over the books in the well-stocked library.

The dining room sparkles with crystal and the table with the high cuisine of Tuscany. Just as fresh flowers and candlelight were my first impression, my first thought was that these, at least, were probably familiar to guests 675 years ago.

Incidentally, the cloister is built of *pietra serena*—that is, I was told, the "stone of quietude."

HOTEL CERTOSA DI MAGGIANO (Relais et Chateaux), Via Certosa 82, 53100 Siena. Tel.: (0577) 288-180. In the U.S.: 212-696-1323. A 14-guestroom and 9-suite (private baths) hotel reconstructed from the ruins of a 14th-century monastery just outside the walls of the old city. European plan. Breakfast included. Fine restaurant open to public. Closed Nov. 15 to Dec. 15. Radio, telephone, and TV. Garden, swimming pool, tennis on grounds. Rates: See Index.

Directions: From Via E.S. Piccolomini, turn right on Strada Certosa and follow signs to the hotel.

LOCANDA DELL'AMOROSA
Sinalunga (Siena)

Here is a place that is hard to describe. Genuine and stylish, it belongs in the pages of *Vogue,* as well as in any art book about Italy. This old Tuscan farmhouse includes a self-enclosed village square, complete with arcades and a chapel, a brick well on a triangular lawn, white canvas chairs under a parasol. Elegance, leisure, and quality are three words to finally sum it all up.

It is strange how each place in the center of Italy—each city, each restaurant—opens up a new variation of the same pleasure. Here the surprise is total; one enters a whole separate world, and a very refined one, too. Maurizio Maffei, the manager, sees to it.

The menu is crowded with numerous delicacies: *filetto di cinghiale* (ham from a wild boar), *crespelle di ricotta e spinaci*, a rolled, hand-drawn pasta enclosing ricotta, a soft white cheese mixed with spinach . . .

The decor features international chic in a typical Italian way. There are also a few rooms along the same line.

LOCANDA DELL'AMOROSA, 53048 Sinalunga (Siena). Tel.: 0577-67-94-97. A luxurious inn and restaurant in an old Tuscan farmhouse, 45 km. from Siena. Rooms have baths, TV, and all necessary luxuries. Closed Jan., Feb.; Mon., and Tues. mornings. Maurizio Maffei, Manager. Rates: See Index.

Directions: Take S-326 out of Sinalunga for 2 km. Watch for the usual landmark—the long alley of beautiful old cypress trees on the right-hand side.

Close to Lake Trasimeno, 25 miles south of Cortona, is the tiny village of Castel Rigone. Perched on one of the lovely hills above the lake at an altitude of 65 meters, Castel Rigone is a picturesque fortified village with a tiny, very pretty piazza and a very beautiful church. Off the piazza is the hotel-restaurant, La Fattoria (the farm), offering good food, comfortable rooms, and a wide open view on the lake.

LA FATTORIA
Castel Rigone (above Lake Trasimeno)

When Aldo Pammelati first came to the Fattoria in 1960, he came to run it as a real farm with 600 hectares of land. As agriculture in the hills was slowly dying, the farm was closed and sold in 1965. Aldo Pammelati bought the main buildings and immediately opened a few rooms to travelers. He then stubbornly set to his task of turning the farm into a pleasant and comfortable hotel.

Now, many years later, it is an undeniable success. The buildings have all been restored to their original simplicity. The rooms are plain but comfortable, most of them with a beautiful view of the lake over the hills; all of them with the pure and cool breezes of the mountains. Even in the midst of summer it's never too warm here. Its perfect location makes this hotel a good overnight place when visiting the center of Italy. Easy access to the lake makes it a nice place to stay for a few days.

Lidia (Mrs. Pammelati) runs the restaurant with the help of her step-mother, who was the cook at the Castle of the Knights of Malta in nearby Magione. Lidia's cooking has kept the simple hearty touch she used when she had to feed all the workers of the farm. But now she caters to a cosmopolitan crowd that fills the impressive dining room on weekends. It is wise to make reservations.

LA FATTORIA, Castel Rigone 06060 (Perugia). Tel.: 075-845-197 or 845-395. A 30-guestroom rustic place. The restaurant is closed on Wed., and the hotel and restaurant are closed in Nov. Tennis and horseback riding ten minutes away. Rates: See Index.

Directions: On the road from Arezzo to Perugia, 58 km. from Arezzo, a sign on the left of the road points to Castel Rigone. The road leaves the lake and winds up to the village. The inn is on the piazza, the highest point in the village.

IF YOU ARE ARRIVING IN ROME . . .

Rome is served by the Leonardo da Vinci Airport, about eighteen miles, or one hour, from the bus terminal. Built more than twenty-five years ago, this airport was never expected to handle the tremendous volume of people that it now accommodates. One needs patience, forbearance, and good humor to negotiate its environs.

The buses to Rome have "A.C.O.T.R.A.L." painted on the sides and leave every fifteen minutes for the central train station, Termini, about an hour away. The fare is about three dollars.

Use only the authorized yellow cabs, and the fare should run about twenty-five dollars. About an eight-percent tip is sufficient. It's a half-hour drive.

Rome has automobile traffic exceeded only by that of Lisbon, so allow plenty of time to get back to the airport, regardless of the method used.

LORD BYRON HOTEL
Rome

I was up to my neck in bubbles in one of the world's deepest bath-tubs. The water was soothing to my tired muscles and exhausted emotions. What a day it had been! At eight-thirty in the morning, I had taken the tour that leaves the front of the hotel and had "done" just a small section of the sights and attractions of Rome in the morning. Returning for lunch, I had followed it with another tour in the afternoon. I had seen Saint Peter's, the Capitoline Hill, the Coliseum, the bridges of Rome, the fountains, and many of the ruins. In the normal course of events it would take another four days to see everything. Now, I was luxuriating in this beautiful bathroom with its mirrored walls, scented soaps, and great, fluffy towels.

A hotel like the Lord Byron is what every traveler needs in Italy. Rome is one of the most energetic, frenetic cities in the world—a fantastic mix of the old and the new in every possible sense. It is certainly one of the most popular tourist attractions because of the presence of the Vatican and all of the incredible ruins of the Old City. After a day on the buses, on foot, bicycle, taxicabs, or what-have-you, it was a pleasure to return to the quiet, efficient service at this conservative hotel.

The Lord Byron is located on a residential dead-end street, which means practically no traffic—and traffic is the one thing that impresses everyone visiting Rome.

I cannot praise the front desk, the concierge, and the management enough for all of the services they provide for their guests, because one thing that everyone needs when they come to Rome is information, advice, and directions.

There are many large hotels in Rome catering to the innumerable crowds of tourists that seem to be there in all seasons of the year, but in many conversations I have had since my return, and sharing experiences with people who have been to Rome, I now know that it was a very fortunate day for me when I discovered the Lord Byron.

LORD BYRON HOTEL (Relais et Chateaux), 5 Via de Notaris, 00197 Rome. Tel.: (06) 360-9541. U.S. reservations: 800-223-6800 or 800-346-5358. A 55-guestroom deluxe modern hotel with first-class service in a quiet section of Rome on the outskirts of the Villa Borghese and near the Via Veneto. Breakfast, lunch, and dinner served all year. Rates: See Index.

Directions: Arriving by air: either take a taxi directly from the airport to the hotel or take the air terminal bus going to the middle of Rome, and then take taxi to hotel. In either case, before paying taxi fare go inside the hotel and check with Lord Byron concierge to make sure it is a fair amount.

Arriving by car from north: Exit Autostrada (A-1) and follow signs that say Salaria, one of the main avenues in Rome. Stay on Salaria (if you have a map of Rome you will notice a large green area to the north of the city—this is Villa Borghese). The most sensible thing to do when you arrive in this area is to hire a taxi and follow it to the Lord Byron.

Note: Don't rent a car at the airport if you are going to be at the Lord Byron. The car-rental company will bring a car to the hotel. The traffic in Rome for the first-time visitor is unbelievable.

Switzerland

GERMANY

AUSTRIA

ITALY

FRANCE

Gottlieben
Stein am Rhein
Appenzell
Chur
ST. MORITZ
ZURICH
LUCERNE
Amsteg
Ascona
LUGANO
Lugano-Paradiso
Kriegstetten
GENEVA

TRAVEL SUGGESTIONS FOR SWITZERLAND

How to Get There

PanAm and Swissair have frequent flights to Switzerland. Your Eurailpass is good in Switzerland.

Introduction to Switzerland

Switzerland is the heart of Europe, the ideal place to start a trip on the Continent. The two main gateways are Geneva and Zurich, each with its own immense lake and pretty ring of mountains; each beautiful in its own right . . . two quiet, refined cities, very cultural, with a high interest in the arts . . . two strange cities where, unlike other capitals, everything works.

Switzerland is like a gigantic music box, minutely tuned. It is a country as serene and peaceful as its most majestic mountains. Don't think you'll be bored, because even the tiny villages are extremely lively and well worth all the time you'll be able to spend there.

Traveling in Switzerland

Switzerland probably has the most orderly driving in Europe, and certainly has one of the best road systems in the world. Most roads are kept open even in the worst winter weather; however, snow tires or chains are needed in the mountains, and it is best to check ahead on road conditions in the Alpine passes.

While renting a car makes getting around easier, distances are very short in Switzerland, and the entire country can be traversed by express train in about four hours. Trains are clean, fast, and always right on time. They can provide some of the best traveling alternatives and some spectacular touring. Detailed information may be obtained through the Swiss National Tourist Office, which has branches in the United States in New York, Chicago, and San Francisco. The New York address is 608 Fifth Avenue, New York, NY 10020; telephone: 212-757-5944.

Country Inns in Switzerland

Switzerland has countless small inns tucked away in mountain villages, towns, suburbs, and even in large cities. If you want to strike out on your own, look for signs that include the words Gasthaus, Gasthof, *or* Wirtschaft—*these places will serve food and usually will have rooms. In the French-speaking sections, the word for inn is* auberge, *and the Italian is* albergo.

Invariably, in a small inn, where the rooms are always dependably neat and clean, the chef is the owner, and his or her reputation is dependent on the quality of the food, which I have been told is excellent and impeccably served.

I encourage you to explore this country and discover for yourself the warmth and hospitality of its people.

Most of the inns in this section are members of Romantik Hotels, and reservations may be obtained by calling 800-826-0015.

Swiss Menus

Breakfast is not a big meal for the Swiss and will rarely be more than the coffee-with-rolls variety. For cereal eaters, sometimes the national cereal staple, Muesli, *is available on request.*

Tearooms abound, with all kinds of marvelous pastries that can be enjoyed at small tables or taken out to be eaten while sitting on a park bench.

Cheese may very well be what Switzerland is all about, and you will find every area has its own special kind. There are restaurants that specialize in fondues; raclette, *a hard cheese, is served hot with a boiled potato and pickles.* Geschnetzeltes und Rosti, *slivered veal in cream sauce, with a pan-fried potato cake, is probably a national dish.*

Menus in out-of-the-way places won't be in English, so sign language usually has to suffice. If you want to see a menu, ask for the Karte. *The word* menu *means the specialty of the day, and that's what you will get if you say it.*

MY ITINERARY IN SWITZERLAND

There are two itineraries in Switzerland, the first one starting in Appenzell and continuing south toward Lugano and then west of Lucerne to Kriegstetten. The second itinerary covers Zurich and some small villages and inns on or near the Rhine.

HOTEL SÄNTIS
Appenzell

On to Switzerland! I cannot imagine a more fetching experience for anyone entering Switzerland for the first time than to visit the mountain village of Appenzell. I came by way of the Autobahn from Imst in Austria; however, Appenzell can be reached from any point in Switzerland.

Although Romantik Hotels has a map of Europe showing all of the locations of every Romantik Hotel, there is a special map, distributed free of charge by the Romantik Hotels of Switzerland. This is a much more detailed map and is invaluable for the Swiss traveler, whether traveling the "Romantik" way or not.

I exited the Autobahn at Götzis, taking the road marked Koblach. Crossing the border into Switzerland, I followed the road to Altstatten, where I found the sign for Appenzell on the left. Most of the road was uphill and above the snowline, and in the early noon sunshine the landscape had a wonderful, shimmering feeling. There are some very typical farm settlements, pretty villages, and artistically painted houses, which lend a unique atmosphere to the country scenery.

After fourteen kilometers I arrived at the village of Appenzell. Sitting in one corner of the square was the Hotel Säntis, named after one of the nearby Alpine peaks, and painted in all the brilliant colors for which the area is noted. I almost used a painting of it on the front cover of this edition. Patrons were dining in the outdoor cafe, grateful for the abundant Swiss sunshine, which can be very capricious in the month of April.

I had lunch upstairs in the dining room overlooking the square. The à la carte menu had an English translation, although the menu for the day did not, and I inquired about some regional dishes. Because it is so close to Austria the hotel menu has a strong Austrian flavor. The menu featured curried minced veal with fruits, English style calves' liver, lots of fish, and beef bourguignon. The special Appenzeller menu had dried beef, noodles with Appenzeller cheese and onions, sausage Appenzell with potato salad, and apple fritters. Desserts were terribly tempting.

The guest rooms of the hotel had been newly furnished in the traditional central-European style, with uniform furniture in all the rooms, but in different colors. Some rooms were furnished in traditional Swiss antiques.

A further word or two about the countryside: these are not the staggering, towering peaks that are usually identified with the Swiss Alps, but a more gentle variety, which still, however, provide all of the typical, pleasant Swiss mountain experiences. Sometimes Switzerland's mountains can be overpowering; these mountains are somewhat gentler and more easily comprehended. The town has an indoor heated swimming pool, saunas, and many museums, including a mechanical music museum and a cheesemaking display. In a country of so many wonderful memories, Appenzell remains one of my fondest.

There are two ways to reach the Swiss Autobahn (N-13); I chose the route that peels off down the mountain with many switchbacks and spectacular views. If you have the opportunity try both ways.

ROMANTIK HOTEL SÄNTIS, CH-9050 Appenzell. Tel.: (071) 87-87-22. A 32-guestroom (all private baths) village inn in one of Switzerland's loveliest areas. Breakfast, lunch, and dinner. Closed intermittently in winter. Many cultural attractions available, including a folklore evening and Swiss bell concerts. Wheelchair access. Open and

covered swimming pool nearby. Cross-country and downhill skiing (not the spectacular kind). Famille J. Heeb, Innkeepers. Rates: See Index.

Directions: From Zurich, exit the Autobahn at Gossau and follow the signs to Appenzell. These are not the same directions that I described in the text above.

HOTEL STERN
Chur

I would hope that everyone who visits the Hotel Stern will have the opportunity for at least a few words with innkeeper Emil Pfister, a sophisticated man, who has been described to me as a "passionate epicure." He is devoted to the Old Grison cuisine and I hope that our readers will seek it out on the hotel menu. (The Grisons is the largest canton, or county, in Switzerland, of which Chur is the capital.)

Emil is also completely tuned in to the needs of travelers from many parts of the world. There are several extremely good brochures with information about the area that is extremely helpful. "Of course," he remarked, "these are the types of things that help our first-time visitors to make a decision to stay longer!" Ah, Emil, there is a method in all of your madness.

At the time of my visit a complete redecorating and remodeling program had been completed in the hotel, and the result was a very agreeable atmosphere, both inside and out. In my guest room there were paneled ceilings and walls of unpainted wood, with beds to match. Throughout the hotel, many original water colors and oils made it obvious that both Herr and Frau Pfister were devotees of art.

A little side note: when I gave Susan Zucco, one of my staff members, one of the Stern's dining room place mats, she was so taken with the original design that she had it framed for her new house.

There are several enchanting things about this little city, including the humorous, life-sized paintings of male and female figures on the walls of some of the buildings. I, like other visitors, had a photograph taken while carrying on a conversation with one of them. The result was very funny.

Chur is one of the many places in Switzerland where you are never away from the mountains; in fact, like Innsbruck, there's a mountain to be seen from every street corner. Of further interest are sidewalk tours through various parts of the town, indicated by red, blue, or green footprints painted on the sidewalk.

The hotel's vintage 1933 Buick is frequently used to transport guests from the railway station and for trips about the area.

Emil Pfister also has a museum of coaches in a little courtyard at the rear of the hotel. There are at least ten or twelve beautifully restored 19th-century horse-drawn coaches of many types, including an old sleigh with very romantic-sounding bells. Emil knows the history of each.

Chur and the Hotel Stern had many pleasing surprises for me, not the least of which was making the acquaintance of Emil Pfister.

ROMANTIK HOTEL STERN, CH-7000 Chur, Reichsgasse 11. Tel.: 081-22 35 55. A 55-guestroom (private baths) in-town hotel in one of Switzerland's smaller attractive cities in southeastern Switzerland. Breakfast, lunch, and dinner. Open every day in the year. The area and city abound in scenic and cultural attractions during twelve months of the year. Emil and Dolores Pfister, Innkeepers. Rates: See Index.

Directions: Exit the Autobahn at Chur Nord and follow the signs to the center. After the fourth light, turn left. The hotel will be plainly visible on the left.

THE ROAD FROM CHUR TO LUGANO

This is a good point in my journey to talk about the roads in the Swiss Alps. In a country that has so many roads curving around and through the mountains, this main road going south from Chur to Lugano has thrilling mountainscapes that far surpass any that I have seen so far. Swiss roads are marvels of engineering with many tunnels and galleries. A gallery is a sort of half tunnel, open on one side. The tunnels themselves provide a sort of between-the-acts experience because you can be in a snowstorm, drive through a tunnel, and come out in the bright sunshine on the other side.

From these roads you can see the many meadows and little villages on both sides, and the pastures are dotted with those tiny, rough sheds found everywhere in both Switzerland and Austria.

In these long mountain valleys it is common for three or four villages to be within sight of the road. Each village has its cluster of houses, churches, and necessary stores; some of them have small hotels with perhaps four or five guest rooms. The same mountain hostelries are called Gasthofs *in Austria.*

Although the road was at 3,000 feet, the tops of the higher mountains

*were obscured. Here and there a bar of sunshine would leap through
for an instant or two before the clouds closed in.*

*In some places, tunnels have been placed beside a mountain, rather
than through it, for the obvious purpose of protecting the road from
being buried by an avalanche.*

*At the San Bernardino Pass, either the outdoor road or the tunnel
may be used, and on the day of my visit, because of the inclement
weather, I decided that it was the better part of discretion to use the
tunnel. Once on the other side of the San Bernardino Tunnel, there
was an entirely different world. The road was above the clouds, and I
could see neither the mountain peaks nor the valley below. I seemed
to be suspended in space midway between the two.*

*As I moved steadily downward, it was possible to see the bottom of
the valley. The stone barns and buildings were quite old, and the road
wound in and out of tunnels through fairly good-sized villages or small
towns. I saw two glaciers and several waterfalls, but the scenery was
now beginning to look quite civilized.*

*Although I did not know it at the time, there would be another
mountain adventure a day later.*

HOTEL TICINO
Lugano

Because I had gotten an early morning start from Chur, I arrived at
Lugano at just about noon. Actually, I enjoyed the road so much it
would have pleased me to have continued on well into the afternoon.

As the reader may have gathered, on my trips through Europe I
usually make at least two stops a day. It would be lovely if I could
stay overnight at every place that I visit. However, I always stay for a
meal and at least a few hours to get acquainted with the innkeepers,
the inn, and the region roundabout.

Lugano and the Hotel Ticino were so interesting that I immediately
wished it had been scheduled for an overnight stop.

Why would I have been happy to spend a longer time in Lugano?
In the first place, it is in the beautiful Swiss-Italian lake country, and
it isn't far at all from several other accommodations that I had visited
earlier, which are included in the section on Italy in this book—the
Villa d'Este and Castello di Pomerio. Second, because of the hotel
itself, which can truly be described as both intimate and elegant, and
third, because proprietors Claire and Samuel Buchmann charmed me
beyond words.

On the ground floor there's an unobtrusive reception area to the left, and the restaurant is through a door to the right. The elevator to the first floor opens up an entirely new aspect, because apparently the hotel is made up of two different buildings, separated by an atrium. This atrium has a skylight roof and a garden that create a wonderful, fresh, light and airy feeling. The glass-enclosed elevator continues to the fifth floor, providing an ever-changing view of the atrium. There is lots of original art and sculpture throughout the hotel with an emphasis on graphics.

I would like to describe many of the guest rooms but suffice it to say all of them have been done beautifully. There are twin and queen-sized beds, and in some rooms you can sit in the window and watch the people stroll by in the plaza. Everything was very clean and warm.

Because I was having a late lunch, both Mr. and Mrs. Buchmann were able to join me. We had an extensive conversation about the Ticino cuisine, which I must say is a bit too complicated for me to include in this account. Trust me, you'll think it's wonderful!

They pointed out that Lugano is well known as both a tourist resort and business and cultural center and is easy to reach by plane, train, or car, including the international Saint Gotthard route. There are museums, art galleries, and beautiful scenery everywhere.

If you can arrange to stay one night or more, by all means do so, but if this is impossible, do what I did and have lunch there.

ROMANTIK HOTEL TICINO, Piazza Cioccaro 1, CH-6901 Lugano. Tel.: (091) 22-77-72. U.S.A. reservations: 800-223-5105. A 23-guest-room (all private baths) in-town hotel in one of Switzerland's more sophisticated cities. Breakfast, lunch, and dinner. Open from Feb. thru Dec. All rooms have radios, telephones, central heating, and most have air conditioning. Claire and Samuel Buchmann, Innkeepers. Rates: See Index.

Directions: If you are arriving for an overnight stay, leave the highway via the Lugano-Sud exit and proceed to the Central-Lago. Now engage a taxi driver and follow him in your car to the hotel. You will then receive instructions about parking. If by some chance you are not remaining overnight and if you're coming from the north, take the second Lugano exit and follow the main road to the railroad station parking area. Park and walk down the nearby stairs, turning left at a sign that says "Altrein." Walk through the underground, and there will be a sign that says "Funiculare." There you board a funny little train that goes downhill into the center part of the city and lets you off at a little plaza. The Ticino Hotel is right there.

ALBA HOTEL
Lugano-Paradiso

This time I was traveling by train on Eurailpass and had no reservations anywhere, preferring to get off as the scene and spirit moved me. So when I arrived at Ticino in March, I did not know the Hotel Ticino was temporarily closed for renovations. I inquired at the railway station hotel-information desk, telling the hostess I preferred small, interesting inns, and was promptly referred to the Alba Albergo, in the Paradiso section of Lugano, south of the central town.

A taxi dropped me at a lacy iron gate through which I could see a garden and palm trees. Less than an hour before I had been looking out on deep snow and waving to passing skiers; now I was in the Swiss Riviera and the villa-turned-inn could have been in southern France or Italy.

Italian is the home language in Lugano, but English was understood at the Alba if not fluently spoken. I was shown a large pink room with bath and balcony on the third floor and was delighted with my quarters.

I took breakfast and supper at the Alba. Good food was nicely served in a small, pleasant dining room, where there were fresh flowers and tablecloths plus attentive service and classical music on the stereo. The menu features regional specialties.

When I went for a walk I found I was at the foot of the funiculare to Monte San Salvatore and quite near the lake. Taking the lakefront promenade, I was a casual ten-minute stroll from the shops and sights of the central old town.

ALBA HOTEL, Via delle Scuole 11, CH-6902 Lugano-Paradiso. Tel.: 091-54 37-31/30. A 21-guestroom (private baths) inn near Lake Lugano in the Paradiso section of Lugano. European plan. Breakfast, lunch, and dinner served to travelers. Telephones, radio, TV, minibars. Open all year. Rates: See Index.

Directions: If you enter town driving on the N-2, continue straight on Via G. Cattori one block to V.S. Salvatore. Go to the end (3 short blocks), and the funiculare station will be straight ahead. The Alba is on your right.

HOTEL TAMARO
Ascona

Although Ascona is in Switzerland, on Lake Maggiore, it really feels like Italy. This is the very same Lake Maggiore that enchanted me a few years earlier.

Truthfully, I'm a little ambivalent about Ascona. I was there at an off-season time, and even so, I had a difficult time finding a place to park. Heaven help us during the high season. I had a feeling that it would be wall-to-wall people. Something like my village of Stockbridge, Massachusetts, on Beethoven Weekend with the Boston Symphony at Tanglewood.

The Hotel Tamaro's interior public rooms, including the dining rooms and sitting rooms, are comfortable and homey, if a little threadbare in spots. The same might be said of the guest rooms. By the way, the guest rooms looking out over the lake and the mountains are noisy at times; those facing the rear are not as picturesque, but definitely more quiet.

I had a very good dinner from a menu that had a decidedly international character. It was a little disconcerting not to have English translations, but the veal scaloppine with risotto and mushrooms was most tasty.

The English discovered Ascona a number of years ago and they've been coming here ever since. There were several English guests in evidence. In fact, it was a little bit like the setting in the first part of the good film of a few seasons ago called *A Room with a View*.

Like all of the Italian-Swiss lake country, Ascona is much too crowded for my personal taste in high season; however, I'd be delighted to return again for a longer stay in April or November.

ROMANTIK HOTEL TAMARO, CH-6612 Ascona Tl. Tel.: 093-3502-82. A 51-guestroom in-town hotel on the shore of Lake Maggiore, a very popular tourist destination. Breakfast, lunch, and dinner. Open March to mid-Nov. Cultural and historical attractions nearby. All varieties of water sports and other recreation easily available. Annetta and Paolo Witzig, Innkeepers. Rates: See Index.

Directions: From Locarno, follow signs to Ascona. Stay on main street, looking for hotel signs. Make a left turn at the lake and the hotel is on the left. Unload your luggage in front of the hotel and then park your car on advice from reception.

THE GREAT SAINT GOTTHARD ADVENTURE

Take a moment to look at the map of Switzerland. After you have located Locarno on Lake Maggiore, follow the road east and north to where the roads separate and one road goes north to the San Bernardino Pass and Tunnel to Chur and the other goes to the west (E-9) through the Saint Gotthard Pass and on to Lucerne.

In a special section preceding the account of my visit to the Romantik Hotel Ticino in Lugano I mentioned the wonderful mountainscapes on the south side of the San Bernardino Pass. However, I was now on a road upward towards Saint Gotthard, which left spring behind and plunged into winter once again. In the high valleys at 2,100 feet there was a full complement of snow on the fields. However, snow is a way of life for this land, and perhaps April is one of the best times to be there because of the opportunity to experience two different seasons.

Continuing north on E-9, I eventually came to the Saint Gotthard Pass/Tunnel. This was definitely a day for the tunnel. Now, however, something very disturbing was happening to my automobile; it was beginning to hesitate. I was reminded of the time my car had completely given out on the West Side Highway in Manhattan. I continued to struggle upward and onward through the tunnel, but it was obvious that things were not right. Finally, actually within sight of the end of the tunnel, the car stopped completely. I had always understood that it would be possible to get help from any of the splendid policemen in the Swiss police stations, so by repeatedly starting the car, shifting into first gear and going about ten feet before it stalled out again, I got to the end of the tunnel and out into the sunshine (surprise!). It took an additional forty-five minutes of coaxing the car up a little hill and then coasting down into (wonder of wonders) the police station.

I eased into an available parking space and sprinted across the blacktop. Opening the door to the station, I was confronted with a microphone arrangement which connected me with a Voice. I pressed the lever down, and after hearing someone at the other end obviously ask me what I wanted, I replied in English (my only real language) that I was having car trouble. Nothing happened. I repeated it again. Still nothing happened. A voice in Italian said something that I didn't understand. Then the same voice spoke in what I assumed was in German. I was now feeling very uncertain, to say the least.

And then the most wonderful sound I have ever heard—English: "Perhaps I can help you." I turned, and there was a very handsome man who explained he was at the police station to arrange some details about a traffic ticket and although he was from Berlin he spoke English.

Thereupon began a series of adventures that added up to wonderful things and generous help from many, many people. Not the least of these was my new friend, whose name is Peter Battenberg. First of all, a mechanic came to look at my car after one hour. He couldn't fix it. He then attached a heavy rubber tow line from his car to my car and explained to Peter that I was to follow him out of the Autobahn to a nearby garage. This was done in relatively short order, although somewhat nervously by me. We arrived at a very efficient-looking garage almost at noon, which is when everyone goes to lunch. I mean everyone goes to lunch.

Peter explained our problem and there ensued some telephone conversations with various people and some nervous waiting on my part. Peter then suggested that since everyone was at lunch, why didn't I join him for lunch at a small Alpine village above the Saint Gotthard Pass, where he and his lady friend were spending the weekend. I accepted with alacrity, and there followed a very delightful lunch and another new friend and a tour of this little ski village, where the ski lift actually starts right from the center of the village.

Full of great expectations, we returned to the garage only to learn that things were not so good. The car would have to be towed to still another garage, where they had more electronic equipment, etc. Furthermore, repairs would take at least two days. This was not good because I had an itinerary to keep, stops to make, and of course a plane ticket back to the United States from Zurich in just a few days.

However, I called the Romantik Hotel Stern und Post in Amsteg, where I was originally supposed to have had lunch, and engaged a room for the night. Peter and his lovely lady drove me to Amsteg, where followed a series of telephone calls to and from AutoEurope and the central Romantik Hotel office in Karlstein, Germany, which had arranged my tour. Peter stayed with me through dinner, then he and his lady friend departed, convinced that all was well. There will be more about him later.

The proprietors of the Stern und Post, Mr. and Mrs. Tresch, couldn't have been more patient, more understanding, or more accommodating. They took many phone calls and really put themselves out. I had a wonderful dinner and a peaceful overnight stay, which I will describe later.

With the cooperation of the Stern und Post, the next morning I was driven to a nearby village to catch a train for Lucerne, where I would pick up another AutoEurope automobile. Settling down to enjoy the matchless Swiss scenery, I breathed a sigh of relief and realized that I had missed only about two visits, although, as it turned out, I couldn't have reached them anyway because they were high in the Alps and the roads were snowed in!

HOTEL STERN UND POST
Amsteg

Spring was just outside my window at the Stern und Post (Star and Post) in Amsteg. This sentence sounds fairly innocuous and so the reader might be led to believe that this was going to be yet another pleasant visit at yet another pleasant Swiss inn. However, there's much more to this visit than meets the eye.

Elsewhere I have described the episode that brought me to this small hotel, where originally I was to have stopped for lunch and then been on my way. However, as it happened I remained overnight.

The Swiss have a well-founded reputation as the "innkeepers of Europe," and this reputation was certainly borne out by the owners and innkeepers of this hotel, because after a very exasperating highway experience I was received in real style, taken care of beautifully, and offered much useful advice on solving the problem.

Amsteg and the Stern und Post are just off the Autobahn, the principal road between Lucerne and Lugano, which traverses the Saint Gotthard Pass/Tunnel. This hotel is ideally situated to permit the traveler to stay overnight and experience all of the breathtaking Swiss scenery in full daylight hours. There are little gardens in both the front and the back and a very interesting peasant house of half timbers and white stucco, which add to the atmosphere. There is a little fountain in the garden and flowers growing everywhere. Looking straight up you can see the mountain and where the snowline begins. The train that runs from Lucerne to Lugano goes by frequently, but not annoyingly.

In spite of the fact that this is a real mountain village, Mr. and Mrs. Peter-Andrew Tresch, the proprietors, are very sophisticated people who are quite at home with the international mix of their hotel guests. Peter-Andrew made wonderful suggestions for dinner, and I was gently guided into the first course, which was fresh trout. The main dish for that evening was beautifully cooked lamb fillets.

There is a rather interesting variation on dining room service here, because all of the vegetables, meats, side dishes, and desserts are placed on two long tables. The meat is sliced right in the dining room, and everybody may watch as the vegetables and other offerings are placed deftly on the plates.

There's a very neat little bar area, which offers entertainment and respite to both locals and hotel guests alike. While I was there a few officers, who were the Swiss equivalent of the National Guard, were having snow maneuvers. Dressed in their trig green uniforms with red trim, they made a most colorful and welcome addition to an evening of good fun.

Had it not been for my automobile trouble I would not have had the opportunity to enjoy a good long dinner and a most restful night at the Stern und Post. I also would have missed the opportunity to see just how friendly, helpful, and hospitable were Mr. and Mrs. Tresch. When you arrive, please give them my warm regards again.

Every traveler should have a Stern und Post in their travel experience.

Reader Comment: "The Tresches are hosts extraordinaire!"

ROMANTIK HOTEL STERN UND POST, CH-6474 Amsteg. Tel.: 044/ 64440. Telex: 866-385. A 40-guestroom (most with private baths) typical small Swiss hotel just off of the St. Gotthard Pass road. Breakfast, lunch, and dinner. Open year-round. Restaurant closed Tues. and Wed. in winter. Amsteg is located in the Swiss Alps and all kinds of both summer and winter recreation are available, including downhill skiing, climbing, and walking. Mr. and Mrs. Peter-Andrew Tresch, Innkeepers. Rates: See Index.

Directions: Use the closest exit from the Autobahn to Amsteg. Hotel is in the center of the town.

HOTEL WILDEN MANN
Lucerne

I'm sure that Susan Rick, the manageress of the Hotel Wilden Mann, eventually chats with almost every guest at the hotel. This is a good thing because she is a very attractive, knowledgeable, sophisticated woman who loves Lucerne and is extremely well acquainted with this beautiful city. Furthermore, she is a most gracious and fitting hostess for this very elegant hotel, whose history dates as far back as 1517. "At that time it was described as a guest house with stables and a general store," she explained. "It was still located within the town walls and boat travelers on the nearby Reuss River as well as those on foot or horseback could easily stop by for a drink. It's too bad that the books only give us information on some of the various innkeepers; there is very little mentioned about the daily activities of those times."

Susan had much to tell me about all of the wonderful attractions, and I regret to say that because of the automobile problem I mentioned earlier I was not able to stay in Lucerne as long as I had planned. Fortunately, she supplied me with much information that I can share with you.

"I guess the thing that most people know about in advance is the Chapel Bridge, with its 16th-century ceiling paintings of old Lucerne scenes, and the little streets nearby that date so far back in history," she commented. "Everybody likes to take a cruise on the old paddle-wheel steamer, and there are many wonderful museums here. People listen to classical music in front of the Lion's Monument and see a fascinating Swiss folklore show, complete with yodeling, flag-throwing, and alphorn-blowing. It's wonderful to walk in the evening through the maze of little streets, bridges, promenades, and plazas. Lucerne is a city of towers. We have towers everywhere, and each one has its own particular meaning."

I learned all of this while having a leisurely walking tour of the hotel, and one of my impressions is of some very romantically designed and furnished guest rooms on the top floor of the hotel. I particularly noticed one room with a little outdoor terrace that overlooks the multi-shaped roofs of the city. Still another impression is of the Burgerstube, a cozy restaurant with lovely Swiss and central-European decorations. The menu runs the gamut from sausage and beer to a chateaubriand with a vintage burgundy. "By the way," Susan remarked, "we have a meal exchange service that allows our overnight guests to take their luncheons or dinners in any of our three other hotels in Lucerne. Our guests may also use the swimming pool at one of them as well as an 18-hole golf course." I also like the fact that it's possible to find a cozy little corner in one of the inn's restaurants and perhaps enjoy a game of chess or a cup of coffee amid the elegant yet homey surroundings. The other of the two restaurants is stylishly decorated with artistic scenes of old Lucerne. It's really most unusual.

The city also has one of the largest transport museums, with an extensive collection of vintage railroad engines, coaches, and antique automobiles, most of them in working condition. Switzerland's only full-sized planetarium is in Lucerne.

The title of this book is *Country Inns and Back Roads*, and it's true that I feel very much at home on the wonderfully kept back roads of Europe; however, I must also confess that I find some of Europe's and England's cities irresistible; to Stockholm, Granada, Vienna, and London I must now add Lucerne.

ROMANTIK HOTEL WILDEN MANN, Bahnhofstrasse 30, CH-6000 Lucerne. Tel.: 041-23-1666. A 50-guestroom (all private baths) city hotel in the old section of Lucerne. Breakfast, lunch, and dinner. Open year-round. Most convenient to enjoy all of the pleasures of Lucerne as well as the numerous surrounding mountains. Lake excursions nearby. Please plan on staying two nights. Fritz Furler (4th generation), Owner; Susan Rick, Manageress. Rates: See Index.

Directions: My suggestion for all major cities is to hire a taxi and follow it to the hotel. It's by far the most satisfactory arrangement.

GASTHOF STERNEN
Kriegstetten

This is an excellent opportunity to point out that Switzerland is a very complex country. There is a great deal more to it than the snow-covered Alpine peaks and bucolic valleys. In the main, I am sure that the image of Switzerland throughout the rest of the world is that of great uphill ski lifts and long ski runs that drop down into glamorous jet-set villages, where everyone skis all day and carouses all night.

Not true. Of course, there are a lot of ski areas and many ski excursions from the United States to the snow centers of all of the Alpine countries; however, to really understand and appreciate the people, traditions, customs, and true heart of these countries, it is necessary to seek out the more quiet places enjoyed by the Swiss and other Europeans themselves.

Such a place is the Hotel Sternen, in a somewhat suburban village and near the larger town of Solothurn. Jörg and Margrit Bohren run it in very much the same way that it has been running since 1845. Actually, Jörg's parents bought it in 1952, and in 1975 Jörg and Margrit took it over.

On arrival, my immediate impression was of a traditional inn with a very pleasant atmosphere, and then I had the wonderful feeling that I was being well taken care of. There is even turn-down service for the beds.

The architectural design of the building was one that I saw many times in Europe. It has three stories, with a sharply pitched, peaked roof. Considering the fact that it has remained practically unchanged since 1847, one does get a feeling of permanence.

Margrit and Jörg seemed to be well acquainted with all of their dinner guests, many of whom, I'm sure, came from the nearby towns of Solothurn or Bern, about which I was becoming more and more curious.

The dinner menu offered three different meats—beef, veal, and pork—on the same plate. It's a sort of sampler, served with vegetables and rice. Jörg was the maitre d' and I could see him moving about, speaking in many languages and making his guests feel at home.

The accommodations were most appealing, and mine looked out a full-length window to a little park area, which had some good swings and slides for children.

It was in a later conversation with Jörg and Margrit that I learned something about nearby Solothurn, which, as they recommended, should be visited by everyone who stays at the hotel.

"It is a town of unique characteristics," Margrit said. "Our guests tell us that they have discovered something very, very wonderful. It has an idyllic quality that invites visitors to wander around and enjoy its charms and the traces of a fascinating past in the many different architectural styles. The ornamental fountains are outstanding."

They told me that the center of Solothurn is closed to traffic, and in summer there are many sidewalk cafes, where visitors can sit and enjoy the sunshine.

The Hotel Sternen is ideally situated as a first stop for someone flying to Zurich and then continuing on to Lucerne and the mountains of Switzerland. It is wonderfully quiet and is just the place to recover from a little jet lag.

ROMANTIK HOTEL GASTHOF STERNEN, CH-4566 Kriegstetten. Tel.: 065-3561-11. A 17-guestroom (private baths) village inn in the Swiss midlands, 8 km. from Solothurn; 30 km. Bern. Breakfast, lunch, and dinner served. Closed first 2 wks. of Feb. Wheelchair access. This is excellent walking, running, and bicycling country. The town of So-lothurn is worth a long visit. Jörg and Margrit Bohren, Proprietors. Rates: See Index.

Directions: From Zurich, take the M1 to the exit for Kriegstetten and turn left. The more adventuresome traveler can follow the Swiss map and go through the countryside.

ZURICH

Zurich is, if possible, more Swiss than Geneva, a more puritanical and sober city—"So clean," James Joyce commented, "that if you spilled your soup on the Bahnhofstrasse (the 'Champs Elysées' of Zurich), you could eat it up without a spoon." While it is true the "Athens of the Limmat" has a friendly, orderly, and hard-working population, it is also true that there are high-class restaurants, discotheques, shops, three outstanding museums, and that this city is the starting point for myriad enchanting excursions.

In fact, the city inhabitants are so welcoming that they have set up a system called "Meet the Swiss," which offers any tourist wishing to visit a Zurich family the possibility to do so—free of charge, of course. You only need to ask the Tourist Office for a list of local hosts happy to invite visitors from other countries into their homes for dinner. A starting point for discoveries and new friendships!

Kloten Airport, Zurich

With the admirable efficiency of the Swiss, visitors arriving at Kloten Airport can deplane and descend to the railroad station and platform with their luggage. There is no charge for carts, and baggage can be transferred to the railway immediately following customs. Porters wear blue uniforms with a Swissair badge.

There are two ways to get to the center of Zurich. One is by train, which takes about ten minutes, with frequent departures, and costs about three dollars. However, the airport station provides connections to many points in Switzerland. The taxi to downtown Zurich is about fourteen dollars.

HOTEL FLORHOF
Zurich

Those who like small hotels will appreciate the Florhof. It possesses all the qualities of a vanishing type of establishment, with a pleasant, just off-center location, quiet surroundings, good service, and good food. An 18th-century patrician building, remodeled ten years ago to provide each of the thirty-three rooms with bathrooms, the hotel still retains some of its ancient atmosphere. Most noteworthy are the ceramic stove with decorative old tiles in the dining room and, on the ceilings of the rooms, the extraordinary plaster moldings in elaborate baroque designs. Both bear witness to the past grandeur of this house. However, there are such modern comforts as color TV and a minibar in the guest rooms.

HOTEL FLORHOF, Florhofgasse 4, 8001 Zurich. Tel.: 01-47-44-70. Telex: 817-364. A 33-guestroom (private baths) unpretentious hotel in a classic building on the bank of the Limmat River. Open year-round. Mr. Schilter, Manager. Rates: See Index.

Directions: Ten min. from railway station.

HOTEL ZUM STORCHEN
Zurich

Paracelsus, Richard Wagner, and Gottfried Keller knew the Stork, as well as many other famous and unknown visitors, in its six centuries of existence. I walked into the lobby, heavily burdened with large packages filled with all the marvelous objects I'd bought at Heimatwerk, an extraordinary shop specializing in Swiss crafts close to the hotel. I was welcomed into the warm and animated lobby by a helpful porter, who instantly helped me with my load. Amiable and efficient people at the reception desk checked me in and gave me all the information I requested, before taking me up to my room.

Strangely enough, although this hotel had been thoroughly rebuilt in the forties and has been remodeled since, it has more of a genuine Swiss atmosphere than older, unremodeled places—tradition does carry a spell. The history of the hotel, which starts in the middle of the fourteenth century, would fill a volume.

The restaurant (*rotisserie*) is one of the best in town. Very well

307

decorated with lots of attractive wood and comfortable chairs, it offers a carefully selected choice of local and some international dishes. The big *spécialité* is venison, in season, of course. My dinner there started with thin slices of smoked young wild boar ham served with fresh figs. I then tried and finished the deer steak with red currants, chives, and green noodles, a very tasty combination. For dessert I chose something also in season, an unusual pasta—a long, fat vermicelli of chestnut paste, all in a tangle on a meringue, and topped with whipped cream. I can say only one thing: try it.

HOTEL ZUM STORCHEN, Am Weinplatz 2, 8001 Zurich. Tel.: 211-55-10. Telex: 81-33-54. Fax: 01-211-6451. A 77-guestroom famous, 600-year-old, traditional Swiss hotel (all modern conveniences) overlooking the river. Rates: See Index.

Directions: Within walking distance of the railway station.

STEIN AM RHEIN

From Zurich, I took a train to Stein am Rhein, a tiny medieval city on the Rhine River, a lovely, lively townlet with colorful, painted facades and extraordinarily well-preserved architecture. If I were arriving from the United States, I would drive there straight from the airport and spend a comfortable day or two at Ilge to settle down to the new feeling of old, quiet Continental Europe.

Stein am Rhein is a real fairyland. The frescoes on the buildings, the buildings themselves, the flowers, the ducks and swans on the river, the chocolate in the chocolate shops, the cows and sheep in the fields, the trees in the forest, the people in the street, and even the food on the plates in the restaurants—all are actually real.

I spent a bright and sunny day there at the beginning of fall. The sky was an intense blue, and a strong, whirling wind carried the old leaves away and wrinkled the waters of the river.

GASTHAUS ILGE
Stein am Rhein

This is a warm and very human place, always a bit noisy and smoky, never empty because the clientele is mostly local. A real inn, in our sense of the word, complete with a welcoming hostess, Rosemarie Benker. She and her husband, Hermann, took over this place ten years ago after running the local youth hostel for a long time. Recently, they transformed the second floor of the house into four homey rooms overlooking the neighboring rooftops. A most romantic place, where it is wise to make reservations in advance.

The restaurant, Hermann's domain, provides hearty meals of *Kalbsleber* (liver of veal), *Rosti* (a special kind of grilled potatoes), and good soups and salads. Don't forget to try the Russian chocolate, *russische Schokolade* (hot chocolate with vodka and cream).

GASTHAUS ILGE, CH 8260 Stein am Rhein. Tel.: 54-41-22-72. A 4-guestroom lively but homey inn with a good restaurant. Advance reservations advisable. Rosemarie and Hermann Benker, Innkeepers. Rates: See Index.

Directions: From Zurich, take the highway to Schaffhausen. Turn off to Stein am Rhein.

There is a pretty path through the vines and the woods, climbing up the hill from Stein, toward the fortress of Hohenklingen. In the fall there are lots of hazelnuts and walnuts on the ground that, along with some excellent pears, provided a friendly sheep and me with a healthy midmorning snack.

HOHENKLINGEN RESTAURANT
Stein am Rhein

It takes approximately half an hour to reach this fortress if one stops to rest on a bench conveniently placed halfway up the hill, with a wide view of the town and the river.

Built in 1050, it has been in the possession of the bourgeois of the town of Stein since 1457. It was then used as a watchtower against possible attacks, and the means of the warning was a huge bell, hence the name Hohenklingen, which literally means "high ring." In 1860, the perils apparently over, the town council converted it into an inn, and they still run the place as such nowadays. It has some of the very few authentic, turn-of-the-century decorations I've seen in the area—wood-paneled walls covered with trophies, flags, and other paraphernalia of hunting or conquest. It is an interesting place for a simple lunch in the preserved atmosphere of a 19th-century inn.

HOHENKLINGEN RESTAURANT, CH 8260 Stein am Rhein. A town-owned fortress-restaurant on top of a hill overlooking the town and the river. Ask the hotel to make reservations.

Directions: Either drive or walk the 3 km. up the hill above Stein am Rhein.

HOTEL KRONE
Gottlieben

The ducks and geese on the Rhine at the Hotel Krone looked as if they hadn't changed one bit since my last visit. The Rhine was calm and, indeed, much the same as it has been for thousands of years. From the marshlands immediately across the river, I could hear sounds of nesting birds, and in the distance a cock was crowing. Dominating the entire scene was a stately swan. I looked around to see if there was a mate nearby, but none appeared. The single swan, with great confidence and self-assurance, paddled out to the middle of the river to see whether or not any of the steamers that ply this part of the Rhine and the Bodensee would be making their appearance.

Now, a passenger boat drifted by almost silently. Strangely enough, I couldn't see anyone on the boat—it seemed to be absolutely empty. Who was steering it? Who was making it go? Oh, there is a head with a hat on it—now I can see it. It cruised by and disappeared quietly.

The new owners of the Hotel Krone have done some important redecorating in recent years, and each guest room has a television set, direct-dial telephones, and an alarm/radio. Furthermore, each is decorated quite differently, as far as colors are concerned. There are fabrics on the guest-room walls instead of wallpaper, and many of the hallways and public rooms have regional paintings. The dining room is very pleasant, with paneled ceilings and walls and an aesthetically pleasing subdued overhead lighting for each table. Fresh flowers were everywhere, complementing the original oils and watercolors.

My dinner that night was beef goulash with a really good red and green pepper sauce. Another excellent dish was shrimp on a bed of spinach. The lobster bisque soup was certainly to my taste, as well as the prawns with a special mushroom sauce. The dessert was an absolutely staggering sample of everything on the dessert cart.

It was great fun to revisit this enchanting hotel on the Rhine River, on the border of Switzerland and Germany.

ROMANTIK HOTEL KRONE, CH-8274 Gottlieben. Tel.: 072-69-23-23. A 22-guestroom (private baths) riverside hotel between Switzerland and Germany. Breakfast, lunch, and dinner served daily. Closed early Jan. to mid-Feb. Famille Schraner-Michaeli, Innkeepers. Rates: See Index.

Directions: From Zurich drive through Winterthur on the road to Konstanz, Germany; Gottlieben is the last village before the border crossing. Coming from Germany, it is the first village after the border crossing.

Austria

INNS AND LOCATIONS

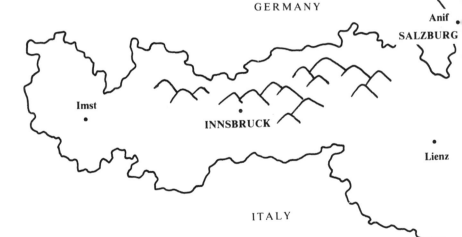

LINZ

Durnstein

VIENNA

St. Wolfgang am See

Semmering

Schladming

GRAZ

Villach

TRAVEL SUGGESTIONS FOR AUSTRIA

How to Get There

Pan Am and several different airlines fly from North America to Vienna. I'd suggest that you talk it over with your travel agent. Eurailpass is also good in Austria.

Country Inns in Austria

Austrian country inns are delightful. Some are simple, less expensive pensions offering the opportunity to know Austrians more readily. The somewhat austere, but pleasant, clean, and comfortable rooms usually have two beds with a private shower and wc. Almost all overnight stays in a pension include a breakfast of rolls, butter, jam, tea, or coffee. Many offer an evening meal (full pension), and special rates are available for longer stays.

Reservations

When a reservation is made for an Austrian accommodation, the agreement is very clear. The hotel owner or pension proprietor must hold the rooms, and the guest (unless he cancels) is positively obligated for the cost of the room. This is the law of Austrian innkeeping.

Reservations for accommodations in this book can be made by mail (a deposit helps) or by telephone. Many of the inns listed here can be booked through Romantik Hotels, and reservations may be obtained by calling 800-826-0015.

Car Rentals

See the section in front of this book entitled "Renting a Car for Europe."

Driving Tips

Driving in Austria is the same as driving in Germany, although speed limits are different. Once again the back roads are beautiful and driving in the Austrian Alps is a marvelous experience. Austrian roads are kept in beautiful condition and it's possible to go everywhere in the country by car.

MY ITINERARIES IN AUSTRIA

One itinerary begins in Vienna and includes a day trip to Dorstein. Then I took the train to Graz and Semmering. Another itinerary starts in Salzburg and works its way to Switzerland.

VIENNA NIGHTS AND DAYS

In every European city there are always "musts." In Copenhagen it is probably Tivoli Gardens; in London, the changing of the guard. In Vienna, the list is so long that there is a temptation to try to see everything. There is the Spanish Riding School, the Vienna Boys' Choir, and the opera. There are almost endless art galleries and museums. There are also the Vienna Woods, the many gardens, castles, memorial sites, and libraries.

There is also the Prater, over 1,300 acres on the Danube River. It is easy to find because it has a 210-foot-high Ferris wheel and the ride is something no one ever forgets. Some of the fun rides in the Prater are the most unusual ever devised by the minds of amusement park operators. It is said that Johann Strauss used to play at the various restaurants and his melodies are heard continually.

One of the most fascinating things about Vienna is the fact that the visitor can go almost everywhere by streetcar or public transportation. At 5 p.m., there were people in evening clothes riding the streetcars toward the center of the city to go to the opera, and at 11:30 p.m., the same people were riding back to the suburbs.

It is possible to go almost everywhere in Vienna and nearby on really well-organized sightseeing tours.

HOTEL RÖMISCHER KAISER
Vienna

This hotel belongs to the Romantik Hotels, a voluntary association of small historical hotels and restaurants, formed to provide an alternative to the standardized facilities of large hotels and catering groups.

I liked this hotel immediately and was very happy to meet the manager, who showed me proudly through many different rooms.

Some of the bedrooms were most romantic, indeed, with ornately carved beds and rather plush furniture. The building is quite old and therefore has higher ceilings and larger rooms than I found in some of the more recently constructed hotels.

The hotel is situated in a pedestrian zone, close to the shopping mall, between the opera house and Saint Stephen's Church.

RÖMISCHER KAISER (Romantik Hotels), Annagasse 16, A-1010 Vienna. Tel. 512-77-51. A 27-guestroom hotel in the center of Vienna. Rates: See Index.

St. Stephen's Church

A back street in Vienna

DINING IN VIENNA

Briefly, Viennese restaurants can be divided into several categories: first-class, middle-class (or restaurant "bourgeois"), the Gasthaus *or inn, the pub, the cellar, restaurants* bon marché *(for cheap meals), and specialty restaurants. Out-of-towners in Vienna can always be seen with two items in their hands—a Viennese restaurant booklet and a map of Vienna. I have discussed Viennese food more completely in describing my visits to various restaurants.*

WIENER RATHAUSKELLER
Vienna

I was wandering across the park to the Town Hall, known as the *Rathaus*. It was built between 1872 and 1885, and has carved figures all around the fourth story of the building. A huge clock was pointing at six o'clock.

The doors opened promptly and I went downstairs into the Rathaus-keller, one of the famous tourist restaurants in Vienna. I was in the cellar, where there was a vaulted ceiling, beautifully carved chairs, many murals, and the sound of music in the background. There were various dining rooms off a long hallway, some of them decorated for parties. In the middle of this hallway I saw a large glass tank filled with fish.

One of these rooms is known as the Grinzinger Keller, where, on each table, there are most unusual wine decanters that look like gigantic medicine droppers. The music I heard was coming from the four musicians at the other end of the dining room. I was told that the atmosphere makes this room very popular with the Viennese and visitors.

The menu was typical of many Viennese restaurants, with quite a few schnitzels and other Austrian dishes featured.

WIENER RATHAUSKELLER, Rathausplatz 1, A-1010 Vienna. Tel.: 421219. A popular "middle class" tourist restaurant in the cellar of the Vienna Town Hall. Open for lunch and dinner. Closed Sundays.

THE THREE HUSSARS
Vienna

I had been told that this was one of the supreme restaurants, not only in Vienna, but in all of Europe. It is located just off the main shopping plaza not far from Saint Stephen's Church, which along with the opera house is the center of Viennese downtown activity.

Here was genteel Vienna at its very best. The restaurant was rapidly filling up with well-dressed, confident-looking people, both Viennese

The Vienna Opera House

and visitors, all of whom seemed very much in place in this rather elegant atmosphere. My table was decorated with a small plant and a lighted candle.

The one thing that everyone always talks about when the Three Hussars enters the conversation is the hors d'oeuvres. There must be at least fifty different varieties and they are all expertly moved by a waiter from table to table on a series of four carts.

I eventually settled for a delicious chicken served Hungarian style, one of the specialties of the house. For dessert I had something that probably could only be born in Vienna. I am not sure it has a name but it consisted of fresh peaches and strawberries intermixed with chocolate whipped cream and nuts.

The Three Hussars is a great adventure in Viennese eating.

THE THREE HUSSARS (Zu den 3 Husaren), Weihburggasse 4, A-1010 Vienna. Tel.: 512-692. A "first class" restaurant especially famous for its hors d'oeuvres. Dinner only. Closed Sundays.

GRIECHENBEISL
Vienna

I visited this very old restaurant in the market district of Vienna on a Sunday morning after church. There was a wedding party in progress with gay accordion music, and everyone was having a very good time.

I was shown to a small table in one corner where I had a vantage point from which to watch all of the people arriving for the noontime meal. All around me were coins embedded in the walls, and here or there was a hole where apparently someone had acquired a souvenir.

The restaurant is made up of many different rooms, some with very low doors, necessitating tall people to stoop as they enter. The furniture, tables, chairs, and fixtures all give the appearance of being antique.

Long before I visited it, I heard it mentioned as the place Mozart frequented. I discovered that not only Mozart, but Beethoven, Schubert, Wagner, Strauss, Brahms, Mark Twain, and Count von Zeppelin had also been guests.

Naturally, a restaurant like this is well known and quite a few visitors find their way to it during a visit to Vienna. I had an excellent cup of *Weiser Melange* and a piece of Viennese pastry for lunch.

The little booklet in English, distributed to each patron, indicates that apparently there has been an inn on this site since 1447. It was once built into the high wall of the outer defenses of the city against the Turks.

GRIECHENBEISL, Fleischmarkt 11, A-1010 Vienna. Tel.: 533-19-77. A "middle class" restaurant two blocks behind St. Stephen's Church. A well-known tourist attraction. Open every day from 10 a.m. to 1 p.m.

HOTEL SCHLOSS DURNSTEIN
Durnstein

On the Sunday afternoon I arrived at Schloss Durnstein, the children of innkeepers Johann and Rosemarie Thiery were on the terrace dressed in their native dirndls and lederhosen to present flowers and sing a song of welcome to an important guest. Obviously innkeeping is a family affair here, which may be why I felt immediately at home, even in a one-time Renaissance palace of the counts and princes of Starhemberg overlooking the Danube.

Not far away are the ruins of the ancient castle where Richard the Lionheart was an involuntary guest in 1192 and 1193. Richard's wily minstrel, Blondel, managed the ransom by trickery, so the story goes, and after thirteen months, Richard went home from the Crusades to England. By the time I considered making the twenty-minute climb from the inn, night was coming on apace. Another day, I decided.

The Schloss was built in 1630 in a prime location halfway between Vienna and Linz. This is the Wachau region, known for fine wines as well as medieval monasteries and storybook villages, and only the fact that the inn was full kept me from changing my plans and staying the night. However, Johann kindly showed me the rooms where guests had not yet checked in and gave me a tour of the premises. I envied all those who had reserved in advance and were spending their holiday in this comfortably luxurious, antique-filled castle-hotel.

At least I had planned to stay for dinner and see for myself why the dining room is so highly recommended. Let me just say this: no prince ever left his table more satisfied.

HOTEL SCHLOSS DURNSTEIN (Relais et Chateaux), A-3601 Durnstein 2. Tel.: (027) 11-212. In the U.S.: 212-696-1323. A 35-guestroom and 2-suite (private baths) historic castle hotel overlooking the Danube in the Walchau, halfway between Linz and Vienna. Buffet breakfast included. Restaurant open to public. Closed Nov. and April. Sauna and solarium on premises. Fishing and sightseeing nearby. Rates: See Index.

Directions: Durnstein is 100 km. from Vienna. Take the winding road to Krems along the Danube if you have time. If not, then take the A-1 to Linz (the highway continues to Salzburg and Innsbruck) and watch for the turn-off to Durnstein and Krems.

GRAZ—THE NATURAL CITY

Almost from the moment of my arrival I felt that Graz had been a great choice of Austrian cities to visit. It was an almost completely "natural" city, neither self-consciously preening itself for tourists nor dominated by some tremendous scenic attraction, such as high mountains or picturebook lakes. I found that it had dozens of extremely interesting scenic and cultural attractions, but on the whole it was relatively undiscovered as far as tourists are concerned.

Graz is the capital of the province of Styria and the second largest city in Austria, with about 239,000 inhabitants. It is situated at the eastern border of the Alps on both sides of the Mur River, about three hours southwest of Vienna by train.

My guide was a young woman who was a student at the university. Incidentally, this guiding service is available at all times through the Graz Tourist Office.

We walked across the river into the Old Town, and immediately I was struck by the many different architectural styles. As she explained, Graz is actually one of the oldest cities in Europe and has one of the best-preserved Renaissance environments.

We walked into the town square, where there were a number of market stalls selling hot chestnuts, soft drinks, fruit, fish, produce, candy—just about everything. Around the square I saw some extremely interesting houses, many of them with hand-painted facades. There were all kinds of small cafes and sweet shops around the plaza and on nearby streets.

One of the most impressive sights in Graz is the Landhaus, built in the middle of the 16th century. Its striking three-story inner courtyard is the scene of many pageants.

We walked up the castle hill to the famous clock tower, the Uhrturm, the symbol of Graz, and from the vantage point of the Herberstein Gardens, the panorama of the city stretched out below us. By this time we were both ready to take a few moments' rest and enjoy a cup of hot chocolate.

   Later that evening, I walked back into the Old Town again, through the town square. The stalls were all shuttered and the stores were all closed. It was a very quiet and peaceful time. The fire engines came through the pedestrian plaza without even sounding their sirens.

   I paid a visit to one of the cafes, and once again experienced people joining me at my table when all the other tables were filled. We all started talking to one another almost immediately, the accordian player struck up a few tunes, and quite a few people began to sing. It was a fitting conclusion to an enjoyable day.

The Landhaus, Graz

ALBA HOTEL WIESLER
Graz

One of the most gratifying rewards for me over the past twenty-two years of writing books about inns in North America, Britain, and Europe has been the enduring friendships that I have made with the wonderful people in this business. Peter Wiesler is a case in point. I met him on a warm, sunny, early spring day a number of years ago, when the train arrived in Graz and we enjoyed a most wonderful lunch. I learned so much from him about the city of Graz and about this section of Austria, known as Styria.

During the ensuing years we have just missed each other in New York on two occasions and have exchanged long letters. I have some colored photographs of Peter and his growing family on the wall right next to my desk.

Although Peter and his wife, Ingrid, sold the Grand Hotel Wiesler to the Alba group of hotels in 1986, they are part of the management of this new hotel and so they are guaranteeing the homelike atmosphere of the old Wiesler. "The hotel is not going to be one of these modern-junk buildings, but is full of atmosphere, combined with every modern hotel equipment and technique'' is the way he put it.

I'm happy to say that the principal restaurant is called The Wieslers', and Peter tells me that it is the leading restaurant of the city.

I'm looking forward to visiting Peter once again at his new hotel. I hope that any of you who visit will be good enough to write me about your experiences.

ALBA HOTEL WIESLER, A-8020 Graz, Grieskai 4. Tel.: 0316-913241. A multi-guestroom five-star hotel in one of Austria's most interesting cities. Well within walking distance of most of the sights and attractions of the city. Rates: See Index.

Directions: Graz can be reached by air, automobile, or train from any point in Europe.

SEMMERING—MY OWN HIDDEN PLACE

Austria will always have a very special niche in my memory. It was the first country I visited in Europe, and Vienna was the first large city. Graz was the first "natural city," and now Semmering was the first "country" experience.

I arrived on a sunny morning after an overnight snowfall. The train ride from Graz had been through the beautiful Alpine foothills, with those remarkable little Austrian villages built along the sides of rushing streams and upland pastures.

I was the only passenger to alight at Semmering and the railroad station was entirely deserted. I had been told that someone would meet me, so I poked around the station awhile, reading the posters. Finally a taxi arrived but the driver did not speak English. So, off we went on the snowy road, curving upward into the village, and stopping in front of the Pension Belvedere.

PENSION RESTAURANT BELVEDERE
Semmering

I will never forget Magda Engelschall. She and her husband are the innkeepers at the Belvedere. From her I received the most heartwarming introduction to Austrian country hospitality that anyone could desire. The first thing she did was to bring me inside, seat me in a booth, and get me a cup of marvelous hot chocolate. She even paid the taxi driver and told me not to worry, we could settle it later. We sat for some time in front of a big picture window overlooking the snow-filled valley with ski-tow areas visible on the other side. I explained to her that I was visiting some out-of-the-way places in Austria to put in a book about inn accommodations, and her face lit up immediately with a beautiful smile. "We have heard about you. I know exactly who to call. Everything will be all right."

In the meantime, I finished my hot chocolate and she conducted me on a short tour of the pension.

The exterior is of a typical Austrian design, with roofs that are made to support considerable amounts of snow, and rooms that have balconies so that guests may enjoy the mountain scenery in any season.

"I'm sorry that it is the wrong season for you to see our garden," she said. "Our guests love to sit out there in the warm weather and also on our terrace in the sunshine. We have many flowers."

The Belvedere is a combination restaurant and hotel, classified as a pension. Magda explained that it is a popular meeting place for all of the people who live in the vicinity and that most of the menu is made up of regional food.

The guest rooms are similar to those that I subsequently found in other pensions—neat and clean, but with no particular style. Most of them have twin beds with those marvelous eiderdown-filled comforters.

Before my Austrian travels were finished I was to meet many other owners of inns and pensions and hotels. I found them generous, understanding, and hospitable. Magda really extended herself to make me feel comfortable. She represents all of the good things about Austrian hospitality. I'm sure that visitors expecting an enjoyable experience in Austria will find their Magdas everywhere.

I have heard from Magda quite regularly since that visit, and it seems that every year some people from America visit because of my story. She tells me that the Belvedere now has an indoor swimming pool and sauna, and all of the guests are enthusiastic about the food.

PENSION RESTAURANT BELVEDERE, 2680 Semmering. Tel.: 02664/ 270. A very cordial restaurant and pension. Wheelchair access. Breakfast, lunch, and dinner served daily. Rates: See Index.

This trip took me from Salzburg and Anif south into the Austrian Tyrol and west to Innsbruck and Imst.

HOTEL GOLDENER HIRSCH
Salzburg

A country inn enthusiast had sent me a copy of Countess Walderdorff's memoirs, *The "Goldener Hirsch,"* so I made a point of stopping by when I was in Salzburg. I was grateful to Count Johannes Walderdorff, son of the famous countess, for taking time to show me around.

"My mother always said she was an amateur," he said, smiling. "For that reason she could not be blamed for breaking rules. For example, she decided *her* hotel would be decorated in the colors and local style of the countryside instead of the modish Viennese formal elegance of the day. She sought out craftsmen from the mountain villages and had everything created to order."

So there are natural beams and painted folk art furniture and wrought-iron locks. Since the name of the inn means "golden stag," the theme is the Alpine hunt and the basic color, hunter green. Waiters wear Austrian loden hunt jackets; the restaurant features game and such mountain trimmings as wild mushrooms and fresh berries.

The Goldener Hirsch was first mentioned in a document of 1407 and is known to have been an inn as early as 1564 (its name dates from the 1600s). However, it was a ruin when Countess Walderdorff began restoration in 1945. An adjacent building was added and, recently, a 14th-century *Kupferschmiedhaus* (coppersmith house) across the street provides additional rooms.

Many famous people have stayed here, especially from the music world. I found it quite humbling to know Mozart was born at Getreidegasse 9 and must have passed this door many times.

HOTEL GOLDENER HIRSCH, Getreidegasse 37, A-5020 Salzburg. Tel.: 662-84-85-11. U.S. reservations, toll-free: 800-792-7637. A 74-guestroom (private baths) inn in the medieval part of Salzburg. European plan. Notable restaurant. Open all year. All amenities, including air conditioning, minibar, TV, radio. Salzburg Festival in July and Aug. Rates: See Index.

Directions: Getreidegasse is a shopping street, and the Goldener Hirsch is more easily entered from Sigmund Platz. From Salzburg Airport, it is 5 km. by taxi or bus; 1.6 km. by taxi from the railway station.

HOTEL SCHLOSSWIRT
Anif

I first met Heimo Graf in Arizona. Heimo and his wife, Hanne, are the innkeepers of the Hotel Schlosswirt, which is just four miles from the center of Salzburg.

Heimo had been on a tour, along with other Romantik hoteliers and Jens Diekmann, of some of the inns in *Country Inns and Back Roads, North America,* and we had all come together at Rancho de los Caballeros in Wickenburg.

Interestingly enough, the second time I saw Heimo he was once again wearing the short lapel-less jacket that is typical of this part of Austria. This time I was visiting his hotel.

When I arrived at Schlosswirt on a late April afternoon, the outlines of a castle set back among the trees on a small lake were just visible through the late afternoon mist. The whole scene had an air of en-

chantment. I subsequently learned that the hotel is directly connected with this castle, dating back to 1607. Heimo explained that as early as 1350 it had been a farm and buildings, and the names of all of the farmers before 1607 and the names of all the innkeepers since that date are well documented. "I am on that list now," he said.

In today's hotel, the ground floor and the first floor date from the late 16th century, and the vaulted ceiling of the passageway, which divides the dining room and the kitchen, and the typically Austrian, simply furnished *Gaststube* always intrigues the visitors. The late-Gothic front door has a cross that was placed there to ward off the plague during the Thirty Years' War.

Heimo, with his great beard and professorial air, may have seemed a little out of place on a ranch in Arizona, but he certainly was very much at home in the dining room of his own hotel. Our evening together with Hanne and occasional visits from his daughter, Chrysta, was delightful. We spent a great deal of time discussing the menu and its Austrian specialties. I had a famous soufflé dessert, known as the *Salzburger Nocker,* that was absolutely ambrosial!

Guest rooms are furnished and adorned in the traditional Biedermeier style of the early Victorian period. They all enjoy a view of the village or the castle grounds.

Hanne mentioned that during the Salzburg Festival reservations must be made considerably in advance. "Salzburg is a beautiful city, and,

as you know, Mozart was born here. It's particularly attractive outside the festival season because then one can admire the sites in a more leisurely way."

It was wonderful to see Heimo once again, and I enjoyed meeting Hanne and Chrysta. In fact, I saw Chrysta a few months later as she was visiting some friends at the Yankee Clipper in Rockport, Maine.

Be sure to order *Salzburger Nocker* at the Schlosswirt.

ROMANTIK HOTELS SCHLOSSWIRT, A-5081 Anif bei Salzburg. Tel.: 06246-2175. A 35-guestroom (all private baths) village inn about 4 mi. from Salzburg. Breakfast, lunch, and dinner served to travelers. Closed Feb. Salzburg Festival. Wheelchair access. Skiing, tennis, golf, biking, sailing, and paths for walking or running nearby. Heimo Graf, Innkeeper. Rates: See Index.

Directions: Exit the Autobahn at Salzburg-Sud.

WHITE HORSE INN
Saint Wolfgang am See
The White Horse Inn!

> *At the White Horse Inn*
> *There's joy the whole summer through!*
> *There's sunshine ever in store there,*
> *For happiness stands at the door there.*
> *The days fly past, you must leave at last,*
> *But still whatever you do,*
> *You'll know when twilight is falling,*
> *The White Horse is calling to you!*

I have visited inns in many parts of the world that have been associated with or are in some way, directly or indirectly, identified with mountains, lakes, oceans, or literature. I have written about inns where novels and music were written, but never before have I visited an inn that was the setting for an operetta!

It all started in 1896, when two German playwrights, inspired by their stay at the White Horse Inn, wrote a romantic comedy about the headwaiter who was madly in love with the sprightly landlady. About thirty years later, the story was made into an operetta and was eventually performed at Radio City Music Hall. It also became a film.

What a setting for an operetta! The inn itself is on the shore of a gorgeous lake with a backdrop of low mountains and Austrian uplands.

While lunching with Helmut Peter, whose family has lived here in Saint Wolfgang for two centuries and has owned this inn since 1912, he remarked that although it was snowing today, two or three days earlier the sun had been strong enough for sunbathing.

A most satisfactory lunch was served in the Kaiserterrasse, with its magnificent view of the Lake of Saint Wolfgang, which is also viewed by most of the guest rooms of the hotel.

"We are really an inn and a resort," Helmut commented. "We have almost everything that a guest would enjoy by way of recreation, both winter and summer, including an indoor swimming pool, sauna, solarium, boats, windsurfers, tennis, and literally dozens of excursions and walking tours. Saint Wolfgang is known as one of the sports centers of Austria, both winter and summer.

"Our guests also enjoy the cog railway ride to the top of Schafberg Mountain and the regular steamer trips on the lake.

"In winter we are within a very short distance of at least three downhill ski areas with plenty of cross-country skiing and other sports, both indoors and out."

The hotel is actually made up of several buildings, and the guest rooms, for the most part, are of generous size. They are decorated in both contemporary and traditional styles. Some of the original rooms have wooden ceilings with heavy beams and painted country furniture. They are all quite pleasant.

There is truly enough about the White Horse Inn to write a book. In fact, a book has been written, containing some of the very early history of the area and the town, dating back to 1430, and explaining how the town became a place of pilgrimage.

The church, just a few steps from the entrance of the inn, is most impressive. Around the turn of the century the village grew into a holiday resort, somewhat assisted by the fact that the Austrian emperor spent his summers at Bad Ischl, nine miles away.

After a tour of everything in the inn and a short visit to the church, Helmut showed me to my car and said, "I hope you will tell your readers that July and August is very high season and I'd suggest that our North American friends who come to Austria in the summertime would particularly enjoy it in September and October or May and June."

Ah, the White Horse Inn!

ROMANTIK HOTEL WHITE HORSE INN (Weissen Rossl), A-5360 St. Wolfgang am See, Salzkammergut. Tel.: (06138) 23-06-0. A 67-guest-room (mostly private baths) resort inn on a beautiful lake approx. 50 km. from Salzburg. Breakfast, lunch, and dinner served. Closed early Nov. to mid-Dec. Indoor swimming pool, lakeshore motorboats, sail-

boats, wind-surfers, tennis, sauna, entertainment, walking tours, golf, skiing, and many more activities available. Lots of amusement for children of all ages. Familie Peter, Innkeepers. Rates: See Index.

Directions: St. Wolfgang is on the main road from Salzburg to Bad Ischl.

HOTEL ALTE POST
Schladming

I left Saint Wolfgang, following the roads on the extremely good maps supplied by Romantik Hotels and locating my next stop, Schladming. It was the site of the world ski championships in 1982. It is a large village right in the middle of Alpine ski country. For the benefit of the hesitant, let me repeat that roads in Europe are superior—well marked and much better signposted then ours in North America, and with very efficient snow-removing machinery.

Hauptplatz is a quiet, tree-shaded, one-way street. The car park is behind the hotel. Hotel Alte Post's lobby and front parlor have over-sized leather couches and chairs. A series of enlarged playing cards have been mounted quite interestingly on the walls in handsome groups of twelve. Apparently, these cards are adapted from a popular local card game, and they show watercolor paintings of objects and people connected with the hotel. Just to prove that all the world is pretty up to date as far as high tech is concerned, there is a VCR in the main lobby.

The name Alte Post goes back to the beginning of the 19th century, when the post office was at the hotel, which had actually been there under another name since 1618. There are many hotel "Posts" in Germany, Austria, and Switzerland, usually for this same reason. As in the case of these old hotels, the Alte Post in Schladming has played an important role in the affairs of the village, being the scene of political rallies and meetings, wedding receptions, and other community affairs.

The hotel has recently gone through a thorough renovation, and has taken on a renewed 19th-century feeling, with the old arches and wooden ceilings on the first floor still intact.

On the morning of my visit, a group of hunters, all dressed in green walking suits and felt hats with little brushes in them, seemed to be celebrating some kind of anniversary, and they were certainly getting off to a great start.

There is a traditional, comfortable *Knappenstube* that has remained unchanged for years and is particularly well liked by the villagers and visitors. Many world-champion skiers and other personalities have placed their signatures on the walls. There is also a small rustic wine bar.

Cuisine is emphasized, with a range of old-style Austrian dishes, which are described in the menu, and more elaborate international cuisine. I particularly remember a dessert called *Kaiserschmarrn,* and I'll never forget the whipped cranberry cream on the top.

It was here that I finally got the German words for "cold milk" firmly fixed in my mind, and since I am very fond of it, I used it throughout my entire trip. It is called *Kalte Milch.*

ROMANTIK HOTEL ALTE POST, A-8970 Schladming, Hauptplatz 10. Tel.: 03687-22571. A 34-guestroom (private baths) mountain village hotel in the Austrian Alps southeast of Salzburg. Breakfast, lunch, and dinner served daily. Closed in Nov. Schladming is a center for winter sports and the mountains provide wonderful recreational possibilities for the summertime visitor as well. Rates: See Index.

Directions: Locate Schladming on the Romantik map and set out with high hopes. Hauptplatz is on the left near the center of town.

FROM SCHLADMING TO VILLACH

The sun was shining brightly as I left Schladming, and by carefully checking the map I knew that I should be stopping in Villach by lunchtime. I had a choice of taking the Autobahn almost the entire way or one of the roads through the mountains at least part of the way. I decided on the latter alternative.

This route threads its way between some of the most magnificent mountains imaginable, and at the time of my visit in April it had been blessed with a light spring snowfall of about four inches. I must say I had some misgivings as I saw a man at the bottom of what appeared to be a very steep section putting chains on his car. However, none of the cars coming down the mountain had chains on, so I decided to continue. I was glad to be here at this time of the year, when I could experience a touch of both spring and summer. There's skiing in this part of Austria until late April, and many cars had skis in their ski racks.

The sun was doing its best to fight its way through the clouds, and the landscape was wonderfully lighted. The temperature was above freezing and the road was not slippery. The road got steeper, the snow got deeper, but everything was still under control and there was one endless succession of fantastic winter panoramas.

At what appeared to be the crest I found the village of Ober Tauern. It was totally unexpected. There were hotels, shops, gondola lifts disappearing into the towering mountains, and people wearing colorful ski clothing. Here was the village ski school, where aspiring skiers were trying to learn parallel turns. (It is not true that Austrians are born on skis, even they *have to learn.)*

Now the road led downhill to the valley floor on the other side and in complete contrast to the four or five inches on the Salzburg side, here the snow was skimpy on the fields.

I'm glad I ignored the first section of the Autobahn; I never would have seen Ober Tauern. It was my first real opportunity to experience what we all see so much of in documentaries and travel literature: a real Austrian ski village.

HOTEL POST
Villach

Villach is a modern Austrian town located in a section called Carinthia. I was much impressed with the appearance of the Post, both inside and out. Everything is done in a very professional but non-commercial way. After seeing a few of the guest rooms, each of which is individually decorated with different designs and furnishings, I was happy to sit down and enjoy a Sunday lunch in the main dining room, where there was a huge flower arrangement under one of the chandeliers.

Some of the local citizens had brought their children for what I'm sure was a real treat. They were well behaved, and it was pleasant to see them.

There were some Carinthian specialties on the menu, including noodles with white cheese. The specialty of the house was fillets of pork, veal, and beef in a fresh pepper sauce with mushrooms. The menu is very large, and I'm happy to say it was in English, because I would have been looking through my cuisine translation for at least half an hour trying to figure it all out. Like other Romantik Hotels, the Post has a special Romantik menu as well.

I found the menu very tempting, but most of the offerings a bit too generous for me in the middle of the day, so I settled for fried white mushrooms in tartar sauce, which were very tasty. I understand the Post is famous for its very extensive menu.

An interesting feature here is the Italian Renaissance garden in the rear of the hotel. The hotel was first constructed around 1500 and has a most impressive history, a description of which is fortunately available in English.

Villach is well known for its thermal springs and lies in the heart of the Kärntner lakes. It's an ideal starting point for excursions into the

magnificent southern Alpine valleys. In wintertime eighteen ski lifts around Villach offer some first-rate downhill and cross-country skiing.

ROMANTIK HOTEL POST, Hauptplatz 26, A-9500 Villach. Tel.: 042 42-26-101. A 65-guestroom (private baths) in-town comfortable hotel in southern Austria in the section known as Carinthia. Breakfast, lunch, and dinner. Open year-round. Centrally located to enjoy all the Austrian summer and winter recreational and cultural attractions. Sauna. Private beach nearby. Rates: See Index.

Directions: Villach is south of Salzburg and east of Innsbruck. Follow the main road into town and the signs for the Centrum. Don't be discouraged if it seems to go out of the way, because there are several one-way streets, both going in and coming out. The hotel is on the left side at the beginning of a very small plaza, right in the business and shopping section. From the north, take a swing around the plaza and park in front of the hotel. They have valet parking.

HOTEL TRAUBE
Lienz

Lienz is in the Dolomites, which are absolutely breathtaking mountains with unbelievable scenery. There is great skiing through all of this area, most of which is adjacent to northern Italy.

I understand there is more sunshine here in Lienz than anywhere else in Austria. The centerfold of the "Ost Tirol" brochure, which is available from any Austrian Tourist Office, shows a panorama of mountains and ski lifts. I think you could be here for three months and never ski the same downhill area twice.

Lienz turned out, as one might expect, to be a rather sophisticated village, and the Hotel Traube fits in very nicely. Its architecture and decor are a combination of both traditional and modern. The traditional decor may be found in the pleasant bedrooms, most of which have a mountain view.

An ideal winter or summer vacation would be to stay here and tour all of this Alpine area. Not the least of the inducements to return is the swimming pool on the top floor. I have seldom seen one like this.

Because the hotel attracts people who are in a holiday mood, the hotel has a program of entertainment, including an orchestra for dancing.

There is a cozy Tyrolean restaurant with wood paneling, which is also patronized by the local people.

The adjacency to Italy may account for the presence of the Ristorante La Mamma, with all kinds of pasta specialties and pizzas.

ROMANTIK HOTEL TRAUBE, A-9900 Lienz. Tel.: (0 48 52) 25 51.
A 60-guestroom (private baths) traditional hotel with many modern
touches located in the Austrian Tyrol. Breakfast, lunch, and dinner.
Open year-round. Many opportunities for both summer and winter
sports nearby. Indoor swimming pool. Gunther and Darinka Wimmer,
Innkeepers. Rates: See Index.

Directions: Please note on the map that Lienz is right near the Italian
border on the road to the Brenner Pass and Innsbruck.

SCHWARZER ADLER
Innsbruck

"If you'll notice on the simplified map in the hotel brochure,
Innsbruck is pretty much in the center of things as far as Austria is
concerned." Harry Ultsch was giving me some most interesting information about Austria in general and Innsbruck in particular as we were
enjoying lunch under a brilliant sunny sky in April. Harry is the manager of this family hotel and the chef is his brother, Werner.

"You see we are on the main road between Garmisch and Salzburg,"
he continued, "and just north of the border of Italy." I found the city
of Innsbruck fascinating. It's a very active cultural and recreational
center with a surprising number of museums, including the Olympia-
museum Innsbruck, which celebrates the winter Olympics of both 1964
and 1976, held in the mountains near the city.

Oh, those mountains! They dominate every street corner, and I'm
sure there's a view of mountains from almost every available window.
They soar as high as 2,500 meters and some of their ramparts have
snow on the crests all year around.

The Schwarzer Adler, whose name means "black eagle," is an excellent central point for excursions to the nearby Alpine valleys and
provides an excellent place for a longer stay to enjoy the spectacular
Austrian scenery, as well as the many cultural delights of the town.

We were joined at lunch by Werner, who came out from the kitchen
in his white chef's uniform long enough to have a glass of wine and
to discuss some of the dishes on the hotel menu. "We have many
Tyrolean specialties," he said. "We think that the garlic soup from
Innsbruck is most superior. We have *Fillet Romantik*, which is veal,
spinach, and mushrooms baked in a crust. We also get many compliments on our rack of lamb."

The interior decorations in this rather smallish hotel are traditional
Tyrolean, and I remember most vividly the impressive vaulted ceilings
in the dining room. Here and there are indications of a Tyrolean her-

itage in the old uniforms on display, as well as painted tiles and walls adorned with such typical things as a zither and a wooden rake. The atmosphere is hospitable and comfortable, but with it there is a distinct air of sophistication.

After a tour of the pleasant guest rooms, I took reluctant leave of Harry and Werner. The Ultsch family is a graphic example of the heritage of Austrian innkeeping.

ROMANTIK HOTEL SCHWARZER ADLER, Kaiserjägerstrasse 2, A-6020 Innsbruck. Tel.: 05222-27109. A 27-guestroom city hotel in the heart of the Austrian Tyrol. Breakfast, lunch, and dinner. Restaurant closed Tues. Open all year. A buffet breakfast included in room rates. Golf, skiing, horseback riding, and tennis nearby, as well as fantastic roads through the mountains. Familie Ultsch, Innkeepers. Rates: See Index.

Directions: After leaving the Autobahn at Innsbruck Ost, turn right at the second light on the Amraserstrasse. Pass under the railroad and take the second street to the right, signposted "Sillagasse," to the front of the Schwarzer Adler.

GASTHOF WEISSES ROSSL
Innsbruck

When I was taken to dinner at the Gasthof Weisses Rossl in the Alstadt (Old Town) section of Innsbruck, I was pleasantly surprised on two counts. First, the Tyrolean house specialties were every bit as good as my host had promised, and, second, I had taken a picture of the inn's flower-filled window boxes and wonderful old white horse cut-out sign when I was wandering about that very afternoon.

The Weisses Rossl dates from 1410, its life as a guest house from 1590, and it has been owned and run by the Plank family since 1919. Total modernization was completed in 1984, so all twelve rooms now have baths (tub or shower), good beds with reading lights, telephones, and radios. Cable TV is available. This is, in fact, the highest-rated guest house in Innsbruck.

The guest rooms are modern, but downstairs on the first floor, the heavy beams and arched ceilings indicate the true age of the house. In the cheerful dining room, a collection of old prints and lithographs, eclectically framed, covers the walls.

Even if you cannot stay here, come for dinner any night but Sunday, when the dining room is closed.

Outside the front door is a cobbled street and next door an antiques shop where I purchased six old pewter buttons and an 18th-century print of Innsbruck at reasonable prices.

GASTHOFF WEISSES ROSSL (White Horse Guest House), Kiebachgasse 8, A-6020 Innsbruck, Alstadt. Tel: 0-52-22 or 23-0-57. A 12-guestroom (private baths) inn in the Old Town section of Innsbruck. Breakfast included. Restaurant serves regional specialties to public. Open all year. Near the Goldenes Dachl, Olympic Museum, and other sights. Werner and Rosemarie Plank, Owner/Innkeepers. Rates: See Index.

Directions: Kiebachgasse is in the heart of the Old Town and comes out at the Old Inn Bridge (Alte Innbrucke). The sign of the prancing white horse will be on your right after the intersection of Seilergasse.

HOTEL POST
Imst

Christl Pfeifer was at her most hospitable. "Our first course will be homemade noodles with spinach," she said. "It is a real Tyrolean dish and one of the specialties of the house. I think you'll also enjoy the sweetbreads, which we serve with boiled potatoes. On the other hand you might find our pot roast with home-fried potatoes and onions quite tempting."

The *Jagerstube* in the Hotel Post is a room decorated with deer antlers, photographs, paintings of the family, and intricately carved chairs and cabinets. It is a warm room, which certainly suits the genial hostess.

One of the more striking features of this hotel is a broad veranda overlooking a portion of the town and some of the high mountains that surround it. With beautiful plants in profusion, in hanging baskets and on tables, this is obviously one of the gathering places for the hotel guests.

The brochure of the hotel (available on request) is a good example of the value of photographs. It has no printing, but does have beautiful views of the hotel veranda, grounds, dining and sitting rooms, swimming pool, and the mountains.

The town of Imst is a center for a great many walking tours, and, fortunately, a small booklet published in English describes some of them in sufficient detail to encourage the visitor to take these small excursions. There are also numerous auto trips equally well described. Although one thinks of Austrian mountains as being confined to winter sports, Imst has many good opportunities for sports in other seasons as well.

The little holiday information pamphlet in English cleverly points out that although Imst has less rainfall than most Tyrolean resorts, it does occasionally rain there, and it suggests that short walks in rainy weather can also be attractive. As the pamphlet says: "We can suggest several ways of passing a rainy day." One suggestion is to go for a swim in the hotel's indoor swimming pool.

ROMANTIK HOTEL POST, Postplatz 3, A-6460 Imst. Tel.: 05412-2554. A 70-guestroom in-town hotel, high in the Austrian Alps. Breakfast, lunch, and dinner. Closed Nov. Indoor swimming pool. Imst is a center of sports activity, including skiing, swimming, horseback riding, tennis, squash, bowling, hiking, cycling, and auto tours. Open-air concerts and Tyrolean evenings with local dances and songs are given frequently. Familie Pfeifer, Proprietors. Rates: See Index.

Directions: Imst is situated in the western part of the Tyrol at the intersection of the north/south highway from Munich to Merano and the east/west highway between Zurich and Innsbruck. Once in the town, make inquiries for the hotel.

Southern Germany

INNS AND LOCATIONS

TRAVEL SUGGESTIONS FOR GERMANY

How to Get There

Pan Am and Lufthansa Airlines provide excellent service from many U.S. cities to several gateway cities in Germany. Your Eurailpass is good in Germany.

Country Inns in Germany

Innkeeping in Germany is a highly respected and traditional occupation. While visiting small hotels, I found three, four, and even five generations of family-owners, and where the ownership has passed through the wife's family, her maiden name has also been retained, linked by a hyphen with her husband's name. For example: Familie Sachs-Stern.

The inn buildings are frequently rich in architectural heritage since many have been in continuous use for centuries. Dining rooms are especially attractive, with many handpainted designs lovingly applied to the mellowed wall panels and chair backs. There are almost always splendid wood carvings as well.

The service is excellent and cheerful, both in the dining room and in the house, although I had to adjust to the idea of frauleins carrying my bags; there are many sons and daughters sharing the responsibilities. Almost everyone speaks English, but I found it fun to practice my German, sometimes with hilarious results.

Visiting these small family-owned hotels provided me with a rich opportunity to learn more about Germany and the Germans themselves. The experience was similar to that of visiting country inns in North America.

Reservations

Most of the accommodations I visited in Germany are members of a well-coordinated group of hotels and restaurants known as Romantik Hotels. They are found in many countries of Europe. These Romantik Hotels have a "Plan as You Go" travel plan that includes a voucher for a minimum of six overnight stays and longer. The first night's accommodation is booked in advance; the following stays can be reserved by each Romantik Hotel. You or your travel agent can book this plan by calling 800-826-0015 in North America. The address in Germany is: Romantik Hotels, D-8757, Karlstein am Main, Postfach 1144. Telephone (0 61 88) 5020, Fax 0 61 88. Some inns in Country Inns and Back Roads, North America are also in the Romantik group as well.

German Menus

What wonderful treats are in store for the visitor in Germany who loves to eat! Here are a few of the Hauptegerichte (main courses) that I enjoyed at the small hotels: Bayerischer Linsentopf (Bavarian lentil casserole with smoked pork and spices); Hasenlaufe in Jägerrahmsauce (rabbit in a hunter-style dark cream sauce of mushrooms, shallots, white wine, and chopped parsley); several different Kalb (veal) dishes, including sweetbreads poached in white wine, veal meatballs, and fricasseed veal. There are many varieties of sausage, Sauerbraten (a beef pot roast that has been marinated several days in vinegar and vegetables and spices), and Zigeunerschnitzel (a gypsy-style preparation of veal cutlets sautéed in tomato sauce with thin strips of pickled tongue, red peppers, mushrooms, and possibly truffles).

The Germans prefer to linger over their delicious pastries and desserts in the late afternoon during the coffee hour. In this case the Konditorei (bakery) also serves as a cafe. Two of the most important words on the dessert menu for me were Schlagrahm (whipped cream) and Schokoladen (chocolate). The varieties of strudels would stretch from Munich to Frankfurt.

Car Rentals

It is possible to arrange for an automobile as part of the "Plan as You Go" program. However, for other travelers may I suggest that you see the section "Renting a Car for Europe" in the front of this book. It is possible to arrange for a car to be picked up in one country and dropped off in another.

Driving Tips

German roads are excellent; even the secondary and back roads are well marked and well constructed. The thinnest lines on the map lead through beautiful farming and mountain country with very little traffic. They may not have route numbers, but the villages are clearly shown.

The international road signs are described in the Michelin Green Guide *for Germany.*

MY ITINERARY IN GERMANY

For traveling in Germany, I have provided a group of five different itineraries, starting from Frankfurt and going in many directions.

ITINERARY 1

From Frankfurt northwest through the Rhine and Mosel River valleys.

These suggestions can also be used by travelers from Berlin, Switzerland, Austria, Luxemburg, Belgium, and the Netherlands. The route leads through the beautiful wine country of both the Mosel and Rhine River valleys.

HOTEL SCHWAN
Oestrich im Rheingau (Rhine)

It was a beautiful morning on the Rhine and I was faced with the problem of getting bathed, shaved, and dressed as rapidly as possible, while at the same time keeping an eye on the ever-changing parade of river traffic. Occasionally, there would be a barge with an automobile perched on it, a popular way to take both car and driver up and down river.

The setting of the Schwan would be worthy of an operetta. Below me were the white tables and gay awnings of the terrace, with the maple trees in bloom. There were already some hotel guests wandering along the river banks, perhaps to look at the old crane that used to be operated by foot power to lift casks of wines to barges. At a table on the terrace, a young couple I had seen in the dining room were sitting close to one another, and I had a feeling they had the bridal suite. If they had cared to, they could have had breakfast in their room.

Now something new was added as a company of local firemen came down to the river, apparently to test their hoses and pumping equipment, and soon there were three or four silvery streams of water arching into the river.

The date on this hotel is 1628, and my host, Dr. Wenckstern, remarked that things have remained the same for a great many years. "We are now, through my wife's family, in the fifth generation of innkeepers and with few exceptions it has been in the family since it was built."

We were joined by Jens Diekmann, and even though he had been here many times, he said that he was learning some things about this beautiful old hotel. We visited the historic wine cellar, where there were long rows of wine casks and dust-covered bottles of the Rhineland's most famous product.

There was one guest room on the top floor with six windows that had an absolutely smashing view of the river in both directions, which

my host said had been described by the famous travel writer Temple Fielding as resembling the bridge of an ocean liner. I wish I'd said it first.

The hotel will arrange a two-day "Romantik Rhine Tour." This includes wine-tasting, a drive through the Rheingau vineyards, and a boat trip on the most beautiful stretch of the Rhine, ending with a candlelight dinner at the hotel.

Because the Schwan is within a very reasonable distance of the Frankfurt Airport, for many people it is either the first or last night in Germany.

ROMANTIK HOTEL SCHWAN, 6227 Oestrich-Winkel. Tel.: 06723-3001. Fax: 06723-7820. Telex 42146. A 64-room rambling hotel directly on the banks of the Rhine River. Breakfast, lunch, and dinner served daily. Rhine River excursions in either direction are available at hotel landing. Many beautiful drives through the wine country. Rates: See Index.

Directions: Oestrich is located on Rte. B42 between Wiesbaden and Koblenz.

RESTAURANT WEINHAUS SANKT PETER
Walporzheim/Ahr (Rhine)

I was seated under the famous chandelier of Saint Peter's Weinkirche. In front of me was the magnificent stained glass window showing Saint Peter holding two keys in his hands, protectively taking care of all the guests.

I couldn't help but be impressed by the interior of this ancient building, which tradition says was built in 1246. The simplicity of the white plaster walls provided a dramatic background for the black wrought-iron work. The main dining room is two stories high with a small balcony traversing the upper story.

The Weinhaus Sankt Peter, along with a few others I visited in Germany, has a reputation for gourmet cooking. The owner, Herr Brogsitter, told me that many of the important members of the government in Bonn hold frequent luncheon conferences here, and the restaurant guest book certainly bore him out with some very flamboyant signatures, photographs, personal business cards, and even a cartoon. The Weinhaus Sankt Peter has obviously played host to a considerable number of political and artistic people.

It was the Saturday midday meal (*Midtag*), and for the most part the guests were families on holiday with their well-mannered children seated around the big tables, obviously enjoying, as children do everywhere, the fun of eating out.

A light repast was all I wanted, and the headwaiter suggested a local fish enhanced by a delicious sauce. One of the young waiters brought a gigantic board holding at least twenty-eight kinds of cheese; I chose a variety and ate them with the usual excellent German bread.

ROMANTIK RESTAURANT WEINHAUS ST. PETER, 5483 Walporzheim/Ahr (Bad Neuenahr). Tel.: 02641-34031. A most attractive restaurant open from 11 a.m. until midnight daily. Closed for holidays and Jan. and Feb. No lodgings.

Directions: Weinhaus St. Peter is located on Rte. 266, which runs east and west from the banks of the Rhine at Linz. Walporzheim is adjacent to the larger walled town of Ahrweiler, which is on most maps.

ITINERARY 2

From Frankfurt south via Heidelberg to the Black Forest.
This itinerary includes some of the most popular vacationing sections
of Germany.

HEIDELBERG

Ah, Heidelberg! A romantic city, where the Student Prince in Lehár's operetta caroused and sang with his fellow students and fell madly in love. Michelin *gives it three full pages, with an extensive description of the Heidelberg Castle and the other impressive sights within the city and its environs.*

Heidelberg is the oldest university town in Germany and the university and the students play an important role in its ambience. There is a student jail (Studentenkerker), *used between 1788 and 1914, allowing certain too-uproarious students to cool their ardor. To be so incarcerated was considered by many of them a mark of distinction. They have left timeless reminders of their tenure with inscriptions and drawings on the walls. It is one of the principal tourist sights in Germany, particularly with thousands of young people finding their way there with guitars and backpacks. I saw quite a few American college T-shirts, although these are sold in stores everywhere in Europe.*

The pedestrian section of the old city, cordoned off from automobile traffic, is a conglomeration of stores blatantly appealing to tourists situated cheek-by-jowl with oriental rug shops, banks, jeans stores (everywhere), ice cream stands, and motion picture theaters. It is a meeting of the old ways and the new. As one Scottish boy responded when I asked him why he came to Heidelberg: "Why mon, this is where it's at!"

HOTEL ZUM RITTER
Heidelberg

Now, Heidelberg and the Zum Ritter! It is hard to imagine Heidelberg without the Zum Ritter.

There are two most uplifting experiences at this hotel. The first is to stand on the street and to become absorbed in the truly magnificent facade. The other is to ascend to the roof garden and enjoy a leisurely view of this historic, romantic city on the Neckar River.

The hotel derives its name from the statue of a young Roman knight (*Ritter*) poised on the uppermost gable of the many-storied facade. Each of the five stories is supported by carved pillars, on which are depicted a variety of figures from Roman history and mythology, as well as representations of the nobility of Heidelberg in the 16th century. The intricate designs of each section could be studied for hours at a time.

The oldest part was built in 1592 by master builder Carolus Belier, and was spared the ravages of a siege 100 years later. It was the only structure in Heidelberg to survive; everything else was burned to the ground.

On the first floor there are high, vaulted ceilings and rather formal dining rooms and sitting rooms that have fragments of sculpture and carvings, including a bust of the builder of the house, who is further commemorated by two large oil paintings.

On the floors above, the rooms in the original section have been furnished with traditional pieces—the honeymoon suite, for example, is positively lavish and has two alcoves overlooking the church across the street. Oddly enough, there is a cradle in the hallway in front of the door. Other traditionally furnished guest rooms have a holiday feeling.

The innkeeper, Georg Kuchelmeister, is an avid hunter, and on the day before my arrival had been hunting in the nearby Odenwald, a beautiful forest just across the river. He explained to me that he provides some of the venison and small game that is served frequently in the hotel dining room.

The view from the roof garden puts it all into perspective; I could see that the city nestles at the foot of the mountains on both sides of the Neckar. The ancient castle still towers above the city, its ruins a continual reminder of bygone centuries.

The Zum Ritter, a late Renaissance masterpiece, is one of the important sights of the city. The Church of the Holy Spirit, just across the cobblestone street; the Heidelberg Castle and gardens towering over the city; and the Philosopher's Walk are all points of interest.

Heidelberg and the Zum Ritter are, indeed, well matched.

ROMANTIK HOTEL ZUM RITTER, Hauptstrasse 178, 6900 Heidelberg. Tel.: 06221-24272 and 20203. A 36-guestroom historic hotel in the center of the old part of Heidelberg adjacent to the university, the Old Bridge, and within a short walk of the cable car to the ruins of Heidelberg Castle. Breakfast, lunch, and dinner served daily. Margarete and Georg Kuchelmeister, Owners. Rates: See Index.

Directions: Motorists should use the nearby multistory parking in No. 12 Parkhaus Kornmarkt (in the direction of the Castle/Schloss). To unload luggage, drive away from the river to the parking place behind the Heiliggeist Church, just opposite the hotel. The pedestrian precinct in front of the hotel may be used by cars only before 10 a.m.

RESTAURANT KATZENBERGER'S ADLER
Rastatt (near Baden-Baden)

Mr. Katzenberger joined me at a corner table for a few moments, and we had a lively talk, frequently interrupted by his greetings to new guests and goodbyes to those departing. During the course of this conversation I assured him I would be quite satisfied with something very light for lunch, and he assured me that he had just the answer to my needs.

Shortly thereafter, a cup of delicious soup was set before me, which, he told me, is served once a year and "tells us that spring is definitely here."

This was followed by two tasty dumplings topped with two small shrimp and accompanied by three crescent-shaped pastries. One bite and I was transported. I ate everything on the plate, and then felt that it would be sensible to order a small dessert.

That's when Isolde, Mr. K's daughter, came with a large platter containing a noodle omelet and veal cutlets. When I protested that she must be at the wrong table, she replied, "Oh no, you have only just started. Besides that, you must also eat your salad."

I restricted myself to a few bites of the noodle omelet and the veal cutlet, although it took a very firm effort on my part not to consume everything on the plate. Isolde returned and I told her I was finished, but she shook her finger at me and told me I should eat more. Before she could take the plate away, Mr. K. came back and looked very upset because he thought I didn't care for the food.

I assured him that it was ambrosial. Well, so much for my eating adventures at this exceptional restaurant originated by such an exceptional man. I hope that perhaps in some way I have conveyed the inherent pride and concern that are expressed there. I would say that Rudolf Katzenberger enjoys a reputation in Germany somewhat akin to that of a cabinet minister, and certainly his tenure has been much more enduring. Many other innkeepers told me that he was the dean of chefs in Germany and possibly Europe.

Since that visit, Rudolf Katzenberger has handed over his business to his daughter and son-in-law, Isolde and Paul Hagelberger. Paul has been in the kitchen of the Adler for over ten years and was responsible for the quality of the cuisine during Mr. Katzenberger's time. Although Mr. Katzenberger is no longer there, the Adler is still an outstanding restaurant.

RESTAURANT KATZENBERGER'S ADLER, Josefstrasse #7, 7500 Rastatt. Tel.: 07222-32103. A distinguished hotel and restaurant. Luncheon and dinner served daily except Sun. Lodging available. Rates: See Index.

THE BLACK FOREST (SCHWARZWALD)

The three sections of the Black Forest contain some of the most popular resort and recreational areas of Germany. The Michelin Green Guide *devotes five pages to it. I visited several Romantik Hotels in which it would be a pleasure to spend an entire vacation.*

The Black Forest has beautiful lakes, high mountains, vineyards, great rivers, graceful bridges, farmhouses crouching under sloping hip roofs, and perhaps one of the continual challenges to photographers: old towns with crooked lanes.

For the active sports-minded vacationer there is downhill and cross-country skiing, horseback riding, tennis, fishing, sailing, hiking, and back roads to content the most lively heart. At various times of the year there are special festivals where traditional costumes are worn and there are many displays of arts and crafts. Black Forest hospitality has a tradition of centuries, and the cuisine in the area features venison, rabbit, and other wild game. Black Forest cake in its many variations is known the world over.

HOTEL OBERE LINDE
Oberkirch (Black Forest)

One of my lasting impressions of this tidy hotel in the central Black Forest is that the names of all the innkeepers dating from 1659 have been painted on one of the rows of beams of its classic half-timbered construction. That means it has been an inn for over 300 years!

The hotel has two restored buildings connected by a small, second-floor gallery. One building houses the dining rooms and the principal public rooms, as well as a few guest rooms; the other is entirely occupied by guest rooms.

Located on the main street, a few squares from the town center, it is a popular hotel, particularly in the height of the vacation season, and it is also a very important town meeting place—for example, the Rotary Club meets here every week. The hotel dining room and gardens frequently have an interesting cross section of both visitors and townspeople. In the rather spacious basement there are two bowling alleys that are slightly different from the American variety. Several local bowling clubs have matches there every week.

The two attractively decorated main dining rooms have a collection of lanterns, rolling pins, ceramics, copper, and pewter ware displayed on plate rails. Also on display is a large collection of photographs of young people, children and relatives of the owners, no doubt—this practice is quite common in Germany.

I arrived at lunchtime and, after looking over the extensive menu, chose a bowl of soup and a piece of delicious homemade Black Forest cake. Accompanied by an ice-cold glass of milk, this chocolaty, creamy concoction was close to divine.

Oberkirch is a small, attractive town and, because of its quite mild climate, it is a center of strawberry growing. There is a strawberry market in town, the largest in Germany, where a strawberry festival is held every year. There is also a sizable outdoor swimming pool and park. During the summertime there are frequent concerts.

A new guest house, in keeping with the old building, with four-poster beds and many other amenities, is now available. An indoor swimming pool, sauna, and solarium are in the planning stages.

In many ways, the Obere Linde in Oberkirch, Germany, reminds me of the Red Lion Inn in Stockbridge, Massachusetts. Each has definite community ties while at the same time providing warm hospitality to travelers.

ROMANTIK HOTEL OBERE LINDE, 7602 Oberkirch. Tel.: (07802)/ 8020. A 44-guestroom family-style inn a few squares from the center of a German town in the Black Forest. Breakfast, lunch, and dinner served daily. Open year-round. Familie Dilger, Innkeepers. Rates: See Index.

Directions: Oberkirch is on Rte. 28, which runs east and west from Freudenstadt to Strasbourg.

I took a few hours to explore some of the scenic views and mountains of the Rhine valley and even got lost. While I was leaning over the radiator of the car examining the map, a man stopped his car and asked me if he could help. He not only showed me the way on the map, but then suggested that I follow him so that I would not lose my way. I had many such instances of courtesy and consideration in Germany. I find it extremely touching.

HOTEL-RESTAURANT STOLLEN
Gutach-Bleibach (Black Forest)

I will always remember this little crossroads inn for its flowers— there were flowers at every window, on all the balconies, and throughout the dining and sitting rooms. The tasteful arrangements bespoke a lover of flowers who, I am sure, was very happy in his or her work. The blooms, many of them geraniums, were set off beautifully against the whitewashed exterior walls and, on the inside, against the traditional brown carved beams and posts, and the white walls and ceilings.

As is the custom in this part of Germany, on the first floor there is a wine room that usually accommodates guests who wish to have light refreshments or the German version of a simple snack. There were also two more-formal dining rooms, one decorated in red and the other in shades of yellow. I saw the familiar corner fireplace.

The guest rooms on the second and third floors were furnished either traditionally or in a contemporary mode. They looked very comfortable and pleasant.

The innkeeper and chef, Herr Jehli, explained that the inn had been built in 1847 and had been in his wife's family for many years. "She and I are the fourth generation of innkeepers," he said. Unfortunately, his wife was not present that day and he had to excuse himself to return to the kitchen; however, he generously invited me to wander around in the hotel at will.

Bleibach is just a few kilometers north of Freiburg, one of the centers of recreation and entertainment in the Black Forest.

ROMANTIK HOTEL-RESTAURANT STOLLEN, 7809 Gutach-Bleibach. Tel.: 07685/207. A 14-guestroom crossroads inn kept in the Black Forest tradition. Breakfast, lunch, and dinner served daily. Familie Jehli-Kiefer, Innkeepers. Rates: See Index.

Directions: Bleibach is a few kilometers north of Freiburg on the upper road to Offenburg (look for Rte. 294).

HOTEL ADLER-POST
Titisee-Neustadt (Black Forest)

The Titisee area is one of the most popular recreational areas in the Black Forest. The main reason is a very beautiful lake that offers a considerable dimension to vacation pleasures. From its shores I could look to the tops of some of the great mountains nearby, and when I was there in April the ski lifts were still running. During the summertime there is sailing, tennis, golf, bicycling, swimming, horseback riding, and the ever-present thermal baths.

Let me explain that there are two towns. One is Titisee, located on the lake, and the other is Titisee-Neustadt, just a few kilometers distant. The "Neustadt" part means "new town" and it was founded in 1251 and has been known as the new town ever since.

Titisee-Neustadt is a business town, and bustles with the air of a prosperous midwestern American community.

Although this squarish stone building seemed rather conventional, I was surprised to find a reception area that was quite rustic in design and furnishings. The twisting staircase to the second floor, with its carved woodwork and painted decorations, reminded me of a similar staircase at the Glen Iris Hotel in Castile, New York.

There were several surprises at the Adler-Post. For one thing, on the second floor there is a small swimming pool, sauna, baths, solarium, and a few unobtrusively placed pinball machines. (Excellent for rainy day entertainment and practicing body balance.) There was also a massage parlor and I was assured by the assistant manager, who had visited

Texas, that any similarity to the kind we have in America is in name only.

Guest rooms, furnished in the traditional manner, were quite handsome, with parquet floors and hand-decorated beds. As usual, there were also a number of rooms furnished in a more contemporary manner.

The Adler-Post is another example of a good, smallish German hotel that, because of its location in a resort area, has a mixture of both vacationers and business travelers. An outstanding feature of its menu is the many different cuts and preparations of venison. "There are many ways to prepare it," said my host, "and I believe our chef knows most of them."

ROMANTIK HOTEL ADLER-POST, Hauptstrasse 16, 7820 Titisee-Neustadt. Tel.: 07651/5066 and 67. A 30-guestroom (private baths) in-town hotel just a few minutes from the resort town of Titisee. Various plans available. Indoor swimming pool, sauna, solarium, and massage available in the hotel. Breakfast, lunch, and dinner served daily. Familie Ketterer, Innkeepers. Rates: See Index.

Directions: The Titisee area is in the upper Black Forest, 28 km. to the east of Freiburg. Titisee-Neustadt is about 5 km. east of the town of Titisee on Rte. 31.

HOTEL SPIELWEG
Münstertal (Black Forest)

Bright sunshine bathed the gentle spring morning with its warming goodness. I paused for a moment to breathe the marvelous Black Forest air and look out over the brook, across the deep valley, and up the steep mountain, where a little girl was leading a cow along the mountain path. The sounds of the cowbell were clearly audible.

"Is it not beautiful?" I turned to look into the brown eyes of a very lovely lady, who introduced herself as the wife of the innkeeper of the Hotel Spielweg. She suggested that we have breakfast together while she told me about the history of this attractive resort hotel.

"This is a very old house," she said. "It has been here since 1650. We built the new section several years ago." (In Germany I discovered that almost all of the innkeepers refer to a hotel or inn as the *Haus,* or house.) "My son, his wife, and my husband and I are trying to preserve the very best of the old ways, while at the same time making improvements and progress with new methods. For example, here in the original building we have maintained the traditionally furnished rooms, with painted doorways, antique beds, chests, and other furniture. In the new building, where you are staying, each accommodation has its

own balcony, or terrace, overlooking the brook and the mountains. We know that a great many of our guests relish that wonderful feeling of being close to nature, so one whole wall of every room is of glass. However, perhaps you have noticed that the ceiling in your bedroom is wood and the beds are decorated with the traditional Black Forest flowers and other designs.'' (I will add a footnote here that my bathroom was an absolute joy.)

"Here, in this building, we've made very few changes. That's my favorite pewter displayed on the plate rail and I'm very particular about even the smallest detail. We place fresh flowers throughout the hotel, and our waitresses wear aprons and blouses made in the same styles that were worn in the middle of the last century.''

She continued, ''The holiday preferences for the average European family have changed considerably during the last thirty-five years, and so we have changed with the times. I have been here for many years, and I sometimes cling to the old ways—fortunately, my son and his wife have joined us and they have shown us that new ideas make for better innkeeping. I think that we make an ideal threesome.

"The alpine and cross-country skiing nearby bring enthusiastic families who must be provided with recreation after a day on the slopes. That's why we have the game rooms and television rooms, and why we also built an indoor swimming pool as well as one outdoors.''

After a most pleasant breakfast we parted, and I went out into the clear Black Forest spring morning to my room to pack my bags and continue my travels through Germany. I am already looking forward to my return trip.

ROMANTIK HOTEL SPIELWEG, 7816 Münstertal. Tel.: 07636/618 and 1313. A 35-guestroom resort-inn in the heart of the upper Black Forest region. Indoor and outdoor swimming pool, sauna, and solarium on grounds. All Black Forest sports and outdoor activities within a few minutes' drive. Breakfast, lunch, and dinner served daily. Familie Fuchs, Innkeepers. Rates: See Index.

Directions: Locate Freiburg on map and then move your eye carefully south to look for Belchen—this is one of the highest Black Forest mountains. Münstertal is just above it.

HOTEL SONNE
Badenweiler (Black Forest)

According to my friend Jens Diekmann, Badenweiler is an ideal place to recover from everyday stress and enjoy a good vacation. "It is the spa," he said, "where knowledgeable Europeans go who wish to have a quiet, tranquil vacation along with the thermal baths."

Although there is parking at the hotel, let me advise you in advance that you cannot park in the middle of the town. There are free parking centers on the outer edges of the town, and one takes a bus into the centrum, where it is so pleasant because there is no traffic.

I was now riding the bus and enjoying a conversation with another traveler, who seemed to be quite informed about this resort community. "The most popular activity is the thermal baths," he said, "although I am sure that many people who visit here never go near them, as there are other things to do. There are some beautiful shops showing the latest fashions and several restaurants and hotels." As we got closer to the centrum, I realized that Badenweiler was a very sophisticated town.

The Hotel Sonne is near the *Rathaus* (town hall) and is distinguished from the other hotels and pensions because of its traditional design—the building is 200 years old. The Fischer family, fourth-generation proprietors, reflected the sophisticated spirit of the town, and were most accommodating when it came to explaining the hotel and the ambience of the area. "It is so easy to drive almost any place in the southern Black Forest within a short time," declared Frau Fischer, "and there are many bus tours that leave on a regular schedule from Badenweiler to dozens of nearby points of interest."

The Hotel Sonne appears to be very comfortable. In particular, I was impressed with the large lobby that had many, many chairs and tables arranged to encourage conversation. The main dining room was rather formal; however, the two side dining rooms were decorated in the traditional Black Forest manner, and the wooden chairs even had hearts carved in their backs.

The rooms, most of them with balconies, overlooked the garden in the rear and there was also a terrace for sunbathing. As I recall, plans were in the works for an indoor swimming pool.

The Hotel Sonne appeals basically to people who are looking for a rest and perhaps a few days in and out of the famous baths, just a few steps away. Frau Fischer explained that it is indeed a very lively place, with concerts, films, theater, folk singing, and many other types of live entertainment scheduled in the town on a continuing basis.

ROMANTIK HOTEL SONNE, 7847 Badenweiler. Tel.: 07632/5053. A 42-guestroom hotel located in one of the Black Forest's famous spa areas. Breakfast, lunch, and dinner served daily. Familie Fischer, Innkeepers. Rates: See Index.

Directions: Badenweiler is located at the southwestern edge of the Black Forest. It is a short distance north of Basel (Switzerland) and is accessible from the Autobahn running next to the Rhine.

ITINERARY 3

Frankfurt, southeast via Aschaffenburg, Buchen, and the Romantic Road. This itinerary includes some of the most picturesque and famous old towns of Bavaria.

HOTEL POST
Aschaffenburg (Frankfurt)

Like other hotels in Germany, the Hotel Post has a history as a stagecoach stop, and this background has set the theme for some of the interior decoration in the inn. For example, in the main dining room, where I was enjoying my first lunch in Germany with Jens Diekmann and innkeeper Karl Seubert, there are many reminders of earlier days, such as several prints and ceramic tile paintings of old coaches. One of the most striking features is the *half* (actually) of a stagecoach, built into one corner of the main dining room. As innkeeper Seubert explained, "The whole coach would take too much space, so we split it in half and put it here for everyone to see." It is possible to open the door and step up on the driver's seat.

The outstanding printed menu of the Post has won a gold medal, not only for the rich and unusual design, but also for the orderly and easily understandable contents, most of which are in both German and English. It has sixteen pages, with a center spread of extremely intricate paintings done in the Bavarian style. The richly decorated pages are done in the manner of an illuminated medieval manuscript.

Here are a few of the menu items that caught my eye. In the hors d'oeuvre section there was corn on the cob, smoked trout, frogs' legs, smoked salmon, and caviar. International soups included Hungarian goulash, turtle soup, Russian borscht, and Indian hotchpotch. There were several different types of salads, many egg dishes, and a variety of fish, including river trout and sole meunière. The meats included pork cutlets, rump steak (very popular in Germany), leg of lamb, and several others. There were also venison and chicken.

After my first meal in Germany we took a tour of the hotel, which included an unusual dining room dedicated to Holland, because the innkeeper and his wife had been married there. In it were Dutch wooden shoes, Delft china, and ceramic figurines. The window paintings on glass were done after the manner of Rubens, Frans Hals, and Breughel.

This hotel has still another unusual feature—an indoor swimming pool. Two of the walls had saucy murals depicting life in medieval Bavaria.

The guest rooms looked very comfortable and tidy, and somewhat contemporary in furnishing, although, as was the case everywhere I traveled in Germany, I found the traditional goosedown-filled comforters that are covered by a sheet and changed after each guest's stay.

Recently, my friend Karl Seubert has been succeeded by Eveline and Roland Hofer as innkeepers; however, Karl is often to be seen in the hotel.

ROMANTIK HOTEL POST, 8750 Aschaffenburg. Tel.: 06021/21333. A 100-guestroom midtown hotel about a half-hour drive from the Frankfurt airport. An excellent, quiet accommodation for Frankfurt visitors. Breakfast, lunch, and dinner served daily. Indoor swimming pool. Eveline and Roland Hofer, Innkeepers. Rates: See Index.

Directions: From Frankfurt airport follow the Autobahn east to Aschaffenburg exit.

THE ROMANTIC ROAD

The Romantic Road links the Main River and the Bavarian Alps by way of some extremely picturesque old medieval towns. There is a complete description of it in the Michelin Green Guide *to Germany and I am certain that the German Tourist Offices in North America will be happy to supply folders in English about this area and the other tourist areas in Germany.*

I have described Romantik Hotels, either on or near this road, a much-traveled highway for Europeans heading south on vacation trips.

The Romantic Road begins in the old cathedral town of Wurzburg and continues through Rothenberg, Feuchtwangen, Dinkelsbuhl, Donauworth, Augsburg, and Landsburg, finally coming to an end at Fussen in the foothills of the Bavarian Alps.

HOTEL PRINZ CARL
Buchen (Romantic Road)

I'll always remember the Prinz Carl, not only for the fact that it was where I spent my first night in Germany, but because we all had such a wonderful, laughing time together. There was Jens Diekmann, innkeepers Werner and Elizabeth Ehrhardt, and Ilse and Bettina, their two very attractive young daughters. A third sister, Waltraut, was unable to be with us. We all quickly became acquainted and they were most courteous in attempting to speak English as much as possible. I, in turn, taught them two ersatz German-American words with which they were not familiar: "Schuss-boomer" and "Sitzmark." Everybody thought this was most hilarious.

Furthermore, I am now a member of the famous *Goldener Kanne* club. Jens Diekmann and I were both inducted by innkeeper Ehrhardt in a very touching ceremony that took place in the main dining room, amidst the congratulations and bravos of the other assembled guests and friends. In order to supply proof of membership, I now possess a scroll on which Herr Ehrhardt has written my name, and I am officially entered in the club rolls. In addition, I have a miniature golden *Kanne* (stein) with a flip top.

The Ehrhardts have kept the Prinz Carl these thirty years, and Werner is the chef. He is particularly well known for the preparation of a saddle of venison and for a range of pastries that include tarts made from sour cherries.

That evening my dinner started with a tasty duck liver paté, which was then followed with their famous "green wheat" soup, also a house recipe. The next course was delicious french-fried shrimp with a Béarnaise sauce in which tomatoes had been mixed. The main course was medallions of veal served with artichokes, and we finished with everybody sampling two delicious desserts: a chocolate mousse, one of my favorites, and a very scrumptious ice cream cake.

The Prinz Carl was a post station for many years. Today, it is a most interesting combination of the old and the new. The dining room and the main reception hall are furnished in a traditional manner, as are several of the lodging rooms on the second floor. However, a new section has very attractive contemporary furniture, reminiscent of the Scandinavian style. My room, number 22, was a studio room overlooking the roofs of the town.

When I left the following morning, the entire family gathered in the center hallway to speed me on my way. I was to have many a warm welcome and companionable experience at German inns for the next several days; however, none would exceed the enjoyable time I had at the Prinz Carl.

There have been some interesting and expected changes since my last visit. I understand that the three daughters of the house are now married and are no longer at the hotel, although Frau and Herr Ehrhardt are still continuing their loving care of *CIBR* readers!

ROMANTIK HOTEL PRINZ CARL, 6967 Buchen/Odenwald. Tel.: 06281/1877. A 26-guestroom village inn, 50 km. south of Frankfurt. Breakfast, lunch, and dinner served daily. Riding, indoor and outdoor swimming, walks through the forest, boat rides on the Main River, and many castles nearby. Familie Ehrhardt, Innkeepers. Rates: See Index.

Directions: Locate Frankfurt on the German road map and then Hei-
delberg about 50 km. to the south. Buchen is east on Rte. 27. From
Frankfurt the road through Miltenburg and Amorbach is very scenic.

HOTEL MARKUSTURM
Rothenburg ob der Tauber (Romantic Road)

"What is *Stammtisch?*" I asked Marrianne Berger, while the two of
us were seated in the reception hall of the Hotel Markusturm. We had
just completed a brief tour of the many different lodging and public
rooms of this truly old hotel. It was just a few moments before dinner.

"*Stammtisch* . . . oh, you will see that in just a moment. I am sure
that you will like it very much."

Her husband, Otto, and their children, Gabriella and Stephan, joined

us and we stepped into a most attractively decorated dining room. The waiters wore green vests, white flowered shirts, red ties, and black trousers. Otto explained that this was the Empire style, worn to commemorate the first 700 years of the freedom of the town. "This was celebrated in 1974," he explained, "but we decided that the men would continue to wear the costumes and the waitresses would wear theirs only on special occasions. Marrianne sewed eight costumes that year and they are all very beautiful and elaborate."

The Hotel Markusturm was constructed out of the first fortified wall of the city of Rothenburg, and is located where Saint Mark's Tower, built in 1204, and the Roeder Arch (1330) formed one of the romantic corners of this medieval city. It is one of the most historic buildings in the town. The hotel served as barracks for soldiers who were assigned to duty in the tower. In later years it was both a brewery and a *Gasthaus.*

Our meal started off with one of the specialties of the house, called *Ratsherrnspiel,* consisting of various kinds of meats, onions, sausage, bacon, and other succulent things served on a skewer with potato croquets. It was served on a special plate that is used only for this particular dish. Gabriella and Stephan, who were studying English in school, explained to me that there were many other plates designed for special menu items at the Markusturm. "We have eight cooks in our kitchen," Stephan declared very proudly.

For dessert I had a local cheese that was very strong and peppery and came wrapped in a napkin. Marrianne insisted upon my sampling some sliced apples that had been dipped in a batter of meal and beer and then dropped in hot oil. They were delicious.

It was during this meal that I learned about the German custom of the *Stammtisch.* While we were discussing the history of Rothenburg, one of their friends came to the edge of the table and knocked three times. Otto and Marrianne smiled and said, "Hello," and the man sat down at the table and lit his pipe. A few minutes later, another man did the same thing. About ten minutes later, a few more men came over, knocked, and we moved a little closer together so that everybody could sit down. Each time, I was introduced briefly, and we went on with our conversation, while some of them started their own.

Marrianne looked at me with a gay smile and said, "Now you know about the *Stammtisch.* It is a custom at almost every hotel in Germany that there is a table where friends and the people of the town come to sit and talk and gossip, or just to be together. Instead of everyone standing up and shaking hands, which you know all Germans love to do, the newcomer simply knocks on the table and everyone says hello and he takes his place."

Before the evening had ended we had a dentist, a factory manager, a folk singer, a bricklayer, a couple from another town (who used to live in Rothenburg), and a bookseller.

A marvelous custom is *Stammtisch*.

ROMANTIK HOTEL MARKUSTURM, Rodergasse 1, 8803 Rothenburg ob der Tauber. Tel.: 09861/2370. A 30-guestroom village inn. Breakfast, lunch, and dinner served daily. Sauna, solarium, garage (if desired). Familie Berger, Innkeepers. Rates: See Index.

Directions: Rothenburg is in central Germany, south of Würzburg and west of Nuremberg. The Markusturm is about three squares from the town hall (Rathaus).

ROTHENBURG OB DER TAUBER

Rothenburg is a walled town and, like Maastricht in the Netherlands, as the town expanded and more walls were built, a series of walled rings were created around the city. Today, so zealous are the townspeople in preserving the ancient atmosphere and quality, that any construction or remodeling in the old part of town must conform to the old architecture. No modern buildings may be built.

The town history started around A.D. 900 and continued through fire, earthquake, and wars. One of these was the Thirty Years' War (1618–1648), when the town was besieged and conquered by three different armies.

There are many yearly events celebrated in the town, including the historic Shepherds' Dances, when members of the Shepherds' Guild meet in the afternoon to perform the historic dances in front of the town hall. The performance of farces, plays by the famous 16th-century shoemaker-poet Hans Sachs, are presented at Whitsuntide.

Rothenburg has gates, churches, castles, fountains, museums, and old houses—all incredibly beautiful and well preserved.

One of the unusual sights is known as the Alte Rothenburg Handwerkerhaus, a remarkably restored and preserved house of a Rothenburg tradesman built in 1270. It contains eleven rooms from the ground floor to the attic, all furnished with original medieval furniture, and shows most graphically how large families, including grandmothers and grandfathers, lived and worked a few centuries ago. The furniture, utensils, stoves, fireplaces, toys, and clothing have all been thoroughly researched by the Berger family, the owners of the Hotel Markusturm. It is truly a glimpse into life in the Middle Ages.

HOTEL GREIFEN-POST
Feuchtwangen (Romantic Road)

I was standing in one of the dining rooms of this very old hotel, and Brigitte Lorentz was explaining the meaning of one of the five murals.

"The first one shows Kaiser Karl, who was out hunting in this area around A.D. 700. He became thirsty and saw a pigeon and followed it to a fountain. He was so enchanted that he caused a Benedictine monastery to be founded on the spot. There you can see King Karl and the pigeon and the fountain."

Other important turning points in the history of the region are also depicted in the murals, and in the final scene I saw a typical 14th-century marketplace scene, when Feuchtwangen flourished as a trade and corn market.

Brigitte and Edward Lorentz are continuing in the innkeeping tradition of Edward's grandfather, who transformed this 1599 building from a brewery *Gasthaus* to a hotel. Most of the old feeling has been retained and there are walls with many exposed half-timbers on the second and third floors.

I discovered that the Greifen-Post is two hotels, with a second-floor bridge connecting the Greifen to the Post. In the Post, the rooms are furnished in the traditional manner, whereas in the Greifen, more modern furniture has been used.

Feeling as if I were stepping back into the Middle Ages, we returned to the main hallway and reception area, where Brigitte pointed out a scroll inscribed with names of such renowned early guests as Emperor

Maximilian, who stayed here; Queen Christina of Sweden, who stopped on her way to Rome (possibly disguised as a man). The mother of Queen Victoria of England was a guest in 1844, and Jenny Lind, the famous "Swedish Nightingale," stopped off for lunch during a tour. Immediately next to the scroll was a notice that the chef at this hotel had won a medal at a recent exposition for preparing what Brigitte called a "farmer's dish."

We walked into the front dining room and discussed the various regional specialties on the menu, like the homemade soups, Bavarian liver and dumplings, goulash-and-garlic creamed soup, a recipe of Edward's grandmother.

"We cook everything with butter and cream, and only use fresh things," she declared. Other regional specialties include mushrooms in cream on toast with Bavarian cheese, and Franconian sausage served with sauerkraut.

Brigitte took me to one corner of the dining room, where there was a mural showing a man in the forest confronting a wild boar. She translated the German saying just above the mural: "I would rather be with the wild pig in the forest than be at home with my scolding wife."

ROMANTIK HOTEL GREIFEN-POST, 8805 Feuchtwangen. Tel.: 09852/2002. A 50-guestroom hotel on the market plaza. Breakfast, lunch, and dinner served daily. Very convenient to Rothenburg. Elevator, swimming pool, sauna, and solarium. Familie Lorentz, Innkeepers. Rates: See Index.

Directions: Watch for signs to Feuchtwangen on the Autobahn a few km. south of Rothenburg.

HOTEL ROSE
Weissenburg (Romantic Road)

If glamour is supplied by political celebrities and guests who are theatrical, then the Hotel Rose in Weissenburg certainly qualifies as being glamorous. I took a look at the rather elaborate guest book under the watchful eye of its owner, Edgar Mitschke, and on the very first page I found that Chancellor Konrad Adenauer had been a guest here in 1957. There was also a most impressive number of television, theater, and musical stars, many of whom included their photographs as well as appropriate sentiments. It reminded me of the registers of old inns from the 19th century in the United States, in which itinerant theatrical troupes took advantage of the opportunity to do a little advertising.

Although Weissenburg is not a large city, the Hotel Rose has a big-city atmosphere with a certain air of elegance about it. Some of the bedrooms, particularly those facing the square, are rather elaborately furnished. The single and double rooms in the back of the house were somewhat austere.

The *Ratskeller* in this hotel dates back to 1320, and the arched brick ceilings have been whitewashed and decorated with animal skins. The light, furnished from candles, created a romantic atmosphere, and in one corner was a small, private fireplace that could supply extra romance for four people.

Over a cup of delicious hot chocolate with whipped cream, Herr Mitschke and I sat in the main dining room and discussed his elaborate menu, which, in addition to offering local German specialties, apparently caters to international tastes as well. He explained that there are certain weeks in the year when they feature a particular kind of cuisine, such as French, Hawaiian, or Swiss.

ROMANTIK HOTEL ROSE, 8832 Weissenburg/Bavaria. Tel.: 09141/ 2096. A 37-guestroom midtown hotel in a very busy central Bavarian town. Breakfast, lunch, and dinner served daily. Familie Mitschke, Innkeepers. Rates: See Index.

Directions: Weissenburg is on Rte. 2 south of Nuremberg and east of Feuchtwangen via many back roads. (Bring magnifying glass for map.)

ITINERARY 4

From Frankfurt east through Bamberg, Wirsberg, Bayreuth, Auerbach, and Munich.

HOTEL ZEHNTKELLER
Iphofen (Romantic Road)

I have visited inns both in North America and Europe with many unusual features, but this is the first time I have ever visited an inn where an opera was written! A well-known German composer, Hans Pfitzner, composed it while he was a guest in this hotel in 1932.

I learned all this from Henry Seufert, the innkeeper. This hotel has been owned and operated by the Seufert family since the late 19th century. Henry is a very interesting man in his early forties and is proud of the fact that he has not only vineyards, but a winery as well. I found Henry's wine in other Romantik hotels in Germany.

The entrance to the Zehntkeller from the road is through an arched gate, and in the early German spring there were pansies and daffodils growing in pots and an old wooden wheelbarrow.

Inside the massive door, I approached the reception desk, which, with wonderful practicality, is right next to the service bar.

I walked about the inn, which at noon had a distinctly bustling air. The waitresses were hurrying back and forth with platters of delicious-looking food with tantalizing aromas. There were two rather small but very attractive dining rooms, both of which had paneling halfway up to the ceiling, topped with the characteristic plate rail with pewter, silver, and ceramics.

When Henry appeared, he and I plunged into history. The old building was originally a monastery, dating back to 1250, and later was occupied by the town tax collector. Just before the turn of the century it was acquired by the Seufert family.

We talked about the menu, and the specialties of the house include chicken in wine, mixed grill, venison, and duck. There are also several veal dishes. For dessert at lunch, I had sliced apples lightly sautéed with flour and cinnamon. I later tried them in my own kitchen.

Henry explained that this was an excellent stopover for people from

Belgium, Holland, and northern Germany, who were headed for Austria or Italy. Many guests returned several times on these trips. Most guests stayed for just a single night. Slightly off the highway, it has a very restful air about it.

In the guest book of the inn, the composer of the opera did something rather novel—he wrote a few musical notes and the legend "Here you have what you want." I have a feeling that many people have found the restful atmosphere, good food, and warm hospitality of the Zehntkeller exactly what they want.

ROMANTIK HOTEL ZEHNTKELLER, 8715 Iphofen. Tel.: 09323/3062. A 40-guestroom inn about 1 km. off main highway. Breakfast, lunch, and dinner served daily. Familie Seufert, Innkeepers. Rates: See Index.

Directions: About 25 km. south of Würzburg. (Rte. 8)

HOTEL WEINHAUS MESSERSCHMITT
Bamberg (Bavaria)

Bamberg is a rather sizable, attractive city with colorful old buildings, a river running through the middle of the town, and a shortage of parking spaces. Although I wasn't certain of the location of the Messerschmitt, I took my chances and rode right into the centrum— and there it was! I joined the rest of the German drivers and parked on the sidewalk.

The hotel has a look of antiquity about it, with wood-paneled ceilings, elaborate chandeliers, substantial furniture, many plants, and gleaming white tablecloths. The menu had quite a few specialties, including different varieties of soups and fish, as well as steaks and veal dishes; among an extensive selection of French and international entrées was Mexican rump steak.

The most tempting and largest dessert menu I think I have ever seen was called "La Dolce Vita" and featured all kinds of ice cream dishes, including banana splits, and quite a variety of crêpes; also coffee with heavy cream, and chocolate. It was tantalizing to someone with a sweet tooth like mine.

Equally tantalizing are the guest rooms at this Romantik Hotel. There are special weekend packages on art and gastronomy during November to March, also a three-day cookery course.

ROMANTIK HOTEL WEINHAUS MESSERSCHMITT, Lange Strasse 41, 8600 Bamberg. Tel.: 0951/27866. A 14-guestroom hotel, restaurant, and Weinhaus in the center of a small, attractive German city.

Lunch and dinner served daily. Familie Pschorn, Innkeepers. Rates: See Index.

Directions: Reaching Bamberg, follow signs to center of city and ask directions.

HOTEL POST
Wirsberg (Swiss Franconia; Bavaria)

Frau Herrmann and I were seated *in* a beer barrel. She was recounting the history of this hotel, high in the Swiss Franconia resort section of Germany, just a few kilometers north of Bayreuth. "My grandfather and grandmother came here and planted the oak tree across the street in front of the church," she said. She showed me some photographs of the inn at the turn of the century and also of her father and mother, who continued in the innkeeping tradition.

"I was born in room 2," she said, and then added with a big smile, "Why, that is the room you are staying in." Room 2 overlooks the triangular-shaped plaza of the town, around which are several shops. In one corner is a church whose bells peal every quarter-hour for twenty-four hours a day; I was a bit shaken at this information, but she assured me I would not hear them after I had gone to sleep, and I did not.

The hotel is furnished with both romantic and contemporary furnishings. My bedroom, as did most, included a television, a small honor-system refrigerator, and a bathroom heater, which I made good use of on a chilly April morning.

At dinner I enjoyed sliced venison served in a gravy-laden casserole

with red cabbage and apple. "We have dishes from Alsace, Yugoslavia, and Mexico," she said. "We also have special weeks when we feature unusual international dishes."

She joined me for breakfast the following morning, and we continued my education on Germany. I enjoyed her very interesting observations, expressed in a combination of English and German. She suggested that I take a walk around the village and also the gardens of the modest castle, which her family was restoring.

Now, how did we happen to be seated in a beer barrel? Because, in one of the dining rooms, a booth that accommodates at least five people has been fashioned from a beer barrel. A decorative lamp hangs from the top, and seat cushions make it very cozy and comfortable.

ROMANTIK HOTEL POST, 8655 Wirsberg. Tel.: 09227/861. A 40-guestroom village hotel in the high hills, about 20 mi. north of Bayreuth. Breakfast, lunch, and dinner served daily. Wirsberg is at a very pleasant high elevation, with many narrow but excellent roads for car touring and miles and miles of walking in the forest. Indoor swimming pool; outdoor swimming pool is nearby in the hills. Familie Herrmann, Innkeepers. Rates: See Index.

Directions: Wirsberg is a few miles west of Berlin-Nuremberg Autobahn (E-6). On the map look for Bayreuth and Kulmbach; Wirsberg is just off Rte. 303.

HOTEL GOLDNER LÖWE
Auerbach (Bavaria)

I was seated in the *Knappenstube* with Frau Ruder. It was like having lunch in a coal mine—overhead were rough beams and planks supported by massive posts from which the bark had been stripped. The walls were rough, raw rock with the streaks of orange iron ore plainly visible.

"We here in Auerbach are very proud of the heritage of the iron miners," said Frau Ruder. "So, we have decorated this dining room to resemble the tunnels in the mines below the city. The word *Knappe* is the German word for iron miners." She pointed out the many miners' lamps and tools, and even a big cart from the mines that had been used to bring up the ore in the mine shafts. Now, it was gaily decorated with greens and Easter eggs, a reminder of the holiday just past. There were several wrought-iron lamps and candleholders. In one corner was a statue of Saint Barbara, who, I understand, is the patron saint of iron miners.

The Goldner Löwe has been in existence since 1144, and until 1898, when a disastrous fire destroyed a great deal of the town, has occupied the same building. It was rebuilt on the same site, and there are some very interesting primitive paintings in one of the dining rooms showing both the old inn and the new. The Ruder family has owned it for almost a hundred years.

In the reception hall, there are some excellent primitive wood carvings of miners, showing the great strength of those men who work beneath the earth.

Frau Ruder translated some of the original Bavarian dishes on the menu, including salted brisket of beef served with horseradish, pigs' knuckles, and fresh trout, kept in a tank in the kitchen. For a rather unpretentious hotel, there were some surprisingly sophisticated dishes on the menu; I never cease to be amazed at the versatility of many of the chefs in these middle-class hotels, who are able to prepare dishes from all over the world.

One interesting dish on the menu is called *Löwentopf,* loin of pork, loin of beef, loin of veal, fresh vegetables, roast potatoes, and a fried egg.

Guest rooms in the Goldner Löwe are furnished in both traditional and modern styles. Several have handmade furniture from local craftsmen. There are very pleasant views of the town. Everything is clean and wholesome-appearing.

Auerbach is not far from the city of Bayreuth, the site of the famous Wagner festival, and the Goldner Löwe would make an ideal quiet place to stop for a few days.

ROMANTIK HOTEL GOLDNER LÖWE, 8572 Auerbach/Oberpfalz. Tel.: 09643/1765. A 28-guestroom village inn in a Middle Ages town. Breakfast, lunch, and dinner served daily. Familie Ruder, Innkeepers. Rates: See Index.

Directions: Auerbach is a short distance south of Bayreuth, about 10 km. east of the Berlin-Nuremberg Autobahn (E-6). Exit is marked Forcheim-Amberg.

ITINERARY 5

Munich, Bad Aibling, west to the Bavarian Alps and on to Lake Konstanz.

This itinerary includes part of the famous Alpine Road, where the traveler may continue into Austria. It leads from Garmisch through Oberammergau, skirting the northern edge of the mountains and continuing into Vangen and Lake Konstanz.

HOTEL VILLA SOLLN
Munich

This small hotel, about fifteen minutes from downtown Munich, has twenty-five guest rooms with direct-dial telephones, television sets, and an inside swimming pool as well as a sauna, garden, and an unusually good breakfast.

HOTEL VILLA SOLLN, Wilhelm-Leibl Strasse 16, 8000 Munich 71. Tel.: 089-792092/93. All reservations to the Hotel Villa Solln should be made directly with the hotel, as it is not part of the Romantik Hotel chain. Rates: See Index.

HOTEL LINDNER
Bad Aibling

The village of Bad Aibling, which has been famous for its "waters," had a very pleasant feeling, with many spreading trees and early spring blooms in the front gardens of the village homes. I turned off the main street and maneuvered into the parking place for the Hotel Lindner.

I was greeted by Erna Lindner, who invited me to have lunch with her and her daughter, Gabi. In earlier times the Hotel Lindner was known as the Castle Prantshausen, and it's been in the same family for 150 years. The house survived a few fires in 1495 and in 1765.

Daughter Gabi was kind enough to explain many of the features of the hotel, including the regional specialties from this part of Germany. These include Bavarian garlic soup, a specialty of the house, as well as sauerkraut and roast potatoes, roast pork, and knuckle of pork with dumplings.

Afterward we had a leisurely walk through the remainder of the hotel and I found that some bedrooms were furnished in contemporary and others in traditional furniture. There are portraits of both the grandparents and the great-grandparents hanging in the reception area. There are many antique tile ovens. Almost all of the guest rooms have television and direct dial telephones.

Gabi told me that the well-known painter Wilhelm Leibl had his *Stammtisch* here during the late 19th century and reprints of his works can be seen throughout the hotel. (For further explanation of the wonderful custom of *Stammtisch*, see the entry for the Romantik Hotel Markusturm in Rothenburg ob der Tauber.)

Later, after an absolutely heavenly dessert and coffee and reluctant farewells to Erna and Gabi, I headed west toward the Bavarian Alps.

ROMANTIK HOTEL LINDNER, Marienplatz 5, 8202 Bad Aibling. Tel.: 08061-4050. A 33-guestroom (mostly private baths) traditional hotel in a quiet spa town in Bavaria, between Munich and Salzburg. Break-fast, lunch, and dinner served to travelers. Open every day in the year. Convenient for the Oberammergau and Salzburg festivals as well as the Munich Oktoberfest. Tennis, horseback riding, golf, skiing, and swimming nearby. Erna Lindner, Hotelier.

Directions: Bad Aibling is just off the Autobahn between Munich and Salzburg.

CLAUSING'S POSTHOTEL
Garmisch-Partenkirchen (Bavarian Alps)

What a beautiful, sun-drenched, blue-skies morning in Garmisch! What a remarkable contrast to the day before, when snow fell upon the Bavarian Alps in mid-April just as it does in midwinter. Certain roads had been closed and it had been necessary to arrive in Garmisch by a different route.

I was having breakfast on the heated terrace at Clausing's Posthotel, where the hot spring sun had re-exerted its customary role and was beginning to melt the ten inches of snow that had accumulated on the tabletops and chairs of the outdoor section. Visitors and townsfolk alike were following the beckoning sounds of Sunday church bells.

I joined some new friends from Iowa whom I had met the night before, who were also traveling in Europe during the off-season.

The waitress brought me tea and a basket of assorted breads, along with a plate of sausage and cheese slices and pots of honey and marmalade. She explained my egg would follow. After a week in Germany I had come to enjoy these German breakfasts very much.

Clausing's, as it is called, is a busy, well-run hotel with a sophisticated, international, yet definitely Bavarian, flavor. My room was comfortable, and decorated, as are many of the guest rooms, in the Bavarian style.

There were a few quixotic touches. For example, during dinner a lady came through the dining room selling flowers, and hot on her heels was a man in a business suit, wearing a Bavarian hat, taking photographs of the guests on request.

Henry Mike Clausing, the innkeeper and a fourth-generation hotelier, explained that about eighty-five percent of all the people who came to Garmisch each year are from Germany, although there is a U.S. Army rest and recreation center here. Clausing's is very popular with American service families. It isn't large enough to accommodate the bus tours, so most of the guests are in groups of two and four. There were several families in the house enjoying the unexpected bonus of a week-

end of late spring skiing. On Saturday night Clausing's casino goes full tilt, and I was happy to see that cheek-to-cheek dancing was still alive and well in Garmisch.

Clausing's has been many things to many people for many years— a place for honeymooning, anniversaries, and holidays in all seasons. Best of all, I think it is fun.

ROMANTIK HOTEL CLAUSING'S POSTHOTEL, Marienplatz 12, 8100 Garmisch. Tel.: 08821/58071. A 45-guestroom in-town hotel in one of Germany's most famous resort towns. Breakfast, lunch, and dinner served daily. Familie Clausing, Innkeepers. Rates: See Index.

Directions: Garmisch is about 1½ hrs. from Munich, also about ¾ hr. from Innsbruck, Austria. The map shows a choice of several roads.

SATURDAY NIGHT IN GARMISCH

It was six o'clock on an April evening in Garmisch. The sun, which had been hidden behind the heavy snow clouds all day, was now providing us with some marvelous shots of gold on the top of the snow-clad mountain peaks, which completely surround this Bavarian Alpine town.

An unexpected heavy snowfall provided Garmisch with another full weekend of skiing, and mingling with the German families dressed in traditional Bavarian garb were American servicemen pelting each other with snowballs.

There is lots of traffic on a Saturday evening in Garmisch, including Mercedes-Benzes with Munich plates, Porsches with U.S. Army plates, local town buses, and many taxis that shuttle back and forth to the train station.

The big attraction in Garmisch is the mountain peaks, like the Zugspitze at nearly 9,000 feet, the Dreitorspitze and the Alpspitze at 7,500 feet, and the Osterfeoderkopf at 6,000 feet. All of them have many ski lifts, tramways, and cable cars. The 1936 Winter Olympic games were held here, and since then Garmisch has been one of the ski capitals of the world. There is also bobsledding, ice skating, and extensive cross-country skiing.

In summer there are the ubiquitous climbing, walking, and excursions. During the warm weather, lakes provide swimming and boating, and the famous castles Linderhof and Neuschwanstein are nearby, as is also the village of Oberammergau, where the famous Passion Play is held.

I came to Garmisch in the spring, hoping for a glimpse of summer, and instead found a generous helping of winter. It was like Christmas on the Fourth of July!

HOTEL ALTE POST
Wangen (Bavarian Alps)

Herr Veile is a man who loves to smile and laugh. As far as I could see he had a great many things to smile and laugh about. For one thing, he and his wife, Louisa, have been keeping this hotel for over thirty years and it apparently has been prospering under their direction. It is located in a beautiful section of Germany, well within sight of the peaks of the Bavarian Alps and only a few kilometers from Lake Konstanz, which has many beautiful drives, homes, castles, and churches.

After meandering through the Bavarian Alps from Garmisch on a beautiful Sunday afternoon, I arrived in Wangen, a baroque walled town, as the bells were tolling six o'clock. The bells of Wangen are still another story. I heard them ring many times, but couldn't make any sense out of them. One seemed to toll four times every hour, and in turn found a response in another, deeper-toned bell that tolled the hour correctly. As soon as this duet was finished, a soprano bell took up the message, apparently just marking time.

The Alte Post, once a post stop, is located just outside one of the town gates, which has a very impressive clock tower. After a most refreshing bath and a short rest, I found my way to the second-floor dining room, where quite a few people from Wangen were enjoying dinner. The atmosphere was very pleasant.

After being shown to a table, I was joined by a German businessman and his wife, who shared the table with me. We became acquainted quite easily, and again I was pleased with the custom in middle-class European restaurants of guests sharing tables when there are no other available tables.

After a most satisfying dinner that wound up with the specialty of the house, an ice cream cake with slivered almonds, I had a long visit with Herr and Frau Veile and learned that there is an annex about a half-mile away on an elevation overlooking the town. We made an appointment to look at it in the morning, and after a short tour of the guest lounge and the hallways, where I found many extremely interesting and attractive pieces of antique furniture, I enjoyed a good night's sleep under my down comforter.

The following morning Herr Veile showed me around the remainder of the house and modestly pointed out the fact that he had received an award as a *Kuchmeister,* which meant that he was a master of the kitchen.

Hotel Alte Post is a beautifully decorated, well-furnished accommodation. It has an interesting history that goes back to 1409, more than 200 years before the formation of the German postal system in 1670.

Yes, Herr Veile has much to smile about.

ROMANTIK HOTEL ALTE POST, 7988 Wangen im Allgau. Tel.: 07522/4014. A hotel with 31 guestrooms in the main building, next to one of the walls of the town, and the annex, on a slightly higher elevation. Breakfast, lunch, and dinner served daily. Familie Veile, Innkeepers. Rates: See Index.

Directions: Wangen is on Rte. 18 approx. 30 km. from Lake Konstanz. It is 2 to 2½ hrs. from Munich.

HOTEL WALDHORN
Ravensburg (Lake Konstanz)

It was Monday morning in Ravensburg. The streets were enlivened by housewives with their shopping bags, and gentlemen of commerce were busy with the affairs of the day.

In the Hotel Waldhorn, the main affairs of the day seemed to be clean, clean, clean! In the front dining room there was a young lady standing on the table dusting off the plate rail and picking up every piece of pewter and china to give it a good swish. She even opened every decorative beer stein and wiped out the inside. Fresh flowers were being arranged on every table; the sweepers were sweeping; the vacuum cleaners were vacuuming.

I was enjoying a cup of tea in one of the dining rooms when I felt

someone jump on the bench next to me and wag a friendly tail. "His name is Bimbo," explained my hostess; "he is also part of the family." The family in this case includes the innkeeper and his wife, along with his son and daughter-in-law.

Frau Bouley-Dressel showed me to the second floor, where the hotel was hosting an exhibition of chocolate manufacturers from Switzerland. I have never seen such an incredible collection of fanciful chocolate. I walked around several of the tables aching to pocket many of the tantalizing morsels.

We progressed to a series of guest rooms, most of which were very pleasantly furnished, several with television sets. We returned to the ground floor and I was asked to sit and have some refreshments where I could watch the activities of the morning.

Albert, the son, joined me and we had a brief discussion about some of the specialties of the newly remodeled kitchen, a splendid example of cleanliness and good organization. He explained that one of the policies of the house was to serve only fresh vegetables. "Nothing frozen or in cans," he said. Consequently, the menu is constantly changing according to the season. One of the popular dishes is chicken Bresse, cooked in a Burgundy wine sauce and served with Gruyère cheese. There is also lamb Bretagne and many fresh fish dishes. I sampled the homemade goose liver paté and truffles, grown in the Strasbourg region a little to the north.

I was seated at what I learned was the *Stammtisch* in the front dining room with its paneled ceilings and walls and interesting carvings and ceramics.

ROMANTIK HOTEL WALDHORN, Marienplatz 15, 7980 Ravensburg. Tel.: 0751/16021. A 30-guestroom hotel in the center of a fairly large town. Quite convenient for many excursions both to the Lake Konstanz region and the Alps. Breakfast, lunch, and dinner served daily. Familie Bouley-Dressel, Innkeepers. Rates: See Index.

Directions: Ravensburg is about 35 km. north of Lake Konstanz via Rtes. 30 or 33.

HOTEL SEESCHAU
Island of Reichenau

Reichenau Island, on Lake Konstanz (*Bodensee,* in German), is reachable by a ferry from Altensbach in Germany, and is also easily reached from Switzerland.

The island itself is really most unusual, almost entirely in cultivation. The island's principal crops seem to be flowers and vegetables. This might be called the island of greenhouses because they are everywhere, and those plants not in greenhouses are protected by large plastic sheets. Even though this was only mid-April there were great quantities of gorgeous blooms everywhere.

We had no trouble locating the Hotel Seeschau because there were several signs indicating that we were on the right road; in fact, the island is quite tiny and it's impossible to get lost. Right on the lakeshore, the hotel had many wildflower-laden terraces overlooking the water. I subsequently learned that Rhine River excursion boats stop off here for lunch or dinner.

As soon as we stepped through the front door, we were taken in hand by a very attractive English-speaking African black girl, who explained that owner-chef Herr Winkelmann was busy in the kitchen, but that he would join us a bit later on at lunch. In the meantime, she was kind enough to take us through the public and guest rooms, many of which overlook the Bodensee. All are furnished with television sets.

Lunch began with a small slice of vegetable quiche and was followed by some sliced salmon and a salmon paté in a piquant sauce. The next course was sliced roast lamb and a variety of island-grown vegetables. I must mention the super-delectable scalloped potatoes that came in a ramekin. I'm particularly fond of potatoes in all of their delicious variations. When a guest orders a meal it is freshly prepared (nothing frozen) and beautifully presented and served. As Herr Winkelmann said when he joined us later on, "You can eat with your eyes as well as your mouth." The cuisine is quite international, with many French dishes, fish from the Rhine, steaks, lamb, and other items reflecting the really cosmopolitan nature of the clientele.

This was the regular noon meal at the Hotel Seeschau, and the dining room is on the sunny side overlooking the terrace, which in turn overlooks the lake. The table was set with a starched, pristine tablecloth and a vase of beautiful, long-stemmed roses. Even though it was early afternoon there was a small candle burning.

Herr and Frau Winkelmann joined us in time for dessert, and this very jolly gentleman explained that the hotel used to be a church, and later on one of the members of the congregation purchased it and made it into a *Gasthof.* Subsequently I trotted behind Herr Winkelmann as we went into the very clean, large, and light and airy kitchen. As he says, "We serve only fresh meals."

The Hotel Seeschau was a pleasant, happy experience and I would like to have stayed longer to enjoy the pleasant walks on the island; and perhaps a return visit in midsummer would find me swimming or sailing on the Bodensee.

ROMANTIK HOTEL SEESCHAU, 7752 Insel (Island) Reichenau im Bodensee. Tel.: 075 34-257. A 13-guestroom (all private baths) island hotel on a lake bordering on Switzerland. Breakfast, lunch, and dinner served to travelers. Closed from mid-Oct. to mid-Dec. and 3 wks. in Jan. Dining room closed from 3:00 p.m. Sun. thru Mon. night; breakfast served on Mon. to houseguests. Fishing, sailing, walking, and swimming all available nearby. Familie Winkelmann, Innkeepers.

Directions: From Germany, take the ferry to the island from Altensbach. From Switzerland, cross the border at Konstanz and take the first main turn left underneath the bridge. Continue about 3 mi., watching for the Reichenau sign. The causeway, lined with beautiful Lombardy poplars, is an indication that you are on the right road.

A FEW SUGGESTIONS
ABOUT THE FRANKFURT AIRPORT

It is necessary to go through customs twice, once for hand baggage and again for luggage from the airplane. Lufthansa has all its domestic and international flights in Hall A.

If you are going to the city of Frankfurt, a train is the fastest and most reasonably priced method.

When departing, non-residents are eligible for a refund of the V.A.T. (value added tax) if purchases exceed 100 marks. Fill out the form and have it stamped at customs.

Your rental car, particularly AutoEurope, can be picked up at the Frankfurt Airport.

381

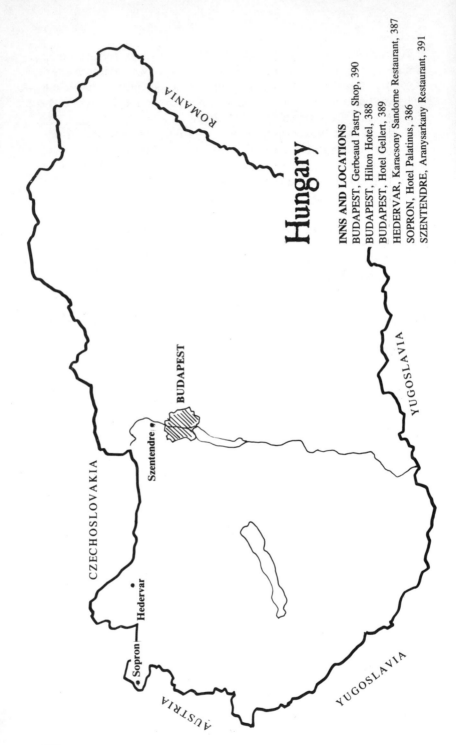

Hungary

INNS AND LOCATIONS
BUDAPEST, Gerbeaud Pastry Shop, 390
BUDAPEST, Hilton Hotel, 388
BUDAPEST, Hotel Gellert, 389
HEDERVAR, Karacsony Sandorne Restaurant, 387
SOPRON, Hotel Palatinus, 386
SZENTENDRE, Aranysarkany Restaurant, 391

ROMANIA

YUGOSLAVIA

BUDAPEST

CZECHOSLOVAKIA

Szentendre

Hedervar

Sopron

AUSTRIA

YUGOSLAVIA

TRAVEL SUGGESTIONS FOR HUNGARY

Hungary represents a venture by this book into an Eastern European country. At best, it might be called a preliminary toe-wetting. If reader response is favorable, I would expect to go farther into the country in the next edition. All in all, it is an adventure and an education.

Visa Regulations
A visa is required of United States and Canadian citizens. A visa can be obtained at the Hungarian Embassy in Washington, D.C., or in Ottawa, and also at the Hungarian Consulate General in New York. Visas are also issued at the Budapest Airport, at border crossing points if you are traveling by car, and at the pier upon arrival by hydrofoil. However, no visas are issued at border points to train travelers. Visas are valid for six months from the date of issue for a stay of up to thirty days.

How to Get There
By Air: There are no direct flights from North America to Budapest. However, the regular flights of Malév Hungarian Airlines link up Bu-

dapest with forty cities in thirty countries. There are twenty-two other airlines in addition to Malév that have regular flights to Budapest.

By Rail: Budapest is easy to reach by rail from any part of Europe.

By Car: Seven of the eight major highways running through Hungary radiate out from Budapest and all are linked up with the international road network.

By Boat: From May to September there is a daily hydrofoil boat running between Budapest and Vienna. Sailing time is four and a half hours. The international waterway is the famous Danube River.

Currency

The Hungarian unit of currency is the forint. Convertible currency can be brought into Hungary in any amount and exchanged at the tourist rate at banks, IBUSZ (Hungarian Travel Company) offices throughout Hungary, and at major hotels.

Credit Cards

Most first-class hotels, restaurants, and shops honor the common American credit cards.

Car Rentals

Have your travel agent rent a car through IBUSZ Hungarian Travel Company, 630 Fifth Avenue, Rockefeller Center, New York, NY 10111; 800-367-7878. Also through AutoEurope: 800-223-5555 (Maine: 800-342-5202).

Traffic rules in Hungary are generally the same as in most European countries. An international driver's license is necessary. The consumption of even the slightest quantity of alcoholic beverages before or while driving is absolutely forbidden.

Clothing

In summer, a lightweight jacket or wrap may be necessary during the evening. In winter, a moderate-weight coat is advisable.

Incidentally, Hungary is six hours ahead of U.S. Eastern Time.

For Further Information and Reservations

The IBUSZ Hungarian Travel Company, 630 Fifth Avenue, New York, NY 10111; 212-582-7412, can supply additional information and send very colorful literature. However, they accept reservations only

*from travel agents and not from individuals. Make your choice and
have your travel agent telephone: 800-367-7878.*

Hungarian Cuisine

*Hungarian cuisine has a long past and has undergone many foreign
influences. During the course of centuries, it has taken in and adapted
many features of Turkish, Italian, and French culinary arts. In addition
to the large restaurants, there are smaller ones at all points in Budapest
and the countryside offering a broad selection. There are also separate
restaurants offering Bulgarian, Romanian, Italian, Cuban, Russian,
German, and Polish specialties.*

*The special taste of Hungarian foods is the result of a blend of red
paprika, black pepper, onions, sour cream, and oil. Some particular
Hungarian dishes include* gulyás *(goulash),* halàszlè *(fish soup), chicken*
paprikás, *stuffed cabbage, Transylvanian meat delicacies, and a variety
of strudels, pancakes, somló desserts, raisin noodles, and dobos cake.*

Inns in Hungary

*There has always been a tradition of country inns in Hungary, the
world-renowned* csárda-s, *where the traveler was always sure to be
welcomed with the sound of the violin and offered a plate of hot "goulash." These had more or less disappeared, replaced by state-con-
trolled hotels that lacked both efficiency and taste. Fortunately, because
they were eager to increase tourism in their country, the Hungarians
have liberated the hotels and the restaurants, and now allow them to
be owned and managed by private individuals. This is part of a new
scheme in the Hungarian economy, so far very successful, of letting
some part of the public sector go private. The result of this is that in
the past couple of years a lot of new places have opened.*

*To find the good private places, just stop someone or ask the local
travel bureau. Everyone knows and will eagerly direct you. Some words
of German will help, especially in the eastern part of the country, but
young people also understand a bit of English.*

*I have included here the first privately owned and run restaurant and
the first privately owned and run inn. They are both very attractive and
their standards are indeed much higher than those of their government-
run counterparts.*

*Another agreeable way to visit Hungary is to use the IBUSZ network,
with rooms and reservation offices in most major cities. Reservations
can be made from Budapest or, as you travel, from one day to the next.
It is better to avoid the Balaton area altogether in the high season of*

July and August unless you have planned your trip and made your reservations long in advance.

AN ITINERARY IN HUNGARY

This trip by auto crosses the border from Austria into Transdanubia, a part of the country called the Dunántul. The journey starts in Sopron at a typical government-run hotel. It continues toward Budapest, stopping at the small village of Hedervar for lunch and also at Györ to see the cathedral.

Route 10 continues on to Budapest. This section on Hungary concludes with a short trip north on Route 11 to visit a restaurant in Szentendre, another wonderful, typical historic town.

HOTEL PALATINUS
Sopron

Here is what is typically the best in government-run hotels. The Palatinus is set on the smallest of the old city squares, in one of the old buildings. It is quite discreet from the exterior, but the renovation is very effective on the inside, achieving both style and comfort. The restaurant, with pink tablecloths, offers good service and good food; the rooms are warm and welcoming. It's a nice place to come home to after a long walk in and around Sopron.

HOTEL PALATINUS, Sopron 9400, UJ utca 23. Tel.: (36-99) 11-395; telex 24-9146 ujhot. A first-class hotel right in the center of an old baroque city. Rates: See Index.

Directions: There are only 2 main streets in the old center; UJ utca is one of the two.

SOPRON AND ENVIRONS

Close by on the same street is a very interesting studio and shop with an equally interesting owner, Andras Orsi. He was originally an engineer and worked as such successfully for many years, until he decided to be what he really wanted and became a sculptor. In this new field also he was very successful. One of the first purchasers of private property in Hungary, he was allowed to buy and renew an old house to transform it into a studio, to which he added a shop.

Budapest is a short and easy drive from Sopron, but I preferred to linger on the way. There are so many interesting stops. Fertöd Castle, for example, the grandest masterpiece of baroque architecture, built by Prince Miklos Esterházy at the end of the 18th century, where one could spend a whole day . . . or the area of the Szigetköz, along the border with Czechoslovakia, the region of islands on the Danube. Although modernized, it retains some old quaint houses, the tanyas, *low and whitewashed, with overhanging thatched roofs. I had a really good lunch in Hedervar, one of the villages there.*

KARACSONY SANDORNE RESTAURANT
Hedervar

If you've seen the Hitchcock film *The Lady Vanishes*, you'll understand exactly what I mean. This place is in a tiny village far off the main road; foreigners never arrive there. No wonder then that everybody turned their heads and stopped talking when I entered. Through the smoke I saw an assembly of darkly clad peasants, all with imposing mustaches, all casting inquisitive glances at me. Suddenly a sympathetic blond lady materialized from the back of the room, and asked what I wanted. Upon hearing that I was hungry, she said that she had little, but would do her best. Her best was marvelous: a thick slice of veal liver cooked to perfection, sweet vegetables from her garden, salads and fruits. I gave her three rosettes.

KARACSONY SANDORNE RESTAURANT, Kocsmaros, 9178 Hedervar, Kossuth L. utca 1. A plain inn offering good food and warmth.

Directions: Midway between Györ and Mosonmagyaróvar. The inn is in the middle of the village.

TO BUDAPEST

On my way to Budapest, I couldn't help stopping in Györ, a must for any lover of the baroque era, if only for the magnificent cathedral.

When I arrived at last in Budapest it was dark already, but I knew where to go, across the river and up to the Var *(castle), close to which is the Hilton Hotel.*

HILTON HOTEL
Budapest

In the heart of the 700-year-old castle district of Buda, the Hilton is the best of all the new grand hotels in Budapest. The hotel stands on the site where a Dominican abbey stood in the Middle Ages, and when the construction of the hotel began, archaeologists unearthed the remains of the 13th-century cloister and it was integrated in the new structure, a rare sight in a Hilton. If you go into the Casino Budapest, you'll find yourself partly in the authentic tower of the Gothic church of Saint Nicholas, newly furnished in the style of the 13th century. A variety of restaurants offer a wide choice of Hungarian and international food. Everything here is up to standard.

HILTON HOTEL, 1014 Budapest, Hess Andras ter 1-3. Tel.: 853-500; telex 22-59-84. One of the most surprising Hiltons in the world. Rates: See Index.

Directions: On the Buda hill, near the castle and the cathedral.

BUDAPEST

Budapest is a surprisingly fizzy city, with rich museums, elegant shops, and animated restaurants where wine and music flow. I found that the tramways were the easiest and best way to go around the city. There are also a lot of taxis, public and private. The private ones are driven by people who double their day's work in the taxi business, but even though they don't usually have a meter, they are not more expensive than the normal taxis. One of the best shopping streets is Vaci utca (street), which runs parallel to the river in Pest, behind the Intercontinental Hotel. Pest is the more commercial part of the city, on the eastern side of the Danube. Most of the shops, restaurants, museums, except the one located in the castle, are on the Pest side. A woman friend tells me there is a new thing going on in Hungary these days: the beauty business. Lots of beauty parlors are blossoming, using the usually good new lines of skin and hair creams and lotions that the Hungarian inventors have come up with. They are, of course, much cheaper than American or Western European similar places and they are fun to try. Another very worthwhile experience in Budapest is the baths. Many different medicinal springs run in Budapest, 123 to be precise. They have many different curative virtues that people have known about for the past 2,000 years. One of the better-known baths flows into the beautiful pool of the Hotel Gellert.

HOTEL GELLERT
Budapest

This is one of the more famous spa hotels in the world. A beautiful building topped with many domes, it was built in 1918 and still retains some Art Nouveau flavor. Surely, it is the most reminiscent of a lost era, and of the specific taste of the Hungary of the beginning of the century. Even if you don't go there to swim, go to see the inside pool—the architecture is startling. The bathers, too, are worth being with, as it is not reserved to the hotel guests, but to anyone who buys a ticket. I enjoyed staying there more than anywhere else in Budapest. Even though it is a luxury hotel, it is really Hungarian, which an international hotel can never be. I learned things about the country there; the atmosphere is more real, the food tastes authentically Hungarian.

HOTEL GELLERT, 1111 Budapest, Gellert ter 1. Tel.: (361) 460-700. An elegant hotel, in the old-fashioned sense. Rates: See Index.

Directions: On the Buda side of the Danube, just below the castle.

HUNGARIAN ATMOSPHERE

For real Hungarian atmosphere, I also like the fruit and vegetable markets with little old peasant women in dark skirts and shawls loudly bargaining over their onions and potatoes. The vegetables were indisputably of the "health" kind, grown naturally and presented for sale with soil and leaves attached. I thought of all the work it would take to prepare them.

For another quite different Hungarian atmosphere, I went to one of the pastry shops that has made the city famous: Gerbeaud.

GERBEAUD PASTRY SHOP
Budapest (Vörösmarty)

Henrik Kugler, a confectioner from Sopron, first opened his shop in Jozsef Square, but as he gained popularity he looked for new premises and finally moved into the present large and beautiful building. The splendid interior and the large choice and perfect quality of the cakes made the place renowned throughout Europe from the last century to today. Kugler's successor, Emil Gerbeaud, set up a chocolate factory and exported the world over. The salons are so spacious they can accommodate hundreds of guests. They are gracefully furnished and decorated with fine paintings and pretty objects. The choice between the myriad colorful and delicious-looking pastries is trying. The best-known cake is the dobos.

FURTHER FACTS ABOUT BUDAPEST

Budapest is the capital of the Hungarian People's Republic. The Danube River flows through the center of the city for twenty-eight kilometers, with the hilly region of Buda on the right bank and the plains of Pest on the left.

The history of Budapest dates from the Celts and the Romans, and there are examples of both Romanesque and Gothic architecture. Even more numerous are relics of the Turkish eras, including some Turkish baths.

Among the most important of the over twenty museums in the city are the National Museum, where the visitor can get an insight into the 1,000-year history of the Hungarian nation; the Budapest History Museum; the Museum of Fine Arts; and the Museum of Ethnography, which displays objects of folklore from the various regions of Hungary.

There are twenty-five permanent theaters in Budapest, as well as a good number of open-air theaters. Budapest musical life is known throughout the world. Liszt, Béla Bartók, and Zoltán Kodály made Budapest their home. The Budapest Festival is held every autumn, and the Budapest Spring Festival is conducted at the end of March.

There are many sporting facilities, including stadiums, swimming pools, boathouses, and much diversion for children, including the Budapest City Park and the Zoological Gardens.

ARANYSARKANY RESTAURANT
Szentendre
This is the first private restaurant in Hungary. Attila Mahr, the owner, has shown a lot of courage and good taste, and has also generated some good publicity for his country. He chose Szentendre, a townlet on the "elbow" of the Danube, as the Hungarians call the area where the river bends.

An ancient settlement of Serbs and Dalmatians, the village is very picturesque—almost a museum in itself, with its baroque and rococo houses, many of which are galleries showing contemporary artists, usually in one-man shows. One of these houses is our restaurant.

The guests all eat at one large table, which makes conversation and meeting easy. The menu offers a wide choice of Hungarian and other cuisines. When I was there, Attila told me that he was going to publish a book with his recipes, and asked whether I thought it would be worthwhile to translate it. I said, "Yes, by all means!"

Shortly before going to press, the cookbook arrived in my office, and a very handsome edition it is.

ARANYSARKANY RESTAURANT, Szentendre. A touristy but quality restaurant. Prices about 500 to 600 forints. Attila Mahr, Owner.

Directions: Take Rte. 11 to the north. The restaurant is in the middle of the village.

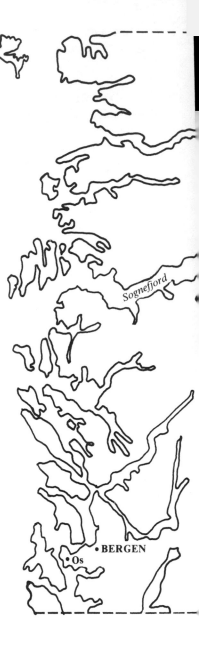

Norway

INNS AND LOCATIONS

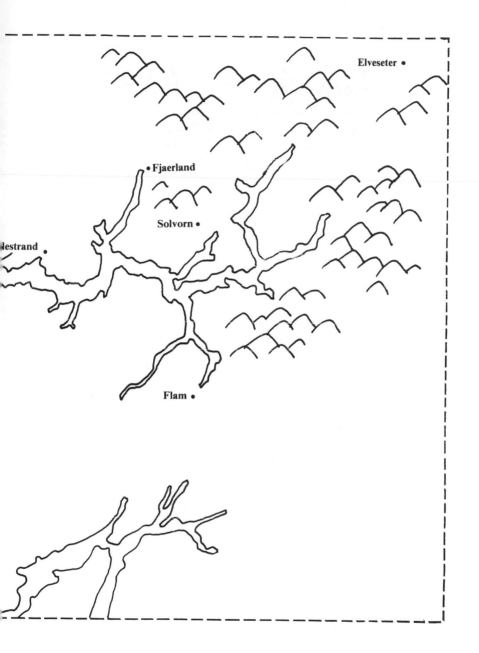

Elveseter •

• Fjaerland

Solvorn •

lestrand •

Flam •

TRAVEL SUGGESTIONS FOR NORWAY

How to Get There

Scandinavian Airlines (SAS) maintains flights from the United States to all Scandinavian countries. SAS has flights to Oslo as does Pan Am. Norway can also be reached directly by car from Sweden and by car/ferry from Denmark. The Eurail pass is good in Scandinavia.

Scandinavian Hospitality

I like to think of this section on these four Scandinavian countries as being a smorgasbord—literally a sampling of the four countries. It is designed to encourage travelers from all parts of the world to visit Norway, Sweden, Finland, and Denmark. I have attempted to elaborate on the type of hospitality in each country and indicate the wide variety of food, services, and accommodations.

Country Inns in Norway

My visit to Norway was confined for the most part to the Sognefjord district, where I found hotels and pensions. In Norway, a hotel is legally classified as having enough bedrooms and reception rooms to adequately house at least twenty guests, and is required also to have a certain number of available wc's. Some Norwegian hotels have many resort facilities on the grounds or nearby.

The pensions share a number of common virtues: most of their rooms have twin beds with down comforters encased in a washable sheeting.

Almost all have running water in each room, and sometimes there is only one wc and one bathroom for seven or eight rooms. All serve three meals a day, and often offer between-meal snacks of delicious homemade cakes with coffee or tea.

All have living rooms where guests can relax before and after meals. Both pensions and hotels have plans that include three meals a day and special rates for three days or more.

Reservations can be made by mail or telephone.

Norwegian Menus

Every hotel and pension has a single-price meal as well as an à la carte menu. The evening meal consists of three courses: soup, usually homemade, a main dish—a large platter with meat or fish and a vegetable, as well as lettuce and tomato or other salad vegetables—and dessert, usually fresh or frozen fruit served with whipped cream.

Breakfast, Norwegian style, is a real eating adventure. This is where I found the many varieties of cold fish, cheese (including delicious goat cheese), breads, crackers, and jams.

Stave church

Car Rentals in Scandinavia

There are many different "Fly-Drive" plans that include automobiles. Travelers for whom Scandinavia is part of a continent-wide itinerary, or those who are not on a "Fly-Drive" plan, will find more information in the section "Renting a Car for Europe," in the front of the book.

Driving Tips

Public transportation in Norway is excellent, and in a great many cases it would be advisable to leave the car in Oslo or Bergen and travel by train, bus, or ferry to a central point, such as Balestrand, and then make a series of daily or overnight excursions into the fjord country, using the carefully coordinated schedules of both ferries and buses. That's what I did. I had to grow accustomed to the long daylight hours and the occasional rain and mist that are part of the fjord country ambience. I was glad that I brought a raincoat. There was, however, plenty of sunshine. Incidentally, gasoline stations and supermarkets close early, usually at five o'clock.

MY ITINERARY IN NORWAY

I took the train from Oslo to Bergen and spent one night nearby before taking the car/ferry to Balestrand. It is also possible to get to Bergen from Oslo by air, ferry, or car and then follow this itinerary. I went to the end of the Sognefjord, up and over the mountains, and down the other side into Sweden.

THE SOLSTRAND FJORD HOTEL
Os, Bergen

My table in the dining room had a perfect view of the Bjornafjord. I could look across the green lawn, past the tennis courts, and out into this water wonderland. The Norwegian flag stirred lightly as breezes from across the water picked up its elegant long tail, making it look like a kite in the sky. The Hardanger Mountains across the fjord had patches of snow, and in the distance, the peaks of higher mountains were almost completely covered with snow.

After an afternoon of learning more about the fascinating city of Bergen, I had set out on Route 14, the road to Os, and now was enjoying my first evening meal in Norway.

It began with a delicious vegetable soup served in a big bowl. The table was laid with old-fashioned silverware. The main course was fresh trout served with a tartar sauce and white potatoes. The dessert was tasty fresh fruit, including oranges, grapes, and peaches, topped with freshly whipped cream. A young man played the piano throughout the entire meal, alternating his selections between such old favorites as Errol Garner's "Misty" and Chopin's "Minute Waltz."

All of the guests in the dining room seemed to be Norwegian. As far as I could tell I was the only non-Scandinavian present. However, the entire staff of this resort-inn spoke English and I was made to feel at home at once.

One of the outstanding features of this waterside hotel is the extensive fitness center, with its heated indoor swimming pool, children's pool, whirlpools, saunas, squash courts, and a variety of exercise equipment.

Guest rooms at this hotel are typical of what I found everywhere in Scandinavia. There are older rooms with traditional furniture and decor, typical of many American and British country inns. Then there is a newer wing of modernized rooms with furniture reflecting modern Scandinavian design, with greater simplicity and austerity of line. The tables, chairs, lamps, and beds are not as decorative as they are functional. I found this functional style almost everywhere I went, for more and more pensions and small hotels have been redecorated and refurnished.

THE SOLSTRAND FJORD HOTEL, N-5200 Os. Tel.: Bergen 30-00-99. Located in a scenic fjord area, 17 mi. from Bergen Airport, 18 mi. from Bergen. Accessible by bus from Bergen. Extensive fitness center with indoor heated swimming pool and saunas, private beach, row-

boats, speedboats, waterskiing, fishing, walking, tennis, squash, mini-golf. Rates: See Index.

BALESTRAND

On the map showing the Sognefjord area I have indicated the lo-cation of the town of Balestrand. Balestrand is the principal stop on the ferries that leave from Bergen each day. There is a car ferry that leaves at 9:30 in the morning and arrives at 6:30 at night, and another ferry leaves at 8:30 a.m., arriving at noon, but does not permit auto-mobiles. Balestrand is approximately a 5-hour drive from Bergen and can also be reached conveniently by bus.

I found that I could use Balestrand as a base for traveling anywhere in this particular fjord system and the nearby mountains. There are ferry, bus, and automobile connections in all directions. The local tourist office, which, by the way, is typical of similar offices everywhere in Norway, is most accommodating. It is open from 9:30 until 6:30 every day, with two hours off for lunch. It is possible to arrive in Balestrand and get assistance at the tourist office in planning either a one-day or a two-week stay in the area. This includes making reser-vations at various hotels and pensions. Travelers are also invited to contact the Balestrand tourist office in the off-season for information, which can be studied in advance of arrival. The mailing address is: Balestrand Tourist Office, N-5850, Balestrand, Norway.

DRAGSVIK FJORD HOTEL
Balestrand, Sognefjord

This fjord hotel is located in a very pretty village just across the Esefjord from the village of Balestrand. It is within walking distance of the Dragsvik ferry stop, which means that guests here have the entire Sognefjord area accessible by water. My room, furnished in a modern Scandinavian fashion, overlooked Balestrand and the main fjord.

I'll take a few moments to describe the dinner served here because it was typical of the pension fare that I enjoyed during my trip. The first course was a piquant homemade asparagus soup. The main course for two was served on a large platter. This consisted of sliced roast beef, cauliflower, pickles, prunes, and generous amounts of lettuce, arranged most artistically. There was a separate dish of boiled white

potatoes, which I found was a staple in the Norwegian diet, and a bowl of tasty gravy prepared from the juices of the meat. Dessert was freshly whipped cream and peaches.

The view from the dining room was lovely, overlooking the fjord and the mountains. In the foreground there were fruit trees in blossom. Overhead, the sky cleared for a short time and a bar or two of sunshine dramatically lighted the fjord.

DRAGSVIK FJORD HOTEL, N-5850 Balestrand. Tel.: 056-94-293. Dragsvik is a hamlet across the Esefjord from Balestrand. All of the fjord outdoor recreation and excursion advantages are available. Rates: See Index.

MIDTNES PENSJONAT
Balestrand, Sognefjord

I stayed one night in this pension in a modest single room that overlooked the flowery hillside. There was running water in the room, and since my visit, nearly all of the rooms have a shower and a wc.

This family-owned pension has a beautiful dining room overlooking the fjord and an outdoor terrace that is very popular on clement evenings. A few steps away it has its own dock and facilities for hiring sailboats, rowboats, and water skis. The owners were most accommodating and I noticed that they spent a great deal of time sitting in the salons, talking with their guests.

I particularly remember the dozens of yellow tulips that were in bloom on the terrace and in the yard of the inn during my stay. It is immediately adjacent to Saint Olav's English church.

MIDTNES PENSJONAT, N-5850 Balestrand. Tel.: 056-91-133. Rates: See Index.

THE FJAERLAND FJORD

A trip by ferry on the Fjaerland Fjord is an exciting way to spend a day, or even a longer visit with an overnight stay at the Hotel Mundal or the Fjaerland Pensjonat. I made the trip for the day and was entranced with this strange and marvelous corner of Norway. The Fjaerland Fjord is one of the most famous and unusual in Norway, with its ever-changing shoreline, from serene pastoral meadows to steep cliffs and snow-topped mountains rising to 3,000 feet on both sides. And at the end of the line, there is a bus trip up to the Jostedal Glacier and its spectacular waterfalls.

HOTEL MUNDAL
Fjaerland
I had a feeling that I had been at this beautiful inn before. Perhaps because of its similarity to so many country inns I have visited in both Britain and North America. As a matter of fact, its atmosphere was distinctly British. When I mentioned this to Marit Mauritzen, she said that quite possibly it was because of their many guests from the British Isles, even as far back as the late 19th century.

"The British are great walkers," she said. "And I think that our proximity to the Jostedal Glacier, the largest ice field on the European continent, makes the prospect of mountain walks and climbing even more attractive. With this in mind, we have always offered courses in glaciology and geology. We're very popular here with botanists and ornithologists as well."

I could feel the innkeeping tradition radiating from this old building and its owners. It was obvious that this hotel had been well cared for by its owners and loved by guests for many years. In the main living room, a fireplace with intricate hand-painted designs of Norwegian flowers was surrounded by deep leather chairs that invited both reverie and conversation. While I was walking through the hotel I could hear someone playing the piano in the background, and there was one particularly interesting room with a circular seat in a beautiful bay window. I also found a billiard room with a wood-paneled ceiling.

In the dining room, there were some large painted panels depicting the fairy tale of the three princes who were turned into bears and could be turned back into princes only if they could find princesses who would be willing to take them into their bedchambers. There is one panel showing the three princesses with their hair literally standing on end upon being confronted by the bears. The happy ending is that somehow or other the bears did turn into princes the next morning!

The guest rooms on the two upper floors were most comfortable, with some rooms overlooking the fjord and the garden below. Until recently the Hotel Mundal and the Fjaerland Pensjonat could be reached only by ferry from either Hella or Balestrand. However, I understand that a road is now completed, and they can both now be reached by ferry or car from Skei.

HOTEL MUNDAL, N-5855 Fjaerland. Tel.: 056-93-101. A country hotel in a beautiful Norwegian village with capacity for 60 guests. All bedrooms modernized. Boating, badminton, fishing, walking, hiking, and glacier excursions. Rates: See Index.

FJAERLAND FJORDHOTELL
Fjaerland

Mr. Ansgar Mundal was my guide through this small hotel with a friendly atmosphere on the fjord side in Fjaerland. He told me that his family has owned this property for many years and that he, in fact, grew up here. There were photographs of his father and mother and grandparents in the reception rooms. Both the main salon and the dining room overlooked this enchanting fjord, and there is a wonderful view of several waterfalls cascading from the mountains.

There were a number of people seated in the salon on this particular day, because there was a slight drizzle. Ordinarily, they might have been walking in the mountains or venturing on to the great glacier, but today they were inside drinking coffee and carrying on enthusiastic conversations. Ansgar explained that the hotel was very popular with the Dutch, English, and Norwegians, many of whom return year after year.

I looked at several of the guest rooms on the second floor and found them clean and comfortable. Some of them have their own baths and wc's. The dining room had paintings of fjord scenes, a sparkling floor, white tablecloths, and flowers on each of the tables.

It certainly looked like a delightful place to me.

FJAERLAND FJORDHOTELL, N-5855 Fjaerland, Sognefjord. Tel.: 056-93-161. A 25-guestroom hotel at the end of the Fjaerland Fjord within 7 mi. of the glaciers. Bathing, rowing, badminton, fishing, walking, hiking, and glacier excursions. Rates: See Index.

A DAY TRIP FROM BALESTRAND

My drive into the mountains north of Balestrand on Route 5 turned out to be a very scenic one, with prosperous farmlands, mountains with rushing brooks and streams, and waterfalls coursing down their sides, carrying melting snow to ponds and lakes below. The frequent bus signs reminded me this beautiful trip can be made by bus in a day, or with an overnight stay at the pension in Vassenden. A bus schedule can be obtained at the Balestrand Tourist Office.

HEIMLY LODGE AND MARINA
Flam, Sogn

The twilight ferry trip through the Aurland Fjord was such a beautiful and tranquil experience I would have been disappointed if there hadn't been an inn that breathed the same kind of atmosphere in this little town at the far end of the fjord. Fortunately, there was—the Heimly Lodge.

It seemed that my head had just touched the pillow when the alarm went off. I wanted to get an early start on the day, since there was really so much to see and do in Flam. I took a quick shower in the bathroom down the hall and joined the other guests for breakfast in a sunny and delightful dining room.

The breakfast was indeed unbelievable. There was a large table in the center of the dining room laden with a wide assortment of fish and many different varieties of cheese, including some delicious cheese made from goat's milk. There were six varieties of Norwegian bread, sliced ham, liverwurst, and other meats. There were all kinds of fresh fruit jams and several varieties of hot and cold cereals. I filled my plate with as many of the breakfast offerings as possible, and took a seat by the window. I was immediately drawn into conversation with people who were pointing out the fact that the morning ferry boat, which was down the fjord, seemed to be floating in space because of the illusion created by the brilliant sunshine, the steep sides of the fjord, and the absence of wind.

As we watched, far down the fjord a huge cruise ship came into view and it was explained that occasionally these luxury liners, which can go almost anywhere on the fjord system because of the deep water, frequently make calls at Flam, and the passengers ride the Flam railway up the mountain to Myrdal or even on to Oslo.

It was an absolutely gorgeous morning, and the sunshine on the garden of the inn found ready reception, from the fruit trees in blossom to the geraniums decorating the terrace and bordering the walk down to the road. I started counting the waterfalls that could be seen from the dining room and finally gave up at eighteen.

Heimly Lodge has the same type of atmosphere that I found at the Hotel Mundal in Fjaerland and the Walaker Hotel in Solvorn. There were many original touches in the salon and quite a few photographs of Norwegian craftsmen and crafts.

After breakfast a group of us went out on the terrace to enjoy the really magnificent presence of the high mountains in this valley and to try to store up some of the incredible serenity. Then, one by one, we all separated to do whatever pleased us for the day. Some were taking off to go hiking, others bicycling, and some would be boating on the fjord. A great many were going to disappear in the mountains with a good book. I was going to take the Flam Railway to Myrdal. We would all gather at dinner for what I knew would be an outstanding experience.

HEIMLY LODGE AND MARINA, N-5743 Flam, Sogn. Tel.: 056-32241. A 40-guestroom inn at the end of the Aurland Fjord in the beautiful Flam valley. All types of outdoor recreation available. Open May 1 to Oct. 30. Rates: See Index.

WALAKER HOTEL
Solvorn, Sogn

Pointing to the right, the sign off the main road read "Walaker Hotel." A road took me past some upland meadows where cows were grazing and I headed for the fjord at the bottom of the mountains. The road looked well traveled and I later found out it was the main road into this village. I passed through some orchards and soon the church spire of the village came into view. It was also lilac time in Solvorn. Norway is captivating in June with all the fruit trees in blossom.

The Walaker Hotel deserves this setting. One thing I learned is that the house is over 325 years old and the old portion of it is called the Tingstova, the Norwegian word for courtroom, and is so called because at one time this is where a judge held trials.

The Walaker Hotel has been owned by the same family since 1690. The present owners, Hermod and Oddlaug Walaker, were married here in peasant costume on Midsummer Eve in 1968, and their photographs were taken on the front porch of the hotel. I was delighted when Oddlaug presented me with a photograph of the event. The 300th anniversary of the hotel will be celebrated in 1990 with the opening of an art gallery and museum in the 100-year-old barn.

I was pleased to see these two energetic people, along with their four children, keeping this country inn in an enchanting village amidst awe-inspiring scenery.

The hotel has a real country inn atmosphere, with some beautiful Norwegian antiques, some of them from the "old church" in the town, which dates back to the 17th century. Open fireplaces, beamed ceilings, a collection of family photographs, and winding staircases add to the comfortable, homelike feeling.

There is also a section that contains new rooms, furnished in the modern mode, with kitchenettes.

Across the fjord from the village is Urnes Stave Church, one of the old stave churches of Norway, and now on the UNESCO Heritage List. There is frequent ferry service to the opposite shore, and Solvorn has direct bus connections with principal Sognefjord points.

The Walaker Hotel is one of the beautiful country inns in Norway.

WALAKER HOTEL, N-5815 Solvorn, Sogn. Tel. from abroad: 4756-84207; in Norway: 056-84-207. A delightful hotel in a secluded fjordside village. Hiking, walking, glacier trips, fjord fishing, rowboats, swimming. Boat, bus, and ferry connections to all points. Rates: See Index.

THROUGH THE MOUNTAINS TOWARD SWEDEN

My time in Norway was drawing to a close. I was driving east on the main highway leading from the fjord country high into the great mountains and snow fields to Lom, on the other side of the mountains. This road, closed for the winter, had been open only four days when I ventured upon it. In some places the snowplows had carved through drifts twice the height of the car, and only continual sanding and filling prevented the cars from being mired down in the spring thaw.

Between Luster on the Sognefjord and Lom, I passed a few small hotels and pensions, most of which were closed. Here are my impressions of one that was open.

ELVESETER HOTEL
Elveseter

This hotel, 2,100 feet up in the great Norwegian mountains, was originally a manor farm that was converted into what are for the most part modern accommodations. A considerable number of new buildings have been added in recent years. A great deal of effort has been made to create the atmosphere reminiscent of an old Norse "Home of the Gods" and every room has a name derived from Norse mythology. All guest rooms are traditionally furnished.

The buildings are grouped together around a square and are linked by heated corridors and an elevator. Each room has a private bath. There is an indoor swimming pool, a gymnasium, and several facilities for meetings. There are also some apartments in an old manor farmhouse nearby.

I was quite surprised to find an accommodation so large and so luxurious in this part of Norway. I wouldn't describe it as a country inn, but it is certainly most impressive.

The hotel is on the road between the Sognefjord and the fertile valley to the east. It is not advisable to take this road after October 1.

ELVESETER HOTEL, 2689 Elveseter. Tel.: (062) 12-000 (May 20–Oct. 1); (062) 54874 (Oct. 1–May 20). Open June 1 to Sept. 20. Indoor swimming pool. Rates: See Index.

It was all downhill from here to Lom. As I descended from the Alpine heights, the wild terrain was replaced by farming country, and quite a few fields had sprinkling systems that were now in use because the rain in Norway stays on the west side of the great mountains.

The Norwegian portion of my trip was, for all practical purposes, completed. There remained only the drive to Lillehammer to cross the border into Sweden.

Sweden

INNS AND LOCATIONS

Sunne •

VARMLAND

DALARNA

Tallberg
•
Siljan

STOCKHOLM

Vanern

Aby •

Vattern

• Granna

• Sunds

• Hok

• Falkenberg

SKANE

• **HJARNARP**

Iolle •

• **MALMO**

409

TRAVEL SUGGESTIONS FOR SWEDEN

How to Get There

SAS has flights to Stockholm and Gothenburg. Pan Am also has flights to Stockholm. Numerous ferries provide service to Sweden from other parts of Europe.

Country Inns in Sweden

Country inn hospitality in Sweden falls roughly into two categories: there are lovely old manor houses and small castles, and there are the more traditional country inns in southern Sweden, in the province of Skane, that are similar to their Danish cousins. The latter I have described more extensively in the section on Denmark.

Those inns to be found in manor houses and castles often have historical or literary connections, with an ambience in which their gardens play a special role. Decorated in harmonizing Scandinavian fabrics and furnished with both traditional and modern furniture, most of the guest rooms have private baths. The food is excellent; it is usually prepared and served by members of the owner's family, who make up the modest staffs.

Swedish Menus

Everything I've ever heard about Swedish smorgasbord is true: it is fabulous. Served as a noon meal, and all day on Sundays and holidays, smorgasbord has many varieties of fish, as well as the famous Swedish meatballs served with lingonberry sauce. Also included are salads, cheeses, marinated meats, breads, and relishes. I found that each chef was proud of his smorgasbord, which involves many hours of preparation.

I had my first taste of small, fresh raw herring for breakfast in Sweden and found them delicious. Evening meals in many Swedish manor houses and restaurants are served in the Continental style, with a great deal of emphasis on French dishes.

MY ITINERARY IN SWEDEN

Because I entered Sweden from Norway, the account in this edition starts in the western part of Sweden called Varmland, and proceeds eastward through the Dalarna region, and thence to Stockholm and south, past Lake Vattern to the resort area of the west coast of Sweden.

VARMLAND, MY INTRODUCTION TO SWEDEN

I crossed the border into Sweden at Eda, and arrived in the rich Varmland country in western Sweden, north of Karlstad. This was an area blessed with most of the good things that Sweden has to offer— great forests, lakes numbering in the thousands, hiking trails, canals, folklore festivals, crafts of all descriptions, and rivers that not only are famous for their natural beauty, but are also avenues of commerce, with many floating logs.

This is a region replete with opportunities for active outdoor sports, including tennis and golf, swimming, canoeing, and boating. In winter there is downhill and cross-country skiing.

The town of Sunne, where I remained overnight, is deep in Selma Lagerlöf country. It is on the straits connecting the upper and middle Fryken Lakes. In August there are nine days of Fryksdal festivities based on Selma Lagerlöf stories.

The fairs and festivals in this area, I am told, are most enjoyable. For further information about Varmland, write the Varmland Tourist Association, Södra Kyrkogat 10, Box 323, S-65105 Karlstad, Sweden.

LANSMANSGARDEN
Sunne

I was completely entranced with this lovely manor house. It is located on the banks of Lake Fryken in Sunne, the center of Sweden's famous Varmland area. It reacquainted me with the Swedish Nobel Prize-winning author Selma Lagerlöf. She had used this inn as a locale for one of her books, and her home, Marbacka, is just a few kilometers to the south.

I arrived about nine o'clock, driving from Norway. My first experience was heartening, indeed. I had arrived long past the dinner hour, but the girl at the desk said that the cook could prepare something for me if I was willing to wait a few minutes. I was. Then an accommodating waiter with a good sense of humor showed me to a table in a most attractive dining room. After a very tasty bowl of soup, he brought me a warm plate with five delicious seafood-filled crêpes accompanied by an excellent tossed salad and some homemade Swedish bread.

The dining room, like the remainder of this inn, is a tribute to Swedish furnishing and decorating. It was a tasteful blend of painted furniture and natural wood. There were flowers on each table, and the cutlery and dishes were Swedish Modern.

After dinner, I went out on the terrace and met a Swedish couple and their English friends, who had been coming to Lansmansgarden for many years. We talked about traveling and promised to meet the next morning for breakfast.

My room in this manor house could be a model for country inns anywhere. It had a lacy bedspread, Swedish designs on the wallpaper,

a blue carpet, and painted furniture. Erik Biorklund, the innkeeper, later explained to me that these were the "romantic" rooms that, whenever possible, were reserved for honeymoon couples. The rooms in this building were named after characters in Selma Lagerlöf's novels.

The next morning, breakfast with my four new friends was great fun because they took delight in introducing me to several typically Swedish dishes, of which there were several. For one thing, I had my first taste of fresh, raw herring. I'll never be satisfied with pickled herring again. I was also introduced to a breakfast porridge made from rye grain, to which I was instructed to add applesauce and a small amount of sugar and milk. Delicious. There were many other dishes, including meats and cheeses.

LANSMANSGARDEN, S-686 00, Sunne. Tel.: 46-565-10301. A 30-guestroom (private baths) manor house in a garden setting in the Varmland section of Sweden. Summer sports include swimming, rowing, badminton, tennis, golf, fishing, walking, hiking. Winter sports include several different ski lifts within a short distance. Rates: See Index.

MARBACKA AND ROTTNEROS

The fact that novelist Selma Lagerlöf was born in this part of the Varmland in 1858, and subsequently made her home here from 1907 until 1940, has asserted a tremendous influence on the area. Her home, Marbacka, is open to the public, and has been preserved exactly as she left it at the time of her passing. It is visited by thousands of people every year.

Rottneros is identified as the "Ekeby" in Selma Lagerlöf's novels. It was probably the residence of an important country squire as early as the 13th century. It is the former garden of an important iron foundry. It covers almost a hundred acres that are in turn surrounded by both natural and formal parkland. In the gardens are more than a hundred sculptures, representing a large part of what Swedish sculptors have created during the past century. These marvelous pieces of sculpture are carefully placed within the natural atmosphere of gardens and trees, and are one of Sweden's foremost tourist attractions.

Marbacka and Rottneros are open from May 15 to September 15. There is a coffee room at Marbacka and a restaurant and cafeteria at Rottneros.

DALARNA

Dalarna covers a considerable area to the northwest of Stockholm.
Dalarna *means "the valleys between the east and west Dal Rivers."*

From my talks with Signe Keyes at Siljansgarden, I learned that the entire area is rich in folklore, history, handcrafts, and the preservation of old Swedish ways. It is also the home of the famous Dala paintings, decorative paintings by self-taught artists who lived between 1780 and 1870. The famous Dala horses, occasionally found in imported crafts shops in the United States, come from a small village near Leksand.

The Leksand area itself comprises ninety villages and the resort towns of Tallberg, Siljansnas, and Insjon. They are all located on the shores of beautiful Lake Siljan, a most attractive natural area.

For further information about Dalarna, write the Dalarna Tourist Association, Bergslagsgrand 1, S-791 00 Falun, Sweden.

SILJANSGAARDEN GASTHEM
Tallberg

I just happened to be walking down a lane toward the shore of Lake Siljan, when I saw a group of several old, sod-roofed houses. The sign said "Siljansgaarden Gasthem." This was the beginning of a most wonderful adventure that included meeting Signe and Kenneth Keys, the proprietors, and several of the guests at this unusual country inn.

This inn, which is really the inspiration of Signe's mother and, later, her father, not only preserves the Sweden of the past, but actually makes it useful and viable today. Many of the living rooms and bedrooms are furnished with antiques. However, there are some lodgings with modern furniture. Perhaps the best description of the inn is found in Signe's words:

"The first question we tend to get here is 'How old is this place?' When you arrive here it seems so settled in its environment and so peaceful that people think it must be an old farmstead. But it isn't. I used to answer that 'the house is much older than the place as you see it.' The oldest house in the group is from the 13th century and that house also has guest rooms in it. We don't know the age of some of the houses. Many of them have dates engraved on them or you can tell from the way they are built.

"When my mother arrived in 1916, there was nothing here—just meadows, forests, and stone heaps. She was born and grew up north of here. She had been married in Stockholm, and for a woman of that time she was very unusual. She was well trained in many subjects and wanted to work among people, as well as have a family.

"In those days it was uncommon to buy a house. You usually tried to find an old one—old houses were of timber. It was common to move houses. The first house she bought had been a mill at the foot of the mountain across the lake here. The millstone we have on the front lawn was one of the millstones inside the house—and it's now used as a coffee table. The house became much bigger than she had intended. She couldn't build the cellar deep enough so the house became higher. That was in 1917. She was well known for her taste in furnishings and art, and the big room is today as it was then. In the old days, people slept, worked, and ate in the one room, therefore it was named the 'Big Room' (*Stor Stuga*). In one corner you had the fireplace; in the other corner you had the beds, similar to what are now known as bunk beds. The bottom was a double bed for the older people and the top for the younger folk. The big drawers were pushed in during the day, and at night were used for the very young children.

"In 1925, my father came here. They found that they had similar interests, and in 1927, they opened this as a guest home where you

could come for rest and recreation, and to meet people. They began to offer summer courses in music, singing, dancing, and literature. When this was started it was very unusual—a pioneer movement.''

I receive lovely letters from Signe every year, and she reports that between ten and twenty-five guests visit her every year as a result of reading *Country Inns and Back Roads*.

SILJANSGAARDEN GASTHEM, S 793 03 Tallberg (Dalarna). Tel.: Leksand 0247-50040. A wide range of rooms, some with private bath. In addition to the preserved Swedish environment, guests can enjoy sauna, tennis, rowboating, table tennis, croquet, badminton, and many walks and hikes throughout the remarkable scenic Dalarna area. Closed from the end of Sept. to Christmas. Open for Christmas. Rates: See Index.

LIDINGOBRO WARDSHUS RESTAURANT
Stockholm

My host and hostess for the evening in Stockholm were Ake and Margaret Gille. Ake, a very gentle man, had been connected with the Swedish Tourist Information Center for some time, and for eight years was located in New York City.

Our first visit was to a lovely restaurant on the water, the Lidingobro Wardshus, just a few miles from downtown Stockholm (Centrum). Apparently, it is located in a former manor house, as are many Swedish inns. My first impressions were most favorable. As soon as we stepped inside the old gates, now permanently opened, I saw three old-fashioned Swedish sleighs loaded with flowers. There were flowers everywhere—in formal gardens, in large tubs placed all around the terrace, and in hanging baskets. The rather formal buildings are wooden, painted in a muted yellow with white trim, and with red tile roofs.

On one of the terraces a cook was barbecuing some meat on a charcoal brazier, and the aroma did amazing things to my already substantial appetite. There were many chairs and tables placed around the terrace, which was not being used on that evening, but was very popular during lunchtime and in the afternoon because of the beautiful view of the pleasure boats and the shore beyond.

Inside this old restaurant there was a series of small connected dining rooms, each with a view of the terrace and the water. Apparently the buildings were in existence before the 1700s and the decorations have been done in the old-fashioned Swedish way.

We walked through the kitchen and had a conversation with a few of the chefs, who were getting ready for the considerable number of people already seated in the dining rooms. I was allowed to sample four or five dishes, including some delicious fish. Because we were going on to dinner, I was not able to eat an entire meal; it took all of my will power to keep from devouring each portion.

LIDINGOBRO WARDSHUS RESTAURANT, Kaknas, Djurgarden 62, Stockholm. Tel.: 08-62-06-94. A country restaurant overlooking the water, just a few miles from central Stockholm. Luncheon and dinner served daily. No lodgings available. Closed July 15 to Aug. 15.

SARA HOTEL REISEN
Stockholm

When I find myself in large cities, I definitely prefer the conservative type of hotel: the Algonquin in New York, the Lenox in Boston, and the Goring in London, for example. In Stockholm, where large hotels are a way of life, the Reisen fits right into my personal preference. Although it is somewhat sophisticated and definitely European in style, this rather small hotel has a very personal air about it, and I found it quite easy to feel at home almost immediately. This was partially because of the friendliness and informality of the staff members who, by the way, are fluent in many languages, including English.

The hotel is housed in three beautiful 17th-century residences in the Old Town section, where there are narrow cobblestone streets and several attractive shops.

Other amenities at the Reisen include music in one dining room, which has been designed to resemble the elegant saloon of a 19th-century ship. There is also a very welcome sauna and an indoor swimming pool.

SARA HOTEL REISEN, Skeppsbron 12-14, S-111 Stockholm. Tel.: 08-22 32-60. Rates: See Index.

I was breezing along on Highway E-4 from Stockholm to southern Sweden, admiring a lake on the left side of the road, when I spied a stately white house and some formal gardens on my right. I was almost positive that I had seen the word "Vardshus" as well. Impatiently, I sought out an exit on my right so that I could turn back for a second look. (E-4 is a divided highway at this point, so there were no left turns.) I drove on for about six kilometers, although in my impatience it seemed like twenty-six. Finally, I turned off and learned from a friendly gas station man that what I had seen was indeed a Vardshus, *or inn. Following careful directions I returned and the result was one of my most memorable adventures in Sweden.*

VARDSHUSET STENKULLEN
Aby

The grounds of this inn were a tribute to the art of gardening. Everywhere I looked there were plants and flowers, well-trimmed hedges, and carefully pruned trees. In mid-June the colors were kaleidoscopic. There were gardens on all four sides, and on the second-floor balconies there were great hanging begonias and containers and tubs of other cascading flowers. There were three or four fountains, some with water lilies in bloom.

While I stood there for a few minutes contemplating camera angles, I discovered I had a companion. A gigantic Saint Bernard nuzzled me, nearly knocking me into a rose bush. For a moment I thought he was going to stand on his hind legs and put his paws on my shoulders, which surely would have been a disaster for me. Just at this crucial point, I heard a voice call something in Swedish and the dog disappeared. A young woman then came out on the rear veranda of the inn and said, "Good afternoon, may I help you?"

The young lady, as it developed, was Maria Svensson, and her family

owns the inn. After I had explained that I was writing a book about country inns in Sweden and that this inn looked like something quite special, she gave me permission to wander around and promised to give me a few minutes later on.

"We are serving a special party right now," she said, "but please make yourself at home."

As soon as I walked into the reception area, I realized that I was supposed to remove my shoes and choose a pair of sandals from a neat collection just inside the door. After I saw the handsome oriental rugs on the floors of every room I knew why.

My next impression was that almost every square inch of wall in the hallways and living rooms was covered with some type of wall hanging, portrait, reproduction, or print. There were also notices of exhibitions of paintings and concerts, past, present, and future. Every room also had many pieces of sculpture placed on the wide windowsills, tables, and among the books on bookshelves that ran from ceiling to floor.

It was obvious that the owners and guests of this lovely inn took delight in music, art, history, and literature.

I could hear the guests in the dining room singing Swedish songs. Between courses, Maria managed to come out and explain a few things to me. My principal regret was that I simply could not take the time to remain there overnight.

The Vardshuset Stenkullen is a family operation, with Maria and her mother and father doing most of the work themselves. Maria explained that nearby Lake Brovikien provided water sports and recreation and that there were lovely walks and drives in the countryside. "Many of our guests," she said, "some of whom have been returning for quite a few years, prefer to just walk in the gardens and sit on the terraces and perhaps read. And, of course, we have music available at any time. Everyone seems to be content."

I certainly had no trouble believing that.

Maria Svensson's letters indicate that things have not changed at this lovely place, and they always take me back to my visit there on a sunny day.

VARDSHUSET STENKULLEN, Aby. Tel.: 011-690-19. Closed Christmas until Mar. 15. Rates: See Index.

HOTELL VASTANA SLOTT
Granna

I always thought of castles as having moats, drawbridges, and crenelated battlements, where men-at-arms in chain mail poured down a rain of arrows from their crossbows at besieging armies. Here, however, was a gentle castle filled with luxurious antiques, paintings, and sculptures and just a low decorative wall on the front, erected no doubt to complete the setting.

I entered, crossing a stone threshold over 300 years old, and found myself in a large reception area with a huge fireplace at one end.

Originally, the "working rooms" of the castle were found on either side—the scullery, pantry, storehouses, and servants' rooms. The owners and their guests occupied the spacious second floor. This is reached by a set of stone steps that have been well worn by many generations. Imagine 300 years of castle visitors, all using these steps to present petitions, or perhaps pay respect to the nobility.

Halfway up the twisting passage, a formidable figure in medieval armor with a battle-axe in its fist confronts and scrutinizes all visitors. When I saw that no one was watching I lifted the visor to see if there was a man inside. There wasn't.

The living rooms, dining rooms, library, and lodging rooms are all lavishly furnished and decorated in the florid castle style that represents 300 years of adding more furniture and seldom removing any. Carved chairs, benches, tables, beds, armoires, and the rooms themselves are all on a larger-than-life scale. Naturally, with so much wall space, many of the paintings, all in the classical style, are tremendous in size and scope.

Today, in these more modest times, the castle is open only in June, July, and August, and the only meal offered is breakfast, although large dinner parties may be arranged.

Most of the bedrooms are very large and many have casement windows that open out to a generous view of the lake. I did see a few smaller bedrooms. No doubt they were reserved in the old days for guests of lesser rank.

HOTELL VASTANA SLOTT, 560 30 Granna. Tel.: 0390-107-00. Golf on grounds. Rates: See Index.

SUNDS HERRGARD
Sunds

There are a few interesting little notes about this inn. For one thing, it is an unusual family arrangement. Two Swedish sisters inherited this property, each married a German fellow a few years ago, and now they all live in harmony, keeping this lakeside inn.

It has prospered and grown in many respects, starting with the main house that has conference rooms, kitchen, and dining rooms. After a few years, additional lodgings were created in some small adjacent buildings that helped to form a kind of open square. More recently, a number of lakeside cottages with all conveniences have been added. It is now an active resort with its own lake recreation and the advantages of being just a short drive from Lake Vattern and Granna.

The surrounding woods and fields that have been left in their natural state, with many trails for pleasant walks, are another reason that this place is popular with families. Children especially like it because there is a large fenced-in area, where deer and wild boar are kept (some of these eventually appear on the menu).

This is where I had my first glimpse of a live wild boar. Although they weren't very big, I must say they did resemble all of the old prints I had ever seen, with those formidable curved tusks.

This inn has a very informal air and most of the guests had been there for a one- or two-week holiday. It is located in beautiful, rolling farming country, and from the sports car badges displayed at the front entrance, it is quite popular with the motoring crowd.

SUNDS HERRGARD, 560 28 Lekeryd. Tel.: 036-82006. Accommodations are in the main house and many bungalows. Horseback riding, fishing, boating, and Finnish steam baths available. Brochure available in English. Rates: See Index.

HOOKS HERRGARD
Hok

I teed up my ball, took a long look down the first fairway, and stopped to speak to my hostess at Hooks. "This looks like an excellent cross-country skiing area," I said. "Do your winter guests enjoy outdoor sports here?"

"Oh, yes," she replied, "winters are really fun here. We Scandinavians enjoy being outdoors then, just as much as we do in the summer. Besides skiing, we have skating on the lake, tobogganing, and curling. Everybody enjoys walking in the snow and our woods are particularly beautiful after a fresh snowfall!"

We then decided that one of the best ways for me to get acquainted with this old manor house/modern resort inn was to play a few holes of golf and enjoy the countryside. It was a most entertaining few hours. In addition to the golf course, the resort offers tennis, badminton, swimming (in the pool and in the lake), bocci, sailing, boating, and fishing. There is also a rather elegant billiard room.

In fact, "elegant" is a good word to describe much of the Hooks Herrgard. In addition to the main building, built in the 1700s, several other buildings have been added, providing rather luxurious accommodations for approximately 120 guests.

When I commented that there seemed to be quite a few guests in the "young married" category, she replied, "Yes, and many of them bring their children. I think that we have guests who enjoy both the old-fashioned and the modern things that they find in Hooks. The setting is romantic, but the facilities are very much up to date.''

HOOKS HERRGARD (Relais et Chateaux), 56013 Hok. Tel.: 46-393-21080. A 100-guestroom resort-inn and conference center in an old Swedish manor house, 370 km. from Stockholm, 230 km. from Helsingborg, and 180 km. from Gothenburg. All summer and winter sports. Rates: See Index.

SWEDEN'S WEST COAST

In the summer it is easy to see why this is also called the Golden Coast. Technically, it extends 250 miles from Laholm to Stromstad, but driving it you undoubtedly will be diverted by the side roads leading to the golden beaches and nearly uncountable islands. There are all the seaside activities: sailing, windsurfing, swimming, sunning, and boating. The restaurants all specialize in fresh fish, though other dishes are also served.

This is one of the oldest inhabited spots in northern Europe and there are cairns and relics from the Bronze Age and before. It was also on the path of Viking invaders, whose boats roamed the waterways and who established early communities along the shore. Today the pleasant climate makes it one of the most popular vacation areas for Scandinavians, though it is just being discovered by Americans.

GOTHENBURG/GOTEBORG: SWEDEN'S SECOND CITY

As the port full of ships will show you, Gothenburg is still important as a waterfront city. Its sea connection to Britain was responsible for the many English customs and names around town. Its fishing industry is why fresh seafood is always on the menus, and there are many fish restaurants as well.

Gothenburg is also the western terminus for a summer pleasure trip on the Gota Canal, either a brief day-jaunt or the relaxing three-day trip to Stockholm. Family pleasure craft on the Canal may also be rented by the week. The "Padden" boats from Kungsportsplatsen will show you the city from the water. It is threaded with waterways.

Liseberg is the largest pleasure park in Scandinavia and has something for visitors of every age. There is Kronhusbodarna, a charmingly restored Old Town with many museums and galleries. There is an enormous antiques center in a former bank, and the 17th-century in-town Hunting Lodge of Queen Kristina, where coffee and waffles are served. At intersections of the landscaped streets and in the many parks and squares you will see the works of the finest modern sculptors.

Among the souvenirs you can acquire is a new Volvo automobile, though plans to do this tax-free and with home shipment are best finalized before you leave the United States.

HOTELL EKOXEN
Gothenburg

Although the Hotell Ekoxen is around the corner from the largest hotel in Gothenburg and next to the air and bus terminals, there is a serenity to the small lobby that told me at once I was in the right place. Maybe it was the cheerful housekeeper picking up tea cups and straightening newspapers as the sun streamed through the windows.

Every room is different, fresh and brightly furnished. Some have adjustable beds, some have refrigerators, and most have cable TV and pick up worldwide broadcasts via the satellite. There is a sauna and a bubble pool, a bar that specializes in oysters, and a pleasant courtyard. The big buffet breakfast is included in the room price, and it's the only meal served. That's all right. The neighborhood is full of restaurants in all price ranges, including the famous Johanna's, only a block away.

The hotel consists of three buildings from the 1880s that were connected a century later. Those on the court side are very quiet, though I did not notice any excessive street noise on the front. Considering the center-city location, this is remarkable until you remember how relaxed and spread out Gothenburg is.

However, here, you are on bus and tram lines to wherever you want to go and an easy walk to the Old Town with its restored workshops and cafes. In summer there are umbrella-topped tables for coffee or light meals in the square and you can pop in to see a glassblower at work or a silversmith hammering out a piece of cutlery or jewelry you can buy on the spot.

On a rainy day, the largest covered shopping mall in Sweden is only steps from the hotel. Even when the sun is shining it's nice to know you can buy a toothbrush or have a camera repaired or buy gifts for everyone you know in one easy stroll.

HOTELL EKOXEN, Norra Hamngatan 38, S-411 06 Gothenburg. Tel.: 031-80-50-80. A 75-guestroom (private baths) hotel in the center of Gothenburg. Very close to train station and bus and air terminals. Car park nearby. No-smoking rooms available. European plan. Buffet breakfast included. No other meals served, but snacks available all times in the bar. Many restaurants nearby. Sauna and Jacuzzi room. Rates: See Index.

Directions: If you come by train or take the airport bus, you will need to walk only two minutes to the hotel, on the north side of the main divided street, Hamngatan. By car, turn off the E3 on Stadtsianareg and loop to Nils Ericsonsgatan, which ends at Norra Hamngatan. Hotel is immediately on your right. Taxi stand in front and standing space to pull in, register, and get directions to car park.

HOTEL LINDSON
Gothenburg

Katie Lindman and Gunnel Andreasson named their gemlike small hotel after themselves when they opened in 1984, and it is run very much like a gracious private home. For example, breakfast is served in a pretty breakfast room opening off the sitting room, and the menu is "anything you like." That means eggs, oatmeal, cheese, ham, fruit, juice, and excellent coffee or tea.

The guest rooms are huge, with white walls, lots of green plants, good art, and nice fabrics. Each is individually done and in the good taste of the owners. Most baths are shared by two rooms, but you are provided with thick terry robes to wear down the hall.

Don't be put off by the rather dark stone exterior. That was the fashion for churches in 1872, and the Hotel Lindson started out as an ecclesiastical structure. Now there are lace curtains at the windows, and it is as handsome inside as any hotel you'll see in Scandinavia—moderately priced too.

Breakfast is the only meal served, but as Katie points out, there are many restaurants close at hand. The neighborhood is full of antiques shops, and the big indoor antiques market of Gothenburg is just a few blocks away. Katie and Gunnel are obviously the right people to direct you to the best shops and buys in the city.

HOTEL LINDSON, Hvitfeldtsplatsen 4, S-411 20 Gothenburg. Tel.: 031-10-19-20. A small elegant hotel (private and shared baths) in a former church in the antiques shopping district of Gothenburg. Breakfast only. Rates: See Index.

Directions: It is five minutes by taxi to the Central Station and bus and air terminals. If you drive, take the Centrum SV exit from the Parkgatan ring, cross the canal, go one block, turn left; two short blocks and hotel is on the corner on your right.

TIDBLOMS
Gothenburg

Tidbloms has a turret with rooms in it, and if you have ever wondered how it feels to wake in a round room, this is where to experience it. Other rooms have more conventional shapes, but each is distinctively furnished and all have coffee/tea-making equipment.

The red brick turn-of-the-century building was originally a bicycle manufacturing plant. When part of it was converted to a restaurant, it proved to be so popular the owners decided to become innkeepers as well. A good decision, I thought, as I walked into the busy lobby. Surely, this is a popular place, especially considering that its location is not in the center of the city.

There is a sunny terrace, sometimes used for conferences but more often for lunch, and a cellar restaurant with vaulted ceilings where dinner is served. Charm, however, is secondary to the cuisine, considered to be some of the best in the city.

Easy access to the European highways from Malmo, Oslo, and Stockholm makes Tidbloms handy for those driving the west coast of Sweden and beyond. Public parking lots are nearby, though I had no trouble parking on the street.

TIDBLOMS (Romantik Hotels), Olskroksgatan 23, S-41666 Gothenburg. Tel.: (031) 19-20-70 (U.S. reservations: 800-243-9420). A 61-guestroom (private and shared baths) unusual hotel with a well-known restaurant. Rates: See Index.

Directions: Take the Olskroken exit from E-3 and follow signs to Tidbloms.

HOTEL HALLAND
Kungsbacka, Halland

I came to this small, attractive new hotel quite by accident. The inn of my original destination on the strand was filled with a weekend conference, and I had not called ahead. However, the receptionist told me I would be well taken care of at the Hotel Halland in nearby Kungsbacka, and she was quite correct.

Hotel Halland would also be a boon to those arriving by train, as the station is visible from the hotel. There is private parking just outside the door.

My room was decorated in blues and grays, had color television, and was very comfortable. Prices are moderate for rooms with private baths and inexpensive for rooms with the shared hall baths.

The dining room was a very pleasant surprise, as I had one of my best dinners in Sweden. The waitress, Suzanne, had lived in the United States, working as a nanny, and when I told her I was enjoying the meal, she brought the young chef out of the kitchen to meet me. There is a cooking school in Kungsbacka, and the graduates often begin their careers here.

The hotel also has sauna, billiards, table tennis, and darts. The village is interesting, with an Old Town and a new. In the town square a market sets up every morning, where you can buy fruit, flowers, sweaters, tablecloths, or whatever else you need.

Kungsbacka is also well located for visits to Tjoloholm Castle, the 18th-century village of Askhult, and many good beaches and islands just offshore.

HOTEL HALLAND, Storgatan 35, 43400 Kungsbacka. Tel.: 0300-115-30. A small modern hotel in a conveniently located town, 28 km. from Gothenburg. European and other plans available. Rates: See Index.

Directions: By train, you will just need to walk across the street to Hotel Halland. By car, follow signs to the train station, and you will see the hotel.

GRAND HOTEL
Falkenberg, Halland

At one time falcons were trained on a local rock, and there are legends of a Viking prince named Hagbard pursuing the beautiful Princess Signe along the shore. Today, however, Falkenberg is a peaceful town on the Atran River where the main excitement is salmon fishing.

Grand Hotel is right on the river, and I looked out my window at the 18th-century bridge. It was no time at all until I had joined the promenaders along the river bank, where there are beautiful gardens and convenient benches for strollers when they tire.

Falkenberg is a small place with a nice Old Town containing a museum, pottery, smokehouse, and cooperage. The Torngrens pottery of Falkenberg is well known and has been in the same family of craftsmen since 1789. In the New Town there is a nice square, many shops, and a congenial attitude toward visitors.

The hotel has a rather severe lobby, and in summer the dining room, which becomes a disco, can be noisy. The guest rooms, however, are pleasant, and most have recently been redone. If the disco becomes too much, there's a tourist information service in town where you can be quickly booked into a guest house or a private home offering bed and breakfast.

GRAND HOTEL, Agatan 1, S-311 00 Falkenberg. Tel.: (034) 614450. A 60-guestroom pleasant old hotel on the Atran River at Tullbron (bridge). Rates: See Index.

Directions: Watch for the signs to Falkenberg on the E-6 and turn off. As you cross the bridge, the Grand Hotel is clearly visible on your right.

KULLAGARDENS WARDSHUS
Molle
I followed the road to Molle, not knowing I would be driving through a nature reserve only about twenty miles north of Helsingborg and the ferry to Denmark. Kullagardens Wardshus was a surprise too, resembling an illustration from a book of fairy tales. Tycho Brahe, the 16th-century Danish astronomer, lived in the house and took care of Kullens

lighthouse in exchange for free rent. Other writers and scientists have resided there, too.

The views across green fields to the sea are serene, and the rooms are handsomely decorated with period furniture. Truly welcoming is the open fireplace, which gets good use if the fog comes in midsummer or in the off season. There are only eleven rooms, so it is wise to make reservations as far in advance as possible. The inn is particularly sought out by golfers intent on enjoying the par 71, 18-hole course next door.

The dining room of Kullagardens Wardshus is an end in itself, however, and wherever you stay, you may want to include an evening meal in this beautiful setting. Fish is a house specialty of note.

A big Swedish breakfast is included in the room rate, and you can add half- or full-pension very reasonably.

There is a flower-bordered terrace and garden where you may lounge away any part of the day you are not otherwise engaged in sightseeing, birdwatching, hiking, golfing, riding, swimming, or playing tennis. It is a place at which I would like to stay for an extended holiday.

KULLAGARDENS WARDSHUS (Romantik Hotels), S-26042 Molle. Tel.: 042-471-48 U.S. reservations: 800-243-9420. A back road country inn on a nature reserve peninsula not far from the ferry to Denmark. Open year-round. Irene and Jan-Ake Hagman, Innkeepers. Rates, See Index.

Directions: From Helsingborg take the road to Kullaberg peninsula (signs will also read Molle), a 30-km. trip that will take about 35 min. From the north, turn at Angelholm and follow signs. Irene and Jan-Ake Hagman say they will come and pick you up if you arrive in Halsingborg without a car.

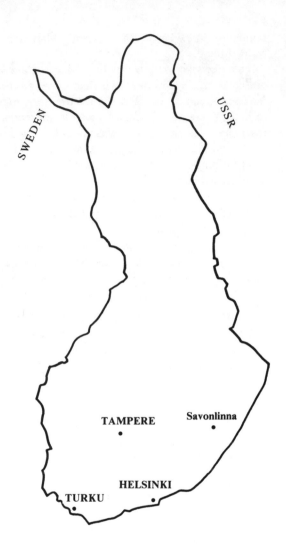

Finland

INNS AND LOCATIONS

TRAVEL SUGGESTIONS FOR FINLAND

How to Get There

Finnair, SAS, and Pan Am fly directly from North America to Helsinki. Overnight ferries will transport you and your car from Sweden in luxury. If you are traveling in Scandinavia by train, your Eurailpass covers your boat fare across the Baltic Sea, but you pay extra for a cabin. Ship, air, road, and rail link Finland to the Soviet Union as well.

Country Inns in Finland

Country inns may occupy old manor houses or be relatively new, but their counterparts in ambience are the small, friendly hotels of Helsinki. While many hotels in Finland are large and ultramodern, with nightclubs, discos, casinos, and multiple restaurants, there are also cottages on islands in the archipelago, where householders welcome guests on a pension basis. Farmhouse accommodations are also available. Since English is widely spoken, you should have no trouble finding a suitable homestay from the lists kept at local tourist offices.

Whether you choose an inn, a hotel, or a private home, you will find there a sauna (pronounced SOW-nah). This relaxing hot box with its pool or shower followup is both an institution and a ritual in Finland, where, indeed, it was invented. You will usually be asked on arrival to indicate the time you would like to use the sauna and often to make a firm reservation.

Finnish Menus

Cuisines of Sweden and Russia meet at the dining tables of Finland, and the Finns have their own culinary specialties as well. The blend is delicious. Fresh wild produce is basic to Finnish cookery, along with the gifts of the sea and forest. Tart and sweet berries grown north of the Arctic Circle come to market in season; more than 500 varieties of mushrooms are culled from the bogs and woodlands. Fish, reindeer, and game are plentiful. A morning visit to Market Square in Helsinki will tell you the menu for the evening meal in the city's finest restaurants. During the Baltic herring run in the first week of October, you will find this delicacy available three times a day.

Finnish smorgasbord is as abundant as Swedish but with a difference. A good place to try it is on an overnight Silja ferry going to or from Stockholm.

Thursday is pea-soup-and-pancake day in Finland. The Helsinki airport restaurant serves a help-yourself luncheon of these specialties at bargain prices.

MY ITINERARIES IN FINLAND

I have come to Finland by sea from Sweden as well as by air from the United States. Taking the overnight ferry between Stockholm and Turku through the archipelago on a long midsummer evening is magical. I have not yet driven to the Arctic Circle, but I would like to follow the Baltic coastline one way and return through the central "Land of a Thousand Lakes." I have visited the glassworks of Ittala and Riihimaki on the way to Tampere, then to Turku with its artisan cottages and castle. Another fine trip is to go northeast of Helsinki to Savonlinna, which is the site of a renowned opera festival every summer. Save several days at least for Helsinki, one of Europe's most charming and unusual capitals.

HELSINKI, THE "DAUGHTER OF THE SEA"

A small city as European capitals go, Helsinki has more than its share of fine public art, like the railroad station designed by Eliel Saarinen and the statue of three smiths by Felix Nylund, across from Stockmann's Department Store. The new city plan on Toolonlahti Bay, including Finlandia Hall and the Concert and Congress Center, was designed by Alvar Aalto. For orientation, you can take Tram 3T for a figure-8 tour of the city with a commentary in English during the summer. The Helsinki Card, which may be purchased at the tourist office, provides free entry to some forty museums, a guided tour, free transport on buses and trolleys, and a number of discounts.

Good design is synonymous with Finland, and the shops of Helsinki are full of examples of high-quality merchandise. The colors are extraordinary.

Central Helsinki is twenty kilometers from the international airport; the train comes into the center of town. Greater Helsinki extends to a number of linked islands. In summer, I highly recommend the folk park on the island of Seurasaari, the National Maritime Museum on Hylkysaari, the fortress of Suomenlinna, where you will find the Nordic Arts Center in a restored 1868 barracks, and Walhalla, a notable restaurant.

PALACE HOTEL
Helsinki

Looking out over South Harbor, with the boats of the islanders pulling in almost at the door to sell their cargoes of potatoes and fish directly to the consumer, I think I can see into the heart of this seafaring northern city. Market Square, where the Esplanadi begins, is steps away, and the hills upon which Helsinki is built rise gently from the waterfront.

The Palace Hotel occupies the upper floors of this convenient building and is probably the most luxurious hostelry in Helsinki. Certainly it has the best dining room and the only Michelin-starred restaurant in Finland, the Palace Gourmet, and the service is excellent.

I fell into the habit of visiting Market Square first thing every morning, so the vendors soon recognized me as a regular. I bargained for and bought some fur-lined gloves that will serve me well in New England winters, and think I would have done equally well had I needed a kilo of red currants or a brace of herring.

When I stay at the Palace, I ask for a room on the ninth floor with a balcony overlooking the harbor.

PALACE HOTEL, Etelaranta 10, 00130 Helsinki. Tel.: (90) 171-114. For reservations: (90) 662-722; or in the U.S., toll free: 800-528-1234.) A 59-guestroom (private baths) exceptionally well-appointed and convenient hotel right on South Harbor in Helsinki. Fine gourmet restaurant and experienced staff. Minibars and color TV in every room. Open all year. Rates: See Index.

HOTELLI RIVOLI JARDIN
Helsinki

"You can tell a top architectural and interior design team created this," my Finnish friend said, and that is saying a lot in a city where high achievement in the public arts is taken for granted. I was even more arrested by the coziness of the lobby, with its arrangements of fresh flowers and the smiling greeting of the staff.

You don't just walk by the Rivoli Jardin either. It is tucked behind street-front buildings in the heart of Helsinki, its views rooftop-intimate rather than sweeping. There is even space for a limited number of cars to park outside the door. As I stood there looking around the courtyard, I thought how distinctively European it was. In winter, frosted by snow, it would be a perfect Christmas card.

The guest rooms are tasteful, many with a sofa and easy chairs worked into small spaces. Triple-glazed windows and walls of Finnish granite insure quietness, while pastels grant peace of mind. Every room has refrigerator, TV, hair dryer, and shower; the suite has its own terrace and a private sauna.

The only meal served is breakfast, in the Winter Garden on the first floor, and it consists of a full range of Finnish specialties. Sandwiches, soups, salads, and snacks are available from the bar at all hours. The neighborhood is so alive with good cafes that a full-service dining room has been ruled out as not necessary.

HOTELLI RIVOLI JARDIN, Kasarminkatu 40, 00130 Helsinki. Tel.: (90)-177 880. In the U.S., toll-free 800-528-1234. A 54-guestroom (private baths) hotel in the heart of Helsinki. Breakfast only meal served; many restaurants nearby. Open year-round. Off-street parking. Rates: See Index.

MARTTA HOTELLI
Helsinki

The first person I saw when I entered the Martta Hotel was Maija, the expert in traditional cookery whom I had met the night before at the Finnish Cuisine Restaurant. She explained she is also a director of the Martta Organization and editor of its magazine. It should have been no surprise that a knowledgeable professional home economist heads this nationwide club dedicated to furthering homemaking and nutritional skills. The Martta Hotel is their Helsinki clubhouse, though you do not have to be a member to stay here.

Rooms are simple and spotless, the atmosphere unabashedly wholesome, and the location right next to the pedestrian-only shopping street, Iso Roobertinkatu. More than half the forty-five rooms are singles, but others are large enough to make this a good choice for families as well as for women traveling alone.

The cafeteria (open to the public and popular with the entire neighborhood) serves breakfast and reasonably priced lunches and snacks, with everything homemade. You can sit on the balcony and have your morning coffee with a very friendly and sophisticated group of guests from all over the world. Every week there is a theme to the menu.

When I visited it was "Lapland Food Week," featuring reindeer and cloudberries. There are also always vegetarian and fish main courses. Even if you don't stay at the Martta, you should try to come to lunch.

MARTTA HOTELLI, Uudenmaankatu 24, 00120, Helsinki. Tel.: (90) 646-211. A 45-guestroom (private baths) hotel that is also the Helsinki clubhouse of the national Martta Organization. Self-service lunch room open to the public. Open all year. Private parking. Rates: See Index.

HOTEL ANNA
Helsinki

Here is a country inn downtown, I thought, when I entered Hotel Anna. The scalloped awning outside, the white lobby with its chintz-covered sofas, and the bowls of fresh flowers were as pleasant as a summer day. There were even sofas and flowers in the upstairs hall-ways, a true country-inn touch.

No surprise, then, to find that each room is different. My favorite was number 613, a sunny corner bedroom with a pleasant sitting area decorated in green and peach. It had not only radio, color cable TV, and a small refrigerator, but its own guest book as well.

On the third floor are ten no-smoking rooms, and the Anna also has three rooms especially equipped for allergy sufferers.

A boarding house in an earlier life, the Anna was completely reno-vated in 1985. In 1988, the small, self-serve, street-level restaurant was added. The guests-only breakfast room upstairs also offers homemade pastry and excellent coffee or tea in the evenings. A money-saving demi-pension arrangement has been worked out with neighborhood res-taurants.

The staff is, well, sweet, and the management obviously caring. This is the hotel I would pick for a long homey stay in Helsinki.

HOTEL ANNA, Annankatu 1, 00120 Helsinki. Tel.: (90) 648-011. A 58-guestroom (private baths) charming hotel in central Helsinki. Non-smoking and allergy-free rooms on request. Self-serve restaurant. Open all year. Rates: See Index.

SAVONLINNA

Probably most famous for its Opera Festival, held in the 500-year-old Olavinlinna Castle, Savonlinna is also popular for the fishing and boating activities. Finland's newest exhibition center, Retretti, features art exhibitions and a recreation area in its halls and caves. Both Re-

Olavinlinna Castle,
Savonlinna

tretti and the Church of the Three Crosses were designed by the famous
architect Alvar Aalto.

HOTEL RAUHALINNA AT LEHTINIEMI
Savonlinna

After observing that Finnish lifestyles appear to be set by proximity to the sea, I discovered lakes so uncountable as to seem an enormous freshwater ocean crisscrossed with spurs of forested land. On the shores of Lake Haapavesi near Savonlinna, I found Hotel Rauhalinna, a romantic late-19th-century villa with seven guest rooms, including a "general's suite" and a watchtower.

Built as a summer retreat for his family and anniversary gift for his wife by the commanding officer of fortresses for the Czar, the villa became an army signal school during the second World War. It was restored in 1973 and made into a country hotel and restaurant specializing in fish, game, and local dishes.

At a time when Finland was an autonomous grand duchy of Russia, skilled woodcarvers were brought from St. Petersburg to make the beautiful cutouts. I found it easy to imagine this a private home with the convenience of boat rental and fishing permits taken care of for me by trusted retainers. You must reserve early for a room at Rauhalinna, especially during the famous midsummer opera festival at Savonlinna and the concert season in the underground hall at Retretti.

HOTEL RAUHALINNA AT LEHTINIEMI, 57310 Savonlinna 31. Tel.:
(957) 253-119. A 6-guestroom and 1-suite hotel on the shore of Lake

Haapavesi near Savonlinna. Open summer only. Swimming, boating, fishing at the door. Finnair has daily flights to Savonlinna. The hotel is 3 mi. from the airport by car or you can take a water bus across the lake to the hotel. Rates: See Index.

TAMPERE

One hundred miles north of Helsinki, Tampere is in the middle of the Western Lake District and is one of the main points of departure for the many lake cruises. In this city that dates back to the 1700s, one of the exciting modern designs is the new library, called Metso ("wood-grouse"), which looked to me like a series of copper-topped mushrooms. The Sara Hilden Art Museum, with the works of outstanding Finnish and other artists is well worth a visit. The Byzantine-style Eastern Orthodox Church and the Sarkanniemi Recreation Center are other interesting sights.

RESTAURANT RAPUKKA
Tampere

I stayed in the new Ilves Hotel in Tampere, an excellent large hostelry on the river, with a fine view from the nineteenth-floor sauna, that cannot remotely be considered a country inn. However, I wanted you to know about Ravintola Rapukka, an extraordinary restaurant in this, the second largest city in Finland.

Finnish cuisine is based on the wild foods of sea, lake, forest, and bog, but nowhere did I find better examples than here. My dinner began with a spruce aperitif (schnapps flavored with spring buds of the spruce tree) and continued with a first course of deep-fried whole mushrooms freshly gathered. I was tempted to try a celery-cheese soup sprinkled with blue flowers, but instead went on to pike-perch with new potatoes, baby carrots cooked and served in leaves, and a salad of bibb lettuce and nasturtiums. A fresh spray of dill scented the plate.

For dessert I had a trio of fresh berry ices (with pansies) and tiny gingerbread hearts.

RAVINTOLA RAPUKKA, Tammelanpuostok 34, Tampere. Tel.: (931) 110-086. A small, distinctive restaurant in central Tampere. Wild, natural foods only, served with unusual flair. Fish, meat, and vegetarian dishes; full-meal salads; special plates for children. Open only midday, from 11 to 4 on Sun., to 6 Tues. through Fri. Closed Sat. and Mon. Moderate prices.

PARK HOTEL TURKU
Turku

The country at the doorstep of this country inn is the beautiful and spacious Puolalanpuisto Park of Turku. Even before I entered the door and saw the attractive living room, I felt right at home.

The Park Hotel was built as a *jugend-house,* or youth hostel, at the turn of the century, and its twenty rooms are individually charming. I particularly liked those tucked under the eaves. The brass-knobbed beds, the bentwood furniture, the flowered carpets, and the quilted bedspreads add to the snug country house quality. The restoration of the hotel has meant private bathrooms throughout, color TV's, and minibars. The suites have whirlpool baths.

The hotel has a good restaurant serving essentially Russian food and a small summer cafe overlooking the green.

Turku is well worth a few days of sightseeing either at the end of the ferry trip to Stockholm or as a destination in its own right. It was the capital of Finland from the 1200s to 1812, when Helsinki acquired both the designation and the university in the aftermath of one of Turku's frequent and devastating fires. In 1827 the only part of wooden Turku that was saved was a small group of 18th-century working-people's cottages on Cloister Hill, now an outdoor museum where artisans work at their trades in authentic surroundings.

The restored stone castle is also a noteworthy provincial museum, where medieval-style banquets are served in the dining hall.

PARK HOTEL TURKU, Rauhankatu 1, 20100 Turku. Tel.: (921) 519-666. A 20-guestroom (private baths) inn by the side of Puolalanpuisto Park in the center of Turku. Restaurant and cafe. Open all year. Rates: See Index.

RESTAURANT BRAHEN KELLARI
Turku

Tucked in the cellar of a century-old building in downtown Turku is the Brahen Kellari, a restaurant famous throughout Finland. Although Turku is a city where Swedish influence has been strong (the Swedish name of the city, Abo, appears so often it seems to be a dual-name as well as a dual-language town), the cuisine here is unreservedly Finnish.

The intimate atmosphere is in part created by the limited number of tables in five small, distinctively furnished dining rooms, each with white-washed walls and brick trusses. Lighting is provided by an intriguing variety of indirect lamps, period chandeliers, recessed "windows," and table candles. Service is warm and attentive.

The house specialty is game (bear, hare, badger, porcupine, pheasant, grouse, ptarmigan, beaver, dove) acquired directly from hunters, both local and from as far north as Lapland. The house aperitif is the "Count's Cocktail," a blend of vodka and buckthorn berry juice from the islands of the archipelago. Patés of game and reindeer are served with cranberry sauce, and the "cream of wild" soup is as remarkable as it is mysterious. Tiny, young vegetables are specially raised for the restaurant.

Fresh wild berries are used extensively in marinades, midmeal sorbets, and dessert mousses. I had a jellied dessert of minced crowberries and cream that was superb.

BRAHEN KELLARI, Puolalankatu 1, 20100 Turku. Tel.: 25-400. A cellar restaurant featuring wild game and Finnish cuisine in the heart of Turku. Extensive wine list. Owner is a member of the international Chaîne des Rôtisseurs. Reservations recommended. Open all year for lunch and dinner. Expensive.

Denmark

Ans •

TRAVEL SUGGESTIONS FOR DENMARK

How to Get There
SAS flights go to Copenhagen. There is a car-ferry from Norway, and a direct road from Germany.

Country Inns in Denmark
Denmark is a country with a tradition of inns, some of which date back 300 to 400 years. A few were designated as royal inns by reigning monarchs, which meant that a bedroom and a change of horses had to be available at all times for the royal party. Some inns have been in the same innkeeping family for generations.

I found these Danish inns in small villages and towns, with the name of the town often included in their own names. Kro is the Danish word for "inn." Although these traditional inns are frequently sought out by foreign travelers, they are principally used by the Danes themselves. All of them serve hearty and wholesome food, with the menus frequently printed only in Danish. The guest rooms are always, as throughout Scandinavia, clean and practical. In the older sections of the inns, the baths and wc's are usually down the corridor. Reservations can be made by mail or telephone.

MY ITINERARY IN DENMARK

From north of Copenhagen I continued through Zealand, proceeding by ferry to Fyn Island and then another ferry took me to Jutland, that portion of Denmark on the European mainland adjacent to Germany.

From here the road leads north and I could have continued on to Norway by ferry from northern Jutland.

HOTEL STORE KRO
Fredensborg

"Oh, yes, the King and Queen are dining here tonight." I stopped short and turned to learn whether I had heard correctly. The innkeeper at Store Kro went on: "Well, the castle is nearby," he said, "and there are strong links between the castle and the inn.

"In 1723, King Frederik IV constructed Fredensborg Castle and at the same time he had an inn built nearby, which was named Store Kro and consisted of two separate buildings. For a number of years the King himself was the keeper of this inn. One of the original buildings is still in use and its exterior has not changed during the many years. It serves as an annex and the interior is equipped with beautiful, modern guest rooms."

The proximity to Fredensborg Castle accounts for the fact that the inn has been the scene of royal receptions and royal weddings. There is one dining room, known as the King's Room, with either photographs or paintings of every Danish king.

Catering to these unusual functions has carried the inn's reputation for good food to places considerably far from Denmark. The innkeeper told me that the chef has traveled widely, preparing meals in other

countries and taking certain Danish specialties with him, such as bread, butter, salmon, and fresh herring.

As we moved into another room with many photographs and paintings of what appeared to be the same man on the wall, he explained the decor to me.

"We Danes are very fond of the theater," he said, "and Olaf Poulsen was probably the most outstanding actor of the Danish stage. He played every major role up to the time of his death in 1923. Some years ago I began to collect photographs, prints, and paintings of him playing various theatrical characters. Now we have put them in this room, where they are well preserved and displayed for everyone to enjoy. I think it's better than a museum because they are in an atmosphere that he, himself, would appreciate."

Store Kro is located on one of the quiet streets in Fredensborg. There are spacious grounds and a garden in the rear of the inn.

Although this inn is larger than many of the inns I visited in Denmark and a bit more formal because of the many functions that take place here, it is nonetheless most hospitable. Each of the rooms has highly individual decorations.

Just imagine the King and Queen would be dining here tonight!

HOTEL STORE KRO, 3480 Fredensborg. Tel.: (02) 280047. A royal inn immediately adjacent to a royal palace still in use. All of the North Zealand recreational facilities and historic castles are nearby. Rates: See Index.

SOLLEROD KRO RESTAURANT
Sollerod

I was wandering about the churchyard immediately adjacent to Sollerod Kro. The rain, which had been spouting all afternoon, had stopped, and scudding clouds frequently opened long enough to light the scene with tints of silver.

All of this was a most appropriate postlude to a delightful evening at the inn across the village road. Actually, it had begun for me just before lunch, when I left Store Kro in Fredensborg to drive to Copenhagen. I located the village of Sollerod with just one inquiry, and after driving through a Danish "Forest of Arden," suddenly came upon a serene and peaceful crossroads with a triangular-shaped flowerbed literally overwhelmed with blossoms. The words "Sollerod Kro" were stretched in large letters across the front of the inn.

The principal entrance was through a cobblestone courtyard, or hollow square, formed by the buildings of this ancient inn. In the center

there was a tinkling fountain and around the edges and in sheltered nooks and crannies were tubs of daisies, pansies, and cornflowers. Much to my surprise there was a large birdcage with colorful exotic birds.

It was too early for lunch, but the innkeeper was happy to explain the history of the inn and invited me to walk through the spacious dining rooms.

It was during this tour that I learned that the church where I was strolling once owned the inn, which dates back to 1677. It has remained unchanged ever since except for certain strengthening of walls and re-thatching of roofs. The building is exquisite, one of the best examples of traditional romantic Danish architecture that I encountered during my trip.

All the rooms are decorated with Danish antiques, and the reception rooms are hung with Professor Aksel Jorgensen's historical paintings and a selection of original manuscripts of the best-known works of Danish writers.

From May to September meals are served in the courtyard, and include dishes from the open grill.

That brings us to where I started—strolling in the churchyard and listening to the organ. To my knowledge, the church does not own the inn any longer. But the tradition remains, and many of the inn guests attend the church and enjoy the church gardens. There are no rooms at this inn, but luncheon and dinner are served continuously from 11:30 a.m. to 10 p.m.

SOLLEROD KRO RESTAURANT (Relais et Chateaux), Sollerod Vej 35, 2840/Holte. Tel.: (02) 802505. A country restaurant just a few kilometers north of Copenhagen. Open year-round exc. Dec. 24. No lodgings.

THE PLAZA
Copenhagen

It is unusual to find a well-known first-class hotel across the street from a central railway station and the airport bus terminal, but the Plaza is remarkable in many ways. It was built originally by the King of Denmark as a royal guest house, which may be why the walls are so thick the trains make barely a whisper.

The rooms are all well appointed and vary from luxurious suites to tucked-in-the-attic doubles. A glassed-in elevator takes you from the paneled reception area, where there are always bowls of fresh fruit and arrangements of flowers. To carry out the theme of feeling at home, the books in the library-bar may be borrowed by guests.

There are two restaurants in the building, and an extensive buffet breakfast is served in the main dining room, or you may order room service.

The Plaza is across the street from Tivoli Amusement Park, and I especially liked rooms facing in that direction. It is also one block from Den Permanente, the Danish craft center, and an easy walk to the Town Hall square and the lower end of Stroget, the pedestrian shopping street.

If you want to know the names of celebrities who have stayed at the Plaza, you can read their names on the pillars in the lobby.

THE PLAZA, 4 Bernstorffsgade, 1577 Copenhagen V. Tel.: (01) 14-92-62 (U.S. reservations: 800-223-6800). A 98-guestroom luxury hotel with an especially friendly atmosphere and a most convenient location. Rates: See Index.

Directions: Arriving by train or airport bus, you will need to walk only across the street to the Plaza. By car, follow signs to the railway station. The hotel has its own parking garage.

HOTEL ASCOT
Copenhagen

This pleasant small hotel is on a quiet back street just a few minutes from Tivoli, the railroad station, the air terminal, and the Stroget shopping district. Built in the 18th century, it was converted to a hotel a few years ago by the present owner. No two rooms are alike, and there are even some efficiency apartments (often taken for the season, so book well in advance).

On the ground floor a pleasant sitting room invites visiting with other guests. There is also a TV room and a breakfast room. Breakfast may also be taken in your room and is included in the daily rate. No other meals are served, but there are many restaurants nearby. The hotel has elevators, and all rooms have private baths.

A car rental agency in the building offers special rates to hotel guests, so if you want to leave wonderful Copenhagen for a few days of touring wonderful Hans Christian Andersen country or drive up into northern Zealand and then take the ferry to Sweden, it couldn't be easier.

Hotel Ascot seems an especially good choice for families since Orsteds Park is also nearby. Roll-away beds are available for children, but I would try for one of those efficiency apartments.

ASCOT HOTEL, 57 Studiestraede, DK-1554 Copenhagen V. Tel.: 01-12-60-00. A small, friendly hotel in an old townhouse near air and rail terminals, Tivoli, and Stroget. Rates: See Index.

Directions: From the railroad station walk one short block up Vesterbrogade to Axeltorv; turn right on Studiestraede. The Ascot is on your right in the middle of the block.

71 NYHAVN HOTEL
Copenhagen

If the rooms are a bit small, blame it on the ship's-cabin atmosphere of this old harbor warehouse on the waterfront in Copenhagen. Nyhavn is the name of the old sailor's district of the city now undergoing a good deal of fashionable gentrification. You will, for example, find antiques in the old tattoo parlors and restaurants in the basements.

The inn is located at the very end of the canal, where the view has not changed in several hundred years. Yet you are only a few minutes' stroll from the Royal Theater, Amalienborg Castle, and Stroget, the pedestrian shopping street of Copenhagen. Many of the old houses along Nyhavn have Hans Christian Andersen associations as well.

After a hearty Danish breakfast from the buffet set up in the dining room, you might consider walking along the waterfront to the Langelinie, where you will find the statue of the little mermaid. Another day, you can walk across the street from the hotel and catch the hydrofoil to Malmo, Sweden. Ferry boats to Norway are just around the corner.

Dining at 71 Nyhavn in summer gives you a choice of either indoors

Danish-French cuisine at Pakhuskaelderen Restaurant or its outdoor fish restaurant, literally moored across the gangway.

71 NYHAVN HOTEL, Nyhavn 71, 1051 Copenhagen. Tel.: 01-11-85-85 (U.S. reservations: 800-243-9420). A 76-guestroom (private baths) hotel in a converted warehouse at the very end of Nyhavn, Copenhagen's old sailor's district. European plan; other plans available. Rates: See Index.

Directions: If you arrive by train, take a taxi; by car, watch for signs to Nyhavn. If you are coming by ferry from Norway, you need walk only one block south; if by hydrofoil from Malmo, Sweden, the hotel is just across the street from your dock.

FALSLED KRO
Falsled

The Falsled Kro is not a conventional Danish country inn. I think it would be outstanding in any country. Like the Solerod Kro, just north of Copenhagen, it is included in the Relais et Chateaux, a directory of rather elegant and exclusive European hotels and restaurants.

The owners of this inn are Jean-Louis Lieffroy and Sven and Lene Grønlykke. Unfortunately, Jean-Louis and Sven were not at the inn during my visit, but Lene and I had an opportunity to get acquainted. It was from her that I learned that although the inn was a farm during the 16th century, it had become a "privileged inn," meaning there would always be room for the king and his horses.

I am certain that it is Lene's experience in the fields of film and fashion that accounts for the exquisite decor of this inn. My room had Danish tables and leather-covered stools, complemented by the white-washed walls on which there were several original paintings. I had the opportunity to look at other rooms during my stay, and one of them in particular was most attractive, with the bedroom on the second floor, reached by old stone stairs. Many of the guest rooms are suites with living rooms and such special features as fireplaces or french windows opening out on a garden.

Outside my door was a broad lawn, and just a few steps away was a very pleasant harbor. There were birds, flowers, flowering bushes, and beautiful trees everywhere.

The main sitting room had a wonderful center fireplace with comfortable low leather seats that invited everyone to stretch out and enjoy coffee after dinner. There are groupings of wicker furniture in various corners and many arrangements of freshly cut flowers. It is the kind of atmosphere that draws people together in conversation.

The cuisine at Falsled Kro is basically French, prepared by Jean-Louis and a team of chefs. My mixed salad, followed by salmon soufflé, would have been at home in Paris. The dessert table had at least eight different types of pastries, including a delicious chocolate mousse.

I had been hearing about Falsled Kro since my arrival in Scandinavia and I was told that it would be a beautiful and idyllic place, and indeed it was. I could only add one further word—sophisticated.

FALSLED KRO (Relais et Chateaux), DK-5642 Millinge. Tel.: 09-68-1111. South of Odense, on the Faborg-Assens Hwy. Rates: See Index.

STEENSGAARD HERREGÅRDSPENSION
Millinge

The clock over the stable sounded twelve times, just as it has been doing for hundreds of years. I paused in my walking tour of this elegant manor house, located just a few minutes from the sunny beaches of South Fyn Island, to watch two colts, hardly more than two months old, chase each other across the meadow.

The hostess at Steensgaard enthusiastically explained that the manor probably belonged to Hartvig Steen, a man most likely of noble means, and that it was apparently mortgaged by him to another family in 1310.

This makes it date back considerably before Columbus discovered America.

After a brief account of owners and mortgagees, I was amazed at how well the manor house-cum-castle appeared today.

"Oh, yes," she agreed. "The original sections were built to last, and the other buildings, which were added to form three sides of the square, are quite in harmony. Don't you agree?"

Indeed, I did. All of the buildings are made of rough stone and half timbers.

Steensgaard is in one of Denmark's most beautiful sections. It offers a magnificent view of fields and forests extending onward to high hills.

"We call it 'smiling countryside,' " said the hostess. "Our guests love to walk in the manor park, which extends through the woods down to the beach. There are fourteen other forests nearby if they really like longer excursions.

"There are also tennis and croquet. By the way, you have never played croquet until you have played with enthusiastic Danes."

The interior of this manor house is quite exciting. I passed from one room to another with original oil paintings, beautiful furniture, and rich rugs. The library has a chessboard in one corner and comfortable chairs drawn close together to invite conversation.

Guest rooms are unusually large, since they were built for private occupancy hundreds of years ago. Many of them have canopy beds.

In a country where there are dozens and dozens of beautiful old country inns, I found Steensgaard Herregårdspension a most interesting contrast. It offers the opportunity to spend a few days in a luxurious manor house.

STEENSGAARD, HERREGARDSPENSION, 5642 Millinge, Fyn. Tel.: (09) 61-94-90. An elegant 15-guestroom (10 with private bath) manor

house serving three meals a day. All types of outdoor recreation avail-
able. Rates: See Index.

RIBE

I could have spent a month in Ribe (ree-ba). To me it is the ultimate
medieval town. It has fascinating 16th-century houses, which are ac-
tually lived in today, intriguing alleyways, unexpected courtyards, and
cobbled streets everywhere.
   Dominating the center of town, just across a small square from Weis'
Stue, an ancient village inn, is the cathedral. It is partly constructed
of stone carried to Ribe from the Rhineland in Germany. One tower
has loopholes, evidence of the war with Germany. The bells of the
cathedral play every day—a hymn at 8 a.m. and 6 p.m., and folk songs
at noon and 3 p.m.
   Ribe's port area, the Skibbroen, is the oldest harbor in Denmark.
The storm flood column marks the height the waters have reached
during some of the worst floods down through the ages. Here is a lovely
town richly endowed with areas of outstanding beauty, and many
charming bridges across, and paths along, the river. There are gar-
dens, museums, castles, fenlands, churches, and a fascinating little
island off the coast, called Mando.

WEIS' STUE
Ribe
   "Yes, the village watchman starts out from here every night during
the summer. He drops in around 9 p.m. and sits here in this room, in
fact in your chair, and enjoys conversing with his friends. At 10 p.m.
he picks up that long pole there in the corner and walks out to the street
singing."
   I, too, was enjoying myself immensely at Weis' Stue. The building
and the atmosphere picked me up almost bodily and carried me back
to medieval times. The very personable innkeeper, Knud Nielsen, was
telling me what great fun it is to be the keeper of an ancient inn.
   "The watchman is an example of the good times we have here," he
said. "He is a great storyteller and also has an extensive knowledge of
the town. People follow him all around the town, just as if he were the
Pied Piper of Hamlin. He tells them about the old buildings and stories
about the town. Everyone eventually ends up here again. The night
watchman is a well-established Ribe tradition."
   Knud invited me to join him on a tour of this modest inn. To go up

to the second floor, I had to duck under a very low doorway and climb steep stairs with the aid of a rope bannister. At the top of the stairs were just four double rooms and one single. The running water for all rooms was available in a wash bowl in the hallway. That's where guests would brush their teeth and do their shaving. There were no private bathrooms and all shared a wc "in the corridor."

When I asked him about his guests' reaction to this old-fashioned mode of innkeeping, he replied, "They love it. Many come back quite often. Actually, we're quite luxurious compared to two or three hundred years ago."

As we returned to the first floor, I became aware of a great number of students who were lounging in one small dining room, playing chess, arguing, and even studying. "This has always been a students' favorite," he said. "For centuries they have been meeting here just as you see them today."

The food being prepared for the evening meal looked sumptuous. There were many Danish dishes as well as a few German and French. We passed through an open courtyard and into the Danish Marine Room, which was very imaginatively decorated with old ship models,

marine sabres, guns, pictures of ships, ship wheels, old brass, maps. He explained that it is given over to the Marine Club about six times a year to members who wish to come and have dinner.

The town of Ribe and the Weis' Stue proved to be a most pleasant Jutland experience. It is hard to imagine one without the other.

WEIS' STUE, Torvet 2, 6760 Ribe. Tel.: (05) 42-07-00. Rates: See Index.

KONGENSBRO KRO
Ans

Mr. Hans Andersen, innkeeper-emeritus at Kongensbro Kro, made it quite clear during the first few minutes of our meeting that his middle name was not "Christian." He was one of the more sophisticated innkeepers that I met in Jutland and the inn reflected the fact that he and his wife had tastes and preferences that would be appropriate in many other settings as well.

We got acquainted in the residents' lounge of the inn, where a small fire was burning at one end, and windows overlooked the river. We soon found that innkeeping joys and tribulations are much the same in Denmark as they are in the United States.

"It is a 24-hour-a-day job," he said, "especially when one wishes to hold a good reputation."

A good reputation is something that Kongensbro possesses in abundance. I had tried six weeks in advance to reserve a room for just one night, but it was impossible. "We take bookings this year for next year," he said. I asked him if there was an explanation for this popularity.

"This is a good place to stay for anyone who wants to take his ease in a time of hurry, and feel in close contact with the peaceful rhythm of nature.

"It is a good place for nature lovers and bird enthusiasts and it is a paradise for anglers," he declared. "Many a lovely hour can be spent fishing and watching the animal life and nature at large.

"The staff at the inn can supply good tips about short or long trips and several of these trips will bring to mind days gone by. One of them is on the old tow path at the bank of the river, which is now able to be used for a distance of twenty-five miles. Incidentally, we also rent canoes for use on the river."

Later on, I had a chance to talk to Ole, whom I met in the garden. He invited me to walk over to a little building next door on the banks of the river, where a special party was being held, and a man who lived in Argentina was cooking barbecued spare ribs.

Hans informed me that he and his wife, after thirty-five years of innkeeping, have turned the inn over to his son, Ole, and his wife. However, he and Mrs. Andersen will be nearby and will drop in frequently to say hello to the guests.

KONGENSBRO KRO, 8643 Ans By, Jutland. Tel.: (06) 87-01-77. A 27-guestroom inn in Danish farm country, 25 km. from Viborg, 18 km. from Silkeborg. Golf, fishing, walking nearby. Rates: See Index.

RANDOM REFLECTIONS ON SCANDINAVIA

Although there are many language similarities, the four countries, Norway, Sweden, Finland, and Denmark, are highly individual. Each year they are becoming increasingly popular with visitors from North America.

Scandinavia is the home of some of the world's famous artisans and craftsmen. Glassware, ceramics, rugs, tableware, handicrafts, and jewelry are to be found everywhere. The performing arts are a great tradition in all four countries, and there is a wide choice among lawn concerts, dramatic presentations, opera, symphony, and folk dancing.

Index/Rates

The following listing of rates varies, with an emphasis on the upper middle range. The rates are meant as guidelines only and are quoted in the currency of the country involved. Basically, they are the cost of one night's lodging for two people and may include a continental breakfast and tax. Please bear in mind the rapid fluctuation in exchange rates makes this listing only approximate, and be aware that advance inquiries should be made for more exact information. Rates are estimated through 1990. Rates are not provided for restaurants, indicated by the abbreviation "Rest."

Denmark

Rates   Page

Amounts shown in krone for two people for one night. These are not firm quotations, but for general estimating.

Finland

Rates   Page

Amounts shown in U.S. dollars for two people for one night. These are not firm quotations, but for general estimating.

France

Rates   *Page*

Amounts shown in francs for two people for one night. These are not firm quotations, but for general estimating.

Germany

	Rates	Page

Amounts shown in marks for two people for one night. These are not firm quotations, but for general estimating.

Hungary

Amounts shown in U.S. dollars for two people for one night. These are not firm quotations, but for general estimating.

Italy

Amounts shown in lire for two people for one night. These are not firm quotations, but for general estimating.

Luxembourg

Amounts shown in Luxembourg francs for two people for one night. These are not firm quotations, but for general estimating.

Norway

Amounts shown in krone for two people for one night. These are not firm quotations, but for general estimating.

Portugal

	Rates	Page

Amounts shown in escudos for two people for one night. These are not firm quotations, but for general estimating.

Spain

	Rates	Page

Amounts shown in pesetas for two people for one night. These are not firm quotations, but for general estimating. For paradores, rates include breakfast and tax.

Sweden

Rates   Page

Amounts shown in krone for two people for one night. These are not firm quotations, but for general estimating.

Switzerland

Rates   Page

Amounts shown in Swiss francs for two people for one night. These are not firm quotations, but for general estimating.